Understanding Nietzsche, Understanding Modernism

Understanding Philosophy, Understanding Modernism

The aim of each volume in **Understanding Philosophy, Understanding Modernism** is to understand a philosophical thinker more fully through literary and cultural modernism and consequently to understand literary modernism better through a key philosophical figure. In this way, the series also rethinks the limits of modernism, calling attention to lacunae in modernist studies and sometimes in the philosophical work under examination.

Series Editors
Paul Ardoin, S. E. Gontarski, and Laci Mattison

Volumes in the Series
Understanding Bergson, Understanding Modernism, edited by Paul Ardoin, S. E. Gontarski, and Laci Mattison
Understanding Deleuze, Understanding Modernism, edited by S. E. Gontarski, Paul Ardoin, and Laci Mattison
Understanding Wittgenstein, Understanding Modernism, edited by Anat Matar
Understanding Foucault, Understanding Modernism, edited by David Scott
Understanding James, Understanding Modernism, edited by David H. Evans
Understanding Rancière, Understanding Modernism, edited by Patrick M. Bray
Understanding Blanchot, Understanding Modernism, edited by Christopher Langlois
Understanding Merleau-Ponty, Understanding Modernism, edited by Ariane Mildenberg
Understanding Nietzsche, Understanding Modernism, edited by Brian Pines and Douglas Burnham
Understanding Derrida, Understanding Modernism (forthcoming), edited by Jean-Michel Rabaté
Understanding Adorno, Understanding Modernism (forthcoming), edited by Robin Truth Goodman
Understanding Cavell, Understanding Modernism (forthcoming), edited by Paola Marrati
Understanding Flusser, Understanding Modernism (forthcoming), edited by Aaron Jaffe, Rodrigo Martini, and Michael F. Miller
Understanding Marx, Understanding Modernism (forthcoming), edited by Mark Steven

Understanding Nietzsche, Understanding Modernism

Edited by
Brian Pines and Douglas Burnham

BLOOMSBURY ACADEMIC
NEW YORK • LONDON • OXFORD • NEW DELHI • SYDNEY

BLOOMSBURY ACADEMIC
Bloomsbury Publishing Inc
1385 Broadway, New York, NY 10018, USA
50 Bedford Square, London, WC1B 3DP, UK

BLOOMSBURY, BLOOMSBURY ACADEMIC and the Diana logo are trademarks of
Bloomsbury Publishing Plc

First published in the United States of America 2019
Paperback edition published 2020

Series design by Louise Dugdale
Cover design by Olivia D'Cruz
Cover image © Getty Images/Luis Argerich/Stocktrek Images

A catalog record for this book is available from the Library of Congress.

ISBN: HB: 978-1-5013-3914-1
PB: 978-1-5013-6759-5
ePDF: 978-1-5013-3916-5
eBook: 978-1-5013-3915-8

Series: Understanding Philosophy, Understanding Modernism

Typeset by Deanta Global Publishing Services, Chennai, India

Series Preface

Understanding Philosophy, Understanding Modernism

Sometime in the late twentieth century, modernism, like philosophy itself, underwent something of an unmooring from (at least) linear literary history in favor of the multiperspectival history implicit in "new historicism" or, say, varieties of "presentism." Amid current reassessments of modernism and modernity, critics have posited various "new" or alternative modernisms—postcolonial, cosmopolitan, transatlantic, transnational, geomodernism, or even "bad" modernisms. In doing so, they have not only reassessed modernism as a category, but also, more broadly, rethought epistemology and ontology, aesthetics, metaphysics, materialism, history, and being itself, opening possibilities of rethinking not only which texts we read as modernist, but also how we read those texts.

Much of this new conversation constitutes something of a critique of the periodization of modernism or modernist studies in favor of modernism as mode (or mode of production) or concept. *Understanding Philosophy, Understanding Modernism* situates itself amid the plurality of discourses, offering collections focused on key philosophical thinkers, influential both to the moment of modernism and to our current understanding of that moment's geneology, archaeology, and becomings. Such critiques of modernism(s) and modernity afford opportunities to rethink and reassess the overlaps, folds, interrelationships, interleavings, or cross-pollinations of modernism and philosophy. Our goal in each volume of the series is to understand literary modernism better through philosophy as we also better understand a philosopher through literary modernism.

The first two volumes of the series, those on Henri Bergson and Gilles Deleuze, have established a tripartite structure that serves to offer accessibility to both the philosopher's principle texts and current new research. Each volume opens with a section focused on "conceptualizing" the philosopher through close readings of seminal texts in the thinker's oeuvre. A second section, on aesthetics, maps connections between modernist works and the philosophical figure, often surveying key modernist trends and shedding new light on authors and texts. The final section of each volume serves as an extended glossary of principal terms in the philosopher's work, each treated at length, allowing a fuller engagement with and examination of the many, sometimes contradictory, ways terms are deployed. The series is thus designed both to introduce philosophers and rethink their relationship to modernist studies, revising our understandings of both modernism and philosophy, and offering resources that will be of use across disciplines, from philosophy, theory, and literature, to religion, the visual and performing arts, and often to the sciences as well.

Contents

Notes on Contributors

Jack Brookes is an independent researcher and graduate of St. John's College, Annapolis. His current work is focused on German Idealism, Ancient Greek philosophy, and poetry.

Douglas Burnham is a professor of philosophy and head of the University Graduate School at Staffordshire University.

SJ Cowan is currently pursuing a PhD in philosophy at University of California, Berkeley. He has a background in photography, theology, and philosophy. His current work is focused on the history of modern philosophy, aesthetics and perception, and contemporary art.

Kaitlyn Creasy is an assistant professor of philosophy at Butler University. Her current work is focused on nineteenth-century continental philosophy (especially Friedrich Nietzsche), nihilism, personal transformation (especially the transformative potential of affect), self-knowledge, and environmental philosophy.

Matthew John Grabowski obtained an AS in Intelligence Operations from Cochise College and a BA in Asian Studies from the University of Maryland. He served as a Platoon Sergeant, and was deployed with the 1/4 Infantry Regiment in support of their mission in Afghanistan. His current works are focused on the classics of Western and Eastern literature, as well as nineteenth-century German and twentieth-century French philosophy.

Sebastian Hüsch is a full professor in History of Ideas at Aix-Marseille Université. Recent publications have been on literature as epistemological model and on religion in the twenty-first century. His current work is focused on nineteenth- and twenty-first-century European philosophy with a special focus on interdisciplinary studies in philosophy and literature, philosophy of existence, and philosophy of religion.

Jeremy Killian is a lecturer in the honors program at Coastal Carolina University. He earned his doctorate at the University of Louisville, where he wrote about Eugene O'Neill and tragic emotions. Dr. Killian's current work is focused on theater studies and philosophy of art, with a particular interest in the paradox of tragedy and the value of tragic theater.

Karl Laderoute is a philosophy instructor at the University of Lethbridge in Alberta, Canada. His current work is focused on the intersections of epistemology, metaphysics, and ethics in the history of philosophy.

James Luchte is a philosopher, author, writer, and poet living in Wales. His publications include *Mortal Thought: Hölderlin and Philosophy* (2016), *Marx and the Revolution of the Sacred* (2015), *Of the Feral Children* (2012), *Early Greek Thought: Before the Dawn* (2011), *The Peacock and the Buffalo: The Poetry of Nietzsche* (translator, 2010), *Pythagoras and the Doctrine of Transmigration: Wandering Souls* (2009), *Heidegger's Early Philosophy: The Phenomenology of Ecstatic Temporality* (2008), *Nietzsche's Thus Spoke Zarathustra: Before Sunrise* (editor, 2008), and *Kant's Critique of Pure Reason* (2007). He has also published dozens of articles on various topics in philosophy, culture, and contemporary politics.

Siobhan Lyons is a lecturer in media at Macquarie University, Australia, where she earned her PhD in 2017. Her book *Death and the Machine* is being published by Palgrave in 2018. She has also been published in *Philosophical Approaches to the Devil* (2015) and *Westworld and Philosophy* (2018). She was awarded a New Philosopher Writers' Award in 2017.

Jill Marsden is a senior lecturer in English at the University of Bolton. She is the author of *After Nietzsche: Notes Towards a Philosophy of Ecstasy* (2002). Her current work is focused on continental philosophy, modernism, and literature.

Bill McDonald is a faculty fellow emeritus of the Johnston Center of the University of Redlands in southern California (1969–2005), where he was also Professor of English and the first holder of the Virginia C. Hunsaker Chair of Distinguished Teaching. He has coauthored two volumes on the Johnston Center (1989, 2004), edited a volume on J. M. Coetzee's *Disgrace* in 2009, and published a book on Thomas Mann's *Joseph* novels (1999). Other publications include essays on Mann, and on Laurence Sterne's *Tristram Shandy*, in edited volumes from MIT Press (2009, 2016). His current work is focused on international modernism, literary theory, ancient Greece, pedagogy, and interdisciplinary studies in the humanities.

Brian Pines teaches courses in philosophy at Monterey Peninsula College. He obtained his PhD from Staffordshire University in 2016, and his current work is focused on continental philosophy.

Ritske Rensma is a lecturer in philosophy and religious studies at University College Roosevelt, an international honors college of the University of Utrecht in the Netherlands. He is the author of the book *The Innateness of Myth* (2010), which traces the influence of C. G. Jung on the American scholar of myth and religion Joseph Campbell. His current work is focused on Jungian psychology, evolutionary psychology, and transpersonal psychology, with a particular interest in the relevance of these disciplines for understanding religious phenomena.

Adrian Switzer is an associate professor in the Department of Philosophy at the University of Missouri-Kansas City where he specializes in teaching and research on Kant and the post-Kantian modern and contemporary traditions. The author of numerous journal articles and book chapters on such figures as Kant, Nietzsche, Benjamin, Merleau-Ponty, Foucault, Deleuze, Derrida, and Irigaray, Dr. Switzer is currently completing *The Events of May 1968: The Art and Philosophy of Revolution* (forthcoming).

Tim Themi is a faculty member at Melbourne University, teaching culture and communication. He obtained his PhD from Deakin, and holds honors degrees in philosophy from La Trobe and the engineering sciences from Melbourne. He is author of *The Neurosis and Nihilism of a 'Life' against Life* (2008), *Lacan's Ethics and Nietzsche's Critique of Platonism* (2014), *Bataille and the Erotics of the Real* (2015), and *Lacan, Barthes, Bataille, and the Meaning of the Eye—or Gaze* (2016). He has presented at the seminar of the Lacan Circle of Melbourne, and taught philosophy and psychoanalysis at Deakin.

Yunus Tuncel holds a PhD from the New School for Social Research. He teaches philosophy and serves on the Board of Directors of the Nietzsche Circle and the Editorial Board of its electronic journal, *The Agonist*. He is a co-organizer of New York Posthuman Research Group and works with trans- and post-humanists. He is the author of *Towards a Genealogy of Spectacle* (2011) and *Agon in Nietzsche* (2013) and the editor of *Nietzsche and Transhumanism* (2017). With Philomobile, an organization he founded, he organizes trips to explore philosophy and the lives of philosophers on location. His current work is focused on aesthetics, philosophy of sport, theories of emotion and affect, psychoanalysis, culture of "gai saber", and philosophy of music.

Patricia Valderrama holds a PhD in comparative literature from Stanford University and a BA in comparative literature from Princeton University. Her dissertation, titled "Reading for the Anthropocene: Twentieth-Century Stories of Resilience and Interspecies Care," elaborates pedagogy of storytelling for our warmer planetary future. Her current work is focused on twentieth-century German, French, and Latin American literatures and philosophies with a focus on representations of humans' interactions with the more-than-human world also known as nature.

Gill Zimmerman holds a master's degree in philosophy and religious studies from the University of Heidelberg. After conducting an independent research project as a visiting research student at Stanford University he is currently preparing his dissertation on the entanglement of ecology and moral philosophy at the Zeppelin University at Lake Constance.

Acknowledgments

There have been some contributors who have given their time and intellectual powers to this volume who are not listed on the preceding pages. We would like to offer heartfelt thanks to Joan, Andrew, and Adam Pines, Boris Shoshitaishvili, and Sepp. In addition, beyond writing glossary definitions, Matthew John Grabowski and Jack Brookes also aided with the editing process.

Abbreviations

References to Nietzsche's work provide title abbreviations and aphorism number. Where applicable, they also contain the full section title, using a "*P*" to indicate a preface (e.g., *TI*, *Skirmishes of an Untimely Man*, 4). We cite the *Kritische Studienausgabe* (*KSA*) by G. Colli and M. Montinari to reference Nietzsche's unpublished notebooks. References to *KSA* include volume, group, and fragment number. We cite the *Briefe: Kritische Gesamtausgabe* (*KGB*) to refer to Nietzsche's letters. We include date, volume number, and letter number in these citations. This way, both the notebooks and the letters can be easily cross-referenced using the *Digitale Kritische Gesamtausgabe Werke und Briefe* (*eKGWB*), freely available on Nietzschesource.org.

A	*Antichrist*
AOM	*Assorted Opinions and Maxims*
BGE	*Beyond Good and Evil*
BT	*The Birth of Tragedy*
CW	*The Case of Wagner*
D	*Dawn*
DD	*Dionysian Dithyrambs*
DS	*David Strauss, the Confessor and the Writer*
EH	*Ecce Homo*
GM	*On the Genealogy of Morality*
GS	*The Gay Science*
HH	*Human, All Too Human*
HL	*On the Use and Abuse of History for Life*
NCW	*Nietzsche Contra Wagner*
PP	*Lectures on the Pre-Platonic Philosophers*
PTAG	*Philosophy in the Tragic Age of the Greeks*
RWB	*Richard Wagner in Bayreuth*
SE	*Schopenhauer as Educator*
TI	*Twilight of the Idols*
TL	*On Truth and Lies in an Extra-Moral Sense*
WS	*The Wanderer and His Shadow*
Z	*Thus Spoke Zarathustra*

High spirits—*It seems to me that most people simply do not believe in elevated moods, unless it be for moments or fifteen-minute intervals at most—except for those few who experience an elevated feeling over a longer period. But to be the human being of one elevated feeling, the embodiment of a single great mood, has hitherto been a mere dream and enchanting possibility; as yet, history does not offer us any certain examples of it. Nevertheless history might one day beget such people, too, given the creation and determination of a great many preconditions that even the dice rolls of the luckiest chance could not put together today. Perhaps the usual state for these souls would be what has so far entered our souls only as an occasional exception that made us shudder: a perpetual movement between high and low and the feeling of high and low; a continual sense of ascending stairs and at the same time of resting on clouds.*

(*GS*, 288)

Introduction: The Heroism of Friedrich Nietzsche

Brian Pines

In this introduction I outline the vision that brought all of us together for *Understanding Nietzsche, Understanding Modernism*. We have each contributed investigations into the correlation between Friedrich Nietzsche and modernity. Taken individually, each chapter portrays one self-contained perspective on the relationship between this thinker and era. Taken together, the book tells a fragmented story of the tragedy of Nietzsche's life, thought, and impact. A more complete narrative might have been composed in which we attempted to understand the modernist era through the influence of an inventor like Nikolaus Otto or a statesman like Otto von Bismarck, but the effects of a technology or system of laws are by nature more definite than the multifarious accomplishments of a text. In our volume we pursue the indefinite: we seek to sympathize with the men and women of the era in order to understand something of the *mood* of modernism.

Most often, modernism is taken to be the cultural products that, with hindsight, appear to be typical of the period from the last decades of the nineteenth century up to at least the 1930s. "Hindsight" is a significant term here, because while Igor Stravinski's *Rite of Spring*, for example, appears to us quintessentially modernist, by contemporaries it was seen as barbaric, infantile, or *anti*-cultural. Emile Cardon, for example, writes in *La Presse* of the first Impressionist exhibition (1874), "In the implementation of [impressionism] artists fall into hopeless, grotesque confusion, happily without precedent in art, for it is quite simply the negation of the most elementary rules of drawing and painting. The scribblings of a child have a naivety, a sincerity which make one smile, but the excesses of this school sicken or disgust."[1] Nietzsche himself was a victim of what, with hindsight, we can characterize as obstinate resistance and misunderstanding on the part of the public. In his last book, an autobiography, he reflects on his persistent obscurity.

> Ultimately, nobody can get more out of things—including books—than they already know. You will not have an ear for something until experience has given you some headway into it. Let us take the most extreme case, where a book talks only about events lying completely outside the possibility of common, or even uncommon, experience,—where it is the *first* language of a new range of experiences. In this case, absolutely nothing will be heard, with the associated acoustic illusion that if nothing is heard, *nothing is there*. At the end of the day, this

has been my usual experience and, if you will, the originality of my experience. Anyone who thinks they have understood me has made me into something after their own image. (*EH*, *Why I Write Such Good Books*, 1)

What makes the case of Nietzsche so fascinating is his astonishing *foresight*—both the prophetic articulations of experiences that were decades beyond what men and women of his time were capable of relating to, and his foresight into his own posthumous fame. The people of his time did not find themselves in his writings, but decades later Nietzsche became a mirror in which priests and painters, conservatives and anarchists, Zionists and National Socialists found a description of their own experiences of modernity. His writings were appropriated for many purposes he would never have sanctioned. More often named than read, and more often read poorly than carefully, Nietzsche's bastards became more numerous than his legitimate children.

This popularity of Nietzsche's writings certainly possesses a set of difficulties for an academic study, but it also makes him an irreplaceable tool for understanding modernism. Nietzsche had articulated the experience of modernity; his writings were a point of reference through which the modernists generations understood their era's complicated moods.

* * *

Our volume is split into three parts. The first part consists of six chapters in which we ask, "What was the experience of Nietzsche?" We recount the outlines of his life along with the development of his thought and how it suggests connections to modernity. The second part is made up of nine chapters, in which we ask, "What was the influence of Nietzsche?" We treat Nietzsche as a messenger of modernism, attempting to connect Nietzsche's message to the figures and movements which emerged near the turn of the previous century. The third part of our collection provides synopses of a selection of pivotal concepts in Nietzsche's writings and serves as a reference guide for the perplexed or the inquisitive.

Nietzsche's experiences

Wherever Stimmung [mood] *penetrates texts, we may assume that a primary experience has occurred to the point of becoming a preconscious reflex.*

—Hans Ulrich Gumbrecht[2]

Nationalism

Precisely four months to the day before Nietzsche was born—on June 15, 1844—the Grand Duchy of Baden opened its rail line from Strasbourg to Basel for business, as part of the *Großherzoglich Badische Staatseisenbahnen* (Grand Duchy of Baden State

Railways). In so doing, it became the first of the Germanic states to attempt to bring modernity up into the foothills of the Alps. Nietzsche moved along this rail line through French Strasbourg to Basel when he was offered a professorship there in 1869. Once up in Basel, Nietzsche regularly traveled on the newly incorporated line into Lucerne in order to visit the court of Richard Wagner—personal musician of King Ludwig II.

As a condition of teaching in Switzerland, Nietzsche had to renounce his Prussian citizenship, and he became officially *Staatenlos* (Stateless). One year later France declared war on Prussia. Out of a sense of duty to his fatherland Nietzsche descended back down into the Germanic states to volunteer in an auxiliary medical unit, the *Felddiakonie* (field deacons). Nietzsche followed the rapid Prussian counterattack through Alsace, traveling past the siege of Strasbourg to the siege of Metz, where what was to be the last successful cavalry charge in central Europe had recently occurred. Outside Metz Nietzsche was entrusted with the care of six wounded Prussian soldiers, and the seven men were enclosed in a cattle car headed back to Karlsruhe. He spent three days and three nights entombed in the gangrenous air with his casualties, writing to Wagner: "That I was able to endure this pestilent air, and could even sleep and eat, now seems to me quite miraculous" (*KGB*, September 1870, II.1:100). His train stopped in Bischwiller, close enough for him to see clouds of smoke and ash rising from the Prussian bombardment of Strasbourg.

The city of Strasbourg was a historical symbol of turbulent times. It had begun as a *Castrum* (Roman military fort) called *Argentoratum*. Just like Basel it was on the Rhine, and Nero had once envisioned it as a check against Germanic invaders crossing the river. During the crisis of the third century Germanic tribes had spilled across the border. Julian, who would become the last pagan Emperor, won a decisive victory over the Alemanni tribes at *Argentoratum* on August 25, 357 CE, restoring the Rhine as the boundary between the empire and the Germanic barbarians. Half a century later, *Argentoratum* was taken by the German tribes, who began to call it *Stratisburgum*. Although it was a nominally free and neutral city throughout the Middle Ages, the bridge at Strasbourg had been used multiple times during the Thirty Years' War by the forces of the (Germanic) Holy Roman Empire to cross the Rhine and invade Alsace. In response, the Sun King, Louis XIV, annexed the city in the late seventeenth century. Louis commanded his *Maréchal de France*, the Marquis of Vauban, to construct a citadel in Strasbourg so that the city could once again be used as a strategic base to halt potential Germanic invasions into France. The Marquis of Vauban is considered to have been one of the greatest military engineers to ever live, but his citadel, completed in 1685, was now surrounded by Germans wielding the artillery of modernity.

Nietzsche had nine hours to contemplate the meaning of the smoke rising from Strasbourg before his train started back up toward Karlsruhe. Once arrived, he transferred his charges and reboarded the same *Staatseisenbahnen* to convalesce in Erlangen; he visited his mother in Naumburg, and then climbed back up to Basel. This experience of war pushed him further into his studies, and he began to work on what would be his first book, *The Birth of Tragedy*: an attempt at forming a Germanic-Hellenic community by uniting the figures of Wagner and Dionysus. While Nietzsche wrote up in the mountains, Strasbourg capitulated to the Prussian armies outside its gates, Bismarck laid siege to Paris, and Wilhelm I was declared Emperor of a united Germany from the palace of Versaille. One would have to go back an entire millennium, to Charlemagne, to find a comparable political event. During the next few years Nietzsche took trips back down to this new Germany to see his mother, to take cures for his ever-worsening illnesses, and to pay homage at Bayreuth.

Bayreuth was Wagner's spectacular attempt at unifying the German spirit through an operatic national myth, his bid to parallel Bismarck's accomplishments. Wagner desired for his magnum opus, *The Ring Cycle*, to be performed in a provincial town, as far away as possible from the swelling cosmopolitan centers of Germany. However, despite the precautions he took to ensure the purity of the rituals performed at Bayreuth, this revival of the ancient Nordic myths became permeated by the mood of modernity. The reforms that Wagner undertook in the theater such as the dimming of the lights, the concealment of the orchestra, and the arrangement of seating were all intended to narrow the audience's focus onto the parade of figures inhabiting the stage. This was the first time audiences were to experience the otherworldly aesthetic of the modern cinema with which we are today familiar. Unlike Greek tragedy—in which the audience socialized with one another as they would at a contemporary sporting event—the audience at Bayreuth was kept in silent observation of a phantasmagoria of water nymphs, ice giants, and old pagan gods. The care taken in detaching these figures from the material conditions of their emergence on stage, from the pulley systems to the submerged orchestra, gave these images the gravity of reality. Theodor Adorno has written of Bayreuth, "Its perfection is at the same time the perfection of the illusion that the work of art is a reality *sui generis* that constitutes itself in the realm of the absolute without having to renounce its claim to image the world."[3] Bayreuth was thus a modern recreation of Plato's cave. Wagner was attempting to ensure that his audience would perceive his world as their only reality. The master's choice to conceal the inner organs of the stagework was symptomatic of modernity: the masses demanded to be presented with a result, an effect, and had no desire to observe the actual production of laws, sausages, or theater.

Nietzsche descended into Germany to attend the first performances of *The Ring Cycle* at Bayreuth in the summer of 1876, but the operas disturbed his delicate health, giving him searing migraines. He would from this point forward reflect upon Wagner using the same discourse of disease that he used to reflect on his experience in the cattle car. He writes in *The Case of Wagner*, "I want to open the window a bit. Air! More air!—" (*CW*, 5).

Nietzsche escaped the atmosphere of Bayreuth on August 27, 1876—the 1466th anniversary of Alaric's Visigothic armies departing from their sack of Rome. Nietzsche writes to Wagner that he "will go to Italy next month, but I do not mean as a land of beginnings, but rather as an end to my sufferings" (*KGB*, September 1876, II.5:556). He passed through the Alps by way of the Fréjus Tunnel: the first railway in Europe that used the marvel of dynamite to bore holes through those colossuses which had always stood between the north and south.[4] The Fréjus Tunnel was a modern monument: explosions, steel, and pneumatic drilling ensured that crowds could migrate through these terrains in comfort and safety; it mocked the triumphs of Hannibal, Charlemagne, and Napoleon, all of whom had endured terrible hardships marching armies through that very same valley. Nietzsche finally came to rest in Sorrento, near Naples—and Wagner followed him south. The two men would speak face to face for the last time in the shadow of Vesuvius on the 6th of November.[5] Wagner headed back across the Alps to the Nordic lands, while Nietzsche remained in what was once *Magna Grecia*, exploring the ruins of Pompeii and Paestum.

Transnationalism

It is hard to overestimate the psychological effect of Nietzsche's break from Wagner. Wagner was the same age that Nietzsche's father would have been, had he not died when Nietzsche was only four. Heraclitus's aphorism "I consulted myself" (*DK*, B101) might be a good enough summary of Nietzsche's life after he loses this father figure. He begins to write in aphorisms, his writing becomes more personal, and more ambitious. He won't remain in one place again for very long until his mental collapse. Nietzsche incorporated into his writings an experience of mobility that was unique to modernity, which would have been unthinkable to the previous century's stationary philosophers, such as Immanuel Kant.

Nietzsche's itinerancy was made possible by his contemporaneity with a great leap toward international integration. Between Nietzsche's birth and death both Italy and Germany unified, the total length of rail laid on the European continent multiplied itself over 150 times, the largest peaceful mass migrations ever to occur took place,[6] the population of most European cities doubled,[7] and time was standardized at the International Meridian Conference—a week after Nietzsche's fortieth birthday. Perhaps the most significant as well as the most subterranean of these events was an unprecedented surge toward price convergence of most major commodities around the world,[8] signifying that the world was rapidly approaching a common valuation of the phenomena which inhabited it. As Kevin O'Rourke states in *Globalization and History: The Evolution of a Nineteenth-Century Atlantic Economy*,

> "the most impressive episode of international economic integration which the world has seen to date was not the second half of the twentieth century, but the years between 1870 and the Great War. The nineteenth century, and in particular the late nineteenth century, was the period that saw the largest decline ever in inter-continental barriers to trade and factor mobility."[9]

Nothing embodied this dizzying race toward modernization more than the new German nation. John Maynard Keynes had written of this time period that "the German machine was like a top which to maintain its equilibrium must spin ever faster and faster."[10]

During Nietzsche's early years as a wanderer, sometimes referred to as his "middle period," he experienced an enthusiasm for all of this dynamic movement and anxiety which composed the mood of the early modernist situation.

> *The European man and the destruction of nations.* Commerce and industry, tragic in books and letters, the commonality of all higher culture, quick changes of

> locality and landscape, the present-day nomadic life of all nonlandowners—these conditions necessarily bring about a weakening and ultimately a destruction of nations, or at least of European nations; so that a mixed race, that of the European man, has to originate out of all of them, as the result of continual crossbreeding ... once a man has understood [that it is in his self-interest], he should be undaunted in presenting himself as a *good European*, and should work actively on the merging of nations. The Germans, because of their age-old, proven trait of being the *nations' interpreter and mediator*, will be able to help in this process. (*HH*, 475)[11]

When Nietzsche speaks of the Germans' historical role as the "interpreters and mediators" between nations, he is perhaps referencing the Peace of Westphalia, which signaled the end of the Thirty Years' War in 1648. The major outcome of this treaty was the establishment of the politics of national sovereignty, with the exception of the German states. The Germanic territories were to be kept as hundreds of decentralized governing units, a perpetual power vacuum in the center of Europe—the perpetual "mediators" of Europe.[12] The smoke Nietzsche had seen rising from Strasbourg, that city which symbolized the boundary between the great powers, signified the end of the terms agreed upon by the Peace of Westphalia. Bismarck had unified Germany, the politics which occurred between sovereign nations were changing form, and "the Concert of Europe" was entering its final movement.

Nietzsche wrote this aphorism in Sorrento at the Villa Rubinacci, a communal house for free spirits such as Paul Rée, Malwida von Meysenbug, and Albert Brenner. He will dedicate the book it belongs to—his first project after breaking with the Francophobic Wagner—to Voltaire. The spirit of the Enlightenment enlivens Nietzsche's middle writings. These works are his most political, they contain his strongest advocations for the power of reasoned discourse, and for a life liberated from all prejudices.[13] This middle period also witnesses Nietzsche's first sustained attacks on Christianity, a traditional target of enlightenment criticism, with the publication of *Dawn*.

The Gay Science is undoubtedly the flower of Nietzsche's hopes during this moment in his life. Nietzsche wrote this book with the ambition of rescuing rationality from "seriousness." While he was writing it, he was simultaneously endeavoring to gather another community of like-minded thinkers. One of these "free spirits" being the beautiful Lou Andreas-Salomé, whom Nietzsche pursued in what would be his last real attempt at love.

Return to war

Nietzsche spent his last and most productive years traversing the area the Romans called *Gallia Cisalpina* (Gaul on the Roman side of the Alps), the province Julius Cæsar had once governed—from which he launched his wars which would incorporate central Europe into the great Mediterranean empire. It was during these last Alpine years that Nietzsche would produce what would one day be his most famous book: *Thus Spoke Zarathustra*. Written in the short bursts of inspiration which interrupted waves of sickness and depression, Nietzsche will later say that in writing *Zarathustra* he lost "all perception of what is imagery and metaphor; everything seem[ed] to present itself as the readiest, the truest, and simplest means of expression" (*EH*, *Thus Spoke Zarathustra*, 3).

Despite his dizzying accomplishments, this era was tortuous for Nietzsche: he lost his closest friends,[14] he reached middle age never having known the love of a woman, and despite the brutal work schedule he kept for himself, he lapsed into greater and greater obscurity. While *The Birth of Tragedy* was moderately successful, *Dawn* sold only 216 copies, *The Gay Science* 212 copies, and the three published parts to *Zarathustra* sold less than 300 copies combined. Nietzsche became more bitter, more warlike, and more hostile to the modern world.

Heinrich Heine, whom Nietzsche had called "the highest concept of a lyric poet" (*EH*, *Why I Am So Wise*, 4), comments on the experience of train travel, which more than almost anything else characterized the mood of modernity, "Space is killed by the railways ... I feel as if the mountains and forests of all countries were advancing on Paris. Even now, I can smell the German linden trees."[15] The rails invaded secluded beaches and remote Alpine villages, crushing any pretense of a "*Pathos* of distance"[16] that could separate a free wanderer from a tourist. Nearly every time Nietzsche ventured to supposedly beautiful locations north of the Alps, such as the *Grunewald*, he found them overcrowded with German vacationers. The lonely philosopher always quickly escaped back south, away from the swarming, "gangrenous," and suffocating urban centers of central Europe which were now overflowing into the countryside. Nietzsche's destructive spirit cast special vehemence toward Germania, "The 'German spirit' is *my* bad air: I have trouble breathing when I am around the instinctive uncleanliness *in psychologicis* that is revealed in German's every word, every expression" (*EH*, *CW*, 3). It was the *mood* of Germans, there was something *in the air* north of the Alps that Nietzsche detested. Nietzsche saw in the rapidly industrializing Germany the "plebeian" spirit of the Reformation, and perhaps the "barbaric" spirit of antiquity, "The Germans robbed Europe of the harvest, the meaning, of the last *great* age, the age of the Renaissance ... Does anyone except me know a *way* out of this dead end? ... a task big enough to *reunite* peoples?" (*EH*, *CW*, 2). He no longer conceived of the Germans as the "interpreters and mediators" of Europe, but instead caricatured them as a barbaric people, who had twice now destroyed the culture of the Mediterranean. Yet this passage also makes clear that the task of unifying the European people still lay before Nietzsche.[17] It should be pointed out, however, that the particular phrasing of "*re*-unite" suggests a dismissal of the republican project that arose out of the Enlightenment, and rather seems to be implying something more closely approximated by the word *imperium*.

Nietzsche prepared to fight the entire modern spirit. He sought out Alpine regions where cleansing winds blew far above the claustrophobic conditions of urban centers, away from communities, away from neighbors, away from "common sense." Nietzsche writes from his mountain recluse to his sister, "The time is forever passed where there is between me and the present any relation other than war to the death!—" (*KGB*, September 1888, III.5:1112).

Despite his hostility toward everything that surrounded him, Nietzsche still saw his own thought projects as essentially positive. He excuses his own misanthropy as a necessary part of his creative process, "Almost every genius has experienced the 'Catilinarian existence' as one aspect of his development: a hateful, vengeful, rebellious feeling against everything that already *is*, that has stopped *becoming* ... Catiline—the pre-existing type of *every* Cæsar.—" (*TI, Skirmishes of an Untimely Man,* 45). Like a lion, Nietzsche tried to bring the tensions he felt between himself and modernity into action; this meant the abandonment of lines of communication, and forsaking submission and mutual exchange with the neighbor in favor of a selfish will to expand. In order to write the last books he would pen during his life—among them *Twilight of the Idols* and *Antichrist*—Nietzsche chose a city with giant open piazzas, "air of the highest purity" (*KGB*, October 1888, III.5:1137), a city "not modern at all" (*KGB*, April 1888, III.5:1013), a city where he finally enjoyed a caesarea from his decades of illness: Turin.

Turin was an auspicious location to launch a war on the heart of Europe. In 58 BCE Proconsul Julius Cæsar had built a *Castrum* in *Gallia Cisalpina*, situated on a flat plain next to the river Po, with a distant view of the western Alps. This *Castrum* was called *Taurinorum*, and was to be a site for gathering Cæsar's military strength prior to his conquest of what lay north beyond the mountains. Nearly two millennia later, on the last day of the year 1888, Nietzsche writes mad letters from the city which has grown out of Cæsar's *Castrum*; he sends one letter to Heinrich Köselitz claiming he has now "crossed the famous Rubicon" (*KGB*, December 1888, III.5:1227), and one to August Strindberg that expresses, "I want to put the young Kaiser in front of a firing squad," signing his name "Nietzsche Cæsar" (*KGB*, December 1888, III.5:1228).

On the first day of the year 1889 there was a total eclipse of the sun; it was around this time Nietzsche is generally considered to have lapsed into complete insanity. His "invasion" took the form of one last train ride through the Alps with his old friend Franz Overbeck and a Jewish dentist. His increasing delusions were fed with promising words and opioids in an effort to get him safely to a psychiatric clinic in Basel. Once arrived in Basel, it was then upon his mother's insistence that he transfer to an institution in Jena. Nietzsche's mother would later write to Overbeck that as the train moved down the Alps and passed into Germany, Nietzsche flew into a bloodthirsty rage, and had to be restrained by attendants.[18]

Europe's experience with Nietzsche

I am neither farmer, mechanic, merchant nor shopkeeper. I believe, however, I am of the first class. I am a farmer of thoughts, and all the crops I raise I give away.

—Thomas Paine to Henry Laurens, Spring 1778

After word of his tragic ending reached the other side of the Alps Nietzsche's fame skyrocketed. The philosopher had been forced to self-publish all of his books after *Beyond Good and Evil*, but by the end of the First World War over a quarter of a million copies of *Thus Spoke Zarathustra* alone would be in circulation. This put *Zarathustra* sales above most best-selling fiction books of the time, an accomplishment almost unheard of for a work of philosophy. We are only given hints of how entrancing Nietzsche was for the modernist generation: as early as 1897, when he had not yet passed away, his followers were already being described as a "cult" in book-length critiques.[19] The war Nietzsche launched was a war of and on the spirit. His writings opened up a new atmosphere; fresh air swept across the continent, and many people took in Nietzsche's mood unknowingly. Nietzsche was neither a heroic engineer, groundbreaking inventor, nor glorious statesmen. He was a "farmer of thoughts," and his influence on European modernism is difficult to quantify.

The magician

On May 17, 1900—exactly 100 days before Friedrich Nietzsche died—Frank Baum published *The Wonderful Wizard of Oz*. Baum's book contains a powerful fantasy, specifically crafted to appeal to the modern imagination. Baum writes in the introduction:

> Modern education includes morality; therefore the modern child seeks only entertainment in its wonder tales and gladly dispenses with all disagreeable incident ... [*The Wonderful Wizard of Oz*] aspires to be a modernized fairy tale, in which wonderment and joy are retained and the heartaches and nightmares are left out.[20]

What if instead of reading "child" literally in the above passage, we instead took this word to refer to the "child" of the modernist century? The new kind of human experience born near the *fin de siè cle*? "Modern education includes morality" essentially means that not only can virtue be taught, but it has already been institutionalized in the school system. Morals no longer need to be wrapped in persuasive and amusing myths. Instead of aiming at sublime engagement with life and suffering, art should be repurposed to distract and entertain. Baum's criticism of modernity was rooted in the spreading Nietzscheanism, "There exists a self-contempt, however, among the moderns: like Schopenhauer, they want to 'lose themselves' in art—escape into the object, 'deny' themselves" (*KSA*, 11:25[164]). Nietzsche's experience at Bayreuth convinced him that the art of the future—the art of modernity—would be spectacular, saturated in sensationalism, and intended to lead the audience away from themselves.

The Wonderful Wizard of Oz is an attempt at describing the conditions of modernist life. Without warning, Dorothy's innocent agricultural existence has been lost in a whirlwind; she experiences the loss of gravity that accompanies being uprooted by an enormous and incomprehensible force. The readers subsequently find themselves in a confusing world, where people have lost their hearts, their courage, and their minds. Based upon gossip and herd-mentality, the protagonists travel to a cosmopolis in search of what they are convinced they have lost, spellbound by the reputation and spectacle of the magician, Oz. As it turns out, Oz was actually more of an industrious entrepreneur, an especially talented propagandist, and even a Wagnerian.[21] The character Oz reflects the author's sentiment that the purpose of the modern spectacle is to intensify, simplify, and universalize a message, and to bring this easily digestible message to a public that yearns for direction and distraction.

Nietzsche had articulated this same conviction that the general loss of orientation in the modern individual and society would be followed by a hunger for distraction. He theorized that the subsequent unmooring of mythology from education and the replacement of centers of meaning with centers of entertainment and gossip would lead to an even more superficial public sphere, and a population who was anxious for the next new stimulant.

> "Modernity" as a parable of nutrition and digestion.
>
> Sensibility fails inconceivably ... The abundance of disparate impressions is greater than ever before:—the cosmopolitanization of food, literature, newspapers, images, tastes, even landscapes, etc. The tempo of this influx is prestissimo; the impressions wipe themselves away; man defends himself instinctively, and resists taking anything in too deep, resists "digesting" anything—and a weakening of the digestive power results. A kind of adaptation to this inundation of impressions occurs: man unlearns to act; *he only reacts* to excitations from the outside. (*KSA*, 12:10[18])

There is no evidence that Baum had ever read Nietzsche, and yet it is hard not to detect his footprints in Baum's writing—both thinkers had a remarkably similar conception of what modernity *was*. This leads us to the question we wish to pursue: what does it mean to "influence"?

It is unlikely that any writer in 1900, even a children's writer, had not at least heard of the exploits of Nietzsche. But there is very little one can gather about an author through hearsay except perhaps the general mood of his writings. As a modernist, Baum's generation forged the links that would interconnect the world: technically with undersea cables, demographically with train travel, politically with "grand politics." Baum himself understood the power of myth to bind his generation socially, with the instruments of mass media. However, all of these wonders were accompanied by dissatisfactions, as should be evident in Baum's cynical introduction. Nietzsche claimed he represented a way out. He offered the outline of an attitude by which the dissatisfied could distance themselves from modernity.

Unlike many other literary trends, the kind of literary modernism we find in Baum should not necessarily be viewed as an affirmative attempt to expand the domain of what it was possible to write about; rather it might be more accurate to view it as a reaction against the encroachment of mass media upon the value of literature. As Peter Sloterdijk has written, "Nietzsche had understood that the phenomenon that would emerge irresistibly in tomorrow's culture was the need to distinguish oneself from the mass."[22] Nietzsche articulated the dissatisfactions a generation of readers had with modernity. Nietzsche was the promise of the new century—the promise that their lives might not become meaningless in the face of the death of God, the promise that capitalism couldn't reach to the bottom of their souls, that humanity could still take on great projects and love their fate. The modernist generation, which would see the supposed demise of the concept of heroism, found one of their last daring champions in the mind of Friedrich Nietzsche.

The Great War

Perhaps Nietzsche's most chilling prophecy is the line in *Ecce Homo* that reads "there will be wars the like of which have never yet been seen on earth" (*EH*, *Why I Am a Destiny*, 1). The question therefore had to be asked, were heroic men of letters still possible in a world of spectacular entertainments and distractions? Could an author like Thomas Paine have the same effect in 1900 that he did in 1776? Could a book still awaken a nation? It was certainly believed by many contemporaries that Nietzsche possessed this same power. In 1914, a month after Germany invaded Belgium, Ashley Dukes wrote a front-page article for the *Globe* entitled "Is it Nietzsche?"[23] Lecture halls across America during the year 1916 heard William Mackintire Salter defend Nietzsche's name against the charges he saw in the headlines—that the Great War was *Nietzsche in Action*, or the *Euro-Nietzschean War*.[24] H. L. Mencken, in the introduction to his translation of *Der Antichrist*, explains that he was detained by the United States Department of Justice, and forced to explain his connection to "the German monster, Nietzsky [*sic*]."[25] Mencken explains his absolute astonishment at how widespread the belief was that Nietzsche was responsible for the Great War, and was only able to attribute it to a case of mass war hysteria.

John Maynard Keynes reflects in 1920 on the effect of the Great War in his short book: *The Economic Consequences of the Peace*. Just as Nietzsche placed Germany at the center of Europe's spiritual modernism, Keynes places special emphasis on the role Germany had in bringing Europe toward modernized economic integration:

> Around Germany as a central support the rest of the European economic system grouped itself, and on the prosperity and enterprise of Germany the prosperity of the rest of the Continent mainly depended. The increasing pace of Germany gave her neighbors an outlet for their products, in exchange for which the enterprise of the German merchant supplied them with their chief requirements at a low price. The statistics of the economic interdependence of Germany and her neighbors are overwhelming. Germany was the best customer of Russia, Norway, Holland, Belgium, Switzerland, Italy, and Austria-Hungary; she was the second best customer of Great Britain, Sweden, and Denmark; and the third best customer of France. She was the largest source of supply to Russia, Norway, Sweden, Denmark, Holland, Switzerland, Italy, Austria-Hungary, Roumania, and Bulgaria; and the second largest source of supply to Great Britain, Belgium, and France.[26]

Keynes prefaces his analysis of the Treaty of Versailles with this exposition of the importance of Germany in order to give more gravity to his conclusive analysis that "the economic clauses of the Treaty [of Versailles] are comprehensive, and little has been overlooked which might impoverish Germany now or obstruct her development in future."[27] The war had destroyed the infrastructure of integration built up in the nineteenth century, but as many others besides Keynes noted, it was the peace which followed that ensured the devastation of this "central support" of European integration, and thus ravaged the *spirit* of "good Europeanism." International lending all but ceased, international migration slowed nearly to a halt, and still has yet to reach pre-World War levels.[28] The urban centers of Europe—which represented the nucleus of modernization—re-encountered the supposedly ancient problem of mass starvation.[29] As Keynes notes, "Even when coal can be got and grain harvested, the breakdown of the European railway system prevents their carriage; and even when goods can be manufactured, the breakdown of the European currency system prevents their sale."[30]

Could this catastrophic disintegration of European society be in any way the fault of Nietzsche? Near the end of the war, Sir Charles Waldstein published a book entitled *Aristodemocracy* (1917), in which he argues that Nietzsche was indeed responsible for the World War. Not at all because of his supposed Prussian militarism (which Waldstein understood Nietzsche opposed), but because "in Nietzsche we have the complete, fearless, and logical construction of this general revolt against the whole fabric of the religious, moral, and social traditions ruling the modern world."[31] Waldstein believed the war to have been caused by "a hiatus, if not a direct contradiction, between our faith and professions and our actions, which did not exist in former ages to the same degree; that civilized humanity is at sea regarding its most important ideas and ideals."[32] Waldstein tries to identify the *mood* which led Europe to devour itself, and concludes that there are none who could have more claims to the destruction of Europe's faith in itself, to pushing humanity out to sea, than Friedrich Nietzsche.

At the end of this first summer of the new century—on August 25, 1900[33]—Nietzsche died. It is therefore a testament to his widespread and enduring fame how many academics as well as members of the popular press cast the blame for the Great War at his feet. Nobel Prize winner and dramatist Romain Rolland reflects that the central problem with Nietzsche's philosophy was, in fact, its popularity: "One Superman is a sublime spectacle. Ten or twenty supermen are unpleasant. But hundreds of thousands who combine their arrogant extravagance with mediocrity or natural baseness become the scourge of god which is ravaging Belgium and France."[34] This is the phenomenon that we wish to study: the writings of this solitary, free wanderer which found admirers and perhaps more strangely—imitators. From devoted disciples such as Thomas Mann to distant messages communicated to the authors of children's literature, Nietzsche's aphorisms spread like an epidemic. In the present volume we endeavor to examine how this virus morphed and adapted from host to host, and explore the various means by which Nietzsche became *popular*.

Overview of the collection

Like the other volumes in this series, our collection is divided into three parts. The first six contributors each discuss the historical context and philosophical importance of one major work that Nietzsche authored. The chapters in Part I are chronologically sequenced according to which text they address. This allows for a certain amount of broad conceptualization concerning the progress of Nietzsche's thought before delving into his relationship with the modernists. In Part II our next ten authors each present a broader refraction of Nietzsche's illumination of the modern condition. Each author in this part discusses the impact of Nietzsche on a figure or movement of modernism. This part opens up into more diverse chapters about Nietzsche's various reappearances in cultural movements associated with modernism. Part III is a series of short chapters, each dedicated to explaining a specific term in Nietzsche's philosophy. This part is a reference guide that aims to dispel confusion concerning specific enigmatic themes that recur within the texts and chapters.

The volume opens with the chapter by Patricia Valderrama on *The Birth of Tragedy*. Valderrama expands the concept of the Dionysian beyond the human realm to encompass a greater community of living beings. Her chapter can be read next to the *Dionysiac* entry in the Glossary. Siobhan Lyons then analyzes Nietzsche's *Daybreak*. She places a heavy emphasis on the nature of dreams in this work, and uses this discussion to explore the connection between Nietzsche and Freud. SJ Cowan authors the next chapter on *The Gay Science*. Cowan compares Nietzsche's project in this work to the basic presumptions of the Enlightenment, and its rational philosophy. Cowan explains how Nietzsche is critiquing a "seriousness" which has pervaded all previous philosophical thought, and therefore reads this work as an attempt to critique the act of thinking itself. This chapter is related to the glossary entry on *Danger.* In the next chapter on *Thus Spoke Zarathustra*, which relates to the glossary article *From Zoroaster to Zarathustra*, Douglas Burnham focuses on the notion of the individual, and specifically the presumed foundational value of the individual person. Moving toward the last works that Nietzsche produces, I analyze the content and form of *Antichrist.* In this chapter I address the question put forth earlier in the introduction: what kind of effect could a writer hope to have in a world that has modernized, and has been filled with sensationalized distractions? My chapter connects with the glossary entry on *The Revaluation of all Values*. Part I concludes with Karl Laderoute's analysis of *Twilight of the Idols*. Laderoute argues that the unusual clarity of *Twilight* in distinction to Nietzsche's other works indicates that Nietzsche wanted to use this text to synthesize and respond to the major themes in the history of philosophy, focusing especially on Greek thought.

Part II of this collection is subdivided into three sections: *The Image*, *Psychoanalysis*, and *Literature*. The first quartet of articles, written on *The Image* connects back to my chapter on *Antichrist* and foreword to the section on *Figuration and Imagery* in the glossary. This section commences with a chapter by Yunus Tuncel on the convoluted nature of Greek theater and Wagnerian opera in Nietzsche's thought. Jeremy Killian furthers this notion of the "modern spectacle," beginning like Tuncel with *The Birth of Tragedy* (both chapters relate to the *Dionysiac* entry in the glossary) and the idea that life is aesthetically justified. Killian's claim is that the eternal recurrence (related to the *Eternal Recurrence* entry in the glossary) offers a new, modernist justification of reality, but one that is also couched in the ancient method of theater and spectacle. Kaitlyn Creasy brings the discussion concerning the nature of the image and the spectacle out of the realm of abstraction in her chapter on the influence of Friedrich

Nietzsche upon the Zürich Dada movement. Reading the Dada Manifesto among other texts, Creasy focuses on the aporia of meaningless which results from the destruction of the limiting human constructs of divinity, purpose, truth, and value in Nietzsche's analysis of nihilism. Adrian Switzer concludes this section by writing on the often overlooked and constitutive role that the theme of "decadence" played in the origins of literary modernism. Switzer situates Nietzsche at the beginning of literary modernism by aligning his decadent stylistic sensibilities with his critique of decadence as an essentially Romantic aesthetic and form of cultural conservatism. This chapter connects to *Decadence* in the glossary.

Switzer's chapter on the declining health of Europe gives us a transition into the new kinds of doctors who were treating the European maladies. The middle section of Part II focuses on Nietzsche's relationship to the psychoanalytic movement; it connects especially to Lyon's chapter on *Dawn*. Tim Themi writes an expansive chapter that reads the surrealists from Bataille to Lacan to situate the position of Nietzsche's influence in the cultural conflict between Athens and Jerusalem. Ritske Rensma authors the second chapter in this section which tracks the influence of Nietzsche on Carl Jung, and mediates on the unconscious motivations for the Great War in Europe. Rensma's chapter looks forward to both Mcdonald's chapter and the glossary entry on *The Will to Power*.

Our final section concerns modernist literature. This section looks backward to Cowan's analysis of *The Gay Science*, and Valderrama's on *The Birth of Tragedy*. We again transition using the concept of physiology into Jill Marsden's chapter. Marsden makes connections between Nietzsche's philosophy and the materiality of writing in the modernist experiments of Joyce, Woolf, and Faulkner. James Luchte then writes about Nietzsche's relationship with Welsh poet Dylan Thomas. Luchte describes a mood that transferred between the two writers, a mood of properly tragic joyfulness that Thomas captured in his poetry and life. In the next chapter Sebastian Hüsch connects Nietzsche's perspectivism to Robert Musil's writings. He elaborates how Musil's approach of "Ironic Essayism" can be read as a microcosm of the response of modernity to Nietzsche's thought. Bill McDonald closes Part II with an chapter on one of Nietzsche's most devoted disciples: Thomas Mann. McDonald's chapter demonstrates just how deeply Nietzsche could affect an author who lived during this period, covering Mann's response to Nietzsche's reception among the political and militaristic classes of Europe.

The volume concludes with Part III: eight chapters on a selection of key Nietzschean concepts. Many of Nietzsche's aphorisms will reference concepts and theories which he never systematically developed, which can only be understood through hundreds of hints and implications that he placed in different contexts throughout his career. These chapters aim to provide succinct entry points into some of the complex subjects in Nietzsche's philosophy, specifically focusing on concepts that are referenced in the first two divisions of the volume. Thus the three divisions of our volume replicate a kind of chronology: Part I examines Nietzsche's life and what he produced during his time; Part II examines the impact his writings had upon the modernists after his death; and Part III reflects back upon and—from a contemporary perspective—synthesizes some of the concepts found deep within Nietzsche's work.

Notes

1 Emile Cardon, "L'Exposition des révoltes." *La Presse* (Paris), April 29, 1874. Accessed January 19, 2018. http://gallica.bnf.fr/ark:/12148/bpt6k514661n/f2.vertical.r=emile.
2 Hans Ulrich Gumbrecht, trans. Erik Butler. *Atmosphere, Mood, Stimmung: On a Hidden Potential of Literature* (Stanford: Stanford University Press, 2012), 20.
3 Theodor Adorno, *In Search of Wagner* (London: Verso, 2009), 74.
4 With gratitude: "Peter Sloterdijk on Friedrich Nietzsche." Interview. *Entitled Opinions* (audio), December 15, 2016. Accessed January 19, 2018. https://entitledopinions.stanford.edu/episodes.
5 This was, in another accident of Nietzsche's life, the 244th death anniversary of "the Lion of the North," Gustavus Adolphus: one of the first European heroes who attempted to retain his heroism in the face of the phenomenon of gunpowder. He died at the Battle of Lützen in 1632 while on a campaign meant to prevent the unification of a German state.
6 Kevin H. O'Rourke and Stephen Broadberry, eds. *The Cambridge Economic History of Europe: 1870 to the Present.* Vol. 2 (Cambridge: Cambridge University Press, 2010), 13. Broadberry and O'Rourke refer here especially to the movements to America from Europe.
7 Adna Ferrin Weber, *The Growth of Cities* (New York: Macmillan company, 1899), 83.
8 "Figure 2 provides similar evidence for another commodity, wheat, and a different pair of countries, Britain and the US.1 The price gap 3 fluctuated widely around an average level of maybe 100% between 1800 and 1840, before falling sharply, and reaching negligible levels by the eve of World War I. (Strikingly, there has been no further price convergence for this commodity and this pair of markets during the twentieth century.)" (O'Rourke, *The Cambridge Economic History of Europe,* 3).
9 Kevin O'Rourke, "Europe and the Causes of Globalization, 1790 to 2000." In *Europe and Globalization*, ed. H. Kierzkowski (Palgrave Macmillan, 2002), 66. Carl Strikwerda also makes this claim (Carl Strikwerda, *The First World War in the History of Globalization*. Proceedings of Legacy of World War One, Chestnut Hill College. 1).
10 John Maynard Keynes, *The Economic Consequences of Peace* (New York: Harcourt, Brace and Howe, 1920). May 6, 2005. Accessed January 19, 2018. http://www.gutenberg.org/ebooks/15776.
11 Gary Shapiro has commented on this aphorism that "in the early 1870s, in the aftermath of the Franco-Prussian War, Nietzsche confronted a German cultural world comparable in some ways to that of the United States and its allies in the 1990s, following the collapse of the Soviet Union and the apparent success of the first Gulf War against Iraq. In both cases, a victorious nation congratulated itself on a newly enhanced position of power and took its victory as an obvious sign of its cultural superiority. Bismarck presided over the founding of the German Reich at Versailles and Bush 41 proclaimed the emergence of a "new world order" (Gary Shapiro, *Nietzsche's Earth: Great Events, Great Politics* (Chicago: University of Chicago Press, 2016), 23). This insightful analysis portrays an analogy between Germany and the

United States as the dominant military powers and France and Russia as the cowed rivals.

12 William Altman believes this to be a reference to The Congress of Berlin (1878) (William H. F. Altman, *Friedrich Wilhelm Nietzsche: the philosopher of the Second Reich* (Lanham, MD: Lexington Books, 2014), 27–28). However, Nietzsche, like Hitler, believed he had a special destiny connected with the Thirty Years' War, writing to George Brandes in 1888, "I was born on 15 Oct. 1844, on the battlefield of Lützen. The first name I heard was Gustav Adolfs." (*KGB*, April 1888, III.5:1014).

13 For an excellent analysis of the Enlightenment's impact on Nietzsche's middle phase, see: Franco, Paul. *Nietzsche's Enlightenment: The Free-Spirit Trilogy of the Middle Period* (Chicago: University of Chicago Press), 2011.

14 Or pushed them away as in the case of Erwin Rhode (*KGB*, November 1887, III.5:950) or Malwida von Meysenbug (*KGB*, October 1888, III.5:1135).

15 Heinrich Heine, *Heinrich Heines Sämtliche Werke*, ed. Ernst Elster. Vol. 6. 7 vols. (Leipzig: Bibliographisches Institut, 1910), 360.

16 See *BGE*, 257.

17 See also *BGE*, 256.

18 Curt Paul Janz, *Nietzsche, Biographie*. Vol. 3 (Hanser, 1978), 82.

19 Ferdinand Tonnies, *Der Nietzsche Kultus*: Eine kritike (leipzig: O.R. Reisland, 1897).

20 Frank Baum,. *The Wonderful Wizard of Oz*. (Dover Children''s Evergreen Classics. Dover Publications, 1996), iii.

21 Peter Sloterdijk, *Nietzsche Apostle*, trans. Steve Corcoran (Semiotexte, 2013), 67.

22 Oz claims that he had built the entire Emerald Cosmopolis (in Baum's usual cynicism) "Just to amuse myself" (Ibid. 161). Mirroring Nietzsche's depiction of Wagner: "I did it only for amusement" (*Z*, *The Magician*, 2).

23 Ashley Dukes, "Is it Nietzsche?" *The Globe* (London), September 1914. Accessed January 20, 2018. https://www.britishnewspaperarchive.co.uk/viewer/bl/0001652/19141008/013/0001. His conclusion, to be fair, was that it was not Nietzsche.

24 Citing *The Unpopular Review*, January 1915, and advertisements of "Why We Are at War," by members of the Oxford Faculty of Modern History, in *The Nation* (New York), September and October 1914.

25 Friedrich Nietzsche, *The Antichrist*, trans. H. L. Menken (New York: Alfred A. Knopf, 1918), 15.

26 Keynes, *The Economic Consequences of Peace*, 111–12.

27 Ibid., 16–17.

28 "Overseas migration to the United States fell from 1.1 million annually in both 1913 and 1914 to an average of only 232,000 between 1922 and 1929 and to only 30,000 in the 1930s. Migration has never been as important in the world again as it was before 1914. The level of migration today is only about a third of what it was before World War One" (Strikwerda, *The First World War in the History of Globalization*, 8).

29 "Internally the population is not evenly distributed, but much of it is crowded into a relatively small number of dense industrial centers. This population secured for itself a livelihood before the war, without much margin of surplus, by means of a delicate and immensely complicated organization, of which the foundations were supported by coal, iron, transport, and an unbroken supply of imported food and raw materials from other continents. By the destruction of this organization and the interruption of the stream of supplies, a part of this population is deprived of its means of livelihood. ... The danger confronting us, therefore, is the rapid depression of the

standard of life of the European populations to a point which will mean actual starvation for some (a point already reached in Russia and approximately reached in Austria). Men will not always die quietly. For starvation, which brings to some lethargy and a helpless despair, drives other temperaments to the nervous instability of hysteria and to a mad despair. And these in their distress may overturn the remnants of organization, and submerge civilization itself in their attempts to satisfy desperately the overwhelming needs of the individual" (Keynes, *The Economic Consequences of Peace*, 227–28).

30 Ibid., 233.

31 Waldstein, Sir Charles. *Aristodemocracy* (London: Murray, 1916), 174.

32 Waldstein, *Aristodemocracy*, 168.

33 The 1643th Anniversary of the last Pagan Emperor of Rome defeating the Germanic Tribes at the Battle of Strasbourg.

34 Quoted from Steven E Aschheim, *The Nietzsche Legacy in Germany: 1890-1990* (Berkeley: University of California Press, 1994), 130.

Part One

Conceptualizing Nietzsche

1

Nonhuman Transcendence: Art and Non-Anthropocentrism in *The Birth of Tragedy*

Patricia Valderrama

Nietzsche's first book, *The Birth of Tragedy*, emerged out of the confluence of several influences and motivations, both personal and intellectual. He pitched it to a potential publisher as a meditation on Wagner, by then the young man's friend, under the guise of a treatise on Greek culture, by then his official academic field.[1] Although Nietzsche held unconventional views on the purpose and aims of the philological profession, his early and extensive education in classics at Pforta left him with a profound knowledge of and lasting love for ancient European cultures.[2] It was also at Pforta where Nietzsche first committed to paper—in poetry and prose—the ideas on life, death, and tragedy that he takes up again in *The Birth of Tragedy*.[3]

Much like Nietzsche advocated for a study of ancient history tailored to understand his present (*AOM*, 218), I read *The Birth of Tragedy* to see what Nietzsche's views on life, death, and art can do for us in the twenty-first century. I propose it has the most relevance in those moments when the twenty-seven-year-old philosopher casts his eyes up, seeking to transcend the material world, and instead locates aesthetic transcendence within human fleshiness, in the particular materiality of our embodiment that intimately connects us to our nonhuman-animal kin. These connections were just beginning to be understood in the West when the book first was published in 1872. Indeed, Nietzsche's education in natural and human sciences at Bonn, including Darwin's *On the Origin of Species* (1859, German trans. 1860), encouraged his turn away from Christianity as well as his embrace of Schopenhauer's philosophy and of Hölderlin's aesthetics.[4]

These emotional-intellectual shifts that Nietzsche experienced in his student days inform *The Birth of Tragedy*: in the way it paraphrases Schopenhauer in the fundamental existential question it poses, and in its attempt to salvage the idea of transcendence from Christian theology by bringing it to the realm of art. As the biographer Julian Young explains, "Fritz's own 'enlightenment' during the Pforta years required him to abandon the naïve theological dogma of his upbringing. ... Fritz's piety became a piety towards art."[5] It is precisely the convergence of the existential question and the metaphysical role that Nietzsche claims for art—like Wagner and Schopenhauer before him—that interests me here. *The Birth of Tragedy* represents Nietzsche's first sustained effort to develop a "purely artistic" and non-Christian "doctrine" for and on behalf of life, a doctrine that he later calls "Dionysiac" (*BT*, *P*, 5). In *The Birth of Tragedy*, he argues that art makes life worth living, despite all the suffering that living entails, and allows humans to experience momentary transcendence precisely because of its non-anthropocentric, multispecies, and embodied character.

As our species confronts a qualitatively different existential threat in the form of anthropogenic climate change, it behooves us to consider what art can do, beyond mimetic representation, to help us face the challenges the next decades and centuries will surely bring. Reckoning with these challenges involves steeling ourselves against unhappy and inconvenient truths, including the possibility of our own extinction within the next eight decades.[6] I believe Nietzsche's insistent and persistent search for the truth, no matter how discomforting the result or the personal consequences, makes him a useful companion in trying to think about art and climate change together.[7] *The Birth of Tragedy* in particular lends itself to this sort of thinking because, in it Nietzsche locates the source of art, and therefore transcendence, in animality and the source of existential suffering in individuation.

Nietzsche begins *The Birth of Tragedy* by identifying the source of art—all art—in nature, rather than in the realm of exclusively human activity. A more-than-human nature channels two agonistic and complementary energies through humans, who Nietzsche conceives of as vessels for nature's impulses, and the product of this channeling is art.[8] Famously, these two vital energies are the Apollonian and the Dionysian. Nietzsche defines them early on as "artistic powers which erupt from nature itself, *without the mediation of any human artist*, and in which nature's artistic drives attain their first, immediate satisfaction" (*BT*, 2). "Artistic pleasure must exist even without human beings," he insists, considering "the bright flower or the peacock's tail" analogous to human-made works of art (*KSA*, 7:7[117]). These early and emphatic claims that art is a wholly non-anthropocentric affair frames his treatment of the Apollonian and, especially, the Dionysian. Rather than viewing humans as the pinnacle achievement of evolution and human culture as the evidence of that status, he evinces a tacit understanding of humans as one kind of being among many, as participants in, rather than dominators of, the more-than-human world he calls nature.[9]

The specific culture that Nietzsche analyzes in *The Birth of Tragedy* lends itself to non-anthropocentrism. The borders of species-being were arguably more fluid for the ancient Greeks: think of the Sphinx, defined by her cleverness and her interspecies body combining human, lion, and bird; or think of Medusa, the only mortal Gorgon, a woman with wings and a head full of snakes, from whose decapitated body Pegasus emerges, and whose dripping blood generates the coral reef in the sea; or, since these interspecies women were both killed by men, think of Dionysus himself.[10] Accompanied by maenads, sileni, centaurs, and satyrs, Dionysus has the horns of a bull, when he is not transforming into one.

Nevertheless, to describe Nietzsche as a full-throated post-anthropocentric thinker *avant la lettre* would overstate the case. A product of its time, in *The Birth of Tragedy*

Nietzsche shows distrust or open contempt for "barbarians" (*BT*, 2, 4, 15, 18); some non-European societies, especially Eastern ones (*BT*, 15); the French (*BT*, 23); would-be revolutionaries threatening social order (*BT*, 18); sexuality, especially women's (*BT*, 2); and "womanish" flights of reason (*BT*, 11); in all those tropes of Western philosophy built up from the nature/culture binary. One of the earliest depictions of the glory of the Dionysian illuminates the uneven texture of Nietzsche's non-anthropocentrism. He writes, "Not only is the bond between human beings renewed by the magic of the Dionysiac, but nature, alienated, inimical, or subjugated, celebrates once more her festival of reconciliation with her lost son, humankind." Nature is personified, not simply linguistically, but in a way that lends the more-than-human world agency and even emotion. For their part, human beings are located on a continuum of life, but according to a European Romantic motif, we remain exceptional for having been "lost." His philosophy continues to enact this human exceptionalism in reverse, arguing, in Vanessa Lemm's gloss, that "human life is the weakest and most fragile form of animal life. The vulnerability of the human animal is related to its relative inferiority."[11] In *The Birth of Tragedy*, he continues, "Freely the earth offers up her gifts, and the beasts of prey from mountain and desert approach in peace. The chariot of Dionysus is laden with flowers and wreaths; beneath its yoke stride panther and tiger" (*BT*, 1). The Dionysian brings peaceful reconciliation with nonhuman animals, so that humans exist on "a continuum of *animal* life."[12] But even after this multispecies reunion has taken place, "panther and tiger" remain in a yoke. Thus, the ontological continuity across species that Nietzsche posits as early as *The Birth of Tragedy* does not entail ontological equality, either before or after humans have rejoined the more-than-human world through the Dionysian. In sum, the young Nietzsche of *The Birth of Tragedy* already espouses the idea of interspecies continuity, but he seems indecisive about the position of human animals on the continuum of animal life.

This vision of the world renewed by Dionysian "magic" already indicates the point where the metaphysical role of art and the existential question converge. Both separately and together, the Apollonian and the Dionysian fulfill specific purposes not just for the more-than-human world that seeks to express them, but for humans, whose experience of the world is characterized by suffering. Nietzsche, going beyond even Schopenhauer, understands existential pain as a structural feature of human life.[13] The more-than-human world, as the source of the Apollonian and the Dionysian, intervenes at the moment when existence would otherwise be unendurable and provides humans with artistically generative modes to cope with and transcend this existential suffering.

Nietzsche recounts an episode from classical Western mythology to define the cause of existential human suffering while differentiating between the remedies the Apollonian and the Dionysian energies offer. After King Midas captures Silenus, the human-horse companion of Dionysus, the king asks the forest "daemon" "what is the best and most excellent thing for human beings." Addressing our whole species, Silenus shares his animal wisdom with a laugh: "The very best thing is utterly beyond your reach: not to have been born, not to *be*, to be *nothing*. However, the second best thing for you is: to die soon" (*BT*, 3). The Dionysian and Apollonian each respond to this existential truth in their own way. The Apollonian mediates the "terrors and horrors of existence" distilled in Silenus's wisdom through dream and illusion. In the plastic arts, for example, "Apollo overcomes the individual's suffering by his luminous glorification of the *eternity of appearance*; here beauty gains victory over the suffering inherent in life; in a certain sense, a lie is told which causes pain to disappear from the features of nature" (*BT*, 16). This is the metaphysical function of Apollonian art: its formal beauty soothes the Greeks in order "to seduce" them "into continuing to live" as if Silenus's wisdom were not true (*BT*, 3). Apollonian illusion, then, masks "the eternal, primal pain, the only ground of the world," but its beauty does not and cannot overcome the Dionysian truth about the pain of existence that Silenus reveals (*BT*, 4). Thus, in the words of Gilles Deleuze, "Beneath Apollo, Dionysus rumbles."[14]

Nietzsche later elucidates the source and cause of primal pain by restating the dynamic between the Apollonian and the Dionysian in the vocabulary of Schopenhauer, whose philosophy so enamored him at the time. "Apollo stands before me as the transfiguring genius of the *principium individuationis*, through whom alone release and redemption in semblance can be truly attained," he explains, "whereas under the mystical, jubilant shout of Dionysus the spell of individuation is broken, and the path to the Mothers of Being, to the innermost core of things, is laid open" (*BT*, 16). Pairing Silenus's wisdom with the reformulation of artistic transcendence in terms of the *principium individuationis*, it seems that it would be best for humans to have never been individuated, materially and biologically. *The Birth of Tragedy*, unique among the other works in which Nietzsche would take up these same questions, singles out individuation as the origin of the terrors and horrors of existence that require the metaphysical balm that art alone can give.[15] "We are to regard the state of individuation as the source and primal cause of all suffering," he declares (*BT*, 10). Because individuation cannot be undone, it would simply be best for humans to die soon. As a return to nothingness, death also entails returning to the pluripotency and plenitude of raw matter. Or as he muses in his notebook, "In so far as contradiction is the essence of the primal One, it can be the supreme pain and the supreme joy at the same time" (*KSA*, 7:7[157]). This alignment of joyful plenitude and pain lies at the core of the Dionysian, in its expression of the truth that the horse-human Silenus reveals as the ground of human existence and in its metaphysical-aesthetic role.

In this metaphysical function, Dionysian art taps into the plenitude of raw matter, allowing us to transcend the individuation that causes our suffering through our very embodiment. The Dionysian achieves the dissolution of individuation through and in humans' bodies, that is, through the materiality that does, in fact, connect us to all nonhuman-animal and plant life. The elder Nietzsche seems aware of the humbling and connective power of corporeality when he writes that "the bowels are the reason why man does not believe himself a God" (*BGE*, 141). It follows that Nietzsche would conceive of Dionysian art as a particularly non-anthropocentric and even multispecies affair. While "singing and dancing," the two Dionysian arts par excellence, "man expresses his sense of belonging to a higher community." Nietzsche continues, "He has forgotten how to walk and talk and is on the brink of flying and dancing, up and away into the air above. ... The animals now talk and earth gives milk and honey" (*BT*, 1).

Evidence of our supposed exceptionalism—bipedalism and language—fade away without much lament as the Dionysian grounds us in our fleshy animality and allows us to understand nonhuman animals, who can, now, "talk." The resultant sensation of "mystical oneness" imparts feelings of "blissful ecstasy" and enchantment (*BT*, 1).

In spite of all the somatic, transcendent pleasure of the Dionysian, Nietzsche also believes it contains the potential for the reckless violence commonly associated with intoxication. As a consequence of expressing the fullness of the more-than-human world, the Dionysian also expresses "the cruelty of nature" (*BT*, 7). Like ecosystems, the Dionysian is beyond good and evil. It asserts the totality of the more-than-human world in all its manifestations and connections, painful and joyous alike. "Everything here speaks only of over-brimming, indeed triumphant existence, where everything that exists has been deified, regardless of whether it is good or bad," Nietzsche explains (*BT*, 3). He distinguishes the Greeks from "Dionysiac Barbarians" in an attempt to differentiate between what is good—music—and bad—"sexual indiscipline"—in the Dionysian (*BT*, 2). While certainly influenced by Nietzsche's cultural and political conservatism, his fear of the drunken, licentious mob and the fear of barbarians he imputes to the Greeks have ecological resonances as well.

Although the full extent of our material-biological entanglements with the more-than-human world were not known when Nietzsche was writing *The Birth of Tragedy*, it is clear by now that the radical connection to the unity of life on our planet that Nietzsche ascribes to the Dionysian does not imply any agency over the matter of which we form a part.[16] Be they Hitchcock's birds, Biblical locusts, or stampeding humans, large assemblages of mobile creatures have their own form of thinking and moving together, seemingly as one. Like the Dionysian, these swarms provoke admiration and terror, for their boundless and internally generated energy seems capable of obliterating any obstacle in their path. Euripides's *Bacchae* serves as a useful illustration of the dynamism of swarms—Nietzsche would certainly disagree (*BT*, 11, 12)—for the play depicts the human women who worship the god Dionysus as a jubilant and fearsome swarm, and their beauty and cruelty alike derive from their alliance with and similarities to nonhuman animals. The Maenads wrap themselves in fawn skins, wreaths of ivy and flowers, and living snakes who "licked their cheeks." The intimacy with nonhuman animals goes further, however. "Some of them held a fawn in their arms, or the wild cubs of wolves, and they gave them white milk, those who had recently given birth and whose breasts were swollen, having left their babies behind."[17] A shepherd recounts these events in awe of this multispecies maternal care, although the implied suffering of the abandoned human infants anticipates his later horror. The Maenads then begin to dance, calling to Dionysus "with one voice," and the whole of the more-than-human world around them—organic and inorganic, human animal and nonhuman animal—join in the dance.[18] Shortly thereafter, the Maenads tear cows and bulls apart with their bare hands, exemplifying the heedless power that also inheres in swarms, as well as a patriarchal fear of women's sexuality and empowerment.[19] In this way, both *Bacchae* and *The Birth of Tragedy* portray the multispecies essence of the Dionysian as containing the joy and horror, the love and cruelty, that do inhere within our species' entanglements with the more-than-human world.

Implicit in *The Birth of Tragedy*'s conceptualization of the Dionysian is the realization that a complete acceptance of our materiality and of our animality also means re-considering ourselves as one moving part, insignificant, in the planet's radically connected ecology—an ecology whose connectivity we still can barely comprehend, which acts as a violent force upon all living beings to the extent that all life ends in death, and which, despite all that, is also prolifically generative. As Lemm claims, in Nietzsche's philosophy as a whole "the totality of life is constituted from an agonistic struggle that involves all forms of life for and against each other in a continuous pluralization of inherently singular forms of life."[20] This prolific yet incomprehensible connectivity characterizes the Dionysian and, because it also characterizes ecology, Nietzsche's concept stands out as a fundamentally life-affirming force and frame for thinking about life on a warming planet. In *The Birth of Tragedy*, "Dionysus is insistently presented as the *affirmative and affirming* god," Deleuze comments. "He is not content with 'resolving' pain in a higher and suprapersonal pleasure but rather he affirms it and turns it into someone's pleasure. ... He affirms the pains *of growth* rather than reproducing the sufferings *of individuation*. He is the god who affirms life" no matter what.[21] Within the non-anthropocentric context and tendencies of the Dionysian, what Deleuze calls "the pains of growth" and what Nietzsche calls "all changing appearances" (*BT*, 7), I interpret as the cycles of our planet's biosphere that engender organic life in all its forms and shape the inorganic elements of our world as well.

The biosphere contains a finite quantity of matter, however, so in order for any organism to live, other organisms have to die, and their materiality must be recycled. This is one way the Dionysian converts the pain (death) of some into the pleasure (life) of others, and it applies as much to predator and prey in the food chain as it does to human corpses and microorganisms in the nutrient cycle. Over the course of geological eons, a single carbon atom in a human body, for example, could have moved between the oceans, the soil, the atmosphere, and any number of nonhuman organisms. I am suggesting that Nietzsche's conception of the Dionysian reflects this ecological truth. Indeed, in 1871, while working on *The Birth of Tragedy*, Nietzsche attempted to define life atomically, jotting down, "Life as a continuous paroxysm projecting appearances and doing so joyfully. The atom as a point ... at every smallest moment becoming, *never being*. ... Therefore we may say that the pain of the smallest atom is at the same time the pain of the *one* will; and that all that pain is one and the same" (*KSA*, 7:7[204]). Considered in light of the biosphere's recycling, life can be seen as an infinite becoming, and a kind of joy can be found in thinking of death as a part of this joyous paroxysm. But our own unique lives, and the lives of the unique human and nonhuman animals we love, remain stubbornly finite. Thus, while the Dionysian offers transcendence over individuation as a kind of metaphysical balm, pain remains, latent, at its center.

Because of the pain that comes with joining with the primordial unity, "one will," or nutrient cycle, the Dionysian needs the beautiful and seductive illusion of the Apollonian as its counterpart and complement. (Indeed, Deleuze's reading of Nietzsche identifies the true opposition of *The Birth of Tragedy* in the conflict between the Dionysian and Socratism, as opposed to the semi-dialectical relation between the Dionysian and the Apollonian.[22]) As Nietzsche states, "What is productive, then, is the pain, which creates the beautiful as a related counter-color" (*KSA*, 7:7[116]). The reconciliation of the two vital energies in *art* neutralizes, but does not eliminate, the pain of the Dionysian. He explains that wherever in Greek culture the Apollonian and the Dionysian can be found together, "the only remainder of [Dionysian cruelty] (in the way that medicines recall deadly poisons) is to be found in the strange mixture and duality in the affects of the Dionysiac enthusiasts, that phenomenon whereby pain awakens pleasure while rejoicing wrings cries of agony from the breast. From the highest joy there comes a cry of horror or a yearning lament at some irredeemable loss" (*BT,* 2). In my interpretation, this dynamic of pain and pleasure stems from the tension and mutual interdependence of the uniqueness and multiplicity of matter, the nutrient cycle and our fleeting, individuated embodiment. Nietzsche himself relates the enduring mixture of pleasure and pain to the more-than-human world, saying it is "as if [nature] had cause to sigh over its dismemberment into individuals" (*BT*, 2). The mutually generative aspect of pleasure and pain also brings Nietzsche to the origins of Greek tragedy, that art form which led him to wonder, first at Pforta and again in *The Birth of Tragedy*, why ancient societies would rejoice in watching their heroes' suffering.[23]

The earliest apotheosis of the metaphysical role of art, Greek "*tragedy arose from the tragic chorus* and was originally chorus and nothing but chorus" (*BT*, 7). Nietzsche traces the origin of the tragic chorus, and thus of art's metaphysical potential, to a collective community that is by no means exclusively human:

> I believe that, when faced with the chorus of satyrs, cultured Greeks felt themselves absorbed, elevated, and extinguished [*aufgehoben*]. ... This is the first effect of Dionysiac tragedy: state and society, indeed all divisions between one human being and another, give way to an overwhelming feeling of unity which leads men back to the heart of nature. The metaphysical solace which, I wish to suggest, we derive from every true tragedy, the solace that in the ground of things, and despite all changing appearances, life is indestructibly mighty and pleasurable, this solace appears with palpable clarity in the chorus of satyrs. (*BT*, 7)

Returning to the book's philological task, Nietzsche argues that, over time, the Dionysian and the Apollonian merged semi-dialectically to create Attic tragedy. In his description of the effect of this merging, Nietzsche effectively locates the origin of Greek tragedy in a community of hybrid human-animals. Even if it were merely a matter emphasizing the Dionysian aspect of the art form—he evinces a clear preference for the Dionysian here and in "An Attempt at Self-Criticism"—he could have chosen any other figure in the *thiasus*. Nor is it the satyrs' heterogeneous species-being that makes them unique within the Dionysian posse, which also contains the Maenads (human women), Silenus (horse-human), and Pan (goat-human).[24] Instead, Nietzsche elects to center and ground his analysis of metaphysical art in a *collective* of Dionysian companions whose bodies, like that of Silenus and Pan, emphasize the animality of humans and the humanity of animals. Given that an essential function of the Dionysian is to undo individuation, it seems intuitive that a collective of some kind, rather than an individual, would give voice to its vital energy. Nietzsche specifies that "the chorus of the satyrs is first and foremost a vision of the Dionysiac *mass*" (*BT*, 8; italics added). It is because of their communal voice as well as the particular form of their embodiment that the satyrs mend the breach of alienation between humans and between humans and "the heart of nature." They do so by revealing the truth of existential suffering to the spectators in the controlled and mediated form of tragedy, which transforms the spectators' "revulsion" at Silenus's wisdom through beauty (*BT*, 7).

The chorus of humanimals does not require recourse to human language to express this wisdom. Indeed, "it is impossible for language to exhaust the meaning of music's world-symbolism," Nietzsche elaborates, "because music refers symbolically to the original contradiction and original pain at the heart of the primordial unity, and thus symbolizes a sphere which lies above and beyond all appearances" (*BT*, 6). The non-linguistic aspect of Dionysian music corresponds to the interspecies-becoming of the satyr chorus as well as to the non-anthropocentrism of Dionysian art, while clearly also gesturing toward Schopenhauer's argument about music as the purest expression of reality. In fact, Nietzsche generalizes the superfluity of human language as a feature of all music. To capture the essence of the more-than-human world, "a new world of symbols is required," he writes, "firstly the symbolism of the entire body, not just of the mouth, the face, the word, but the full gesture of dance with its rhythmical movement of every limb" (*BT*, 2).

As a collective of humanimals, the satyr chorus is uniquely qualified to reflect the spectators' own animality, and thus their participation in the nutrient cycle, back to them as an existential truth. In the recognition of their animality, the spectators experience a three-stage *Aufhebung*. First, they feel "extinguished," or fully mortal, then "absorbed" by the biosphere, and, finally, "elevated," transcendentally at one with the more-than-human world. But the process doesn't conclude there, for having "*acquired knowledge* ... they find action repulsive, for their actions can do nothing to change the eternal essence of things; they regard it as laughable or shameful that they should be expected to set to rights a world so out of joint" (*BT*, 7). Once the observer of the satyr chorus "has gazed with keen eye into the midst of the fearful, destructive havoc of so-called world history, and has seen the cruelty of nature," malaise, paralysis, and depression would be the only resulting affects, Nietzsche speculates, were it not for the metaphysical property of tragic art. "Art saves him, and through art life saves him—for itself" (*BT*, 7). Underscoring the non-anthropocentric quality of tragedy, Nietzsche claims the satyr chorus intervenes not on behalf of the spectator, to save her from her existential nausea, but on behalf of life itself.[25] In this way, the life-affirming yet painful qualities of the Dionysian subtend the truth tragedy expresses, while the beauty of Apollonian form and moderation make it tolerable.[26]

Art intervenes in both the playwright who acts as a vessel for more-than-human impulses and in the bodies of the satyrs who provide the spectators with "metaphysical solace." I propose that it is the collective interspecies-being of the satyrs—a community of creatures becoming human and becoming animal—that conveys the metaphysical solace that "life is indestructibly mighty and pleasurable" to the spectators, in spite of their suffering. I also propose that, by putting humanimal collectives at the root of the metaphysical role of art, *The Birth of Tragedy* suggests not only that transcendence of individuation occurs by crossing species boundaries through shared materiality, but that artistic practice originates in our animality.[27]

If individuation is the source of existential suffering and of human estrangement from the more-than-human world, then individuation may just be the young Nietzsche's word for what we now call "human exceptionalism and bounded individualism, those old saws of Western philosophy."[28] Life-affirming and collective, the Dionysian reveals the fundamental absurdity of those notions: it affirms life for life's sake, not for humans' ideas about themselves. Denying the notion of our inherent species exceptionalism, Dionysian art forces us "to recognize that everything which comes into being must be prepared for painful destruction" in death, but "the struggle, the agony, the destruction of appearances, all of this now seems to us to be necessary, given the uncountable excess of forms of existence thrusting and pushing themselves into life" (*BT*, 17). By focusing on the vitality and multiplicity of the recycling of matter, as the Dionysian does, we can appreciate, without fear, the "lust for life" that the more-than-human world demonstrates (*BT*, 1, 15). In this sense, Nietzsche's vitalist rendering of the Dionysian considers the totality of life from the perspective of deep time, the atom, or, as Lemm has suggested, the cell. Admittedly, these perspectives are more easily maintained for the duration of a tragedy than that of a humanimal life, especially since it remains unclear whether ethics or politics fit into the world from this vantage point.[29] As Nietzsche framed it in his 1886 preface, "This book burdened itself with a whole bundle of difficult questions. So let us add the hardest question of all! What, when seen through the prism of *life*, is the meaning of morality?" (*BT*, *P*, 4).

He does not answer that question in *The Birth of Tragedy*. When he was writing it, he considered one of its goals to be "*the rebirth of German myth!*" through Wagner's music (*BT*, 23). He later disavowed *The Birth of Tragedy* as "an impossible book," overly ambitious for a young man who did not have the courage or capacity to go beyond Kant, Schopenhauer, and, although unnamed, Wagner (*BT*, *P*, 3, 6). Nevertheless, "An Attempt at Self-Criticism" does not repudiate his first book's outline of an "*anti-Christian*" doctrine for life, an outline which he would later elaborate in *Zarathustra*, *Twilight of the Idols*, and elsewhere (*BT*, *P*, 5). Nonhuman animals continue to play a fundamental role in this doctrine, especially as embodied by Zarathustra, whose only community is a multispecies one. This life-affirming doctrine emerges out of and goes beyond a nineteenth-century understanding of modernity.

Nietzsche's insistence on the pain caused by individuation and his desire to return to a primordial origin shares many features of European Romantic fears about the alienation provoked by modernity, an alienation from "nature" and among (almost invariably) men. The young professor writing *The Birth of Tragedy* saw an enviable cultural unity in the Greeks and conversely saw egoism, cultural fragmentation, and "feverish and uncanny agitation" for all things new around him (*BT*, 23). In his sustained critique of Socratism, he blames an unshakable faith in the power of the empirical sciences and of progress for the death of Dionysian tragedy. By defining beauty along the parameters of reason, aesthetic Socratism eliminated art's life-affirming qualities and nullified its metaphysical purpose and potential (*BT*, 12). Thus, with the fall of Dionysian tragedy came the "degeneration and transformation of the national character of the Greeks" (*BT*, 23). Correspondingly, Nietzsche calls for a return to the Dionysian in German culture and claims its stirrings can be found in Wagner's music (*BT*, 19). He would later break with Wagner and move away from the nationalism that *The Birth of Tragedy*, written during the Franco-Prussian War, espoused. But the end of Nietzsche's career vividly displays the enduring importance of the Dionysian and its non-anthropocentrism to his philosophy and his life.

By the winter of 1888–89, Nietzsche's mania had convinced him he was Dionysus. He even recreated the "Barbaric Dionysian" festivals he had analyzed in *The Birth of Tragedy*, in all their explicit sexuality, by himself in his rented room.[30] The story goes that, while thinking himself the wine god, Nietzsche witnessed a coachman violently whipping a horse in a plaza and wrapped his arms around the horse's neck, sobbing. There are good reasons to be skeptical about this account of Nietzsche's final psychological break, not least because it was reported for the first time eleven years later in an anonymous newspaper article. The biographer Julian Young believes Nietzsche may have "scripted" this encounter in a letter he wrote in the summer of 1888, and that the epistolary "script" was itself inspired by a remarkably similar scene in *Crime and Punishment*. Scripted or not, and regardless of its veracity, it remains plausible. To me, Nietzsche's encounter with a horse in Turin illustrates that compassion for nonhuman-animal kin follows from the Dionysian.

As we humans are causing the sixth mass extinction of more-than-human animal life and, with regard to anthropogenic climate change, continue to behave like the nauseous, paralyzed Hamlet Nietzsche describes, the affirmative pessimism and potential for interspecies compassion in Nietzsche's early elaboration of the Dionysian find renewed relevance. For instance, the science writer Dorion Sagan's non-anthropocentric essay, "Beautiful Monsters: Terra in the Cyanocene," succinctly narrates millions of years of planetary history from the perspective of a bacterium, and Sagan finds room in that history for Nietzsche's vitalism. He writes, "When Nietzsche, in his posthumous writing, holds up a mirror for us and describes the world as a monster of force beyond good and evil, he is emphasizing life's monstrous and necessary connection to energy in an energy-steeped cosmos without beginning or end. But … ."[31] Sagan feels the need to qualify his comment and, with that qualification, he shifts perspective, from that of the universe to that of the organism.

In order to affirm life, Dionysian vitalism steps so far back, and takes such a long view, that unequal patterns of pain and joy fade away, but the Dionysian aesthetic Nietzsche describes in *The Birth of Tragedy* balances this affirmative vitalism with an emphasis on materiality rooted in the mundane realities of joy and suffering experienced in and by humanimal corporeality. Those mundane realities necessarily lead to a different perspective, one close enough to lived experience that they can reveal those patterns of injustice inhering in which human and nonhuman-animal bodies experience suffering and why. The satyrs—as multispecies humanimals, as emblems of Dionysian vitalism, and as comic participants in tragedy—bring together these multiple perspectives and affects. As Tracy Strong concludes, the science-art-life optic used in *The Birth of Tragedy* emphasizes "the consequences of perspectives for what counts as life."[32] As we reform the way we inhabit this warming planet—not only to ensure our (human) continued survival for the centuries to come, but also to allow more-than-human lives to flourish—we would do well to remember that. When we consider the ethical dimensions of life on a warming planet, it must be done at multiple scales and from multiple perspectives simultaneously, with the awareness that each one is necessarily insufficient and incomplete.

The Dionysian compassion and grief Nietzsche may have felt for the Turin horse and that I feel for the more-than-human ways of life being lost forever can be, in the words of the philosopher Donna Haraway, "a path to understanding entangled shared living and dying; human beings must grieve *with*, because we are in and of this fabric of undoing," the undoing that climate change already is and will continue to be.[33] Dionysian tragedy, in its non-anthropocentrism and in its transcendence through animality, works as one way to grieve with our nonhuman-animal kin. It also allows us to rehearse, to think with and through, the shifting, multiple perspectives needed to consider the ethical questions we must ask ourselves as we face the punishing math of planetary boundaries and the challenges of living in a damaged biosphere. I hope the modicum of relief its vitalism offers suffices for us to move from the paralysis of despair to planetary triage and multispecies care.

Notes

1 Julian Young, *Friedrich Nietzsche: A Philosophical Biography* (New York: Cambridge University Press, 2010), 124.
2 Young, *A Philosophical Biography*, 28, 125.
3 Ibid., 40–41.
4 Ibid., 40–41, 61, 86–87. I do not want to exaggerate the influence of Darwin on Nietzsche's thought, especially since it is unclear whether or not he read *On the Origin of Species*. What is certain is that he had learned about Darwin's evolutionary theory by 1868. Young, *A Philosophical Biography*, 576n44.
5 Young, *A Philosophical Biography*, 39.
6 Probabilities of the extinction scenario come from Yangyang Xu and Veerabhadran Ramanathan, "Well Below 2°C: Mitigation Strategies for Avoiding Dangerous to Catastrophic Climate Changes," *Proceedings of the National Academy of Sciences* 114, no. 39 (2017): 10318, http://doi.org/10.1073/pnas.1618481114.
7 For different takes on Nietzsche's philosophy and its relationship to climate change, see Gary Shapiro, *Nietzsche's Earth: Great Events, Great Politics* (Chicago: University of Chicago Press, 2016), ix–xii; Graham Parkes, "Staying Loyal to the Earth: Nietzsche as an Ecological Thinker," in *Nietzsche's Futures*, ed. John Lippitt (New York: St. Martin's Press, 1999), 167–88.
8 What I call the more-than-human world would be considered precisely the opposite, that is, the less-than-human, and what is more-than-human, in eighteenth-century

Europe, would be the divine. Instead of Nietzsche's term, "nature," I use "more-than-human world" as much as possible, in order to avoid the supposition of the nature/culture binary that humans can exist somehow apart, and to underscore the magnitude of life forms that exist on our planet in addition to humans.

9 See Vanessa Lemm, *Nietzsche's Animal Philosophy: Culture, Politics, and the Animality of the Human Being* (New York: Fordham University Press, 2009), 1; Alphonso Lingis, "Nietzsche and Animals," in *Animal Philosophy: Essential Readings in Continental Thought*, ed. Matthew Calarco and Peter Atterton (New York: Continuum, 2004), 9–10, 14.

10 Donna Haraway, *Staying with the Trouble: Making Kin in the Chthulucene* (Durham: Duke University Press, 2016), 53–54.

11 Lemm, *Nietzsche's Animal Philosophy*, 6. In *The Birth of Tragedy* specifically, the traditional kind of human exceptionalism is also present. Nietzsche refers to humans as "the noblest clay, the most precious marble" that nature can sculpt (*BT*, 1). Across his work as a whole, Nietzsche maintains a degree of anthropocentricism in his treatment of nonhuman animals, by tending to associate them with one dominant, observable trait, and therefore denying them the full interiority and capacity for variability given *a priori* to human animals.

12 Lemm, *Nietzsche's Animal Philosophy*, 1, italics added.

13 Young, *A Philosophical Biography*, 124–25.

14 Gilles Deleuze, *Nietzsche and Philosophy*, trans. Hugh Tomlinson (New York: Columbia University Press, 2006), 12.

15 Young, *A Philosophical Biography*, 40, 124–25. Nietzsche vacillated on this point while he was working on *The Birth of Tragedy*. Between the end of 1870 and the spring of 1871, he also wrote that "individuation is the *result* of suffering, not its cause" (*KSA*, 7[117]).

16 For a full explanation, see Jane Bennett, *Vibrant Matter: A Political Ecology of Things* (Durham: Duke University Press, 2010).

17 Euripides, *Bacchae*, trans. David Franklin (Cambridge: Cambridge University Press, 2000), lines 587–92. Despite the fact that Nietzsche disparages Euripides as partly responsible for the death of tragedy, his descriptions of Dionysian glory do not deviate much in content from those of the playwright.

18 Euripides, *Bacchae*, lines 608–10.

19 Ibid., 620–22.

20 Lemm, *Nietzsche's Animal Philosophy*, 3.

21 Deleuze, *Nietzsche and Philosophy*, 13.

22 Ibid.

23 Young, *A Philosophical Biography*, 40.

24 Silenus is sometimes considered to be the proper name of a human-horse hybrid that raised the young Dionysus, and sometimes considered to be term for a kind of forest demon. Nevertheless, Nietzsche treats Silenus as an individual forest creature and the satyrs as a troupe of singing goat-men, and that is what I am commenting on here. Friedrich Nietzsche, *The Birth of Tragedy and Other Writings*, ed. Raymond Guess and Ronald Speirs, trans. Ronald Speirs (Cambridge: Cambridge University Press, 1999), 22n37.

25 Lemm makes the same point using *Assorted Opinions and Maxims*, writing that "the perspective of continuity posits that human life does not play a central role in the totality of life, but is only a small and insignificant part of it. Nietzsche even

speculates that nature uses human life as a means toward its own completion rather than the other way around." *Nietzsche's Animal Philosophy*, 3.

26 Nietzsche summarizes the process thus: "This insight leads us to understand Greek tragedy as a Dionysian chorus which discharges itself over and over again in an Apolline world of images. ... This primal ground of tragedy radiates, in a succession of discharges, that vision of drama which is entirely a dream-appearance; ... on the other hand, as the objectification of the Dionysiac state, the vision represents not Apolline release and redemption in semblance, but rather a breaking-asunder of the individual and its becoming one with the primal being itself" (*BT*, 8).

27 For more on human artistic practice emerging from our animality, see Lemm, *Nietzsche's Animal Philosophy*, 10–29; Lingis, "Nietzsche and Animals," 13–14; Margot Norris, *Beasts of the Modern Imagination: Darwin, Nietzsche, Kafka, Ernst, and Lawrence* (Baltimore: John Hopkins University Press, 1985), 5, 73–100.

28 Haraway, *Staying with the Trouble*, 30.

29 For differing arguments on violence, animality, and Nietzschean vitalism, see Lingis, "Nietzsche and Animals," 10; Norris, *Beasts of the Modern Imagination*, 4–10; Lemm, *Nietzsche's Animal Philosophy*, 33; Shapiro, *Nietzsche's Earth*, 139.

30 Young, *A Philosophical Biography*, 530–32.

31 Dorion Sagan, "Coda. Beautiful Monsters: Terra in the Cyanocene," in *Arts of Living on a Damaged Planet*, ed. Anna Tsing et al. (Minneapolis: University of Minnesota Press, 2017), M172.

32 Tracy B. Strong, "The Optics of Science, Art, and Life: How Tragedy Begins," in *Nietzsche and the Becoming of Life*, ed. Vanessa Lemm (New York: Fordham University Press, 2015), 27.

33 Haraway, *Staying with the Trouble*, 39.

2

Nietzsche's Dawn of Dissent: *Morgenröte* and the Modernist Impulse

Siobhan Lyons

Friedrich Nietzsche's relatively obscure book *Daybreak*, or *The Dawn: Thoughts on the Prejudices of Morality* (1881), written in his middle or "positivist" period, sees the philosopher's work develop greater maturity between *Human, All Too Human* (1878) and *The Gay Science* (1882). *Daybreak* is, as Clark and Leiter note, "sadly neglected," overshadowed by his more popular works including *Thus Spoke Zarathustra* (1883–84) and *Beyond Good and Evil* (1886). Yet, as Nietzsche himself pronounced, it was the book that would begin his campaign against morality.

Daybreak features, in scattered but energetic form, Nietzsche's burgeoning skepticism regarding European and Christian morality, which informed his later works such as *The Genealogy of Morality* (1887). His writing in itself is, as Michael Tanner observes, characteristically "mischievous."[1] Within the work Nietzsche attacks the suffocating values of Christianity and the tyrannical adherence to custom that defined his age.

Many of Nietzsche's views in the work, particularly on human drives and the subjective concept of "evil," were clearly instrumental to the theories of twentieth-century writers and thinkers, particularly Sigmund Freud, who famously challenged Victorian morals. Nietzsche's influence can also be found in modernist writers such as Franz Kafka, Gertrude Stein, Thomas Mann, James Joyce, Marcel Proust, William Faulkner, and Joseph Conrad, whose avant-garde writing similarly rejected social morality.

For the modernists, as for Nietzsche, life was not defined by one singular moral reality. The modernists fundamentally rejected the rhetoric of morality as espoused by their times, looking at the inner life of the human as complex and uncertain. This is where the modernists owe a debt to Nietzsche's views on morality and the irrational status of the human being.

Although it isn't one of Nietzsche's most popular pieces, *Daybreak* is invariably one of the most important works of the philosopher's oeuvre, a transitional piece that develops Nietzsche's anti-morality stance, informing much modernist thought. While the idea of Nietzsche as a modernist, or "pre-modernist," has gained increasing attention in the last few decades, few have examined the influence and significance of *Daybreak* on the philosopher's continued project on morality. This chapter will analyze Nietzsche's *Daybreak* and its underestimated influence on and connection to the philosopher's work and modernist thought, particularly in regards to the work of Freud.

Nietzsche and the modernist impulse

For many theorists, Nietzsche is not representative of modernism; his relationship with modernism is, if not ambiguous, then certainly open to interpretation, as is his relationship to the period of modernity more broadly. As Robert Gooding-Williams puts it, "Disagreement about Nietzsche's relation to modernity is pervasive among intellectual historians and social scientists."[2] Patrick Bridgwater too notes that "if Nietzsche stood for modernism in his 'campaign against morality' and in his metaphysics and theology, he stood no less resolutely against modernism in the political context."[3] He writes that "even more bitter than his attacks on Christianity are his repeated attacks on democracy as such."[4] Yet he argues that whether Nietzsche himself was in any way defined as "the champion or the opponent of modernity, however does not matter."[5] Instead, what matters, for Bridgwater, "is the fact that it was precisely the 'transvaluation of values' that was, in one way or another, the central problem facing the generation of 1890-1914,"[6] making Nietzsche's theories regarding one's place in the shifting moral landscape overwhelmingly important. Paul de Man similarly addressed the question regarding Nietzsche's place in philosophy, stating that "Nietzsche's ruthless forgetting, the blindness with which he throws himself into action lightened of all previous experience, captures the authentic spirit of modernity."[7]

One of the issues that Nietzsche focuses on particularly in *Daybreak* is the construction between Christianity, guilt, shame, and repression. And one of the defining characteristics of the modernist impulse was the prominence of psychic turmoil, guilt, isolation, and a radical break with conformist attitudes with which society blindingly engaged. Authors such as Kafka, Proust, Mann, and Joyce often used stream-of-consciousness narratives, or focused on the inner turmoil of many of their characters, who were quite often at odds with the society in which they lived.

The extent to which Nietzsche influenced specific modernists has been keenly debated, chiefly due to the aforementioned fact that Nietzsche was not technically a modernist. And yet his feverish writing style and unabated assault on moral conformity and the unexplored depths of the psyche resonate particularly strongly with many of the writers instrumental to modernist thought. Nietzsche's influence on Sigmund Freud is particularly notable; many of the themes that are more often associated with Freud were previously explored by Nietzsche, and emerge with prominence in *Daybreak*, as I will discuss.

Background

While writing *Daybreak*, Nietzsche's relationship with his mother, Franziska Nietzsche, went through various stages of estrangement and reconciliation. A major source of tension was Nietzsche's move away from Christianity, which is remarkably noticeable in *Daybreak*. But it was initially in 1864, when Nietzsche was an undergraduate student at Bonn University, which "began [Nietzsche's] journey of alienation from his mother and sister by refusing to take communion."[8] His mother also disapproved of Nietzsche's relationship with Lou Salomé and Paul Rée in Tautenberg, which made the philosopher furious.

During his writing of *Daybreak*, however, Nietzsche nevertheless maintained a steady correspondence with both his mother and sister, Elisabeth, and when Nietzsche would finally succumb to madness after a now-infamous mental breakdown in 1889, his mother and sister both took care of him. His relationship with Elisabeth too was often fraught with tension, as his sister developed strong anti-Semitic ties with Hitler and the Nazi party.

While Nietzsche's father, Carl Ludwig Nietzsche, died in 1849 following several months of illness, his brother Karl Ludwig Joseph died in 1850. In his father's absence, Nietzsche developed a strong idolization of Richard Wagner, who was the same age as Nietzsche's father, both men having been born (along with Søren Kierkegaard) in 1813. Nietzsche made frequent visits to Wagner and his mistress (and later wife) Cosima in Tribschen, Lake Lucerne between 1869 and 1872.

By 1876, however, "Nietzsche publicly began to distance himself from the Wagner cause and articulate the serious doubts he had held for some time about Wagner as an artist."[9] This was partly since Nietzsche had struck up a new friendship with Paul Rée, but also because Nietzsche himself was breaking with his previous philosophical tradition of deriding "theoretical optimism and the Socratic faith in knowledge."[10] Nietzsche's break with Wagner seemed to be confirmed in *Human, All Too Human* (1878), which repulsed Wagner and even Nietzsche's closest friends, for the philosopher suddenly adopted a radical shift in tone and outlook, where he was now embracing scientific truths. His next work, *Daybreak*, would prove to be a decisive yet overshadowed work in the positivist period.

Daybreak's obscurity

Curtis Cate, in his book *Friedrich Nietzsche: A Biography* (2003), translates Nietzsche's *Daybreak* as "Morning Glow," from the original German title *Morgenröte*. The word was used to "symbolise the glowing dawn of a radically new form of thinking about moral judgements."[11] Martin Heidegger, meanwhile, noted that with *Daybreak*, "a light dawns over Nietzsche's metaphysical path."[12] Cate shares Clark and Leiter's sentiments regarding the book's unpopularity, stating that "because it was later overtaken and overshadowed by briefer and more stridently anti-Christian works, *Morgenröte* [*Daybreak*] … has remained to this day one of Nietzsche's least known and least read books."[13] *Daybreak* became Nietzsche's attempt to "define and analyse the general problems and principles of a new, less incoherent, less idealistic, more rational and realistic system of morality."[14] Comparing *Daybreak* to Nietzsche's other works, Cate argues: "Here, even more than in *Human, All Too Human*, Nietzsche kept stressing the extent to which human beings, far from being a completely separate and superior species, are related to the animal and even to the vegetable world of Nature."[15] Magnus and Higgins similarly note that *Daybreak* "goes further than *Human, All Too Human* in elaborating Nietzsche's critique of Christian morality. It is perhaps also more masterful than the earlier work in its artful use of 'aphoristic' juxtaposition to engage the reader in his or her own reflections."[16] Pearson and Large also argue that the work demonstrates Nietzsche's "creative evolution as a critic of morality," and that in *Daybreak*, Nietzsche is "carrying out a revaluation of all values and disclosing the nature of his interest in the question of the origin of moral values: it is a question of a future vitality in which the unegoistic is revalued."[17]

Nietzsche began writing *Daybreak* in Riva, northern Italy, and also wrote parts of the manuscript in Venice, Marienbad, Stresa, and Genoa. While writing *Daybreak*, Nietzsche also stopped in Bolzano—a favorite vacation spot of Freud's, who, like Nietzsche, admired the mountainous surroundings. During this time, Nietzsche's health was poor—frequent bouts of vomiting and a paroxysmic fit while heading through the Gotthard tunnel stalled Nietzsche's intellectual progress. He abandoned a trip to southern Italy, fearing, according to Cate, of "putting too great a distance between himself and his invaluable transcriber and proof-reader, Heinrich Köselitz, at a time when he felt a new book germinating inside him."[18] Settling in Genoa, Nietzsche spent the first few days moving from one lodging to another, until he finally found acceptable lodgings in a room at the top of a house which required Nietzsche to walk up 164 steps. This particular place "afforded [Nietzsche] an extraordinary degree of quiet and the creative seclusion he needed from the teeming world below him."[19] Yet Cate also notes that if Nietzsche's health proved more acute in Genoa than in Venice, it was likely due to the philosopher being "in the prenatal throes of cerebral 'labour.'"[20]

There are perhaps numerous reasons for *Daybreak*'s relative obscurity beyond being eclipsed by Nietzsche's major works; Cate insists that the Middle Period was characterized by inconsistency and literary commotion: "None of his books," Cate argues, "from *Human, All Too Human* on, had had a single aim. All of them had been marked by a chaotic plethora of mini-essays on a large number of subjects."[21] *Daybreak* is, certainly, more sporadic and less thematically coherent than later works, jumping from topic to topic without much synthesis in between. And yet his aphorisms are undeniably invigorating, and Nietzsche's intensity and fervor is evident throughout the book. *Daybreak*, therefore, finds its allure in Nietzsche's developing voice, despite the erratic quality of his essays.

Moreover, Cate notes that despite the book's "rosy title," *Daybreak* "was not a joyous book."[22] He argues that its fourth chapter was "almost grim in denigrating 'altruism' and stressing the importance of selfishness in the constitution of strong, healthy, self-reliant, free-thinking, unbigoted individuals."[23] Magnus and Higgins, too, note that in *Daybreak*, Nietzsche's "picture of Christian morality seems dismal."[24] Indeed, discussing altruistic acts, Nietzsche argues that thinking only of ourselves resides at the center of all thought: "Pleasure arises at the sight of a contrast to the condition we ourselves are in; at the notion that we can help if only we want to; at the thought of the praise and recognition we shall receive if we do help" (*D*, 133).

Nietzsche's flagrant rejection of altruism and selflessness, too, could be cited as a reason for the book's comparative obscurity in the philosopher's oeuvre. But despite these elements, and despite the book's absence from major philosophical discussions regarding Nietzsche and his influence, *Daybreak* is an underestimated accomplishment in Nietzsche's philosophy, exhibiting his burgeoning attack on morality and astute critique of culture.

Against Christian morality

Book I of *Daybreak* is primarily taken up with Nietzsche's vibrant and uncompromising attack on Christianity. Nietzsche discusses at length in *Daybreak* the compulsion to avoid vice and propagate feelings of guilt at Christianity's insistence: "Misfortune and guilt—Christianity has placed these two things on a balance: so that, when misfortune consequent on guilt is great, even now the greatness of guilt itself is still involuntarily measured by it" (*D*, 78). Discussing the liberating forces of the Greek tragedy in this manner, Nietzsche notes that they did not produce an "adequate relationship" between guilt and misfortune.

Indeed, in *Daybreak*, Nietzsche argues: "Christianity has succeeded in transforming Eros and Aphrodite—great powers capable if idealization—into diabolical kobolds and phantoms by means of the torments it introduces into the consciences of believers whenever they are excited sexually" (*D*, 76). He also asks: "And ought one to call Eros an enemy?"

For Nietzsche, there is within Christianity a "great popular protest against philosophy," which manifests itself in "*love* of God, *fear* of God, as fanatical *faith* in God, as the blindest *hope* in God" (*D*, 58). Nietzsche continues his attack in earnest, claiming:

> These serious, excellent, upright, deeply sensitive people who are still Christians from the very heart: they owe it to themselves to try for once the experiment of living for some length of time without Christianity, they owe it to their faith in this way for once to sojourn "in the wilderness"—if only to win for themselves the right to a voice on the question [of] whether Christianity is necessary. (*D*, 61)

And yet Nietzsche acknowledges that Christianity has an immense attraction to those who have never lived without it: "How many there are who still conclude: 'life could not be endured if there were no god!' … The truth, however, is merely that he who is accustomed to these notions does not desire a life without them" (*D*, 90).

Toward the end of Book I, Nietzsche claims that "really active people are now inwardly without Christianity" (*D*, 92). For Nietzsche, Christianity is filled with unresolved contradictions and undermines free, intellectual thought. He finds numerous inconsistencies with the concept of god. In an aphorism on "God's honesty," Nietzsche posits:

> A god who is all-knowing and all-powerful and who does not even make sure that his creatures understand his intentions—could that be a god of goodness? Who allows countless doubts and dubieties to persist, for thousands of years, as though the salvation of mankind were unaffected by them, and who on the other hand holds out the prospect of frightful consequence if any mistake is made as to the nature of the truth? Would he not be a cruel god if he possessed the truth and could behold mankind miserably tormenting itself over the truth? (*D*, 91)

Indeed, Nietzsche continuously reflects on the ambiguous role that doubt plays in Christian beliefs, noting that Christianity "has done its utmost to close the circle and declared even doubt to be a sin. One is supposed to be cast into belief without reason, by a miracle, and from them on to swim in it as in the brightest and least ambiguous of the elements" (*D*, 89). More specifically, Nietzsche persuasively argues against the "price of believers," in which "he who sets such store on being believed in that he offers heaven in exchange for this belief … must have suffered from fearful self-doubt and come to know every kind of crucifixion: otherwise he would not purchase his believers at so high a price" (*D*, 67).

For Nietzsche, believers are pulled into belief without sufficient reason, and those who lack, doubt, or question that belief become stranded—morally and spiritually. There is, for Nietzsche, an emphasis on punishment—severely illogical in nature—within Christianity. For Slavoj Žižek, this works in a peculiar manner, one that he calls the "temptation of meaning." For Žižek, as for Nietzsche, the element of punishment in religion is preferable to the lack of any understandable meaning:

> When something horrible happens, our spontaneous tendency is to search for a meaning. It must mean something. … Even if we interpret a catastrophe as a punishment, it makes it easier, in a way, because we know it's not just some terrifying blind force. It has a meaning. It's better when you're in the middle of a catastrophe, it's better to feel that God punished you than to feel that "it just happened." If God punished you, it's still a universe of meaning.[25]

This is precisely why punishment is more appealing than meaninglessness in Christianity, and upon which their entire ethos in based. The stifling nature of Christianity on individualism is found in the baseless allegiance many followers have to its ambiguous structure, and the habitual use of punishment as a tool for both believers and nonbelievers alike corresponds to a method by which to control behavior and stifle expression, passion, desire, and thought. In this way Nietzsche work epitomizes Karl Marx's famous edict that "religion is the opiate of the masses." As Magnus and Higgins argue, "Psychological damage to the believer results from the Christian-moral worldview's insistence on absolute conformity to a single standard of human behaviour."[26]

It is unsurprising, therefore, that Nietzsche was so influential to both the modernist sensibility—which eschewed moral conformity and challenged universal meanings—and to Freud especially, for whom desires, primarily sexual, are socially repressed.

Nietzsche and Freud

Nietzsche's anti-Christian stance in *Daybreak* accorded strongly with Freud, who developed a theory of the mind that moved away from an essentialist philosophy of the soul, and toward an idea that somewhat aligned humans with animals. This is where Nietzsche's influence on Freud begins to take shape.

While Freud is almost uniformly associated with the notion of the unconscious, numerous passages in *Daybreak* suggest that Nietzsche was very much interested in the concept before Freud. In fact, prior to Nietzsche, philosophers including Karl Robert Eduard von Hartmann and Arthur Schopenhauer explicitly and repeatedly used the term *das Unbewusste*. Hartmann's first book, *Philosophy of the Unconscious* (1869) established him as a philosopher, while Schopenhauer too was strongly affiliated with the notion of an "unconscious": "Nearly a century before Freud ... in Schopenhauer there is, for the first time, an explicit philosophy of the unconscious and of the body."[27]

Interestingly, Freud is noted as having said that he never read any of Nietzsche's work. Yet as Chapman and Chapman-Santana argue, this contradicts much of Freud's own references to Nietzsche: "Nietzsche wrote about mental functions in ways Freud was to duplicate later."[28]

According to Chapman and Chapman-Santana, Freud first stated that he had never read Nietzsche while at a meeting of the Vienna Psychoanalytic Society in 1908, and would repeat this statement throughout his life. Yet they note that Ernest Jones, a colleague and friend of Freud's, claimed that Freud had told him in a conversation that "Nietzsche was one of the authentically great men of all time."[29]

Paul Katsafanas, too, has argued that "although contemporary philosophers often assume that the unconscious arose as a major topic only with Freud, in fact the eighteenth and nineteenth centuries are replete with work on this notion."[30] In fact, according to Katsafanas, Nietzsche credited Leibniz with the discovery of the unconscious. Moreover Freud was, he insists, "no doubt influenced by Nietzsche's conception of drives."[31]

In a specific segment in *Daybreak*, Nietzsche discusses the notion of drives, in terms that seems to prophesize Freudian concepts. Discussing what he calls the "so-called ego," Nietzsche writes of "inner processes and drives," arguing that "we are none of us that which we appear to be in accordance with the states for which alone we have consciousness and words" (*D*, 115). It is here that Nietzsche alludes to a state of being which, years later, Freud would identify as the unconscious processes of the id, the ego and the superego.

Despite Freud's insistence that he did not read Nietzsche, a couple of references to the philosopher can actually be found in Freud's *The Interpretation of Dreams* (1899), first published a year before Nietzsche's death. In one passage, Freud writes: "We begin to suspect that Friedrich Nietzsche was right when he said that in a dream 'there persists a primordial part of humanity which we can no longer reach by a direct path.'"[32] He references Nietzsche in another passage, stating: "What I have called dream-displacement might equally be described [in Nietzsche's phrase] as a 'transvaluation of psychic values.'"[33]

The phrase "transvaluation of psychic values" is one that frequently appears in Nietzsche's work, including in *The Genealogy of Morality* and *The Will to Power*, and is also borrowed numerous times in Freud's own writings:

> This expectation is also destroyed by a comparison of the dream and the dream material. The intensity of the elements in the one has nothing to do with the intensity of the elements in the other; a complete "transvaluation of all psychic values" takes place between the dream-material and the dream.[34]

Freud also writes of dreams in a distinctly Nietzschean fashion in *The Case of Schreber*:

> In dreams and in neuroses, so our thesis has run, "we come once more upon the *child* and the peculiarities which characterize his modes of thought and his emotional life." "And we come upon the *savage* too," we may now add, "upon the *primitive* man, as he stands revealed to us in the light of the researchers of archaeology and of ethnology."[35]

In a significant passage from Book IV of *Daybreak*, a similarity can be found between these two streams of thought:

> In outbursts of passion, and in the fantasizing of dreams and insanity, a man rediscovers his own and mankind's prehistory: *animality* with its savage grimaces; on these occasions his memory goes sufficiently far back, while his civilized condition evolves out of a forgetting of these *primal* experiences. (*D*, 312)

While the similarity can certainly be seen as coincidental, Ronald Lehrer, in his book *Nietzsche's Presence in Freud's Life and Thought* (1995), notes that at a Vienna Psychoanalytic Society meeting in 1911 there was a reading on the topic of dreams specifically taken from *Daybreak*. According to Lehrer, Freud "refers to these ideas of Nietzsche in a 1919 addition to *The Interpretation of Dreams*," though he states that "of course we do not know when Freud first read or learned of such passages in Nietzsche."[36]

Nietzsche was himself noticeably intrigued by the notion of dreams, and several passages in *Daybreak* clearly indicate his eager deconstruction of the dream process. Indeed, at the beginning of *Daybreak*, Nietzsche argues: "The greatest accomplishment of past mankind is that we no longer have to live in continual fear of wild animals, of barbarians, of gods and of our own dreams" (*D*, 5).

In a particularly significant segment, Nietzsche discusses the phenomenon of dreams and responsibility, arguing: "You are willing to assume responsibility for everything! Except, that is, for your dreams! What miserable weakness, what lack of consciousness courage! Nothing is *more* your own than your dreams!" (*D*, 128). In *The Interpretation of Dreams*, Freud similarly notes: "All those who allow the continuance of the morality in the dream nevertheless guard against accepting full responsibility for their dreams."[37] He argues that there is a "mixture of rejection and recognition of responsibility for the moral content of the dream."[38]

Referring to his subjects, Freud discusses the ambiguous relationship of the dream and the dreamer, quoted here at length:

> They could just as calmly reject the attempt to hold the dreamer responsible for his dreams, and to draw inferences from the badness of his dreams as to an evil strain in his nature, as they rejected the apparently similar attempt to demonstrate the insignificance of his intellectual life in the waking state from the absurdity of his dreams. The others for whom the "categorical imperative" extends also into the

> dream, would have to accept full responsibility for the immoral dreams; it would only be desirable for their own sake that their own objectionable dream should not lead them to abandon the otherwise firmly held estimation of their own morality.[39]

The question of whether one ought to accept responsibility for the seemingly random sequence of events in one's dreams is one that both Nietzsche in *Daybreak* and Freud in *The Interpretation of Dreams* are concerned with. The question of responsibility stems from the question of morality, and the extent to which we are our dreams. Again, there arises the notion of guilt and repression of which Nietzsche routinely speaks, and the desire to separate oneself from the morally questionable content of their dreams seems, to Nietzsche, to register as yet another element of Christian control and self-denial. Nietzsche specifically refers to Oedipus, a figure who operated at the center of Freud's philosophy: "It is precisely here that you rebuff and are ashamed of yourselves, and even Oedipus, the wise Oedipus, derived consolation from the thought that we cannot help what we dream!" Nietzsche reasons that the majority of society "must be conscious of having abominable dreams" (*D*, 128).

Moreover, both Nietzsche and Freud look at the ambiguous causes of dreams and where they arise in regards to one's waking life. In *Daybreak*, Nietzsche claims:

> Waking life does not have this *freedom* of interpretation possessed by the life of dreams, it is less inventive and unbridled—but do I have to add that when we are awake our drives likewise do nothing but interpret nervous stimuli and, according to their requirements, posit their "causes"? That there is no essential difference between waking and dreaming? (*D*, 119)

Freud similarly discusses the relationship between waking life and dreams and the presence of stimuli: "Dreams would accordingly be residues of waking mental activity which were disturbing sleep."[40] He also asks: "Why does mental life fail to go to sleep? Probably because there is something that will not allow the mind any peace. Stimuli impinge upon it and it must react to them. A dream, then, is the manner in which the mind reacts to stimuli that impinge upon it in the state of sleep."[41]

For both Freud and Nietzsche, dreams originate through a physiological or psychical process. For Freud, dreams are "psychical phenomena, [and] in that case they are products and utterances of the dreamer's, but utterances which tell us nothing, which we do not understand."[42] In *Daybreak*, Nietzsche similarly writes: "Our moral judgments and evaluations too are only images and fantasies based on a physiological process unknown to us, a kind of acquired language for designating certain nervous stimuli" (*D*, 119).

Indeed, in Nietzsche's notebooks from his later period, he writes: "The whole of our dreaming is the interpretation of total feelings with a view to possible causes, and in such a way that we only become conscious of a state when the chain of causality we've invented for it has entered out consciousness" (*KSA*, 13:15[90]).

In his 1886 notebooks, Nietzsche also asks, "to whom do you tell your night thoughts?" (*KSA*, 12:4[5]). Freud offers something of an answer in his *Introductory Lectures to Psychoanalysis*: "It is the dreamer himself who should tell us what his dream means."[43] For Freud, although he acknowledged the greater ambiguities at work in dreams, he argued that the dreamer can uncover the dream's meaning, "only he does not know that he knows it, and for that reason he thinks he does not know it."[44] Nietzsche similarly discussed the unconscious aspect of the intellect in his early notebooks: "The intellect just does not know this: he asks: *why* this desire?" (*KSA*, 9:11[127]). For both Freud and Nietzsche, then, there is not only desire at work in the intellect, but it is unconscious and subsequently expressed in dreams.

Nietzsche's influence

The similarities between Nietzsche and Freud are notably stark; both identify the similarities (and differences) between dreams and waking life, while they also argue that the dream stems from a psychic yet ultimately unknowable cause.

In his work *Freud and Nietzsche* (2000), Paul-Laurent Assoun finds a number of key parallels between the two philosophers, particularly in regards to what he identifies as the therapeutic work in *Daybreak*. He argues that "having described the symptoms of the illness of both individuals and of civilization, Nietzsche and Freud naturally turn to confront the final question which will close the process. *What does one do* in order to remedy the illness?"[45] He posits that in *Daybreak*, "We find the most complete exposition of what could be called a Nietzschean therapy. There, Nietzsche poses the question of mastery over the Self; what does one do in order to combat the 'violence of an instinct'?"[46] Freud's work on instinct and on our drives can clearly be seen as stemming, however indirectly, from Nietzsche's work.

Peter Bornedal argues that "we see the parallel to Nietzsche, who had already in *Morgenröte* introduced the disciplining effects of work."[47] He notes that "Nietzsche and Freud are narrating a story that (phylo-genetically) starts in our prehistoric past, and presupposes the existence of an original freedom, which is gradually restricted, finally resulting in the psychological crippling, the systematic destruction, of contemporary man."[48]

Moreover, he argues that "it is both Nietzsche and Freud's claim that in the history of civilization a *servile configuration* has been formed out of the malleable human psyche. The human psyche has been deepened and hollowed out, in order to finally split the human into two: a supervisor and a supervised."[49]

For both Nietzsche and Freud, there is a gap between man and its self: "The modern human has become fundamentally alienated from its self."[50] Bornedal also argues, "We notice that not only does Freud in several cases employ the exact same vocabulary as Nietzsche—'feeling of guilt,' 'conscience,' 'aggression,' 'internalization'—also the plot-structure of his foundational narratives is in several cases the same."[51]

Bornedal argues that when reading Nietzsche, particularly his work on guilt, "it is hard to believe that Freud was never directly influenced by Nietzsche."[52] Indeed, why Freud would choose to deny a familiarity with at least some of Nietzsche's work appears initially confusing. Yet despite having denied reading Nietzsche, Freud is also quoted as having been tremendously influenced by the philosopher, offering insight into this separation: "In later years I have denied myself the very great pleasure of reading the works of Nietzsche, with the deliberate object of not being hampered in working out the impressions received in psychoanalysis by an sort of anticipatory ideas."[53] Freud's continuous denial of having read Nietzsche, therefore, appears symptomatic of a desire to assert himself as the father of the unconscious, to distinguish himself as a philosopher whose work on unconscious drives is uniquely inspired.

Indeed, as David Frost puts it, Nietzsche's insights and his "doctrine of drives" have informed "almost all aspects of human behavior and psychology." "If this looks Freudian," he argues, "that's because it is. Freud said he had to stop reading Nietzsche for fear of finding his own idea presaged there."[54]

Hence it is clear that Nietzsche was indeed *too* influential in the development of Freud's own philosophy, to the extent that a separation needed to evolve between their respective ideas. As Borendal states, "It is clear that this deliberate attempt to forget Nietzsche is an attempt to rid his mind of a potential rival psychologist. Freud aspires to establish a 'master-discourse,' and it is all-important to avoid influence."[55] But he also notes that "it seems difficult to entirely avoid influence from a rival who, in the very instance of being dismissed, is recognized to have had the same insights as psychoanalysis. How does one decide to suppress something without first recalling that which is to be suppressed?"[56]

Indeed, it is somewhat ironic that Freud attempted to "suppress" Nietzsche and his influence, given Freud's well-known work on the ill-advised method of suppression. It seems clear that although Freud attempted to distinguish himself from Nietzsche, the German philosopher's thoughts nevertheless (perhaps unconsciously) impinged themselves on Freud's own thinking and writing. The notable similarities between Nietzsche and Freud suggest that Freud's work, in part, exists as an homage to Nietzsche's early work on dreams and the unconscious, but with evident deviations and characteristics. To this end Nietzsche's influence on Freud and the psychoanalytic project cannot be overstated, helping to inform a branch of psychology that nevertheless became more Freudian than Nietzschean. Moreover, it is in *Daybreak* that such crucial ideas begin to crystallize, emphasizing the need to reintegrate, if not prioritize *Daybreak* as a significant book in Nietzsche's oeuvre, rather than relegating it to a supplementary interest.

* * *

Daybreak sets the scene for Nietzsche's later work, and astute readers observe how Nietzsche is critically and imperatively developing his voice and view within *Daybreak*, making the work fundamentally important in developing Nietzsche's philosophy as a whole. Without *Daybreak*, Nietzsche's later, more coherent foray into morality would arguably have been insufficiently developed. It is within *Daybreak* that Nietzsche begins to formulate his opposition to Christian morality, delving into concepts such as the unconscious and emotional drives that would have an unprecedented impact not only on Freud, but on the modernist project in literature and art. As the aforementioned theorists attest, Nietzsche's influence on modernist writers, and the influence of

Daybreak, is notable. While *Thus Spoke Zarathustra*, *The Genealogy of Morality* and *Beyond Good and Evil* are among Nietzsche's most well-known and influential works, the themes that reside at their core are first developed in *Daybreak*, in which Nietzsche begins his earnest and forthright attack on morality. Despite various criticisms of the book, the aphoristic rhythm of *Daybreak* and its vehement attack on morality acts as something of an encyclopedia of varying topics, illustrating the broad scope of Nietzsche's interests and, consequently, the broad reach of his influence.

Notes

1 Michael Tanner, "Introduction," *Daybreak: Thoughts on the Prejudices of Morality* (Cambridge: Cambridge University Press, 1982), ix.
2 Robert Gooding-Williams, "Nietzsche Pursuit of Modernism," *New German Critique*, No. 41, Special Issue on the Critiques of the Enlightenment (Spring-Summer, 1987), 96.
3 Patrick Bridgwater, *Nietzsche in Anglosaxony: A Study of Nietzsche's Impact on English and American Literature* (Leicester: Leicester University Press, 1972), 15.
4 Bridgewater, *Nietzsche in Anglosaxony*, 15.
5 Ibid.
6 Ibid.
7 Paul de Man, *Blindness and Insight: Essays in the Rhetoric of Contemporary Criticism* (Abingdon: Routledge, 2005), 147.
8 Keith Ansell-Pearson and Duncan Large, *The Nietzsche Reader*, Malden (Oxford and Carlton: Blackwell Publishing, 2006), xxii.
9 Pearson and Large, *Nietzsche Reader*, xxiv.
10 Ibid.
11 Curtis Cate, *Friedrich Nietzsche: A Biography* (London: Pimlico, 2003), 301.
12 Heidegger, Martin. *Nietzsche: Volumes Three and Four: The Will to Power and Knowledge and as Metaphysics and Nihilism*, 188.
13 Cate, *Friedrich Nietzsche*, 304.
14 Ibid.
15 Ibid., 305.
16 Bernd Magnus and Kathleen M. Higgins, "Nietzsche's Works and their Themes," *The Cambridge Companion to Nietzsche* (Cambridge: Cambridge University Press, 1996), 33–34.
17 Pearson and Large, *Nietzsche Reader*, 156.
18 Cate, *Friedrich Nietzsche*, 300.
19 Ibid., 301.
20 Ibid.
21 Ibid., 353.
22 Ibid.
23 Ibid.
24 Magnus and Higgins, *Cambridge Companion to Nietzsche*, 35.
25 Slavoj Žižek, cited in Astra Taylor, "Slavoj Žižek: Ecology," in *Examined Life: Excursions With Contemporary Thinkers* (New York: The New Press, 2009), 157–58.

26 Magnus and Higgins, *Cambridge Companion to Nietzsche*, 35.
27 Rüdiger Safranski, *Schopenhauer and the Wild Years of Philosophy* (Cambridge, MA: Harvard University Press), 345.
28 Arthur Harry and Miriam Chapman-Santana, "The Influence of Nietzsche on Freud's Ideas" (*British Journal of Psychiatry*, 1995, 166), 252.
29 Chapman and Chapman-Santana, *Influence of Nietzsche*, 252.
30 Paul Katsafanas, *The Nietzschean Self: Moral Psychology, Agency, and the Unconscious* (Oxford: Oxford University Press, 2016), 17.
31 Katsafanas, *The Nietzschean Self*, 100.
32 Sigmund Freud, *The Basic Writings of Sigmund Freud*, ed. A. A. Brill (New York: Modern Library, 1938), 497.
33 Sigmund Freud, *The Standard Edition of the Complete Psychological Works of Sigmund Freud, Volume V (1900-1901): The Interpretation of Dreams and On Dreams* (London: Hogarth Press, 2001), 655.
34 Sigmund Freud, *The Interpretation of Dreams* (Mineola: Dover Publications), 525.
35 Sigmund Freud, *The Standard Edition of the Complete Psychological Works of Sigmund Freud, Volume XII (1911-1913): Case History of Schreber, Papers on Technique and Other Works* (London: Vintage Books, 2001), 82.
36 Ronald Lehrer, *Nietzsche's Presence in Freud's Life and Thought: On the Origins of a Psychology of Dynamics Unconscious Mental Functioning* (Albany: State University of New York Press, 1995), 125.
37 Freud, *Interpretation of Dreams*, 110.
38 Ibid.
39 Ibid., 109.
40 Sigmund Freud, *Introductory Lectures on Psychoanalysis*, Volume 1 (London: Pelican Library, 1981), 118.
41 Freud, *Introductory Lectures*, 118.
42 Ibid., 129.
43 Ibid., 130.
44 Ibid.
45 Paul-Laurent Assoun, *Freud and Nietzsche* (New York: Continuum, 2002), 172.
46 Assoun, *Freud and Nietzsche*, 172.
47 Peter Bornedal, *The Surface and the Abyss: Nietzsche as Philosopher of Mind and Knowledge* (Berlin: Walter De Gruyter, 2010), 398.
48 Bornedal, *The Surface and the Abyss*, 398.
49 Ibid., 399.
50 Ibid.
51 Ibid.
52 Ibid.
53 Sigmund Freud, "The Psychoanalytical Movement," *The Pelican Freud Library*, Vol. 15 (London: Penguin Books, 1986), 73.
54 David Frost, "Nietzsche's Therapy," *Philosophy Now*, Issue 93, 2012.
55 Bornedal, *The Surface and the Abyss*, 400.
56 Ibid.

3

On the Way to Nietzsche's "Ticklish Truths": Comedy, Poetry, and Chance in *The Gay Science*

SJ Cowan

In elaborating their thoughts, philosophers have long relied on metaphors of land, constructing concepts from a lexicon of grounds, landscapes, or terrains. The sea, in contrast, represents not only an uncontrollable chaos, but also presents an image of an infinite, indefinable surface. In his 1781 *Critique of Pure Reason*, for instance, Kant imagines "travel[ing] through the land of pure understanding … and survey[ing]" it completely. He conceives the land—"the land of truth"—as an island surrounded by a broad, stormy ocean, "the true seat of illusion." His fear is that "many a fog bank and rapidly melting iceberg [will] pretend to be new lands" and draw voyagers into "adventures from which they can never escape."[1] The absence of surety and definition in water are Kant's concern. Were he to leave his island, he assures readers, his passage would merely be for the sake of finding more land. And so it has been: when serious thinking is called for, philosophers have set to work upon dry ground.

It is against this impulse that Nietzsche wrote his 1882 *The Gay Science*. For him, philosophers have too long failed to question the ground upon which they labored. In *The Gay Science* Nietzsche operates under different premises: "We have forsaken the land and gone to the sea! We have destroyed the bridge behind us—more so, we have demolished the land behind us! … Woe, when the homesickness for the land overcomes you … and there is no more land!" (*GS*, 124). Refusing to remain landlocked, Nietzsche risks himself, betting that somehow, somewhere on the horizon of the infinite, he will be transmuted. His hope is to become an altogether new kind of philosopher, whose object—as he describes—is a new of kind of happiness, and a new kind of truth. Whereas the truth of land is firmly planted, Nietzsche pictures himself plunging into frigid waters, confronting truths so "shy and ticklish, [they] can't be caught except suddenly." On the way to such truths, he warns, "One must either *surprise* [them] or leave [them] alone" (*GS*, 381).

In the years leading to the writing of *The Gay Science*, Nietzsche's health had been in decline, leading him to resign from professional teaching. Yet, he had never been satisfied living the regimented life of an academic. In order to recover, and regain his freedom of spirit, he spent much time near open water. He traveled to Italy—Sorrento, Genoa, and Messina—living among friends, inspired by landscapes and the wide-open horizon of the ocean. Thus, while overused as literary devices, metaphors of land and sea help expose a target of Nietzsche's criticism in *The Gay Science*. Namely, "serious thinking"—the grounded, severity-of-thought that philosophers typically demand. Calling for thinkers to "take leave of every wish for certainty," and to dance "beside abysses," Nietzsche hopes to create a new expression for philosophy (*GS*, 347).

Animating Nietzsche's method in *The Gay Science* are the themes of comedy, poetry, and chance. Historically, readers have treated these themes as valuable topics spanning Nietzsche's corpus. But these themes have yet to be read in conjunction with one another. Moreover, they are often treated as secondary to, for example, his critique of morality and his metaphysics (or lack thereof). Comedy, poetry, and chance not only undergird the method of Nietzsche's joyful science, but they also provide coordinates for approaching his "ticklish" truths.

* * *

Nietzsche opens *The Gay Science* by observing the way humans attach grave amounts of meaning to their endeavors, and by challenging the tendency to treat life as unquestionably significant. Be they philosophical, religious, or moral, Nietzsche notices that the great teachers in history have promoted a similar belief: that the question of the meaning of existence is something to take seriously. "To be sure," these teachers "in no way … want us to *laugh* at existence, or at ourselves" (*GS*, 1). They forbid laughter, Nietzsche explains, from the conviction that one should be concerned to find one's purpose, the reason behind one's being.

The desire to settle questions of purpose and being—the "Why?" of existence—is a product of what Nietzsche calls the "age of tragedy" (*GS*, 1). Paradigmatic of the tragic age are, to his view, the religious and philosophical-moral worldviews dominating ancient Greek and Hebrew thought, through Christianity, up through his own day. Central to these systems is the belief in something external to worldly happenings (be it God, Truth, Reason, etc.) that renders otherwise random events meaningful. As with Oedipus, whose unhappy demise became nonetheless significant, tragedy represents the deeply rooted faith that life inevitably produces meanings or morals. From the very beginning of his career Nietzsche had argued that such faith has made us too serious in our thinking because it encourages us to search for certainty with utmost reverence. Already in 1872, with his *The Birth of Tragedy*, he criticized the Socratic-philosophical tendency to prize knowledge above poetry and all else. For him, the naïve trust in human thought constituted the problematic supposition in the development of tragic thinking. Seeking an answer to "Why?" naively assumes that, behind the chance occurrences of life, a transcendent source gives life significance and order.

Nietzsche's goal in *The Gay Science* runs contrary to this tradition. Inspired by the medieval troubadours—whose artful, lyric expression characterized their poetic culture, their "*gaya scienza*"—Nietzsche means to develop his own *fröhliche Wissenshaft*, "gay" or "joyous" science. One finds in *The Gay Science*, for the first time in Nietzsche, a mature blend of poetry, rhetorical wit, and philosophical acumen. Such a science, he believes, will allow him to think against the tendencies of tragedy, and allow the "comedy of existence to 'become conscious' of itself" for the first time (*GS*, 1). His guiding principle is learning "to laugh [at oneself] *from the whole truth*" (*GS*, 1).

To understand Nietzsche's ideas of the comedy of existence and laughing from the whole truth, it is helpful to turn to a text he wrote in 1873, "On Truth and Lies in an Extra-Moral Sense." He opens as if telling a fable...

> In some remote corner of the universe poured out into countless flickering solar systems, there was once a star on which some clever animals invented *knowledge*. It was the most arrogant and most untruthful minute of "world history"; but still only a minute ... the star solidified and the clever animals died. ... There were eternities in which it did not exist; and when it is gone nothing will have happened. (*TL*, 1)

Nietzsche here inhabits a voice of nihilism that sounds grim to tragic thinkers. Our power *to know* has made us arrogant, convincing us that our knowledge links us to the heart of reality. "The proudest of men, the philosopher," he continues, "believes the eyes of the universe are trained on his ... thoughts like telescopes from all sides." In this story, readers face the futility of humankind's pursuit to know the truth of existence. With an undo confidence that there is a sure order to being, we unblinkingly hold out for truth. All the while we blind ourselves to the universe's indifference to our fragility and our finitude. From the nihilist perspective it is not meaning, but a loss of a sense of order, that takes center stage.

Opposing tragic thought, therefore, is nihilism. If the tragic perspective is naively optimistic that existence has a natural order and meaning; then nihilism offers a contrasting pessimism wherein even history's pivotal moments are reduced to naught. Nihilism allows one to fixate on one's lack of ultimate direction: *when we are gone, nothing will have happened*. True, nihilism provides a clear alternative to tragedy. But it is not a satisfactory substitute. Nietzsche criticizes tragedy for its uncritical acceptance of life's significance. Equally and oppositely, nihilism remains serious, rooted firmly in dry ground: the nihilist uncritically assumes that if life and meaning have no transcendent order, then there has no order at all.

To locate comedy in this, one must focus on the potential for a dynamic ebb and flow between tragedy and nihilism. Comedy includes both the recognition of the absurdity of life and participation in meaning-making activities. Despite rejecting life's providential order, "we must constantly give birth to our thoughts and maternally endow them with all that we have of blood, heart, fire, pleasure, passion, agony ... disaster" (*GS*, *P*, 3). The double movement of comedy involves a nihilistic destruction of meaning and order, and a tragic trust in their restoration. The struggle, however, is to restore meaning to life without recourse to transcendence. Always on-the-way-upward out of tragedy's faith in life, and always on-the-way-back-down from nihilism's resignation, the comic is at home in the experiences of both.

Though never explicitly laying it out, Nietzsche offers clues as to how to become conscious of life's comedy. In *Daybreak*—a book Nietzsche associates with *The Gay Science*—he poses two questions meant to prompt a change in one's perspective. "What am I really *doing*? And why am *I* doing it?" (*D*, 196). The first involves reflecting on one's goals, cares, occupations, and so forth. But (given his use of "really"), the question is not just about the mere fact of one's activities, but it also serves to undercut one's naïve, tragic faith in the value of them. The question is thus directed to the existential significance of one's activities, and allows one to segue from tragedy to nihilism: in answering it, one must stand back and observe (with the nihilist) how the pivotal moments of one's life serve no more of a higher purpose than habitually repeating one's daily, mundane routine.

The second question—"why am *I* doing it?"—moves one's thought in the opposite direction. One is prompted to wonder, "Of all the chance circumstances in history, why it is *me in particular* with my specific set of goals, cares, etc.?" This question is posed from a nihilistic distance. Yet, to provide an answer one must regain an intimate, up-close relation to one's world. "*I* am an artist (or nurse, or teacher, etc.)" one responds, "because it's what I love doing (or it brings meaning to my life, or it's all I *can* do, etc.)." To provide an answer, one must (alongside the tragic) consider the shape one's life has taken and decide which habits are worth developing.

Together, these questions provoke the insight that humanity's defining feature is not simply a coupling of the desire for meaning with the recognition of life's absurdity. Also defining humanity is an awareness of our own improbability. Somehow humanity has emerged from the chaos of an expansive, indifferent universe; yet we are able to compose our lives, achieving a sense of reason and a predictable degree of order. When the comic laughs "from the whole truth," they laugh at the perpetual oscillation between an excess and an absence of meaning. The comedic tension between tragedy and comedy allows one to focus on the infinitesimal probability of one's existence, "the inexplicable fact that we live precisely today, when we had all infinite time in which to come into existence" (*SE*, 1). If humankind were merely mortal, life would not be funny. But the comic laughs, valuing life anew because life is so very unlikely. Comedy involves lifting oneself out of one's immediate circumstances, surveying life's vanity, and participating nonetheless, finding joy in one's finitude.

* * *

It is our prejudice, as thinkers in general, to favor serious thought over cheerful or humorous thought. Whether it be in analysis, evaluation, or formulation, serious thinkers "put in the labor," proving a thought worthy of development. From ancient to modern, the prejudice runs deep. Plato charged that comedic "representations be left to slaves … and that they should receive no serious consideration whatsoever"; Hobbes warned, "They that are intent on great designs have no time to laugh."[2] Joy is associated not with real work but with moments of release. Nothing central to intellectual investigation is done out of appreciation for amusement-for-its-own-sake.

The Gay Science—Nietzsche's most elevated, energetic work—provides a breath of fresh air, departing from the prejudice that taking thought means *taking it seriously.*

In the preface Nietzsche remarks, "This entire book is really nothing but an amusement," signifying "the saturnalia of my mind" (*GS*, *P*, 1). Indeed, the book means to undermine the prejudice entirely:

> *Taking seriously.*—For most people, the intellect is an awkward, gloomy, creaking machine that is hard to start: when they want to work with this machine and think well, they call it "taking the matter *seriously*"—oh, how taxing good thinking must be for them! The lovely human beast seems to lose its good mood when it thinks well; it becomes "serious"! And "where laughter and gaiety are found, thinking is good for nothing"—that is the prejudice of this serious beast against all "gay science." Well, then, let us prove it a prejudice! (*GS*, 327)

A joyful science means shattering the icon of the thinker as pensive and solemn. Nietzsche takes a chance in *The Gay Science*, wagering that there is more advantageous mode of inquiry and attempting to demonstrate such a possibility. A promising way of reading *GS*, therefore, is by asking whether it lives up to the task.

In doing so, the following questions arise: Why is Nietzsche so determined to include gaiety in philosophy? And, what motivates his critique of seriousness? These questions are difficult for two reasons. First, they originate from within the framework that Nietzsche is distancing himself from, and so they calls for answers grounded firmly in reason, not resting atop an unstable surface. A second difficulty is that Nietzsche spells out neither his underlying motivation nor the contours of his method. And so it is a challenge to know where to even begin. Fortunately, however, *The Gay Science* contains resources to supply answers to these questions, consisting of reasons for both not being serious-in-thought and for thinking-joyfully.

* * *

One can find in *The Gay Science* a motivation to not take thought so seriously. For Nietzsche, our prejudice for seriousness rests on the intellectual fear that, without rationality, madness—an "outbreak of arbitrariness in feeling, seeing, and hearing"—would ensue, giving way to "joy in unreason" (*GS*, 76). In its modern iteration, this fear stems from eighteenth-century Enlightenment ideals, wherein the powers of reason and rationality were believed to provide not just a stable foundation for theoretical disciplines, but also a coherent order for life more generally. Consider the distinction between the rational and irrational. The latter is associated with earthiness, animality, and base desires; the former is viewed as the means by which humanity transcends the animal, inhabits a world, and finds truth. Rationality, it is thought, makes us more than animal, and if we fail to take it seriously, we fail to cultivate our unique nature. The fear, therefore, is of losing our singular place in nature.

To be clear, Nietzsche is not criticizing the fear of unreason as unjustified. He readily admits that without rationality "humanity would have perished long ago!" (*GS*, 76). Yet (similar to the fable above) he points out that the "discipline of their heads" has made humans prideful, leading us to pursue rationality as if it were a natural obligation. We have begun to think that any semblance of ambiguity in thought represents a shortcoming. With a faith in rigor, thinking has become laborious, aimed at eradicating falsehood and taming the chaos of our animal nature. Thus, Nietzsche concedes that the fear of unreason is justified. But he believes our overconfidence has led to a twofold confusion. In prizing rationality we come, on the one hand, to fix the opposition between the rational and irrational, and we thereby lose touch with our animal origins; on the other, we too quickly assume that, in leading away from madness, rationality must instead lead to truth. Equipped to dissolve these confusions, Nietzsche aims to disabuse readers of the intellectual fear of joy.

Nietzsche did not favor the traditional divisions between the rational and the irrational, and the human and animal. Early in his career he argued there was a "lack of a cardinal distinction between man and animal" (*HL*, 9) and that "humanity" is wholly interwoven in "animality." This means that the definitive features of humanity (like rationality and language) are in fact animal expressions. In *Daybreak*, for example, his answer to the question "How did rationality arise?" is blunt: "Irrationally, as might be expected" (*D*, 123). Likewise in *The Gay Science* he wonders, "What is the origin of logic?" No less direct, he answers, "Surely it arose out of the illogical" (*GS*, 111). Without a cardinal distinction between the two, rationality is nothing other than a highly developed animal expression. Moreover, in *The Gay Science* he argues that it is only thanks to the fact that humans are social, herd-like animals that we have achieved our faculties of both language and self-consciousness. Nietzsche's argument is intricate, and not as direct as one might hope. Thankfully the basic point is clear. Being less equipped to endure the severity of nature (e.g., being weaker, slower, and without claws, etc.) humans "needed [the] help and protection" of one another. In order to outwit predators humans came to cooperate, and learned, in Nietzsche's words, to "express [our] neediness and to make [ourselves] understood" to one another (*GS*, 354). Humans gradually mastered the tools of communication and eventually developed full-scale languages and systems for self-conscious reasoning.

Certainly, humans differ from other animals in the use and application of rationality. Nietzsche does not doubt that. His worry is that by approaching thought in such a serious way we confuse ourselves, positioning humanity above animality rather than within it. We thereby lose touch with our nature. "I fear that animals," Nietzsche laments, "see man as a being … who has in a most dangerous manner lost his animal common sense" (*GS*, 224). Our stress for rationality has not made us not into more complete humans but into burdened, self-alienated, sick animals. We have become "the miserable animal" that has lost sight of the irrational conditions of life.

The second confusion is thinking that, since rationality is capable of providing order, it leads toward truth. For Nietzsche, this assumption is false. Rationality is not a vehicle to *truth*, he argues, but only to a communal *faith* in the power of agreement:

> The opposite of the world of the madman *is not truth and certainty*, but the universal bindingness of a faith; in short, the non-arbitrary in judgment. And man's greatest labor so far has been to … lay down a *law of agreement*—regardless of whether these things are true or false. (*GS*, 76)

Here, Nietzsche detaches the question of truth from the issue of rationality. Rationality is not a faculty linking humanity to the order of the universe. It is merely an expression of humanity's herd instinct: allowing us to survive, to agree, and to establish frameworks for judging in a consistent way. Our prejudice to take thought so seriously too comfortably assumes that there is a rational basis to thought. Under this delusion we are driven to treat "life itself [as] *a problem*" to be solved, something requiring an answer (*GS*, *P*, 3).

Nietzsche goads his readers to lose their pride in the activity of thinking. Asking us to lose the faith that "reality stands unveiled" before the rational (*GS*, 57). He hopes instead to consider the ways that the patterns of human thinking "still carry around the valuations of things that originate in the passions … of former centuries" (*GS*, 57). In this case, the passion is our animal fear of chaos. This fear has been beneficial, allowing humans to "arrange for ourselves a world in which we are able to live." Yet, by leaving it unexamined we remain ignorant to the realization that life is *not* an argument: the "conditions of life," Nietzsche recognizes, "might include error" (*GS*, 121). If truth and rationality are separate affairs, then thinkers can move free from the bias of "taking the matter *seriously*." Moreover, if we fear losing hold of what makes humans special among animals, then fear works against us: rigor has not made us superior to animals; it has distanced us from our own nature.

* * *

It is one thing to criticize a mode of thought, and another to provide an alternative. If, as Nietzsche argues, thinking has become too serious a business, then how should it be conducted instead? Even if one agrees with his diagnosis, the realm of prescription lies open. Why not adopt more curiosity? How about passion? Artfulness? Why make thought joyful? Nietzsche reasons that if our severity in thought has turned us into sick, self-oppressed animals, then the alternative must be to develop thought that is healthy. As mentioned at the outset, Nietzsche wrote *The Gay Science* during a period of recovery from sickness. In the course of writing it, he had begun to catch the "first glimpses of the sunlight of returning health" (*KGB*, July 1887, III.7:872). What is more, it is also during this time that a close friendship was forged between Nietzsche, Peter Gast, and Lou Salomé, the latter being the woman who would become the closest thing to a lover that he would ever know. With his spirits on the rise, his attention to health and its connection with joy are thus not just theoretical concern, but something that his practical, physical conditions necessitated.

Nietzsche discusses health in (at least) two ways in *The Gay Science*. First, he argues that health is a context-dependent notion. There is no "health" per se. What counts as healthy "depends, on your goal, your horizon, your powers, your impulses, your mistakes, and above all on [your] ideals" (*GS*, 120). Whether physical or mental, one's health depends on one's ends. Recall that *The Gay Science* aims to establish a comedic-philosophical stance, one at home in, yet exceeding, the worlds of both tragedy and nihilism. The comic's impulse is not stability, but motion: longing for the "ice sheets of his soul" to be melted, so that he might "speed toward the ocean yearning for [his] highest hope and goal" and rise "ever healthier" more. Likewise, health, in *The Gay Science*, involves promoting vitality in flux, a continual shifting of thought.

Additionally, Nietzsche also focuses on the significance of health for philosophy itself. He presents two images of philosophizing, from sickness or from health. Sick thinkers need philosophy in order to survive; healthy thinkers choose to philosophize in order to flourish. Philosophy is sick insofar as it is an outgrowth of our fixation on rationality and our dissociation from animality. Sick philosophy approaches life as something that must be treated by thought, like a condition in need of restoration. In contrast, Nietzsche characterizes healthy philosophy as being a luxury, a joyful expression of gratitude in life. From health, a philosopher thinks abundantly, excessively, and amusingly. To the sick, healthy thought appears inexpedient, sick thought always hungers for more, taking hold of whatever it can get. Healthy thought, in contrast, does not hold tightly to its ideas—healthy is the thinker who recognizes that "it takes more genius to spend than to acquire" (*GS*, 21). For Nietzsche, healthy thought is rare, "sick thinkers are in the majority in the history of philosophy" (*GS*, *P*, 2).

Keeping spirit with his critique of seriousness, Nietzsche's exposition of healthy and sick philosophy does not center on argumentation but is more focused on presentation, and registers more affectively than rationally. His method prioritizes the experience and dramatization of an idea over its analysis. He held out hope that a renewed method of thought would engender a new feeling of life for thinkers. As he had stated in *Daybreak*, "We have to *learn to think differently*—in order … to attain even more: *to feel differently*" (*D*, 104). The feeling of a thought and its affects, no less than the thought of a thought, are at issue in *The Gay Science*. So, when approaching the work of others, Nietzsche is careful to ask, "Is it hunger or superabundance that have become creative here?" (*GS*, 370). One's method, of course, conditions the effect a thought will have within one's system. What Nietzsche emphasizes, however, is the way one's method conditions the affect that a thought carries into the world.

Nietzsche laments the seriousness that has normalized itself in philosophy. "In a scholar's book," he writes, "there is nearly always something oppressive, oppressed" (*GS*, 366). In a cartoon-like way, he pictures the thinker conceiving thought in a state of unremitting pain.

> Seated before the inkwell, stomach clenched, head bowed over the paper; and oh, how soon we're done with the book! Cramped intestines betray themselves—you can bet on it—no less than stuffy air, cramped spaces.—Those were my feelings as I closed a decent scholarly book—grateful, very grateful, but also relieved. … The "specialist" emerges somehow—his eagerness, his seriousness, his ire … his hunched back—every specialist has his hump. Every scholarly book reflects a soul that has become crooked. (*GS*, 366)

According to this picture, the standard way of thinking requires sickly conditions. We have come to identify with our pain to the extent that we have lost sight of how to think a thought separate from it. Becoming vain with our status as unique creatures, we wound ourselves: ever grinding the gears of our mind; hunching our backs, breaking them on scholarly books. We even desire such suffering, imagining that it provides the justification to continue thinking. As Nietzsche puts it, we are so "busy turning [our] unhappiness into a monster ahead of time only so that afterwards we have a monster to fight" (*GS*, 64). We kill ourselves in order to confirm that our power for thought makes us dominant among animals. Even Kant, Nietzsche explains, lured modern philosophers to "turn the critical will against itself, so that, like the scorpion, it drives its sting into its own body" (*D*, *P*, 2). Nietzsche's hope is to undo our pain by teaching thinkers to think excessively, reintroducing the irrational into the rational.

Nietzsche recognizes that any sustained project, no matter its nature, leaves its mark on one's body or mind. "Every craft," he states, "makes one crooked." This is not to suggest that he believes that scholars and specialists are altogether in the wrong. "No," he continues, "my scholarly friends, I bless you even for your hunched backs!" He praises them for enduring pain, and for pursuing though more than money, comfort, and ease. Nevertheless, Nietzsche did not believe thinking necessitated self-oppressive circumstances. A gay science intends a world where thinkers no longer "fill the world with their clamor about distress," and consequently "with the *feeling* of distress." His call for joy, his emphasis on health, bears witness to good news: thinking can "become more refined and their satisfactions sound like good music." *The Gay Science* is Nietzsche's attempt to lead by example, using it to "paint [his] *happiness* on the wall," reminding thinkers that they need not contort themselves in order to think well (*GS*, 56).

As the contrast between health and sickness illustrates, at issue is not *what* a thinker thinks, but rather the *way* a thinker produces thought. Nietzsche's focus and his methods became entangled with his habits: he was not under the restrictions of professional teaching duties, his chronic illness showed signs of decline, much of his time was spent near the ocean in Italy, and he found joy in his personal relationships. It is thus no wonder that he referred to *The Gay Science* as "his most personal" book. Again, Nietzsche's point is not to disregard the profoundly serious insights of scholars—for *The Gay Science* contains discussions of many of his most serious teachings. So, it is worth highlighting that his critique of seriousness and affirmation of joy centers on the activity of thought itself and not necessarily on the content of thought. A thought itself may be serious, but the thinking that produces it need not be. Take, for example, Nietzsche's idea of the death of God. The idea itself was exceedingly serious. But thinking the death of God was, for him, a liberating experience, wherein he felt "illuminated by a new dawn" (*GS*, 370). Joy is the disclosing of a thought's health, its abundance.

A text produced from health is, for Nietzsche, clearly marked: written with a transgressive freedom, by "a spirit that plays ... with everything that was hitherto called holy, good, untouchable, divine" (*GS*, 382). A thinker displaying health is like a comedic thinker, free to revalue what is otherwise holy (for the tragic) or meaningless (for the nihilist). The comic exemplifies health by being able to think serious thoughts "through excess" rather than sickness. Not originating in distress, the comic's health maintains cheerfulness by sharing not in the pain of life—in the endless pursuit for an answer to "Why?"—but by sharing in joy with others, creating meaning even as it passes away.

* * *

The Gay Science is an index of Nietzsche's life with thought. "I'm still alive; I still think." The book is a back-and-forth dialogue between Nietzsche and thinking as such, "I must still be alive because I still have to think" (*GS*, 276). Thought, it seems, is inevitable for the one who is *thinking*. One's encounter with thought must therefore occur in some fashion. As Nietzsche tells it, the great teachers of history have shared a bias on the issue. They "all try to talk people into thinking they are in a very bad way and need some severe, final, radical cure" (*GS*, 326). If this is the narrow straight in which our encounter with thought is fated to transpire, then life remains will remain painful and serious. Sure of his love for life, *The Gay Science* chronicles Nietzsche's attempt to think new circumstances.

Above, I sketched an account of Nietzsche's dissatisfaction with philosophy's stance toward thought, and I described his alternative joyful, comedic vision. His joyous science, as mentioned at the outset, prepares the way for a new kind of philosopher whose object is a new kind of truth ("so shy and ticklish one must either *surprise* or *leave alone*"). A method limits not only the shape of one's thought and arguments, but also what counts as a convincing presentation of thought. To risk stating the obvious: a new method of thinking means a new way of conducting thought. So it is not surprising that Nietzsche develops a new expression for philosophy in *The Gay Science*.

There are many facets to Nietzsche's method in *The Gay Science*: his use of multiple voices, his sourcing from vastly differing disciplines, his gnomic style—to name a few. However, I want to draw attention to the themes of poetry and chance. These themes comprise only a small portion of the whole of *The Gay Science*; they are, no doubt, insufficient to the task of understanding *The Gay Science* as a complex totality. Fortunately, that is not what is at stake. Together, poetry and chance provide a glimpse of the animus of Nietzsche's method in *The Gay Science*, helping make sense of his "ticklish" truths.

Nietzsche warned readers not to follow too closely after him. For him, learning involves overcoming—rather than imitating—the ideas of a teacher. He encouraged readers to cultivate their own encounter with thought. "This is *my* way," he speaks through the mouth of Zarathustra, "where is yours?" (*Z*, *On the Spirit of Gravity*, 2). What follows is thus not intended as a directive for how to continue Nietzsche's project. But this is not to say the methodological principles in *The Gay Science* are unworthy of attention. Taken at a general level, poetry and chance can be embraced by readers wanting to think with Nietzsche, and modified by those seeking to think after him in their own way.

* * *

In the face of rigor, poetry brings to philosophy an unwanted quality: ambiguity. There is an ancient dispute between the two. Early on, Plato clarified the issue through the voice of Socrates.

> Conversation about poetry reminds me too much of the wine parties of second-rate and commonplace people. … No one can interrogate poets about what they say … some say the poet's meaning is one thing and some another, for the topic is one on which nobody can produce a conclusive argument. (*Protagoras*, 347c-d)

The problem (for philosophy) is that poets do not prioritize rationality. Indeterminacy is a function of poetry. A poem can always mean something other, something more. Philosophers also find poetry problematic because poetry presents ideas intuitively rather than discursively. For a poet, words are things to conjure with—material to evoke ideas, experiences, affects—not tools for constructing chains of explanation. A poem is indifferent to serious argumentation, and external to decisive reasoning.

The Gay Science is Nietzsche's first published work that grants poetry a prominent place, and his method takes steps to bridge the gulf between philosophy and poetry. Importantly, however, his turn to poetry in *The Gay Science* was not his first affair with the art. In fact, among all his literary endeavors, he took up poetry the earliest and it stayed with him the longest. He wrote his first poems in 1855 at the age of eleven, and his last written work, *Dionysian Dithyrambs*, was being prepared for publication just before his breakdown in 1889. In his valuing the art of poetry, Nietzsche does not shy away from ambiguity. Yet he does not bring ambiguity to philosophy simply to counter its prejudices. Rather—as can be seen in the poems included in *The Gay Science*—poetry is a means of reflecting on writing in general. He distances himself from his poems, taking a meta-poetic stance toward writing, self-consciously noting that his poems are "songs in which a poet makes fun of all poets in a manner hard to forgive" (*GS*, *P*, 1). His poems are stubborn, written with a respect for poetic form but not without authorial remove.

Of interest is how Nietzsche's meta-poetic stance surfaces in *The Gay Science*. His consideration of poetry is wrapped up in his philosophical approach to writing. In a striking passage he elaborates:

> It is remarkable that the great masters of prose have almost always also been poets … verily, one writes good prose only *face to face with poetry!* For this is an uninterrupted, courteous war with poetry: all its attractions depend on the fact that poetry is constantly evaded and contradicted. (*GS*, 92)

Writing good prose, Nietzsche argues, requires keeping sight of the poetic power of language, metaphor, and the space between words. He cites writers like Goethe and Emerson—poets not lacking in philosophical prowess—as mastering prose precisely because of their engagement with poetry. Prose is written face to face with poetry in that, with the placement of every word and idea, there remains, ever-present, the chance of miscommunication. Good prose does not forcefully repress poetic potentiality, ridding it of ambiguity. On the contrary, it is by keeping poetry alive and in tension with prose that prose utilizes poetry's absence to its advantage. Philosophical prose establishes meaning by contradicting the poetic option. Yet, the absence of poetry is not found in its erasure, but instead in the trace of one's hesitation before the poetic. In writing, there is always a moment of decision of how to move forward—Poetry, or prose? Without an intimacy with poetry, prose withers—it conveys meaning, but only out of obligation to convention. By keeping an eye always on the poetic option one is able to develop what Nietzsche elsewhere calls the "great and rare art of giving style" to one's work (*GS*, 290).

Immediately noticeable in *The Gay Science* is his use of the aphorism. He began using this form in the two preceding books, but it is not until *The Gay Science* that he mastered the form's poetic potential. A challenge facing any writer using aphorisms is learning how to exploit breaks in thought. As with the lines of a poem, there is always something indirect, something left unsaid, between aphorisms; there is always an element of ambiguity in why an author chooses to write what comes next. In *The Gay Science*, Nietzsche demonstrates his recognition that the spaces between aphorisms contain an important moment of indirect communication. While *The Gay Science* lacks a linear progression, its developmental structure and tempo is clearly a matter of focus for Nietzsche. In *The Gay Science*, poetry's ambiguity is left present in the organization of his prose, allowing the work's content (i.e., his comic approach to philosophy and critique of seriousness) and form to harmonize.

To illustrate, in an exemplary stretch of aphorisms, Nietzsche simultaneously presents his philosophical views and celebrates his method of writing. He begins by imagining the figure of a "*Homo poeta*" (the poet-human), suggesting that such a being occupies a comic position. In a moment of authorial remove he occupies the poet-human's voice, wondering how he ought to progress. "Should I start considering a comic solution?" (*GS*, 153). What follows are nearly 125 brief passages, involving three discernible (though, not precisely defined) movements. First, Nietzsche begins with straightforward, traditional aphorisms. To illustrate:

> *An uncomfortable trait.*—To find all things deep—that is an uncomfortable trait: it makes one constantly strain one's eyes and in the end always find more than one had wished. (*GS*, 158)

Or:

> *Being deep and seeming deep.*—Those who know they are deep strive for clarity. Those who like to seem deep to the crowd strive for obscurity. For the crowd takes everything whose ground it cannot see to be deep: it is so timid and so reluctant to go into the water. (*GS*, 173)

Before long, Nietzsche shifts tack, initiating a second movement. His thoughts move quicker and become more visceral and compressed: "*Thoughts.*—Thoughts are the shadows of sensations—always darker, emptier, simpler" (*GS*, 179); "*Books.*—What good is a book that does not even carry us beyond all books?" (*GS*, 248).

Continuing in a collage-like fashion, Nietzsche evokes imagery of flying fish, skimming the crest of waves (*GS*, 256); comparing wakefulness and dreaming (*GS*, 232); and considering the power of poetic language (*GS*, 261). By writing on such variegated topics in a rapid way, Nietzsche purposefully puts distance between himself and his readers. He then jumps, in the third movement, becoming his own reader, transforming the act of writing into one of reading. Rather than stating the aphorism's topic in the title, he uses them to interrogate himself.

> *What do you believe in?*—In this: that the weight of all things must be determined anew. (*GS*, 269)
>
> *What do you love in others?*—My hopes. (*GS*, 272)
>
> *What is the seal of having become free?*—No longer to be ashamed before oneself. (*GS*, 275)

This threefold movement of aphorisms illustrates Nietzsche's meta-poetic methodological stance, his ability to make poetry's absence present in prose. In the first movement the aphorisms function generically and Nietzsche states his thoughts directly. In the second movement, he capitalizes on the aphorism's power for indirect communication. Here, he widens the space between author and audience, forcing readers to look outside his prose to decipher its meaning. Finally, he performs a gestalt shift. No longer is there a distance between author and audience, but an identity. He begins writing in, and as a, direct response to his own writing. Like the comic caught in the waves between tragedy and nihilism, his prose pulls in two directions at once. Just as direct as the first movement, but just as enigmatic as the second, the third movement's aphorisms turn in on themselves. In the act of formulating a question, Nietzsche professes his thought. Together, the movements demonstrate his creative response to the challenge of activating the breaks in thought. No longer is the blank space representative of a gap, but is now the domain of what he left unwritten, which always has the potential to comically invade the written. Despite Socrates's aversion to poetry, Nietzsche confesses his admiration for everything he "said—*and did not say*" (*GS*, 340). It is here, in the space of the unsaid—the open sea—wherein the "war between poetry and prose" is fought.

* * *

The comedic thinker inhabits the space between tragedy and nihilism, choosing to engage life's affairs and give them meaning apart from any transcendent, providential source (be it God, reason, truth, etc.). Yet, the comic is in danger. "No matter how much we have confronted the chaos of existence and denied it all providential reason," Nietzsche warns, "we still have to pass our hardest test" (*GS*, 277). As he recognizes, comedic thinkers may (like serious thinkers) fall into the trap of becoming too confident in thought. Because they have not lost connection to tragedy, the comic is able to give meaning to life, but that does not imply that they can assume their skill in "interpreting and arranging events has reached an apex" (*GS*, 277). Recall that comedy is a perspective in motion: always on-the-way-up from tragedy, placing oneself above one's world, and always on-the-way-back-down into the activities of life. The danger is thinking that, in the upward movement, one gains a privileged perspective, a vantage external to one's world. But there is no leaving the world. In always coming back down, the comedic thinker embeds themselves in activities that are out of their control. To suppose that the vantage of comedy allows one to interpret and arrange without flaw would be to misconstrue the shape of comedy. Without sure order and without the illusion of control, comedic thought involves an element of chance.

In *The Gay Science*, Nietzsche contrasts chance against providence (both transcendent and personal). Using musical imagery, he highlights the fundamental role chance plays in our activities:

> We [should not] think too highly of the dexterity of our wisdom when at times the wonderful harmony created by the playing of our instrument surprises us all too much—a harmony that sounds too good for us to dare to give credit to ourselves. (*GS*, 277)

There is in every endeavor a possibility of being surprised with the outcome. No matter how skillful or rigorous one is, there are moments wherein one strikes just the right chord, or has a brilliant thought, unexpectedly. In moments like these, it is as if the thinker is the instrument, and chance the musician. "Indeed, now and then someone plays *with* us—good old chance." Nietzsche sees the guiding hand of chance as basic to ingenuity. "The essential part of every invention," he wrote in *Daybreak*, "is the work of chance" (*D*, 363). It would be wrong to think, however, that the possibility of chance provides excuse to fall into resignation. Instead, Nietzsche sees chance as offering unanticipated ways forward and opening the potential to think with an openness toward the unknown, and a readiness to yield to the unexpected. When "chance guides our hand," he continues, "the wisest providence could not invent music more beautiful than what our foolish hand then produces" (*GS*, 277). The chord, the thought, unintended, fulfills. In a chance occurrence, one cannot take full credit: one was not planning the encounter. But the chord, the thought, persists nonetheless.

Of course, even the most rigorous thinkers would yield to an unplanned breakthrough. … And then go on, regimented as before. Nietzsche's tactic is not merely to allow for chance: he goes further, reserving space for it in advance, incorporating it in his method. His writing encourages his readers to nurture their relation to chance. A gay science is not like a puzzle, in which every piece is accounted for and needs proper assembly. Instead, it is like a natural force, always *in medias res*. "We are all volcanoes approaching their hour of eruption," Nietzsche explains. "How near or distant" the eruption is, "of course, nobody knows" (*GS*, 9). A volcano is not an argument, a problem in need of a solution. No: it is a presence of pure potential, of chance, on earth.

Likewise, in contrast to the tradition of serious thinking—which has come to view life as problematic—Nietzsche imagines, "life could be an experiment … not a duty, not a problem" (*GS*, 324). As a principle, chance animates the gay scientist's tireless dedication to experimenting in thought. "I approve of any form of skepticism to which I can reply, 'Lets try it!'" (*GS*, 51). Nietzsche's poetic method of writing is again revealing. The aphoristic form lends itself to covering many topics at once, allowing him to borrow ideas from one discipline (say, philology or theater) and to try to apply them to another (say, psychology or ethics). He realizes that some investigations may not prove fruitful. But, he does not fear making mistakes. Throughout *The Gay Science*, one sees Nietzsche discovering and uncovering his thought along the way of its writing. Like any science, it is the doubtable and the unknown that drives a gay science forward: "I want to hear nothing more about things and questions that don't admit of experiment" (*GS*, 51). However, unlike other sciences, which presuppose a framework for thinking and experimenting within, *The Gay Science* is Nietzsche's attempt to think the breakdown of framework, wagering on the possibility of thinking in the wake of its collapse. A consideration of the most well-known claim in *The Gay Science*, the death of God, gives substance to this idea.

It is in *The Gay Science* where Nietzsche's "madman" first causes a commotion in the marketplace. Despairing, he cries, "I'm looking for God! ... Where is God? ... I'll tell you! *We have killed him*—you and I! We are all his murderers" (*GS*, 125). In Nietzsche's view, God represents more than the figure of religious devotion. For him, God is the name of the stable, transcendent coordinates of the world—the fixed points of reference by which truth, morality, rationality, and so on are constructed. The madman thus worriedly considers the magnitude of the event of God's death, "the wiping away of the entire horizon," asking, "where are we moving to now?" If we have killed God, what will take God's place? The temptation (still alive today) is to immediately say, "nothing": to move from tragedy to nihilism. One searches *The Gay Science* for his answer, only to find no direct response. Is it that that Nietzsche has none to give? Not quite.

The key to understanding Nietzsche's answer to the question of what fills God's place is found in the aphorism, "How to understand our cheerfulness" (*GS*, 343). There, he explains that "at hearing the news [God is dead]" he feels "the opposite as one might expect": not despairing, he is taken by a "new and barely describable type of ... happiness ... and amusement." Where the madman found the situation frightening, Nietzsche finds it inspiring. As if watching a new dawn break, his "heart overflows with gratitude, amazement, forebodings, and expectation." Thus, his response to the question of what will take God's place is not an answer, but a feeling: joy. Nietzsche does not see, as did the madman, God's death as signifying the horizon's closure, but as its pure unfolding. "The horizon," he marvels, "is now infinitely open." Such openness, however, does not guarantee that something "better" or "more healthy" will take God's place. The horizon may seem clear, but that does not mean it is bright or without danger. What will take the place of God?—Only chance can say. The indefinite horizon must first be traversed before any determinate content emerges. By embracing chance-in-thought, Nietzsche is able to clear the space for new thought without determining in advance the shape that it will take; about its future, the Nietzschean answer is, "I don't know."

What makes Nietzsche's answer troubling is that he treats the death of God not merely as a thought experiment, but as a world-collapsing event. The position of unknowing involves a real risk: what comes next—what is put in God's place—could potentially be worse. For those living in the wake of the Second World War, for instance, the possibility of something worse became an actuality: it stripped culture of its naïve fascination with the open horizon, and it stole, in the wake of Auschwitz, the ability to give voice to the pain caused by the violent hands of modern power.

* * *

Thought, for Nietzsche, is as much an experience as it is anything else. And *The Gay Science* is a complicated, tangled experience. In the preface, Nietzsche reflects on the challenge the experiences of *The Gay Science* pose to its readers. He begins by doubting that "someone who has not experienced something similar" will understand the book. Jesting, he considers composing multiple prefaces—perhaps *that* would bring unfamiliar readers "closer to the experiences of the book" (*GS*, *P*, 1). In particular, Nietzsche has in mind the "high spirits, unrest, and contradictions" that make *The Gay Science* the unique book it is. Such experiences are reflected in Nietzsche's turn to joy and his critique of seriousness. Moreover, Nietzsche notes in Book V that a central feature of *The Gay Science* that may impede readers is its brevity in style, his method of writing on multiple topics in brief bursts (*GS*, 381). For this reason, I focused on his willing acceptance of poetry and chance.

For someone not sharing in these experiences, *The Gay Science* appears to lack a decisive element: depth. Not far behind the prejudice for seriousness follows the assumption that an idea must be worked through completely for it to be worthy. Relying on the firmness of land, serious thinkers dig deep foundations for thought. By contrast, Nietzsche risks himself, shifting from topic to topic, grazing only the surface. Nietzsche deliberately writes in this way, as a form of protest: "That [brevity] is no way to get to the depths, to get deep *enough*, is the superstition of those who fear water ... they speak without experience" (*GS*, 381). He doubts that ideas must be brooded over in order for them to be understood. Instead, he quips, "I approach deep problems like I do cold baths: fast in, fast out." Counter-intuitive for the serious, the tragic or the nihilist, the "depth" Nietzsche is interested in simply rests there, on the surface: a gay science stops prematurely, before it settles within frame, in order to give value to surface, skin—the way things merely appear. As a comedic thinker, Nietzsche recognizes that depth is intrinsic to nothing in life; it is sourced not in transcendence, but in human finitude and the way one chooses to engage it. For him the superficial *is* the profound. There is no deeper meaning.

This chapter has been an attempt *on the way* to grasping Nietzsche's claim that *The Gay Science* charts an open course toward philosophical transformation. In *The Gay Science* there is speed, a lightness of touch, found at the heart of philosophy, which represents his project of thinking critically while simultaneously embracing chance with high spirits. In aiming to think philosophy apart from its traditional weight, Nietzsche sets himself new objects: among them, a new kind of truth. He believes his use of brevity and attention to the surface has a positive value. Namely, giving him access to a kind of truth that usually goes unnoticed. The truths that he has in focus are what he calls shy, ticklish. In approaching them, one must always move swiftly or not at all—lest they recede, obscuring their comprehension. Nietzsche's method of writing is no accident to his joyful science, nor is it merely a psychological predilection: "I must say things briefly so that they will be heard even more briefly." When touched upon, ticklish truths veil themselves, like an organ tensing up in response to a prodding hand. To catch them, one must remain in constant motion—no less sensitive than the truths one seeks—touching them in flight, catching one glimpse at a time.

The experience Nietzsche presumes necessary in *The Gay Science* is fraught with contradiction: neither meaningful nor meaningless; neither rational nor irrational; not poetry but not prose alone; dedicated cultivation, but leaving room for the rupture of chance. The work of a joyous science presents the comedy of attempting to dismantle the world without being sure of what will take its place. Meaning is found where one puts it. But there is also always a constant shifting, posturing, and re-posturing from position to position. So reluctant to expose themselves, the truths Nietzsche is after reveal themselves in motion, in their opposites—the unsaid within the said: poetry in prose, the rational in the irrational, the comedy between tragedy and nihilism, and so on …

Notes

1 Immanuel Kant, *The Critique of Pure Reason* (Cambridge: Cambridge University Press, 1999), A236/B295.

2 Plato, *Laws*, 7: 816e; Thomas Hobbes, *The English Works of Thomas Hobbes of Malmesbury*, 11 vols. (London: Bohn, 1845), 4:455.

4

"What Do You Matter?": Nietzsche's *Zarathustra*, Individualism, and Modernism

Douglas Burnham

Thus Spoke Zarathustra is the strangest book Nietzsche wrote, which probably also means one of the strangest ever written. It is a fictional religious or sacred text, and this pretense is meant *both* as mockery of religion and as genuine prophetic sentiment. It tries to imagine a future, but does so by reimagining the past. It is serious but also childish, bombastic but also lyrical, of titanic universality but also deeply personal.

In this chapter I will aim to illuminate something about this book, by way of its relationship to modernism, broadly speaking, and more especially by way of the problem of the nature of the *individual* in modernism. This period sees the starkest contrasts between ways of evaluating the nature, value, and role of individuals. On the one hand, an apparent triumph of liberalism in politics and economics; while on the other hand, the Russian Revolution finally puts a major power in the hands of communism. Or again, consumer culture brings individualism to the masses, while at the same time leading thinkers and artists are questioning the very nature of the individual. The influence of Nietzsche's *Zarathustra* turns out to be no less ambiguous.

* * *

So, a strange book with a strange history. Nietzsche spent a long time working on the project, from late 1882 to 1885—the longest period on a single work of his career—although the text is not correspondingly lengthy (Nietzsche later claimed that the various parts were in fact written in short creative bursts). One should at any rate not underestimate the care he lavished upon it. Given that any wider intellectual credibility Nietzsche enjoyed in the 1870s was long gone by this period, the first three (of four) parts not surprisingly sold very poorly in the 1880s. Nietzsche circulated the fourth only privately; this fourth was then published in 1892, after his mental collapse (i.e., after he had lost control of his literary estate). However, within just a few years and certainly by the end of the century, when modernism had caught up with it, the work became very popular and influential indeed. By then, three major young composers had set aspects of *Zarathustra* to music (Mahler and Strauss c. 1896 and Delius in 1898), the first English translation appeared already in 1896, and Nietzsche together with his Zarathustra were practically household names (in certain circles, at least) across Europe and the United States. None of which, of course, means that either Nietzsche or his strangest book was also well understood.

As mentioned, the work is in four parts, with first also having a prologue. If one were forced to choose a genre in which to pigeonhole it, it would be a novel. Specifically, a fictional, ancient "religious" narrative, nominally set in ancient Iran. Not least in its ancient, oriental setting and its episodic nature, Nietzsche was no doubt influenced by Voltaire's fine short novel *Zadig, or Destiny. A Tale from the Orient*, which comes complete with pretend dedications. Zarathustra is the Iranian spelling of the real historical figure more commonly known by the Greek version of his name, Zoroaster. Zarathustra/Zoroaster was an ancient philosophical or religious leader who lived in what is now eastern Iran, and after whom the still-practised religion Zoroastrianism is named. Nietzsche chose to make Zarathustra his chief character, likely because he represents a non-Greek and non-Judaic intellectual tradition; that is, he comes from "outside" the intellectual and religious structures that Nietzsche so often criticizes (thus also the use of the Iranian rather than the Greek version of the name). Nevertheless, historically Zarathustra's teachings were moral in nature, positing as competing, real cosmological principles good and evil, indeed perhaps the first time in intellectual history that such strong and universal moral principles had been posited. Nietzsche thus saw Zarathustra representing exactly the point where the broader philosophical tradition went wrong, where morality became inseparable from both philosophy and religion. Zarathustra stands at a kind of fulcrum point for Nietzsche's comprehensive critique of morality. Thus, the novel is an imaginative historical intervention, a "thought experiment" if you like. With it, Nietzsche is asking: what if instead, this outsider Zarathustra had preached a doctrine that was truly outside and (in terms of Nietzsche's next publication) "beyond good and evil," how then would subsequent, especially European culture be challenged and changed?

The prologue and each part are made up of a number of short episodes, most only a few pages long. Most of the episodes are written as a series of brief paragraphs, averaging roughly two dozen words and sometimes a single sentence, which mimic both the historical style of Zarathustra and texts like the Psalms in the *Old Testament*. They are notably akin also to many of the surviving fragments of the pre-socratic philosophers. The overall type of writing varies, including narrative passages and various interspersed poems, but the most common form is Zarathustra's didactic voice—that is to say, his speeches delivered either to the "people" or to his disciples. In style, the work is almost always highly imagistic and allegorical, although the tone can vary from parody and crude humor, through energetic exhortation to calm reflection.

The plot is not terribly involved. Zarathustra has spent a decade becoming wise, in a cave in the mountains. He comes down to teach the people that the human is not an endpoint, but rather a transition to the "overhuman." However, he realizes quickly that the people are unable to understand him, so resolves instead to accumulate disciples. He travels, and the places he visits (all of which are allegorical and at least highly fictionalized if not actually fictional) are occasions for elements of his teachings. He sometimes returns to his cave, for reflection or solace. By the end of Part Two,

Zarathustra becomes painfully aware that there is an element of his teachings of which he has refused to speak, and indeed has not even acknowledged to himself. This is the thought of eternal recurrence (or "return"), the destructive or transforming thought, which leads Part Three to an ultimately positive mystical conclusion. In Part Four, Zarathustra brings to his cave a group of "higher men" who he believes may be his true followers (they are in fact exaggerated satirical portraits of more or less contemporary figures, such as Schopenhauer and Wagner), but who end up disappointing him; Part Four again ends with optimism that his "children" are soon to come.

As a whole, the book elaborates on two overarching philosophical ideas. The first is the "overhuman" (sometime translated as "overman" or, especially in early translations, it is rendered as "superman)—this is the idea that human life should be continually developing rather than arriving and remaining at some particular stage. The "overhuman" is thus an image of the unrealized potential of the human to develop beyond its existing nature or limits. The second theme is what Nietzsche calls "eternal recurrence" (or "eternal return"). The exact nature of this idea is a matter of considerable debate in the scholarly literature but, broadly, here Nietzsche invites us to reflect upon the notion that the entire cosmos repeats itself endlessly and, if so, what this does to our cherished values, and our sense of personal or collective worth. Nietzsche's hypothesis is that this thought, if we allowed it fully to penetrate every corner of our being, would likely destroy us (by eliminating every value that we formerly believed in and gave our life meaning)—or, if not, transform us beyond the human and toward the overhuman.

Given that both of the just named themes are huge, as much in their scope as their intended impact, here I will focus on one subsidiary notion, a part of this grander enterprise. This is the idea of the self or the individual, and the identity or unity of that self, considered as a *problem* rather than a *foundation*. Our focus in turn will require us briefly to touch also on Nietzsche's critique of moral values insofar as these relate to the unity of the self. I have chosen this subsidiary notion because of its significance both for Nietzsche, obviously, but also because shortly after Nietzsche is writing, it becomes a prevalent feature of modernism.

* * *

Earlier still in the nineteenth century, the theme of individuality was prominent too. There were three clear sources for this. The first was the Enlightenment individual, whether as understood in political discourse as the bearer of inalienable human rights, or as in Kant's ethics, as morally autonomous, or in empiricism as the focus point of the accumulation of data, and thus as the foundation of knowledge (in the political and economic spheres, this broad movement is clearly an ancestor of liberalism, to which I will return). The second, and by no means unconnected, source was romanticism, which tended to depict the individual as in a broadly heroic if perhaps doomed struggle against a society characterized by staid and restrictive traditions or utilitarian values, and generally an uncomprehending world. This romantic tradition is exemplified in Goethe's version of the Faust story, in Byron's *Manfred* and *Don Juan*, and in the attitude of many contemporary figures to Napoleon (e.g., Beethoven's initial dedication of his third symphony to Napoleon); it becomes formalized in the writings of Thomas Carlyle who saw history as revolving around "great" men. The third source and one again that is by no means completely distinct from the others is the work of Hegel. Historically, however, Hegel's philosophy turned out to be ambiguous with respect to the individual. For example, in Hegel is found one origin of the "great men" theory (specifically in Hegel's notion of the "world-historical individual"). Divergent readings of Hegel are possible, and indeed proliferated in the second third of the century. Are world-historical individuals genuine grounds qua individuals, or just historical effects? Similarly, strands of Hegelianism end up, more or less simultaneously, in Max Stirner's radically individualist *The Ego and His Own*, and in the first mature works of Marx and Engels, who insist upon the primacy of the social.

The case of Stirner is particularly interesting, and merits a brief further comment. This is because the early reception of Nietzsche often viewed him as an imitative disciple of Stirner. *The Ego and His Own* (a slightly more revealing rendition of the title might be *The Unique Ego and Its Possessions*) argues that there are in fact no causal, moral, or logical claims upon the unique self—for example, no idea of human nature or psychology, no power, and even no truth claim compels it. The self possesses its thoughts, experiences, and its world in complete independence. A second-rate thinker albeit a first-rate dropper of intellectual bomb-shells, Stirner should probably be thought of more as a belated romantic than a genuine member of the Young Hegelians. The identification at the time of Stirner and Nietzsche's thought is understandable, but in fact relied upon an interpretation of Nietzsche that pre-judged his stance on individualism. Stirner only helps us *not* to read Nietzsche well.

The Left Hegelians aside, this early-nineteenth-century individual was a *foundation.* To be sure, it may require liberation, or may struggle against its world and time, nevertheless its existence and importance were unquestioned, and that existence provided a ground upon which other philosophical, moral, or political edifices could be constructed. So, for example, liberalism built a system of moral and political thought on the basis of the value of the freely acting, equal individual; likewise, on the foundation of such an individual lies the romantic valorization of independence, genius, self-subsistence, and iconoclasm.

In the late nineteenth and the first half of the twentieth centuries—roughly the period that I am calling "modernist"—the Enlightenment notion of the individual becomes dominant, but in surprising new ways. In the political and economic spheres, especially, individualism considered as foundational experienced a growth as in no other period, and the liberalism as envisioned by J. S. Mill, for example, achieved extreme new manifestations. Universal (or near-universal) enfranchisement in Western democracies placed the foundation of the validity of the State on the "consent" of the governed—but not (as John Locke clearly intended that phrase) where this means simply for the protection of the governed, but where it means, quite literally, quantity of votes cast by individuals.

Mass production meant individual consumerism in at least two senses. First, reduced production costs meant the democratization of style of dress, transportation, housing, tourism, theater (by way of cinema), and so forth; while expanding universal education made everyone a reader of books and periodicals. The incomes not just of the middle class but even of workers in many Western countries became more than was needed for basic necessities, meaning that it was no longer merely the minority who were such consumers. Thus, the meaning of work and of payment for work done became identified with access to consumer goods and leisure, rather than mere "livelihood," that is, subsistence living for oneself and one's family. Individual purchases were thus the foundation of the value one assigned to any innovation, including in the narrower cultural sphere. Second, individuals competed to display their expenditure, profligately if necessary, in what Veblen at the end of the nineteenth century called "conspicuous consumption." In other words, to be an individual (or a member of a distinct class) became identified with visibly being more successful in having and especially consuming one's aptly named "disposable income." The former mode of consumerism emphasizes *equality* (as of course does political enfranchisement); the latter emphasizes *difference*. For both of these reasons, however, the value of some new product (whether it be a novel or a design of car) became increasingly identified with the quantity of sales to individuals; it is notable that the term "bestseller" is invented and comes to be in common use during this period. In summary, then, in the political and the economic spheres, respectively, the individual as voter or consumer becomes the foundation of value and the basic unit of the political and economic order.

In all the above instances of modern individualism, however, the nature and value of the individual itself is not questioned, no more than it had been in the most of the nineteenth-century trends that I discussed above. It is *assumed to be* the rightful place of political or economic choice, and the capacity of that choice to be free (to be the authentic expression of that individual), and thus for the overall effect of those choices to be the best outcome or the most efficient economy, is likewise unquestioned.

However, there are of course two others sides to modernism. First, which I will not discuss here, what many saw as the culmination of Marx's thought in collectivism, in various forms. Second, and more important for us here, are those celebrated radical new forms of thought and expression that go under the umbrella "modernism." A chief characteristic of this modernist thought and cultural practice was a questioning of precisely this foundational character of the individual. Rather than being the ground of some greater edifice, the self becomes a problem, perhaps indeed *the* problem. This is most obviously exemplified in the work of Freud, for whom the self is fissured. It is as if we are invited to ask: which of these forces making up and competing for the psyche is the "real me"? While the answer is unclear and always changing—and depends upon a relationship to another, namely the therapist—nevertheless the *problem* is absolutely important, for in it lies the engine of change and development of societies and cultures, Freud argues.

One finds the theme of the self as a problem also in the fractured identities of characters in Woolf (most famously in *Mrs Dalloway* or *Orlando*). The fragile appearance and rapid dissolution of "stable" characters in Kafka similarly (his short story "The Judgement" being a particularly obvious example of this, as the young man, initially projecting an image of happiness, confidence, and success, is somehow unraveled by a confrontation with his father). Likewise, the central character of Hans

Castorp in Mann's *The Magic Mountain* would initially appear a ripe candidate for a *Bildungsroman*—a standard novel type that relates a young person's individual character reaching its final, adult form. But Hans never actually develops, nor stays constant, in his health neither well nor ill, neither coming nor going—and the novel ends with him as an anonymized soldier in the First World War. Somewhat later in this period, the same effect is found in the relentless stripping away of the trappings of character in Beckett (e.g., *Murphy* from 1938). For a final example, in Sartre's existentialism, the freedom of the self is to be sure an inescapable feature of the self, but not a *foundation*, rather at best a kind of always possible clearing within which actions could construct an individual identity, and even this identity must be both fragile and a burden, and in turn requires constant re-affirmation. The individual could only be a foundation, for Sartre, in the case of inauthenticity.

In literary and theatrical naturalism, human beings are understood as determined psychologically or socially in decipherable ways. This movement began prior to the modernist period, but it became fully mainstream only at the end of the nineteenth and beginning of the twentieth centuries. In naturalism, the individual was already not a foundation per se. In Zola or Strindberg, for example, there are "strong" individually sculpted characters, but it is clear that these are not only at the mercy of forces beyond them, but originally formed as characters by those forces. The naturalist individual, then, while not a problem in the above-mentioned typically modernist ways, nevertheless leads us decisively away from the liberal or romantic individual.

Furthermore, several important strands of modernism ultimately included a decisive turn away from naturalism. This modernist turn away thus involved the rejection of conventional psychology in either the understanding of character or the experience of a readership/audience. So, albeit in completely distinct ways, Maeterlinck (insofar as he gives a symbolist, rather than a naturalistic, version of fatalism; an approach that was influenced by Wagner and is taken up, later, in the more experimental works of O'Neill), Brecht (through distancing techniques that point out the artificiality of the theatrical reality), and Artaud (through the direct immersion of the spectator in the events of the play, intended to dissipate identities) all rejected naturalism and created theater that ended the reliance on both character types and psychology. They thus further broke up any calm confidence in the identity of the self.

The above proliferation of examples is meant to indicate the prevalence of this problem in modernism, as well as signaling the variety of ways in which it appears. What is clear, then, is that the modernist period carried with it an inner contradiction. Politically and economically (in consumerism at least), one finds an entrenchment of the foundational value of the individual. Moreover, shall be shown below, a pseudo-Nietzschean version of individualism was also very widespread in the period. At the same time, there were any number of cultural projects underway in psychology, philosophy, theater, and the novel that understood the individual as insubstantial, questionable, fragile, originally fractured, or some kind of mere effect of other forces.

* * *

One of the origins of this new way of conceiving of the individual or the self is of course Nietzsche. Although Freud was uncomfortable with the idea, it seems likely that Nietzsche's view of the self did indeed influence his work, if only indirectly. Of the figures mentioned above, the influence is acknowledged to be direct at least in the case of Thomas Mann, Antonin Artaud, Eugene O'Neill, and Jean-Paul Sartre.

It is not difficult to find in Nietzsche's works clear statements that think of the self or the individual in problematic terms. In *The Birth of Tragedy*, for example, one finds Nietzsche conceiving of both individual and cultural identities in terms of the competing basic drives of Apollonian, Dionysian, and Socratic. In other words, what might appear to be a genuine foundation are in fact multiple drives, rather than drives being transient "possessions" of some individual unity. (The notion of the Dionysian just on its own had an enormous and well-known influence on modernism and the portrayal of individuality, but that is a slightly different story to the one I will be pursuing below.) Similarly, much later in *Beyond Good and Evil,* Nietzsche insists that the "soul" is not something individual, but something multiple and social (*BGE*, 12). While the famous frontispiece of Hobbes's *Leviathan* shows the many subjects of the state unified in the body of the monarch, Nietzsche inverses this idea, suggesting that even the individual subject is in fact always multiple.

No less difficult is it to identify clear statements of this idea in *Zarathustra*. The point is made philosophically in "On the Despisers of the Body" in Part One, where "the body," "reason," "spirit," the "I" are all names for *distinct* and by no means harmonious aspects of the "self." Moreover, it is illustrated by way of staged dialogues between aspects of the self. For example, in the eighth section of the Prologue, where Zarathustra speaks to his "heart" and again his "hunger"; or the last section of Part Two where he is addressed by "the stillest hour." To be sure, interior dialogue is hardly unique to Nietzsche (and that is part of the difficulty of interpretation), but in conjunction with the philosophical claims concerning the multiplicity of the self, the conclusion is unavoidable that such dialogues are more than a conventional device. Zarathustra addressing his "heart," then, is not a metaphor for a high-level conscious reflection and decision-making, or even some kind of uncertainty, but rather a genuine multiplicity of the self, either on the level of drives (as back in *The Birth of Tragedy*) or on the "social" model of the self (as in *Beyond Good and Evil*).

To be sure, Nietzsche sometimes adds that the originally dispersed individual may be subject to a unifying destiny, but it is not one that any "I" chooses in any ordinary sense of the word "choice." The content of the interior dialogue in "The Stillest Hour" makes this clear. To the extent that such individuals have any genuine unity, it is not a foundational one (i.e., is it not inalienable or autonomous) but rather a manifestation of historical forces that extend far beyond the individual per se and were never the object of a "choice" in the liberal sense. History demands the emergence of an individual so that the current condition of human beings might change. (This idea of individual as destiny might be thought of as a Nietzschean version of Hegel's notion of "world historical individual," mentioned above.) Thus the peculiar affects ascribed to the "over" (or "super") "human": it knows both the entitled voice of command together with the humility of being an instrument of broader destiny. In *Zarathustra* this notion is reflected in the famous passage where the overhuman must inhabit dragon, lion, and child (*Z*, *On the Three Transformations*); and is repeated later in different terms by way of the contrast between the masculine hero of knowledge, and the feminine beauty of form (*Z*, *On the Sublime Ones*), or between stillness and action (*Z*, *At Midday*).

Self-identity, Nietzsche finds, is a moral and often also indeed a theological concept, this is most clearly illustrated by Locke, for whom the continuity of the self is guaranteed by the need of God to judge men. Likewise, a moral system can provide the self with a pseudo-unity because it provides a purpose, or a fixed order of values. So, the Enlightenment view of the self as foundational in turn depends upon the value attached to *reason* as the highest and purest aspect of the human (Kant), or upon the highest valuing of individual *equality*—enlightenment human rights theories often assume such equality—or again upon the *collective* valuing of the welfare of all humans, as in utilitarianism. The romantic conception rests upon a valuing of freedom, but now understood as creativity or self-definition. In all these ways, the reliance upon the unity or identity of the self, inherited by the nineteenth century, is tied to moral values.

Each of these unities Nietzsche could call "pseudo" because at bottom they are in turn founded upon either a self-contradictory basis or a hidden theological one. Thus, such moralities by no means provide a unity to the self in the manner Enlightenment and romantic thought hoped. Not surprisingly, *Zarathustra* explicitly makes such claims. So, for example, the Kantian view of reason Nietzsche reveals as both a hopeless abstraction and also akin to asceticism, a cutting of life off from the body. In other words, it is a longing for death (this is the main theme of *On the Despisers of the Body*, early in part one, and it is developed much further in *On the Three Evils* in part three). Again, what the majority call "equality" is illusion, and in fact founded upon the emotion of revenge (found in *On the Flies of the Market Place*, and often throughout part two). Utilitarian concern for welfare yields not a healthy, growing culture but rather a soporific stagnation (these are the themes of sections three and five of the prologue, and again in part two *On the Tarantulas*). Romantic genius and cult of the "great man" is a mistaking of the loudest for the most important moments in history, and more generally a huge oversimplification of the notion of creativity (again, see *On the Flies in the Market Place* and especially *On Great Events* in part two). It follows that, to the extent Zarathustra can achieve a crumbling away of traditional moral values, this will also achieve a crumbling of the corresponding identity and foundational role of the individual self, as conceived of in eighteenth- and nineteenth-century culture.

* * *

However, *Thus Spoke Zarathustra* is an unusual case. Not only does the philosophical content of the work dispense with a foundational individual, but in both the key ideas of the book (the overhuman and the eternal recurrence) lies a powerful instrument for the dissolution of the individual as foundational. Nevertheless, from the beginning, Nietzsche and especially this book were frequently interpreted in a very different way.

In a manner similar to the portrait of the modernist individual above, let us adduce several examples of this misinterpretation. Zarathustra's vision of the overhuman, considered as the ultimate individual, was a key premise of many of Nietzsche's early English-language interpreters, such as H. L. Mencken. In 1901–03, Russian composer Alexander Scriabin began drafting sketches for an opera to dramatize the overhuman as a self-proclaimed epitome of creation; his slightly later *Poem of Ecstasy* has a similar organizing idea. George Bernard Shaw borrows the word "superman" directly from *Zarathustra* for his monumental *Man and Superman* (1903), but thinks of it as the endpoint of evolution, to be achieved by the loosening up of human breeding, which is currently restricted by social mores such as monogamy. This superman is not, to be sure, a great individual, but rather a species of great individuals. Shaw accordingly writes: "Until there is an England in which every man is a Cromwell, a France in which every man is a Napoleon, a Rome in which every man is a Cæsar, a Germany in which every man is a Luther plus a Goethe, the world will be no more improved by its heroes than a Brixton villa is improved by the pyramid of Cheops. The production of such nations is the only real change possible to us" (295). Jack London's *The Sea Wolf* (1904) has as its main protagonist a radically individualist, amoral Wolf Larsen who was quite explicitly based on how London—and by no means only London—interpreted the "superman" described in *Zarathustra*. In science fiction, one of the important new genres of popular culture in the modern period, there was a whole tradition of "superman" stories, which have as their common ancestor a very loose interpretation of Zarathustra's teachings concerning the overhuman. These include *The Hamdenshire Wonder* in 1911 or *Odd John* in 1935. The eponymous character of the latter conceives of himself as an individual above human morality. And, of course, the comic book superhero himself (who was not originally conceived of as an alien) first appears in 1938. Ayn Rand's first novel *We the Living* (1934) is quite explicit in its employment of Nietzsche to justify the elitist—and at least here in this first novel quite violently elitist—individual. In short, for many in the modern period, *Thus Spoke Zarathustra* was Nietzsche's main work, and its main theme the promotion through the notion of the "superman" precisely the foundational and inalienable value of the individual. This, as I shall try to show below, is a misunderstanding (although perhaps an understandable one). And there remains, even today, a widespread misunderstanding of Nietzsche's thought on just this point.

This misinterpretation is to a degree understandable because there appears to be a tension between the philosophical "content" of *Zarathustra* and its genre, style, and form. It turns out that one needs to take extra care in interpreting *Zarathustra* because the genre, style, and form can set up certain expectations in the reader that are demonstrably though subtly *not* to be ascribed to Nietzsche. The book's subtitle gives us a clue to the fact that Nietzsche was well aware of, *and indeed counted on*, playing this dangerous game: "A book for everyone and no one." In other words: a book everyone could read, but few—perhaps none, yet—will understand or be able to take to heart.

One might expect *Zarathustra* to contradict in practice what it preaches in theory since it appears to be a novel, and one that has a clear main character (Zarathustra himself). In other words, the mere fact that here is a narrative with an identifiable chief protagonist suggests that in its form at least *Zarathustra* cannot sustain its philosophical ideas concerning identity or the nature of the individual. However, all this would be to overlook peculiar features of the narrative in question. In order to see this, let us crudely speculate that a narrative might provide a character with unity in two main ways, either the character emerging as the constant in shifting events of the picaresque or the character emerging as a coherent development given the events of the story. The latter is an idea that goes all the way back to Aristotle's *Poetics*, but which became increasingly prominent in the nineteenth century. The nineteenth-century novel in various ways continued the tradition of the *Bildungsroman*—that is, the novel of the development of a character, usually over the course of his or her youth. Even realism and later naturalism, while it went out its way to depict the often arbitrary external forces that operated on a character, did so with equally careful attention to psychological mechanisms. Such a character may not have had the heroically persistent unity, nor the stubborn freedom of a romantic hero, but did have an understandable continuous coherence, as defined by the sociology and psychology of the day. Even were Nietzsche's book to be classed as a naturalistic novel—which it certainly is not, in anything like the normal sense—there would still be some available identity to Zarathustra's character, although that character be hollowed out by external forces. Alternatively, this coherence may be correspondence to one of the known character types or subgenres, most obviously in comedies or melodramas. When Dickens presents us with the avaricious and cruel man who runs the workhouse, we know what to expect. Types have a constancy that depends upon generic norms, rather than upon psychology or social forces. In brief, the nineteenth century expected its characters to exhibit some kind of evident unity across their development.

The character of Zarathustra certainly at first looks as though it will take the form of the hero of the picaresque—or perhaps the romantic hero—having some kind of constancy as events unfold around it. The first sentence of the Prologue tells us that Zarathustra left his home and spent ten years alone in a mountain cave, becoming wise. Such a character one might expect is now fully formed, and his adventures will only reveal to us the character and that character's wisdom, both of which are *already the case*. Moreover, the pattern fits a stock character, and he is also known: he is the wise man, the prophet, the speaker of perhaps cryptic but very important truths, the archetypes including the blind seer Tiresias in Sophocles, Moses, and other prophets in the *Old Testament*, or the fool in *King Lear*. As a stock character, we know, or think we know, several things about this character's identity: he will, for example, be unique (there is rarely a need for *two* seers). That the book is called *Thus Spoke Zarathustra*—that is, indicating its primary content being a record of Zarathustra's teachings—only adds to these impressions.

However, Nietzsche is fully aware of all this, and takes evident delights in bursting all these bubbles within two pages. Still in the Prologue, the first-person Zarathustra meets upon coming down from his cave is yet *another*, quite different wise old hermit, which is a surprise to the reader as it calls into question our initial simple identification of Zarathustra as *the* wise man. Equally importantly, the first thing Zarathustra says he immediately takes back, as though it were spoken in error ("What did I say of love," Zarathustra says in section two, and Nietzsche adds an exclamation mark, as if to stress Zarathustra's frustration with his own error). Again, this runs very much against our expectations of the character type: the prophet may be misinterpreted, but surely cannot misspeak. Now, Nietzsche of course would not be the first writer to subvert his reader's expectations in such a way—playing on the reader's expectations is a key part of any writer's arsenal—but for him to do so in so comprehensive and clear a manner, and so directly against our thinking of Zarathustra as a recognizable type, right in the opening pages, surely means something. I suggest it means not just that the character of Zarathustra will be surprising, but that Zarathustra should not be understood as a character *in this sense* at all.

Well, then, despite the ten years in the mountain cave, perhaps this Zarathustra is in the process of development, and his not-yet-being-unique and his making mistakes are all part of that development? Rather than a fixed or otherwise resilient character, maybe he is still young and growing. Perhaps, this is a *Bildungsroman*. If so, then the expectation is that the development will follow understandable paths. Even stock characters may have expected paths of development, of course (e.g., the innocent being corrupted by the city) but more to the point, I mean some psychological or sociological description of development under particular circumstances, as in for example Stendhal or Dostoevsky. Any such intelligible development would entail that one has to see Zarathustra as a recognizably developing character, and perhaps in that way also an independently acting individual.

There are barriers in the narrative to accepting this solution—for example, Zarathustra's supposed "development" occurs in curiously precipitate fits and starts. However, the most important barrier to accepting that the narrative of Zarathustra is a version of traditional character development is philosophical in nature. For precisely the traditional mechanisms of character development are ruled out: there is and could be no general psychological law, nor sociological description of structure or development, that leads to Zarathustra, either as he is at the beginning of the book, or at the end. Zarathustra changes, to be sure, but this (Nietzsche repeatedly insists) is *transformation* and not development. That is to say, it is a kind of change for which there are no rules or expectations, like the "sea change" in Shakespeare's *The Tempest*, or the coming to life scene in *The Winter's Tale*.

As before, Nietzsche clearly signals this right at the beginning of the book. In the same meeting with the hermit that I discussed above, the hermit "recognizes" Zarathustra—this is repeated twice for emphasis, and the hermit also adds "Zarathustra he was called." However, in direct contradiction to this recognition, the hermit *also* sees that Zarathustra has been transformed in ways that Nietzsche describes in deliberately paradoxical ways: "Then you were carrying your ashes to the mountains; would you today carry your fire into the valleys?" and again "Zarathustra has become a child." Both of these things are indeed impossibilities, if taken literally: ashes cannot return to being fire, nor an adult become a child. These images imply a reversal of cause and effect and more generally a reversal of the direction of time; in fact the former is an impossible reversal of that which is already a classic symbol of transformation (fire to ashes). The direction of time and the reliability of cause and effect are precisely the minimum conditions needed to devise a psychological theory of development. The point is that

Zarathustra is the same qua continuous physical organism, perhaps, but his "character" has transformed in a way impossible to both achieve and anticipate. Of course it is possible to dismiss the images of ashes and child as mere poetic hyperbole, and not to take them so literally. However, it is surely disingenuous to accuse Nietzsche, on the book's second page, of such back-to-back carelessness. Moreover, both images recur in the book, and with the same meaning and the same implied paradoxicality: see for example, Part One *The Three Transformations* and *On Believers in a Behind-the-World.*

This notion of transformation is underscored by the concept of the "overhuman" being achieved through the thought of eternal recurrence—such that in Part Three's famous "On the Vision and the Riddle" Nietzsche writes that the transformed one is "no longer human." It is important to realize that this famous passage concerning the impossible outcome of the thought of eternal recurrence is near the beginning of Part Three, and is thus a response to the problem Nietzsche elaborates at the end of Part Two (beginning in *On Redemption*): that is, the problem of willing backward. And this in turn is a problem precisely concerning identity of the self, the ability of the self to gather itself from disconnected pieces. Thus, Zarathustra proclaims in *On Redemption*: "Verily, my friends, I walk among human beings as among fragments and severed limbs of human beings." Eternal return addresses this disturbing fragmentation not by discovering or creating a wholeness, but through a test of whether one is a piece of destiny within an essentially ascending mode of human life. The thought of eternal recurrence, and its unpredictable, transformative consequence, is thus not so much a "solution" to the problem of individual identity, recasting such identity as the essential problem of existence..

Nietzsche's *Thus Spoke Zarathustra* is a complex and subtle text, and its relation to modernism no less so. To some in the period, it was Nietzsche's great statement of the individual as hero, and thus continuous with one or the other of the modes that individualism took in nineteenth-century thought. However, philosophically *Zarathustra* involves the destruction of the individual as in any way a foundation of value or meaning. Human identity is an abyss: foundationless. Moreover, narratively Nietzsche lays traps for his reader in order to disabuse that reader of any presuppositions concerning the coherence or development of individual character. The human individual is not a solid ground, nor even a sensible goal, but a set of phenomena deeply related to religious and moral thinking, and thus to the decay of culture. Because of these deep relations, however, the human individual is also not simply a phantom or a distraction, but forms the central problem of human existence.

5

Der Antichrist: A Book for Barbarians, Slaves, and Cave Dwellers

Brian Pines

Der Antichrist is one of Nietzsche's last works. He began composing it in Sils Maria in August 1888, finished writing the next month in Turin, and by January of the next year he had been admitted to a psychiatric institution in Basel. For a long time this book was read as a hyperbolic or even ad-libbed diatribe.[1] The essential problem readers tended to have with *Antichrist* is that it engages in little recognizably philosophical activity compared with Nietzsche's other works. Instead it castigates, exaggerates, and rambles. The usual explanation for the style of *Antichrist* was that Nietzsche's mind was already tainted by the madness to which he would soon succumb.[2] This seemed confirmed by certain biographical details, for example the extreme speed with which the work was written, or the completely unrealistic predictions the author made of its success.[3]

Recently there has been a resurgence of interest in this once unpopular work. Michel Serres, Babich Babette, Weaver Santaniello, and most especially Andreas Urs Sommer and Gary Shapiro have found philosophical substance beneath the uncultured diction of *Antichrist*.[4] However, this wild style which presents itself on the surface of *Antichrist*, a style which Shapiro calls "Nietzsche's graffito," still remains one of the text's main problems. I propose an explanation for "Nietzsche's graffito" that does not rely on the concept of Nietzsche's madness, but instead finds philosophical justification for this style in the text of *Antichrist*. I will argue that Nietzsche did not intend for his book to appeal to philosophical audiences, rather, he intended it to be read by those who in other works he calls "the herd." The *Antichrist* contains an underlying meditation on the nature of "the herd," and they, not the philosophers, are its target market. By revealing Nietzsche's rhetorical methodology through an analysis of the content of *Antichrist* I ultimately hope to explain Nietzsche's bewildering belief that this text would be more popular than any he had published hitherto.

Images and instincts

There is a hypothesis running throughout *Antichrist* which puts forward a theory of how "the masses" become enchanted by an idea: "In all fairness, people should ask themselves whether it was not really an aesthetic taste that kept humanity in the dark for so long: people demanded a *picturesque* [pittoresken] effect from the truth, they demanded that the knower make a striking impression on their senses" (*A*, 13). Amid all the bombastic, attention-grabbing aphorisms in this work, many more subtle concepts could be overlooked. What is it that Nietzsche is trying to convey here? Following Nietzsche's usage of italics, the concept of the "image" ("picturesque") is what should be concentrated on. Nietzsche is trying to communicate to us in this aphorism the importance of an *image* for convincing "humanity," "the people," of an idea. Nietzsche repeats this slightly cynical thought later on in *Antichrist*:

> When one reflects how necessary it is to the great majority that there be regulations to restrain them from without and hold them fast ... then one at once understands conviction and "faith." ... The grand poses struck by these [men of fanatical faith and conviction], these conceptual epileptics, can affect the great masses,—fanatics are picturesque, humanity would rather see gestures than listen to reasons. (*A*, 54)

This aphorism helps to solidify the link between the nature of the image and the convictions of the masses. It is through the faculty of imagination, not reason or understanding, that the masses of human beings attach themselves to a cause or idea. But why should this be the case? What is the nature of the image and the faculty of imagination that gives it such power over the beliefs of the many?[5] This is the question Nietzsche is exploring in *Antichrist*. In order to investigate this problem Nietzsche examines one of the most impressive mass persuasion events in history: the Christianization of the Roman Empire.

The regions and subjects Nietzsche chooses to analyze in his re-telling of this event were picked to support the theory of mass persuasion that he is developing. In his discussions concerning the conversion of the Germanic barbarians[6] Nietzsche analyzes the state of the Christian god after their religion expanded to include these Nordic souls. He claims that the Christian god transformed into a "hybrid image of decay [Verfalls-Gebilde], made from nullity, concept and contradiction, who sanctions all the instincts of decadence, all the cowardice and exhaustions of the soul!" (*A*, 19). Nietzsche is once again describing a serious and precise concept despite the brevity and theatrical flourishes of this passage: namely, that an *image* has the capacity to "sanction" certain *instincts*, to encapsulate and protect them.

This postulation that images "sanction" instincts is one of the central theses of *Antichrist*. Nietzsche is arguing that the success of Christianity can be attributed to the way in which it catered the images it produced to the instincts of the people it was trying to dominate. Nietzsche is even more explicit on this point in his notes, writing that

> a spell had been cast on the strongest, most natural, and even more, the only real instincts [Triebe]—one must henceforth deny the presence of these drives in any action in order to find that action praiseworthy. ... Of course, the psychology of the saint, the priest, the "good man" had to be purely phantasmagoric. The real

> motives of action had been declared bad: in order to perform any action at all one must describe and sanctify that action. (*KSA*, 12:10[57])

This note is a meditation on the relation between instincts, images ("phantasmagoric"), and action. The import of this aphorism is that the image of any action acts as a kind of membrane that regulates which instincts express themselves in said action. The instincts must first be "sanctified" in the image of the action in order to be released; the image of a good or moral action has the instincts under its spell. His use of the term "phantasmagoria" [*phantasmagorie*] here is especially significant for its association elsewhere in his works with the project of Bayreuth, Wagner's attempt to unleash the Nordic instincts in the modern German masses through hours of pure imagery and sound.

The image of the cross

Nietzsche identifies one image in particular to focus his analysis on. The cross is the central image he uses to explain the *effectiveness* of Christianity at winning over the inhabitants of the Roman Empire.

> Every time Christianity expanded to greater and cruder masses of people whose presuppositions were increasingly remote from the presupposition under which it arose, it became increasingly necessary *to vulgarize Christianity and make it barbaric*,—Christianity soaked up doctrines and rites from all the *subterranean* cults of the *imperium Romanum* and bits of nonsense from all kinds of sick reason. (*A*, 37)

The point Nietzsche is making in this paragraph is that Christianity needed to make itself *barbaric* in order to take over the inhabitants of the Roman Empire. "Barbarian" is a term the Romans and Greeks famously used to indicate anything that was *not* them; Christianity needed to portray itself as foreign to the culture of Rome, as *against* the Roman culture. And the Romans originally *did* think of Christianity as barbaric: suspicious and fearful, they spread rumors that Christian rituals involved cannibalism and incest.[7] Nietzsche is implying here that Christianity was *purposefully* presenting itself as the "anti-Roman" religion, thereby representing and taking into itself what was "subterranean" [unterirdischen] or repressed in the Roman Empire and "sanctioning" it. His assertion is that before Christianity there weren't symbols, images, or practices that sheltered the "servile" instinct of pity, for example. So that when Christianity eagerly identified itself in opposition to the Roman Empire, becoming "barbaric," or "slavish," it gathered to itself the instincts of all the unrepresented masses—by the use of one image in particular.

> [Christianity] took the cross, which was generally reserved for the rabble,—it took this horrible paradox to bring disciples face to face with the true riddle: "*Who was*

> *that? What was that?*"—The feeling of shock and profound offence, the suspicion that a death like this might *refute* their case. ... At this point, people started to feel as if they were in revolt *against* the order, they started to understand Jesus as having been *in revolt against the order*. (*A*, 36)

"The order" that Nietzsche refers to is imposed by the Roman Empire. It is cultural order, whose upper classes place value in ethical concepts such as *dignitas* and *libertas*. Nietzsche believes that it was the cross—a symbol of a kind of death absolutely irreconcilable to a citizen of Rome,[8] a symbol that was meant to be a *warning* to the disgruntled rabble of the Empire—that established Christianity as a haven for those marginalized by the Empire. The cross was an image that rallied all the instincts which had been repressed underneath Roman cultural domination.[9]

We can now follow Nietzsche's attempt to see deeper into the mechanisms of this relation between images and instincts with this specific example he provides. If images sanction instincts, then specifically what instincts did the image of the cross sanction, and how?

"People have gone even further, making [pity] into *the* virtue, the foundation and source of all virtues,—but of course you have to keep in mind that this was the perspective of a nihilistic philosophy that inscribed the *negation of life* on its shield" (*A*, 7). Given that Nietzsche is discussing the ascendancy of Christianity over paganism in the Roman Empire, it is impossible to ignore the reference to Constantine here, who famously had his soldiers draw a "☧" on their shields at the battle of the Milvian bridge. The "Chi-Rho," as this symbol was known, was an early depiction of the cross made from the Greek "CHR."[10] Nietzsche references this early incarnation of the cross again later on in the text: "Decadence was victorious *in hoc signo* [in this sign (you will conquer)].—*God on the cross*—have people still not grasped the gruesome ulterior motive behind this symbol?" (*A*, 51; brackets added). The point of these quotations is that the Christians chose as their symbol an image that was offensive and paradoxical in the context of Roman cultural milieu.[11] The cross represents an injunction to *imitate* God's martyrdom, "[Paul] seeks to bring the persistence (the blessed, atoned persistence of the individual soul) as a resurrection in causal connection with that sacrifice (after the type of Dionysus, Mithras, Osiris)" (*KSA*, 13:11[282]). Nietzsche means here that by imitating Jesus's martyrdom, Christians are endowed with immortal souls, and thereby connected causally and ontologically with the immortal God. The significance given to this representation of God's bodily suffering in an image of his martyrdom is precisely why Nietzsche associates Christianity so strongly with the instinct of "pity" (*mitleid*: literally "suffering with"). It was the image of the cross which allowed the instinct of *mitleid* to express itself in action.

By representing the possibility of "suffering with" an immortal God, the image of the cross represents the idea "that as immortal souls, everyone is on the same level as everyone else, that in the commonality of all beings, the 'salvation' of *each* individual lays claim to eternal significance, that the small-minded and the half-mad can imagine themselves [sich einbilden] well" (*A*, 43). This comment—that it is important for the small-minded to imagine themselves well—appears almost improvised, and seems at first to be philosophically unimportant. I have to assert that it is a mistake to read a comment such as this as textual garnish, extraneous to Nietzsche's philosophical stance in *Antichrist*. In precise wording, Nietzsche is asserting here that the fundamental action required for Christianity to take power over the dregs of the Roman Empire was to establish an *image*. The image of equality in the transcendental, in contradistinction to the inequality of the material world, "'God on the cross' is a curse on life, a hint to deliver oneself from it" (*KSA*, 13:14[89]). The instinct of pity, of "suffering-with," which was so foreign to the eyes of the Romans, is given sanctuary in the image of the cross, and any sequence of actions which results in martyrdom.

To preview what I develop below, Nietzsche insists that this was all done *intentionally*, claiming "The cross as the mark of the most subterranean conspiracy that ever existed" (*A*, 62). He sees this "conspiracy" as originating in the machinations of one man in particular, behind the image of the cross was "Paul's invention, his method of priestly tyranny, of forming the herds, the belief in immortality" (*A*, 42).

The propagandist and the hero

Having recovered the theorem of images and instincts that Nietzsche is putting forward in *Antichrist*, and applied it to the most significant image in Christianity, I can now begin to explore Nietzsche's inspiration for this theory, which at this point might still seem unsubstantiated and somewhat arbitrary. The first step toward that goal will be to discuss Nietzsche's analysis of Jesus's relationship with Paul, which he conceived of as similar to the relationship between Socrates and Plato, or even Achilles and Homer. I will call the figures in these relationships the "hero" and the "propagandist." Achilles, Socrates, and Jesus are the heroes: they have left us no writings and so cannot speak for themselves. Thus they required a propagandist such as Homer, Plato, or the apostle to propagate and popularize their message.

This is not my own schematic, but rather is a relationship that we find expressed at least obliquely in *Antichrist* (with the qualification that while Homer is a very important figure for Nietzsche, he does not play a significant role in this work). Consider the manner in which Nietzsche describes Jesus, "Before [Jesus' crucifixion], his image [Bilde] had not had any belligerent, no-saying, no-doing features at all; in fact he was the opposite of all this. The small congregation had evidently *failed* to understand the main point, the exemplary [Vorbildliche] character of dying in this way, the freedom, the superiority *over* every feeling of *resentment*" (*A*, 40). Isn't this manner of dying reminiscent of the death of Socrates as it is described by Plato? "He does not offer any resistance, he does not defend his rights, he does not make a single move to avert the worst, what is more, *he invites it*" (*A*, 35). These qualities Nietzsche uses to describe Jesus's approach to his own execution are mirrored in Plato's description of the death of Socrates. Although Socrates does in a certain sense defend his rights in *Apologia*, he refuses to take an opportunity to escape his execution in *Crito*. The most significant portion of the description: his "invitation" to die, his refusal to offer any resistance, is present in abundance in *Phaedo*. Nietzsche links these two heroes, Jesus and Socrates, in other instances in his work as well.[12]

I will return to the figure of the hero in our conclusion and for now focus on the methods and psychology of the propagandist, which is the main subject of my chapter. In *Antichrist* Nietzsche is competing with Homer, Plato, and Paul, not Achilles, Socrates, or Jesus. He is competing with these guardians of the heroes' *Kleos* [κλέος], the propagandists who dramatically illustrate the message of their hero for the masses to consume and absorb. One of Nietzsche's criticisms of these figures is that these illustrations they make of their heroes are not devoid of *intention*. Nietzsche sees the propagandist as a kind of artist who paints the hero according to his agenda, "Think with what freedom Paul deals with the personal problem of Jesus" (*KSA*, 13:15[108]). Peter Sloterdijk expresses this same cynical interpretation of these figures: "Language's self-laudatory energies could no longer be aimed directly at orators who were specialized in function of public speech, such as the elder, the priest, the rhapsodist. Rather, they had to take a detour and praise the lords, heroes, gods, powers, and forces of virtue, from which a refracting ray came to fall on the orator."[13]

Nietzsche will continually assert in *Antichrist* that Plato and Paul cynically formed the images of their respective hero in order to further their own projects, "With Paul, the priests wanted to return to power,—he could only use ideas, doctrines, symbols that would tyrannize the masses and form [bildet] the herds" (*A*, 42). It is this constant implication throughout *Antichrist* that Paul has cynically connived to pull off this mass persuasion that I think demands an explanation. Nietzsche claims that the early Christian writings "are the *opposite* of a naive corruption" (*A*, 44), meaning they are an *intentional* corruption. He writes that "the type of the redeemer has been preserved for us only in a distorted form ... retroactively enhanced with features that can only be understood as emerging from war and intended as propaganda" (*A*, 31). Why do we find this conspiratorial tone in *Antichrist*? On what grounds does Nietzsche think he can determine what Paul's *intentions* were?

Eikon and eros

In pursuit of a philosophical explanation for the style of *Antichrist*, "Nietzsche's graffito," we have formulated two major questions: "Is there some deeper philosophical rationale for Nietzsche's belief that images 'sanction' instincts?" and "Why does Nietzsche believe that he has some insight into the intentions of St. Paul?" I believe I can answer both of these questions through an interpretation of what I consider to be the most important aphorism of *Antichrist*. Too long and complex to be quoted in its entirety, aphorism fifty-seven reads in part,

> Nature ... separates out predominantly spiritual people from people characterized by muscular and temperamental strength from a third group of people who are not distinguished in any way, the mediocre. ... The highest caste—which I call *the few*—, being the perfect caste, also has the privilege of the few: this include representing happiness, beauty, and goodness on earth. ... The ones who are second: these are the custodians of the law, the guardians of order and security, these are the noble

> warriors. ... Let us not underestimate the privileges of the mediocre ... [which include] Crafts, trade, farming, *science*, most of art—in a word, *employment*. (*A*, 57)

Ostensibly this passage is commenting on the *Manusmriti*, one of the earliest Hindu texts, which Nietzsche had first read in May 1888. However, Andreas urs Sommer—in the second mammoth volume of his interpretation of Nietzsche's 1888 works—has observed a much closer resemblance in this description to Plato's tripartite division of the soul and society in *Republic* than anything in the *Manusmriti*. The same observation has been made by Julian Young,[14] Roger Berkowitz,[15] and Thomas Brobjer.[16] Sommer writes that Nietzsche is "Platonizing" Manu,[17] first of all noting the similarity between Nietzsche's characterization of the types of humans as "spiritual," "muscular," and "mediocre" and the three classes of citizens sectioned out in Plato's *Republic*. Secondly, Sommer observes that Manu actually describes *four* castes, not three, meaning that Nietzsche is distorting Manu.[18] Sommer cites Nietzsche: "[The ruling caste] do not rule because they want to but because they *exist*, they are not free to be second" (*A*, 57) and comments, "That's exactly the fate of Plato's philosopher-king."[19] Sommer expresses concern that there is never justification for why the tripartite division is "natural" and further questions why Nietzsche is referencing Plato at all. He speculates that it might have been due to some influence by Friedrich von Hellwald or Viktor Hehn. He also notes that the addition of "science" to the duty of the Chandalas is particularly odd, as there is nothing in the *Manusmriti* to indicate that the Chandalas were responsible for scientific labors.[20]

I agree completely with Sommer, Brobjer, and Young that this aphorism is a reference to Plato's tripartite division in *Republic*. I further believe my interpretation may provide an answer to this anomaly. Plato's *Republic* touches on the same question which is at the heart of *Antichrist*: how does one sway "the masses," the lowest of the three divisions? A central interest of *Republic* is the question of how to organize *eros*[ἔρως] as perfectly as possible (see *Republic*, 6, 500 D for example).[21] I believe that Plato's problem of *eros* is picked up by Nietzsche in *Antichrist*, with his term "instincts": "To achieve a perfect automatism of the instinct,—this is the presupposition of every type of mastery" (*A*, 57). To draw this connection to its conclusion: Plato approaches the problem of the organization of *eros* in *Republic* by recommending that *eros* be controlled through *eikon* [εἰκών], images. The core of my argument is that *Republic* uses the same cynically aristocratic method to approach the problem of "the masses" that *Antichrist* does. Plato concludes that the *instincts* of inferior, mediocre people in a city are moved and collectivized most through *images*, which affect the inferior part of the human soul.[22]

> Is it, then, only poets we have to supervise, compelling them to make an image of a good character in their poems or else not to compose them among us? ... Are we to allow someone who cannot follow these instructions to work amongst us, so that our guardians will be brought up on images of evil, as if in a meadow of bad grass, where they crop and graze in many different places every day until, little by little, they unwittingly accumulate a large evil in their souls? (*Republic*, 3, 401 B-C)

Plato's genius here is to provide an *image* of cows for those readers of his who do not have the philosophical education to understand him otherwise. He will employ the same method with the divided line and the allegory of the cave, providing a numerical explanation of a concept for his philosophically inclined readers, and then go through the same story in images in order to persuade his readers who are not as philosophically inclined, who are still dwelling in the cave. As we will see, *Antichrist* engages in the same imaginary rhetoric.

With this reference to Plato's methodology of utilizing *eikon* to organize *eros* we can answer our two questions mentioned above ("Is there some deeper philosophical rationale for Nietzsche's belief that images 'sanction' instincts?" and "Why does Nietzsche believe that he knows the intentions of St. Paul?"). Nietzsche found this theory of images and instincts in Plato, and is applying it to the Christianization of the Roman Empire *because he believes that the early Christians found these techniques in Plato as well.* Nietzsche's conspiratorial claim in *Antichrist* is that the early Christians, especially Paul, utilized the methods they found in Plato.[23] This is how Nietzsche ties together Plato and Paul: one Propagandist inherits the techniques of the other.[24]

Postulating some kind of general Platonic influence in the writings of Paul wouldn't in itself be an unwarranted speculation. Paul was trained as a rhetorician, and wrote in Greek. His birthplace of Tarsus was cosmopolitan, and known as a center of Greek learning. Athenodorus, Zeno, Antipater, and Nestor all lived and studied there; Strabo even goes so far as to claim that it surpassed Athens and Alexandria as a center of philosophical study (*Geography*, 14.5.13). Nietzsche was clearly aware of all this, noting that Paul's "homeland was the center of Stoic Enlightenment" (*A*, 42). This information would make it seem more than likely that Paul would have become acquainted with the works of Plato at some point during his life. More specifically, we also find Paul using Platonic language in his letters. The most relevant example would be his use of the term *eikon* to refer to Christ's relationship with the Father, "The god of this age has blinded the minds of unbelievers, so that they cannot see the light of the gospel that displays the glory of Christ, who is the image [εἰκὼν] of God" (2 Cor. 4:2-4). And "The Son is the image [εἰκόνα] of the invisible God" (Col. 1:15). This use of the term *eikon* to refer to Christ as a kind of manifestation of the father (and therefore potentially being ontologically "lower" in some way than the transcendental God he is representing) could possibly be inspired by Plato's style of dialogue in *Republic*, where he uses dramatic images like the cave (thus influencing the lowest parts of the soul) to lead his readers toward the transcendental forms.[25]

Nietzsche only ever implicitly points out similarities between Paul and Plato in *Antichrist*, which require some speculation to discern. However, taken together and in context especially with aphorism fifty-seven, it is clear that Nietzsche was linking these two figures. For example, what is the great question that Adeimantus presents Socrates with in Book II of *Republic*? This is a serious query which Plato revisits over and over in his dialogues: "How is it that being just benefits someone more than being unjust, disregarding the appearance of justice?" (*Republic*, 2, 367 A-D). Socrates's answers in this section are problematic, but in the last book of *Republic*, where Plato writes his myth and speaks of the need to control the mediocre population of the city, he has Socrates give a different answer to this question. The answer given is that justice benefits the just man because the soul is immortal (*Republic*, 10, 608 C-D), and that because the soul is immortal the just man would eventually be rewarded (*Republic*, 10, 613 A). This promise of immortality, of conjoining with the transcendental god, was also the meaning behind the image of the cross. Nietzsche believes that *Paul himself* was the propagator of the doctrine of immortality, and that *he got the idea from Plato*. After clarifying his belief that Jesus had never preached a personal immortality, Nietzsche writes: "The *outrageous* doctrine of personal immortality ... Paul himself still taught it as a *reward!*" (*A*, 41). Nietzsche isolates the responsibility for the adoption of a doctrine of personal immortality by Christianity to Paul.

There are other implied connections that Nietzsche makes between Paul and Plato throughout *Antichrist*. For example, he will make references to Plato's "noble lie," found in *Republic* 3, 389b. Nietzsche goes on to state that "Paul understood that lying—that 'belief' was necessary" (*A*, 47). These potential references to the connection between Paul and Plato may be subtle, but should be carefully considered, especially given statements Nietzsche makes in other works such as "Christianity is Platonism for 'the people'" (*BGE*, *P* [noting especially the bracketing of the term "the people"]).

Negation—rebranding

The evidence just presented concerning the connection between Paul and Plato will be supplemented as we move forward with our explanation of the style of *Antichrist*. In order to do so, we need to discuss further the effect of the method used by our two propagandists. What exactly does Nietzsche means when he says that Plato was "Anti-Greek" (*TI*, *The Problem of Socrates*, 2)? Michael Sugrue discusses this issue of Plato's untimeliness—the method by which he waged war against his own Greek culture—in his lectures on the Platonic dialogues,

> Plato will supplant the old forms of tragedy and epic with a new art form. ... It vindicates the new hero, the Socratic hero of knowledge, as opposed to the Homeric hero of violence. ... Socrates will be the new epic hero, he is the new Achilles for this new kind of art.[26]

The juxtaposition Sugrue makes between the heroes Socrates and Achilles is also a juxtaposition between their propagandists: Plato and Homer. Using the language of the themes we have been discussing above, we could say that the image Plato was painting of Socrates as a hero was an attempt to represent the unrepresented instincts of the mediocre, exhausted, and ugly masses in war-torn Athens. The key here is that Plato's project is not entirely positive, Socrates is not *just* modeled as a new hero. Plato also has Socrates disparage the violent heroes of the Homeric myths, famously banning myths from his city which contain "bad images [εἰκάζῃ τις κακῶς]" (*Republic* 2, 377e).

Nietzsche's disagreements with Plato were many, but he must have admired the "Overabundant and dangerous health" (*GS*, 372) Plato required for his cultural war on the Homeric values. He will often talk about Plato in terms that might seem approving, if one was not aware of his caustic criticisms elsewhere: "[Platonism] was the greatest of rebaptisms; and because it has been adopted by Christianity we do not recognize how astonishing it is" (*KSA*, 12:7[2]).[27] Nietzsche is asserting here (much more explicitly) that Christianity was attempting to follow the model of Plato.[28] Just as Plato demonized and banished the Homeric images and instincts, Christianity bans

> all the basic instincts of [the higher] type, [Christianity] has distilled "evil" and "the Evil One" out of these instincts—the strong human being as reprehensible, as "depraved." Christianity has taken the side of everything weak, base, failed, it has made an ideal out of whatever *contradicts* the preservation instincts of a strong life; ... by teaching people to see the highest spiritual values as sinful, as deceptive, as *temptations* [Versuchungen]. (*A*, 5)

Christianity has adopted a Platonic policy of intolerance toward the images and instincts of the Roman Empire. It exiles these instincts to the image of the devil: "The word 'devil' was a real boon to [the Christians]: they had an overpowering and terrible enemy" (*A*, 23). The Roman emphasis on *dignitas* was described as "vanity" (Mt. 5:39), *felicitas* dismissed as "lust," or "greed" (Col. 3:5), and *libertas* replaced with an injunction to submit to authority (Rom. 13:1-7). Nietzsche laments the destruction of the Roman idols, this reversal of values: "Morality as the thorough deterioration of the imagination ... *what* is Christian morality? Chance robbed of its innocence; happiness polluted by the concept of 'sin'; well-being as danger, as 'temptation' [Versuchung]" (*A*, 25).

The Roman instincts which had been sanctioned under national mythology are now seen as having originated in the devil, as being temptations by the devil. The Christian community "fights health as a type of enemy, devil, temptation [versuchung]!" (*A*, 51). Nietzsche is describing a kind of cultural fight to the death. "Every society has the tendency to reduce its opponents to caricatures—*at least in imagination*—and, as it were, to starve them. Such a caricature is, for example, our "criminal." Within the aristocratic Roman order of values, the Jew was reduced to a caricature" (*KSA*, 12:10[12]; emphasis added). The Christians thought of the Romans as "sinful," and the Romans referred to everything that was not them as "servile" or "barbaric." In *Antichrist* Nietzsche is describing the methods by which the Christians *won* this fight; as Edward Gibbon writes, "The reproach of *Barbarian* was embittered by the more odious epithet of *Heretic*."[29]

This Christian victory was followed by a purge, a policy of absolute intolerance for the sinful instincts. Nietzsche conceives of this purge as a narrowing of culture, a cutting off of the fat, an iconoclastic movement, in which the images of old heroes are broken. The meaning of one of Nietzsche favorite Bible verses "*One thing* is necessary" (*A*, 43; *GS*, 290; *GM*, *What Is the Meaning of Ascetic Ideals*, 16; *D*, 132),[30] is essentially that the Romans could no longer worship at the altars of the Egyptian goddess Isis on Monday and sacrifice to their Jove on Tuesday; Christianity required a stricter obedience. Nietzsche thus asserts that one of the effects of the Christian cultural victory was the transformation of the Roman Empire from a polyculture into a monoculture. To understand this transformation let us return to aphorism fifty-seven.

> A book of law never describes the uses, the reasons, and the casuistry in the prehistory of the law: this would make it lose its imperative tone, the 'thou shalt,' the presupposition for being obeyed. This is precisely where the problem is. At a certain point in the development of a people, its most circumspect (which is to say far-sighted and hind-sighted) class declares that the experience according to which life should be conducted—that is, *can* be conducted—, is over. Its goal is to harvest the richest and most perfect crop possible from the ages of experiment and *bad* experience. Accordingly, what now needs to be prevented at all cost is any further experimentation, the continuation of values in a fluid state, scrutiny, selection and criticism of values *in infinitum*. (*A*, 57)

The meaning of this section of aphorism fifty-seven is that Nietzsche believes this "harvest" did not just occur once with the ancient Aryan race of the *Manusmriti*, or Homer and the *Iliad*, or the Bible, but as the term "harvest" implies, it must have recurred perennially. Nietzsche is associating the early Christians, and especially Paul, with this "circumspect" class of aristocrats who declare an end to liberality, experimentation, and work to streamline culture. The Pauline project was an attempt to *stop* experimentation, to keep society static—the same project we find in Plato's *Republic*.

This is an occasion where I respectfully disagree with Sommer and some of the other scholarship. In his reading of this aphorism, the Christian religion does not create the same hierarchical aristocratic distinctions as the system they are overturning. Rather, Sommer contends that Nietzsche is using the example of Manu as a "hypothetical contrast [*Gegenmodell*] to the Christian reality."[31] Manu conforms to the "natural tripartite order" discussed later in the aphorism, whereas Christianity professes a radical equality. The *Manusmriti* propounds aristocratic values, whereas the Bible expresses chandala sentiments.[32] As opposed to this reading, I interpret Nietzsche as positing a conspiratorial continuity between Manu, Plato, and Christianity. From Nietzsche's notes: "The scheme of an unchanging community, with the priests at the top: the oldest great cultural product of Asia is this field of organization, must, of course, have prompted reflection and imitation in every respect. Plato: but above all the Egyptians" (*KSA*, 13:14[204]). Further commenting in the same notebook "Plato is entirely in the spirit of Manu: he was inaugurated in Egypt. The Morality of the caste, the God of the good, the 'eternal individual soul'" (*KSA*, 13:14[191]). These notes I believe establish a strong connection between Plato and Manu. I think there is also fairly good evidence that Nietzsche believed Christianity followed in this line of succession. He writes in his notes, "The 'holy lie'—this is common to Confucius, the law book of Manu, Mohammed, and the Christian church: and it is not absent from Plato either" (*A*, 55); "Here too the Jews seem merely 'mediators'—they invent nothing" (*KGB*, May 1888, III.5:1041); and of course the line that "Christianity is Platonism for 'the people'" (*BGE*, *P*). Therefore, I interpret Nietzsche to be lumping together these three traditions.

Nietzsche as propagandist

Now that I have given my interpretation of Nietzsche's story of the Christianization of the Roman Empire and its Platonic inspiration, I can begin to answer the question of Nietzsche's method that I began with, and reflect these theories I have been describing onto the style of the text. There is certainly precedent for this kind of reflective reading, Nietzsche's very first published book begins with an invitation to read him in this way.[33] This postulation of authorial intention might be especially warranted in the case of Nietzsche. Nietzsche's books had *goals*, he writes that *Antichrist* intends to break time in half (*A*, 62), he intends for this book to achieve something outside of itself. Nietzsche deployed rhetorical strategies in line with what he wanted the text to achieve, and if we consider these rhetorical strategies we can begin to account for some of the aspects of this work that were once dismissed as products of madness.

What are some of the specific issues with the book which might stop a philosopher from taking *Antichrist* seriously? Aside from a general haste and superficiality which seems to pervade the book, two major philosophical shortcomings attract my attention in this text. The first is that Nietzsche's advocation of science appears two dimensional, "Christianity, which is completely out of touch with reality ... would be mortally opposed to the 'wisdom of the world,' which is to say *science*" (*A*, 47). We see here a strong connection made between the terms "reality" and "science," as if the story were as simple as "Christianity is lies, science is truth." In his other works, Nietzsche at least places a germ of doubt in his estimations of the capabilities of science to attain the truth (e.g.: *BGE*, 24; *GS*, 344; *GM, What Is the Meaning of Ascetic Ideals*, 24) as well as making well-known criticisms of truth as such (such as: "The conditions of life might include error" in *GS*, 121). These previous reservations concerning the duty of science seem to have disappeared:

> All the presuppositions for a scholarly culture were [present in antiquity], all the scientific *methods* were already there, the great, incomparable art of reading well had already been established—this presupposition for the tradition of culture, for the unity of science; natural science was on the very best path, together with the mathematics and mechanics,—the *factual sense*. (*A*, 59)

This aphorism can be interpreted as saying that the reason "reading well" was a presupposition for science is because the world is a text, and it was the "factual sense" that is being championed as the ultimate interpretation of it. This vocal insistence on science's use of "facts" to achieve an ultimate interpretation about "reality" is startling to read in a work of Nietzsche's, who had repeatedly attacked the concept causality, and had written that there *were* no facts "only interpretations" (*KSA*, 12:7[60]).

The second most prominent philosophical deficiency of *Antichrist* is the idea of the "natural." Despite his critiques of this concept elsewhere in his work (such as *BGE*, 188) he uses this term just as bluntly as "science." This echoes Sommer's criticism of Nietzsche's assertion that Plato's tripartite division is "natural," with no further justification. Nietzsche will only provide a slight clarification by also asserting that the "natural" is "the real."[34]

This would mean that he is using the concept of "the natural" in the very way he had criticized in *Beyond Good and Evil*, 188. Even more puzzling he uses "the natural" to describe some of the very things he has elsewhere criticized: "The parasitism of the priest (or the 'moral world order') takes every natural custom, every natural institution (state, judicial order, marriage, care for the sick and the poor), everything required by the instinct of life, in short everything *intrinsically* valuable, and renders it fundamentally worthless" (*A*, 26). Is this really Nietzsche? Every assertion here would have most Nietzscheans cringing: to name the "state," "marriage," "care for the poor," of all things as examples of these "natural institutions" (not to mention this phrase "intrinsically valuable")?

I have addressed these deficiencies to remind us why this text was found problematic at first. I believe that these two problems can be explained with reference to the question of method that this chapter has been working toward addressing. "The 'holy lie'—this is common to Confucius, the law book of Manu, Mohammed, and the Christian church: and it is not absent from Plato either" (*A*, 55). My essential claim about the style of *Antichrist* is that it is Nietzsche's attempt to construct a holy lie (or a noble lie); Nietzsche as the author is playing the role of the propagandist: he is modeling his intentions after Plato and Paul. "'The truth is there': wherever you hear this, it means that the *priest is lying*" (*A*, 55). Where does Nietzsche say the "truth" is in this text? As I have just explained, he is bewilderingly obstinate in his assertions that the truth resides in "science," and the "natural." This would mean that Nietzsche considers himself a priest in this text, his advocacy for these concepts is a part of his "holy lie."

If we return again to aphorism fifty-seven we can now place these two major philosophical deficiencies in Nietzsche's "holy lie." First let us focus on the concept of the natural, which Sommer also identified as problematic in this passage. Nietzsche says that in order for the more circumspect classes to control the masses one of the necessary steps is to impose "*tradition*, which is to say the claim that the law existed from time immemorial, that it is irreverent to cast doubt on it, a crime against the ancestors. The authority of the law is grounded in the theses: ... the ancestors *lived* by it" (*A*, 57). This is the same advice that Plato gives in *Republic*.[35] Recalling that Plato's noble lie was used to keep the *non-philosophers* in line, the reason that Nietzsche presses this concept of "naturalness" so forcefully is to convince *his expected readers* that what he is advocating represents the way things were "naturally," from time immemorial. The second deficiency, science, can also be explained under this interpretation. If we continue further into aphorism fifty-seven Nietzsche lists the tasks that the mediocre masses are responsible for "crafts, trade, farming, *science*" (*A*, 57). This is another section Sommer points out as puzzling, in that science was not actually a duty of the Chandala caste according to Manu, and yet here it is the one duty Nietzsche italicized for emphasis. Nietzsche champions the pursuit of science throughout *Antichrist* in order to appease the profession of the mediocre, to organize their instincts into more manageable image containers.

Nietzsche gives hints concerning his intentions with these two concepts in a note he writes in the spring before he composed *Antichrist*:

> What is now to be prevented, especially, is new experimentation. A double wall is set against the desire to continue testing and selecting: 1) Revelation 2) Tradition.

> Both are Holy lies: the intelligent state that they invent, understood as well as Plato understood. The revelation: the assertion that the reasoning of those laws is not of human origin, not slowly and blundering sought and found, but that it was imparted by divinity ... Tradition: that is the assertion that since ancient times it would have been so. (*A*, 57; *KSA*, 13:14[213])

I claim that he is setting up science to appear not as an invention of human knowledge, but as a superhuman wisdom, that touches upon a true reality; likewise that his emphasis on "tradition" in this note will later crystallize into an insistence on the "natural" lifestyle. All cynically conceived, all designed to play to the instincts of the target audience of *Antichrist*: the mediocre, the non-philosophers, the barbarians, slaves, and cave dwellers.

Thus if we read Nietzsche as engaging in a "holy lie," and we refuse to take his endorsements of science and the natural seriously, we can explain some of the philosophical deficiencies found in *Antichrist*. We do this by asserting that Nietzsche's audience for *Antichrist* was not philosophers, but the modern herd. The stylistic problems that many readers have with *Antichrist*, the bombastic tone, full of resentment, lacking in philosophical acumen, is Nietzsche intentionally imitating the tone of the circumspect class from aphorism fifty-seven who "never describe their reasons." This is important because it puts Nietzsche in the tradition of Paul and Plato. This is why, in his self-eulogizing biography, Nietzsche states: "I am the opposite of a heroic nature" (*EH*, *Why I Am So Clever*, 9). He is not the hero, but the propagandist.

Some Nietzsche scholars may instinctively reject the notion that Nietzsche would ever imitate anything Platonic, based off of Nietzsche denunciations of Platonism, which are numerous and severe.[36] Nonetheless, I claim that Nietzsche imitates at least portions of Plato's philosophical style. Thinking of the dramatic content of Plato's dialogues, Nietzsche at least must agree with Plato on the necessity of popular writings to stir the imagination. If it isn't abundantly clear that his style accomplishes this, he says it outright, "I have letters that can make even blind people see" (*A* 62). The fact that this is overdone in this work, that there is less philosophy and more rambling flourishes of language, is precisely the complaint early Nietzsche scholars made about *Antichrist*. Consider passages such as this: "The cranny God, the God of all dark nooks and corners, of unhealthy districts the world over! ... His empire is as it ever was, an empire of the underworld, a hospital, a basement-kingdom, a ghetto-kingdom ... and he himself, so pale, so weak, so decadent" (*A* 17). My interpretation is that this phantasmagoric method of writing is essential to the project of *Antichrist*. *Antichrist* was not written for a philosophical audience, but for the modern masses.

GötzenDämmerung

Now that we have begun to situate Nietzsche's role as author of *Antichrist*, we can begin to understand how he conceived of this book's project. I chose the term "propagandist" over the more classical term "mythologist" because I wanted to convey a sense of cynicism about the modern era that pervades *Antichrist*. Nietzsche characterizes the attitude of modernity in the very first aphorism of *Antichrist*: "'I don't know where I am; I am everything that doesn't know where it is,'—sighs modern man. ... *This* modernity makes us ill,—this indolent peace, this cowardly compromise, the whole virtuous filth of the modern Yes and No. This tolerance and *largeur* of the heart that 'forgives' everything because it 'understands' everything is *sirocco*[37] for us" (*A*, 1). This description of the mood of modernity is prescient, it describes a society which yearns for a direction, which looks backward and imagines that it sees a more vital force animating its ancestors. It describes a society in the midst of experimentation, a society that is tolerant, democratic, and chaotic. "The modern ideas as wrong: 'Freedom' 'equal rights' ... 'Democracy' 'Tolerance'" (*KSA*, 13:16 [82]). Nietzsche's cynicism toward the moods of modernity in his final productive years transformed into anger and frustration: "The *modern spirit lacks discipline*" (*KSA*, 12:9[165]). *Antichrist* is Nietzsche's attempt to instill discipline, *his* governance over the modern masses.[38]

Nietzsche saw himself as living at the end of one of the perennially recurring ages of experimentation which he described in aphorism fifty-seven. He asserted in this aphorism that it is precisely during these eras of weakness and decline that an opportunity is offered to a prescient member of a "circumspect class," "Whenever the will to power goes under [neidergeht] ... [the subjugated] take revenge by demonizing their master's god" (*A*, 17). Modern life seemed to Nietzsche to have lost its vitality: its will had gone under. This means that it was a period of opportunity for Nietzsche to *demonize* and destroy Christianity. We recall that he analyzed how Christianity destroyed Roman culture by making a negative image of the "natural Roman instincts"? We recall how this image was characterized as *vice* and *sin*? This is precisely what Nietzsche is attempting to do to Christianity, to take the instincts that find sanction in the image of the cross, and expel them to images of vulgarity, egoism, and vice. "All in all, we have become the officers of their [mentally unhealthy races] instincts, for us it is dishonorable, cowardly, unclean in all the highest degree, to be a Christian. ... The law against Christianity has as a headline: war to the death: the vice is Christianity" (*KGB*, December 1888, III.5:1170). He repeats this maxim in the last aphorism of *Antichrist*: "*War to the death against vice: the vice is Christianity*" (*A*, 62). The images Nietzsche creates in this work are not arbitrary, they are not just designed to gain him popularity among the uneducated. Rather he is intentionally crafting negative images of Christianity in order to *attack* the instincts among the uneducated which it sanctions. *Antichrist* is a work of negativity and no-saying, its very title is a negation. It demonizes Christianity, relegating the instincts which with images of Christianity sanctioned to images of *vice*. In my reading the goal of the text is almost entirely destructive and iconoclastic, the spirit of the book is *GötzenDämmerung*.[39]

Modern propaganda

To conclude this chapter I would like to address a lingering question, to which I do not have a conclusive answer. If Nietzsche is embodying the figure of the propagandist, then who is his hero? One candidate would be Zarathustra: Reto Winteler has argued that *Thus Spoke Zarathustra* constitutes Nietzsche's positive supplement to the "negative" text *Antichrist* (see concluding paragraph in glossary definition *Revaluation of All Values*). Especially given that both books engage deeply with the biblical tradition, Winteler's argument seems very plausible to me. Another candidate might be Nietzsche himself, given that he will soon create a literary caricature of himself in *Ecce Homo*, explicitly putting himself in the tradition of Christ's heroism. However both these candidates come from outside of the text of *Antichrist*. If we take as a presupposition that the book is complete in itself there is really only one option: Jesus of Nazareth.

Antichrist could even be called "pious" in this sense—supposing that the latin *pius* is related to *purus* (clean)—there are portions of *Antichrist* which try to rescue the *Kleos* of Christ, which try to purify the image of the redeemer. Nietzsche takes exception to the interpretation of Christ found in Paul and the Gospels, and he claims to be describing a more faithful form of Christianity when he writes

> The concepts of guilt and punishment are completely missing from the psychology of the "evangel"; so is the concept of reward. "Sin," any distance between god and man: these are abolished,—*this is what the "glad tidings" are all about*. Blessedness is not a promise, it has no strings attached; it is the *only* reality—everything else is just a symbol used to speak about it. (*A*, 33)

These are some of the only positive characteristics that emerge attached to any figure in *Antichrist*.[40] Nietzsche represents Jesus as an experimenter who in some ways exemplified the kind of life Nietzsche champions: the life which is a risk, and a creation. Nietzsche says Jesus is "New and completely original" (*A*, 42), and a "Free Spirit" (*A*, 32). Most strangely, he calls him an "idiot" (*A*, 29). It has been noted many times that this is probably a reference to Dostoevsky, however I have not seen it mentioned that this is also a possible reference to Siegfried, Wagner's experimental, idiotic, immoral hero of *The Ring Cycle* (or even Parsifal, Wagner's archetypal "pure fool").

Nietzsche was certainly still thinking frequently of Wagner in 1888. In the summer before and the winter after he composed *Antichrist*, Nietzsche wrote two books reflecting on Wagner's celebrity, one of which is a brief reflection on Wagner's place in history and culture, the other an edited collection aphorisms that he had previously published. In the former, *The Case of Wagner*, Nietzsche meditates on Wagner's "hypnotic" powers using language very reminiscent of the themes of *Antichrist*, "Wagner begins with a hallucination: not of tones but of gestures. ... Wagner invented his musical devices to persuade the masses" (*CW*, 8). This term "gestures" is used in *Antichrist* to reference what I have been describing as the image. Nietzsche continues, explaining the noise of Bayreuth: "The *People*—they all need the sublime, the profound, the overwhelming. They all use the same logic. 'Anyone who knocks us over is strong; anyone who lifts us up is divine; anyone who gives us vague presentiments is profound'" (*CW*, 6). Isn't this a description of what Nietzsche is attempting in *Antichrist*? To overwhelm his audience with an avalanche of imagery, to "lift up" his audience by exalting their positions as the mediocre of the world, and to write nothing but vague presentations that *appear* profound? Nietzsche will write around this time period "Wagner understood how to accommodate the three basic needs of the modern soul with his heroes—they wanted the brutal, the sick, the innocent" (*KSA*, 13:14[63]). This is very reminiscent of Nietzsche's description of Christ in *Antichrist*, he calls him a "child," diagnoses in him a "condition where the *sense of touch* is pathologically over-sensitive and recoils from all contact, from grasping any solid objects. Just follow this sort of physiological *habitus* [condition]" (*A*, 29). Therefore, it is very possible that Nietzsche's description of Jesus in *Antichrist* is a borrowed image of one of Wagner's central Heroes.

It seems that in the last year of his productive life Nietzsche was meditating on the methods by which an individual could gain control of a crowd, whether through Wagner or Paul. William H. Schaberg writes that the 1888 works are "desperate cries for recognition; the kind of worldly recognition so generously heaped upon [Wagner] yet completely denied to the philosopher."[41] It is hard not to refer to the loneliness and obscurity that Nietzsche still suffered in 1888. Nietzsche writes to Carl Spittler, a former student of Franz Overbeck's, "My '*Case of Wagner*' has actually created the first truly public interest in me" (*KGB*, December 1888, III.5:1189). Nietzsche might have been attempting to seduce the way he saw Wagner seduce, by pulling his readers into a world of images, convincing them that this is the only world there was. If *Antichrist* is a methodical attempt by Nietzsche to seduce the modern masses then it would most likely make some reference to Bayreuth. For Nietzsche, "Wagner sums up modernity" (*CW*, *P*).

Notes

1 For example: "It is almost as though the work of diagnosis were over, the time having now come to combat. The *Antichrist* is unrelievedly vituperative, and would indeed sound insane were it not informed in its polemic" (Arthur Danto, *Nietzsche as Philosopher* (New York: Columbia University Press, 2005), 164).

2 "The ending of the Antichrist and much of Ecce Homo certainly show so strange a lack of inhibition and contain such extraordinary claims concerning Nietzsche's own importance that, knowing of his later insanity, one cannot help finding here the first signs of it" Walter Arnold. Kaufmann, *Nietzsche: Philosopher, Psychologist, Antichrist* (Princeton: Princeton Univ. Press, 2013), 66.

3 For example, Nietzsche writes to Helen Zimmerman: "An assassination attempt on Christianity will make an immense sensation in England: I have no figures in my head for the number of editions" (*KGB*, December 1888, III.5:1180).

4 There is also a forthcoming volume *Nietzsche and the Antichrist* (Bloomsbury February 2019) which I anticipate will successfully place *Antichrist* as an essential Nietzsche text.

5 There is a lengthy note from this time period where Nietzsche appears to be working out this problem (*KSA*, 13:14[117]). However, given all its references to Wagner, Darwin, and tragedy, as well as the haphazard manner in which notes are generally written makes dissecting this passage an inefficient use of space in this chapter.

6 I believe the persecution in Lugdunum (Lyon) is the earliest reference to the Christianization of people Nietzsche might have considered Germanic, or central European. This would mean that by 177 CE at least, there were converts to Christianity north of the Alps.

7 Adrian Goldsworthy, *How Rome Fell: Death of a Superpower* (New Haven: Yale University Press, 2010), 179.

8 "But the executioner, the veiling of heads, and the very word 'cross,' let them all be far removed from not only the bodies of Roman citizens but even from their thoughts, their eyes, and their ears. The results and suffering from these doings as well as the situation, even anticipation, of their enablement, and, in the end, the mere mention of them are unworthy of a Roman citizen and a free man" (Cicero, *Pro Rabirio Perduellionis Reo*, 16).

9 "And I, brethren, when I came to you, came not with excellency of speech or of wisdom, declaring unto you the testimony [*μυστήριον*—meaning witness or proof, this is also the word that indicated an object of a mystery religion] of God. For I determined not to know anything among you, save Jesus Christ, and him crucified. ... And my speech and my preaching *was* not with enticing words of man's wisdom, but in demonstration [*ἀποδείξει*—showing] of the Spirit and of power: that your faith should not stand in the wisdom of men, but in the power of God." (1 Cor. 2:1-5).

10 Standing for χριστός ("christos"), which is a Greek translation of the Hebrew: מָשִׁיחַ ("massíaḥ").

11 It is perhaps not widely understood how subversive and distasteful the image of the cross was. It is not just that the Christians were worshiping a man who had been convicted and executed under the direction of the state, but the Tanakh itself resisted the choice of Jesus as the messiah: "Cursed is anyone hung on a tree" (Deut. 21:23). Paul addresses this specific question, writing, "For the preaching of the cross is to them that perish foolishness; but unto us which are saved it is the power of God ... hath not God made foolish the wisdom of this world? ... For the Jews require a sign, and the Greeks seek after wisdom: but we preach Christ crucified, unto the Jews a stumbling block, and unto the Greeks foolishness (1 Corinthians 1:18-23)." This quote nicely references the dual attitudes of misunderstanding and mockery that characterized the early responses to the symbol of the Cross.

12 Nietzsche also compares Jesus and Socrates much earlier in his career, "*Judicial murders*—The two greatest judicial murders in the history of the world are, to put it bluntly, concealed and very well-concealed suicides. In both cases someone wanted to die; in both cases he allowed the sword to be plunged into his breast by the hand of human injustice" (*HH*, 94). Also see "[Socrates] distinguishes himself from all previous philosophers by his plebeian origins and by an altogether meager education" (*PP*, *Socrates*).

13 Peter Sloterdijk, *Nietzsche Apostle*, trans. Steve Corcoran (Semiotexte, 2013), 14.

14 Julian Young, *Friedrich Nietzsche: A Philosophical Biography* (Cambridge: Cambridge University Press, 2010), 515.

15 Roger Berkowitz, "Friedrich Nietzsche, The Code of Manu, and the Art of Legislation." *New Nietzsche Studies* 6–7 (2005–06).

16 Thomas Brobjer, Nietzsche's magnum opus. *History of European Ideas*, 32, no. 3 (2006): 278–94.

17 Andreas Urs Sommer, *Nietzsche-Kommentar: "Der Antichrist," "Ecce homo," "Dionysos-Dithyramben" und "Nietzsche contra Wagner"* (Berlin: De Gruyter, 2013), 274–75.

18 Even though he is getting his information on Manu from *Louis Jacolliot*, who himself distorted Manu, Sommer notes that Jacolliot does mention four castes. Meaning this is indeed Nietzsche's distortion.

19 Sommer, *Nietzsche-Kommentar: "Der Antichrist," "Ecce homo," "Dionysos-Dithyramben" und "Nietzsche contra Wagner,"* 277.
20 Ibid., 278.
21 See for further discussion: Paul W. Ludwig, "Eros in the Republic." Chapter 6 in *The Cambridge Companion to Plato's Republic*, ed. G. R. F. Ferrari, Cambridge Companions to Philosophy (Cambridge. Cambridge University Press, 2007), 201–31.
22 "We say that a maker of an image [εἰκών]—an imitator—knows nothing about that which is but only about its appearance (*Republic*, 10, 601B); "Therefore the part [of our soul the image exerts power upon] is the inferior part in us" (*Republic*, 10, 603a.); "Clearly, then, an imitative poet isn't by nature related to the part of the soul that rules in such a character, and, if he's to attain a good reputation with the majority of people, his cleverness isn't directed to pleasing it. Instead, he's related to the excitable and multicolored character, since it is easy to imitate" (*Republic*, 10, 605A).
23 Noting that "the methods, it should be said ten times over, *are* the essential thing" (*A*, 59).
24 "The cause of holy lie is the will to power. ... Establishment of dominance: for this purpose the dominance of concepts, which in the priesthood a *non plus ultra* [go no further] of power establishes this power through the lie. In light of the fact that they do not possess physicality, the military, a lie, a supplement of power, a new concept of 'truth.' One is mistaken, if one presupposes an unconscious and naive development, a kind of self-deception ... . The fanatics were not the inventors of such systems of thought oppression. ... Here the most cold-hearted prudence is at work, the same kind of deliberateness that Plato had when he thought of his 'state'" (*KSA*, 13:15[45]).
25 This would be assuming an early interpretation of the nature of the trinity which was later deemed heretical: "For the Son is a thing created, and a thing made: nor is He like to the Father in substance; nor is He the true and natural Word of the Father; nor is He His true Wisdom; but He is one of the things fashioned and made" (Alexander of Alexandria, II *Catholic Epistle*, 2).
26 Michael Sugrue, "Tragedy in the Philosophic Age of the Greeks." Lecture. https://www.thegreatcourses.com/courses/plato-socrates-and-the-dialogues.html. Given the title of Sugrue's lectures, and his occasional references to Nietzsche throughout the lectures, he might even have had the idea of a "revaluation of all values" in mind when he discusses Plato's attempt at overturning the values of Homeric society.
27 Nietzsche is even more specific in his notes: "Plato, the man of the Good—he solved the instincts of the polis: the Agon. Military competence, art and beauty, the mysteries, faith in tradition and grandfathers ... his example was the most complete detachment from the old instincts" (*KSA*, 13:14[94]).
28 Further evidence that Nietzsche was connecting Christianity and Plato's "revaluations": "The great *Lies* in History: as if it was the *corruption* of paganism that paved the way for Christianity! Instead, it was the weakening and *moralization* of the man of antiquity! The reinterpretation of natural drives as *vices* has already occurred before!" (*KSA*, 12:9[22]).
29 Edward Gibbon, *The History of the Decline and fall of the Roman Empire*. Vol. 4 (Paris: A. and W. Galignani, 1840), 277.
30 The full context being that Jesus is invited to the home of Martha and Mary (not his mother), and while Martha makes preparations Mary sits and listens to the teachings of Christ. Exasperated, Martha Exclaims, "Lord, don't you care that my sister has left me to do the work by myself? Tell her to help me!" "Martha, Martha," the Lord

answered, "you are worried and upset about many things, but only one thing is necessary, Mary has chosen what is better, and it will not be taken away from her" (Luke 10:40-42). I'll admit that the context does not seem particularly enlightening to me in any of the instances where Nietzsche uses the phrase.

31 Sommer, *Nietzsche-Kommentar: "Der Antichrist," "Ecce homo," "Dionysos-Dithyramben" und "Nietzsche contra Wagner,"* 277.

32 Sommer does state that "Christianity has, in its own way, automated behavior" (Ibid. 271) meaning that he believes that there is a similarity to be drawn between Christianity and Manu, even if he contends that Nietzsche is using this example primarily as a contrast.

33 "We shall have gained much for the science of aesthetics when we have come to realize, not just through logical insight but also with the certainty of something directly apprehended, that the continuous evolution of art is bound up with the duality of the Apolline and the Dionysiac" (*BT*, 1).

34 Once the concept of "nature" had been opposed to the concept of "God," the word "natural" necessarily took on the meaning of "abominable"—the whole of that fictitious world has its sources in hatred of the natural (—the real!—)"(*A*, 15).

35 "So, do you have any device that will make our citizens believe this story? I can't see any way to make them believe it themselves, but perhaps there is one in the case of their sons and later generations and all the other people who come after them" (*Republic*, 3, 415 C-D).

36 This is probably the main critique that could be leveled at this interpretation. First I would say that Nietzsche is aware of some of his excesses in his criticisms of Plato as a pure villain, "Plato, for example, becomes a caricature in my hands" (*KSA*, 12:10[12]). Second I would refer readers to an article by Brobjer where he gives an account of Nietzsche's relationship to Plato that does an excellent job of articulating the complex relationship between the two thinkers. *Nietzsche Wrestling with Plato and Platonism*. In *Nietzsche and Antiquity: His reactions and Response to the Classical tradition*, ed. Paul Bishop (Rochester, NY: Camden House, 2004), 205–19.

37 Literally meaning "Southernly," referring most often to a cold mediterranean wind.

38 "The 'believer' does not belong to himself; he can only be a means to an end; he must be used up; he needs some one to use him up" (*A*, 54).

39 Shapiro agrees that this is primarily a negative text, a reactionary text (Gary Shapiro, "Nietzsche"s Graffito: A Reading of Antichrist." *Boundary 2* 9–10, no. 3–1 (Autumn 1981): 119–40, 138). This is also a crucial element of Reto Winteler's thesis, that *Antichrist* represents the negative aspect of Nietzsche's *Hauptwerk*, as a necessary complement to the positive. "It was as the image of judge and destroyer of the surrounding culture that Nietzsche could identify as the author of *Antichrist*" (Reto Winteler, "Nietzsche's Antichrist Als (Ganze) Umwertung Aller Werte: Bemerkungen zum 'Scheitern' Eines." *Nietzsche-Studien* 38 (2009): 229–45, 239.f).

40 Gary Shapiro offers an interpretation of the role of Jesus in his 1981 essay which interprets Jesus as the antihero of *Antichrist*. Shapiro, "Nietzsche's Graffito: A Reading of Antichrist," 127.

41 William H. Schaberg, *The Nietzsche Canon: A Publication History and Bibliography* (Chicago: University of Chicago Press, 1995), 155.

6

Twilight of the Idols and the Dawn of Modernity

Karl Laderoute

> *People are not the products of some special design, will, or purpose ... We have invented the concept of "purpose": there are no purposes in reality*
>
> —*Twilight of the Idols, The Four Great Errors, 8*

Twilight of the Idols is one of the last texts Nietzsche authorized for publication. Although written as a break from toiling on his masterwork, *Revaluation of All Values*, *Twilight of the Idols* is one of Nietzsche's most important works. It offers a relatively clear articulation of many of the core themes present throughout his earlier works. Despite its brevity, the book is one of Nietzsche's most accessible works, and it offers an excellent summation of his mature philosophy.

This chapter is broken into two parts. The first part provides a brief consideration of the chronological position of *Twilight of the Idols* in Nietzsche's oeuvre. The second part of this chapter offers an explication of the various sections of the work, elucidating Nietzsche's views and reasoning. Many key themes of Nietzsche's earlier writings find clear expression in this late text: an assessment of Socrates and the decline of the ancient world; an assessment of the positive influence of antiquity on Nietzsche's thought; a criticism of traditional metaphysics and epistemology; the critique of traditional morality and a call to a revalue values; a focus on psychological investigations and explanations; the endorsement of causal determinism, the rejection of free will, and a focus on physiology; and a critique of modern (German) culture. Despite a rearticulation of core Nietzschean themes, notably absent in *Twilight of the Idols* are lengthy expositions of what some may consider to be key Nietzschean concepts: the will to power, the *Übermensch*, and eternal return. Below, I show how the arguments put forth in *Twilight of the Idols* criticize the errors Nietzsche sees enshrined in the philosophical-moral tradition and elucidate his suggestions on how we may overcome those errors. I conclude that *Twilight of the Idols* should be considered an indispensable work for those interested in Nietzsche's mature philosophical position.

Approaching *Twilight of the Idols*

The year 1888 saw a flurry of writing activity from Nietzsche after several years of steady publishing. From 1878 to 1888, he published at least part of a book each year. The years 1881–87 were particularly productive, seeing the publication of *Daybreak* (1881), *The Gay Science* (1882), the four-part *Thus Spoke Zarathustra* (1883–85), *Beyond Good and Evil* and new prefaces for some of his earlier works (1886), *On the Genealogy of Morality* and a fifth book for *The Gay Science* (1887). In his final productive year (1888), Nietzsche penned *The Case of Wagner*, *Twilight of the Idols*, *The Antichrist*, *Ecce Homo*, and *Nietzsche contra Wagner*.

Twilight of the Idols is the most important—though not necessarily most novel—work Nietzsche produced in 1888. Its importance lies in the fact that it stands as a summation of his mature philosophy. The book was published on January 24, 1889, twenty-one days after his mental collapse in Turin. The work was written in a mere twenty days between August 18 and September 7, 1888, during Nietzsche's seventh, and final, summer stay in Sils Maria.[1] The preface of *Twilight of the Idols*, written after Nietzsche left Sils Maria for Turin, is dated "30 September 1888, the day that the first book of the *Revaluation of All Values* [i.e., *The Antichrist*] was finished."[2] Nietzsche indicates that *Twilight of the Idols* is a "form of convalescence ... a recuperation, a sunspot, a little light adventure into a psychologist's idle hours" *(TI, P)*. As Julian Young explains, this work "incorporates notebook material that was originally intended for the masterwork, [but] there are no notebook sketches of this specific work."[3]

For a hastily produced piece, the work exhibits refinement, and its basis in Nietzsche's earlier notebook material supports the view that *Twilight of the Idols* is more a repackaging of Nietzsche's mature views than an exposition of substantively new positions. In an 1888 letter to Georg Brandes—who gave the first lectures on Nietzsche's philosophy from April 10 to May 8, 1888 in Copenhagen—Nietzsche calls *Twilight of the Idols* "my philosophy in a nutshell" (*KGB*, October 1888, III.5:1134).[4] In *Ecce Homo*, Nietzsche describes the work as having a broad scope and offering determinate positions on issues he treated more suggestively in the past: "There is no reality, no 'ideality' this work does not touch. ... But you do not get hold of things that are questionable any more, you get hold of decisions" (*EH*, *TI*, 2). *Twilight of the Idols*'s format marks a hybrid of the styles used in Nietzsche's earlier works. "Arrows and Epigrams" and "Skirmishes of an Untimely Man" are reminiscent of Nietzsche's discursive, aphoristic works, such as *Human, All Too Human* and its sequels, *Daybreak, The Gay Science*, and *Beyond Good and Evil*. The longer expositions found in the other sections are closer in style to his more focused works, such as *The Birth of Tragedy* and *On the Genealogy of Morals*.

Philosophizing with a hammer

Although the work is "a little light adventure into a psychologist's idle hours" (*TI*, *P*), the philosophical import of Nietzsche's theses is anything but light; it marks nothing short of a conceptual revolution in Western thinking whose impacts were felt throughout Western culture in the twentieth century. As Nietzsche himself indicates, "What the word 'idols' on the title page means is quite simply what had been called truth so far" (*EH, TI*, 1). The first section of *Twilight of the Idols, Maxims and Barbs*, is a series of short aphorisms that reiterate themes from Nietzsche's earlier works. However, instead of unpacking the meaning of these terse statements, it is more valuable to turn to an exegesis of the sustained articulations of the views offered in the longer sections of *Twilight of the Idols* that follow this opening cannonade of his "*great declaration of war*" (*TI, P*).

The Problem of Socrates offers a psychological and physiological diagnosis of the Western philosophical tradition's original martyr. Before examining Nietzsche's diagnosis of Socrates, let me share an anecdote. Several years ago, at a conference on ancient philosophy, I had a discussion with a young scholar about Socrates. This scholar explained that they used to be interested in Nietzsche, but that over time their focus shifted to Socrates and Plato. I enquired why they had such a change of heart, especially if they were already familiar with Nietzsche's critiques of Socrates, Plato, and the history of the Western philosophical tradition. They responded that if we cannot save the Socratic project, then there is no point in doing philosophy. For this thinker, as for much of the Western philosophical tradition, philosophy simply *is* the Socratic quest for truth. Of course, this quest is not the quest for just any truth; if it were, then there would be no differentiation between philosophy and the sciences. Philosophy is the quest for wisdom, the highest truths, the most important insights capable of being garnered by humans that are promised to result in moral improvement.

Socrates (as presented by Plato) was not merely committed to discovering nature's secrets, but to discovering the best way of living. In Plato's *Phaedo*, Socrates provides an account of his intellectual history. He reports that he read a work by Anaxagoras "saying that it is Mind that directs and is the cause of everything. ... I thought that if this were so, the directing Mind would direct everything and arrange each thing in the way that was best."[5] Socrates goes on to lament that Anaxagoras's theory of *nous* was merely concerned with explaining the operations of the natural world (i.e., natural science), and not concerned with teleological explanations that showed that all things in the world are ordered for the best (i.e., revealing a moral world order). Socrates's (or, more likely, Plato's) own method of explanation invokes the Forms to meet this explanatory *desideratum*.[6] Socrates's teleological view of nature (human nature included) is taken up by Plato.[7] Aristotle also assumes that nature is inherently teleological, and considers it absurd that humans would lack a natural function.[8]

That nature has a purpose, that humans have a natural purpose, that nature is designed for the best, are all assumptions. These assumptions were taken up by the most influential intellectual movements of the late ancient world—Stoicism, (Neo-) Platonism, and Christianity—and jointly shaped the dominant movements of Western thinking for two millennia. Nietzsche's problematization of Socrates marks nothing less than a problematization of the assumptions underlying the Western intellectual tradition. In Nietzsche's wake, twentieth-century thinkers have recast what it means to do philosophy. One example comes from Deleuze and Guattari's aptly named *What*

Is Philosophy? Deleuze and Guattari hold that philosophy, instead of being the pursuit of truth, is instead "the art of forming, inventing, and fabricating concepts."[9] Deleuze's oeuvre is influenced by his reading of Nietzsche, as is the thinking of numerous twentieth-century thinkers.[10] In many ways, these thinkers are building on the ground prepared by Nietzsche, whose "posing questions with a *hammer*" and "*sounding out idols*" helped overturn over two millennia worth of assumptions (*TI*, *P*). Those assumptions are the ones taken up by the scholar mentioned above: that philosophy is, in essence, the pursuit of wisdom (which itself consists of knowing certain truths), and that attaining wisdom results in moral improvement.[11] Twentieth-century philosophers have doubted—in some cases rejected—both assumptions, taking the path that Nietzsche laid out.

Nietzsche begins by pointing out that "the wisest men in every age have reached the same conclusion about life: *it's no good*" (*TI*, *The Problem of Socrates*, 1). While this remark may sound exaggerated, it is anything but baseless. As Nietzsche points out, Socrates's last words in the dramatized death scene of the *Phaedo* are "Crito, we owe a cock to Asclepius; make this offering to him and do not forget" (*TI*, *The Problem of Socrates*, 1).[12] Asclepius, god of medicine, was invoked by the ill hoping for a cure. As Nietzsche explains, Socrates's dying remark reveals his own self-assessment that "Socrates is no doctor ... death is the only doctor here ... Socrates was only sick for a long time" (*TI*, *The Problem of Socrates*, 12).

In what way was Socrates ill? What allows Nietzsche to generalize the claim that Socrates was ill from the closing remark in the *Phaedo*? Nietzsche suggests that Socrates, along with the wisest men of history, "are *types of decline*" (*TI*, *The Problem of Socrates*, 2). Nietzsche holds that the consensus of the wise that life is an ill is ultimately a non-cognitive expression of their physiological condition. He contends that "*the value of life cannot be estimated*. Not by the living, who are an interested party, a bone of contention, even, and not judges; not by the dead for other reasons" (*TI*, *The Problem of Socrates*, 2). Nietzsche's explanation indicates that a necessary condition for a proper estimation of the value of life is objectivity. As he explains in a later section, "Even to raise the problem of the *value* of life, you would need to be both *outside* life and as familiar with life as someone, anyone, everyone who has ever lived: this is enough to tell us that the problem is inaccessible to us" (*TI*, *Morality as Anti-Nature*, 5; cf. *GM*, *What Is the Meaning of Ascetic Ideals?*, 12).

Nietzsche here rejects the possibility of evaluating the value of (human) life in general. One may judge particular lives—albeit always from a partial, biased, and limited perspective—but to proffer an evaluation of life in general amounts to nothing more than an expression of one's own attitude because it is impossible for a human to assess the evidence objectively. What determines one's attitude? Nietzsche answers that it is one's physiological condition that determines their assessment of life:

> The *consensus sapientium* ... proves least of all that the wisest men were right about what they agreed on: instead, it proves that they were in *physiological* agreement about something, and consequently adopted—*had* to adopt—the same negative attitude towards life. Judgments, value judgements on life, for or against, can

> ultimately never be true: they have value only as symptoms, they can be taken seriously only as symptoms. (*TI*, *The Problem of Socrates*, 2)

Nietzsche here expresses his view that psychological (mental) states are epiphenomenal, that is, mental states are causally inert, unable to influence an agent's actions, and are themselves effects of causal processes. As Nietzsche here explains, an organism's psychological states are determined by its physiological states.[13]

Nietzsche points to Socrates's ugliness as "a sign of crossbreeding, of *arrested* development due to crossbreeding," potentially even a sign of criminality (*TI*, *The Problem of Socrates*, 3).[14] Socrates suffered from a "chaos and anarchy of his instincts" as well as from "auditory hallucinations, interpreted religiously as 'Socrates's daemon'" (*TI*, *The Problem of Socrates*, 4). Recalling the *ressentiment*-fueled slave revolt in morality in *On the Genealogy of Morality* (*GM*, *'Good and Evil,' 'Good and Bad,'* 10–11), Nietzsche suggests that Socrates's irony is "an expression of revolt" rooted in "plebeian *ressentiment*," and that his use of dialectics was in fact "a type of *self-defense*" wielded due to an inability to otherwise defend himself from his opponents (*TI*, *The Problem of Socrates*, 6–7). Socrates's dialectics turned into a new type of contest that appealed to "the agonistic drive of the Greeks" (*TI*, *The Problem of Socrates*, 8). However, instead of interpreting the sudden popularity of the dialectical method as a signal of Socrates's wisdom, Nietzsche interprets it as signaling the degeneration of Greek instincts. "Wherever authority is still part of the social fabric, wherever people give commands rather than reasons, the dialectician is a type of clown: he is laughed at and not taken seriously" (*TI*, *The Problem of Socrates*, 5). Had Greek instincts still been intact during Socrates's time, he would have been rejected *tout court*—perhaps killed much sooner—instead of spawning a new intellectual movement.

Socrates appealed to so many Greeks because he promised a cure for their degeneration and the anarchy of their instincts. This cure was the tyranny of rationality. "The fanaticism with which all of Greek thought threw itself on rationality shows that there was a crisis: people were in danger, they had only one option: be destroyed or—be *absurdly rational*" (*TI*, *The Problem of Socrates* 10). Socrates's cure was to let reason act as a tyrant, subjugating all of the unruly drives and instincts. Nietzsche points to Socrates's formula that "reason = virtue = happiness" as summing up the promise of this cure (*TI*, *The Problem of Socrates* 4, 10). Nietzsche sees Plato taking up this teaching, with Aristotle, the Epicureans, and the Stoics following suit thereafter.

Nietzsche contends that "Socrates was a misunderstanding; *the whole morality of improvement, including that of Christianity, was a misunderstanding*," because degenerates like Socrates are unable to overcome their decadence (*TI*, *The Problem of Socrates*, 11). To fully understand Nietzsche's problematization of Socrates, we must turn to the following five sections of *Twilight of the Idols*, which move between criticisms of traditional metaphysics and epistemology (*'Reason' in Philosophy*, *How the 'True World' Finally Became a Fable*, *The Four Great Errors*) and criticisms of morality and moralists (*Morality as Anti-Nature*, *The 'Improvers' of Humanity*).

Criticizing Socrates for prizing reason and believing that "reason = virtue = happiness" may appear ill-founded. After all, the great technological advances we enjoy today are the result of an evidence-based process of inquiry. Reason has also long been identified as a key element in virtuous activity. But Nietzsche's criticism of reason focuses on its role in the philosophical and religious traditions; in fact he goes out of his way to note that "we have science these days precisely to the extent that we have decided to *accept* the testimony of the senses,—to the extent that we have learned to sharpen them, arm them, and think them through to the end" (*TI*, *'Reason' in Philosophy*, 3).[15] Socrates is identified as ill, as representing the decline of Greek instincts and the decadence in Greek culture.[16] Nietzsche equates the antique esteem for reason with a devaluation of the world; those who followed in Socrates's footsteps, including the most influential philosophical movements of the ancient world (such as Platonism) and ultimately Christianity, concurred with this devaluation, which is actually a revaluation of values. Whereas the older Hellenic instincts are representative of master morality, Socrates and his ilk invert values, making what was good (the world, instincts, change) into something evil. Here again (as we will see when examining the penultimate section of *TI*) Nietzsche's archrival turns out to be Plato, with Socrates acting as the impetus and representative of the movement toward the fetishization of rationality.

The key to Nietzsche's criticism of the Western philosophical tradition of rationalism is his identification of a twofold movement: the denigration of reality, regarding it as a secondary world of appearances, and the positing of a fictional "true" world of ultimate value to justify this denigration. "To divide the world into a 'true' half and an 'illusory' one, whether in the manner of Christianity or in the manner of Kant ... is just a sign of decadence,—it is a symptom of life *in decline*" (*TI*, *'Reason' in Philosophy*, 6). As Nietzsche notes, philosophers "see death, change, and age, as well as procreation and growth, as objections,—refutations even. What is, does not *become*; what becomes, *is* not" (*TI*, *'Reason' in Philosophy*, 1). Nietzsche believes the central features of human existence—and of reality more generally—are rejected by philosophers. Rather than embracing the world of constant change, philosophers posit a separate, "higher" world of being to redeem existence. Although the senses constantly attest to the immutable change characteristic of every element of the world, philosophers have done their utmost to reject the senses as deceptive and evil: "These senses *that are so immoral anyway*, now they are deceiving us about the *true* world. Moral: get rid of sense-deception, becoming, history, lies,—history is nothing but a belief in the senses, a belief in lies" (*TI*, *'Reason' in Philosophy*, 1).

Nietzsche's critique of the philosophers' lack of historical sense in *Twilight of the Idols* is not novel. This critique found early expression in the opening passages of *Human, All Too Human* (1878); there he identifies "historical philosophy" as "the youngest of all philosophical methods" (*HH*, 1). He elaborates that

> all philosophers have the common failing of starting out from man as he is now and thinking they can reach their goal through an analysis of him. They involuntarily think of "man" as an *aeterna veritas*, as something that remains constant in the midst of all flux, as a sure measure of things. Everything the philosopher has declared about man is, however, at bottom no more than a testimony as to the

> man of a *very limited* period of time. Lack of historical sense is the family failing of all philosophers. (*HH*, 2)

Nietzsche connects this lack of historical sense with art:

> It is true, certain metaphysical presuppositions bestow much greater value upon art, for example when it is believed that the character is unalterable and that all characters and actions are a continual expression of the nature of the world: then the work of the artist becomes an image of the *everlastingly steadfast*, while with our conceptions the artist can bestow upon his images validity only for a time, because man as a whole has become and is changeable and even the individual man is not something firm and steadfast. (*HH*, 223)

In the face of a tendency to dehistoricize human morals, concepts, and tendencies by covering up the irrational, contingent, historical developments that have shaped them, Nietzsche operates as a "subterranean man," drawing attention to historical countercurrents of the dominant narrative in his works after *Human, All Too Human* (*D*, *P*, 1). The opening aphorism of *Daybreak* is clear on this score: "All things that live long are gradually so saturated with reason that their origin in unreason thereby becomes improbable. Does not almost every precise history of an origination impress our feelings as paradoxical and wantonly offensive? Does the good historian not, at bottom, constantly *contradict*?" (*D*, 1). In that work Nietzsche also points toward the history of morals and indicates that "*the definitive refutation*" of a concept is the historical (i.e., genealogical) refutation (*D*, 95).[17]

In *Twilight of the Idols*, Nietzsche repeats his earlier criticism that philosophers treat historically conditioned, contingent ways of thinking as eternal, immutable, and sublime:[18] "You want to know what the philosophers' idiosyncrasies are? … Their lack of historical sense for one thing, their hatred of the very idea of becoming, their Egypticity. They think that they are showing *respect* for something when they dehistoricize it, *sub specie aeterni*,—when they turn it into a mummy" (*TI*, *'Reason' in Philosophy*, 1). Following his own genealogical method, Nietzsche attributes this way of thinking to Parmenides and the Eleatics. The subject-predicate structure of language enshrines the Eleatic error of positing a world of being, as declarative sentences that indicate change simultaneously indicate stasis, some subject (substance) that exists through the change, despite all the evidence of the senses attesting otherwise. For example, Descartes's (in)famous wax example in his *Meditations* shares the assumption of the Eleatics: although every sensory property of the wax has changed, Descartes takes it to be obvious that it is still the same piece of wax. No argument is given for this conclusion; in fact, Descartes takes the conclusion to be so certain, and its rejection so absurd, that he takes it as definitive evidence that knowledge is a product of the understanding and not of the imaginative faculty.[19] The assumption in favor of substance is also conceptually tied to the belief in the immortal soul. Although the body dies, decays, and ultimately disintegrates, it is still believed that something persists throughout the changes.[20] Nietzsche famously sums up this view with his claim

"I am afraid that we have not got rid of God because we still have faith in grammar" (*TI, 'Reason' in Philosophy*, 5).

But why does the subject-predicate grammatical structure of language prevent a rejection of God? It is because the concept of God is the final product of the "reasoning" process that abstracts from the testimony of the senses. What the senses show us is a world of constant change. However, our limited cognitive abilities make it impossible for us to make sense of these changes as distinct events. As a coping mechanism, we develop abstract ideas of enduring entities (substances) that persist through changes. The same process of abstraction gives rise to abstract concepts of properties as well: "all the highest concepts, Being, the Unconditioned, the Good, the True, the Perfect" (*TI, 'Reason' in Philosophy*, 4). Nietzsche's obvious target is Plato, whose theory of the Forms aims to explain what is similar across various cases where the same linguistic terms are thought to designate the same property.[21]

Nietzsche's aim here is not entirely negative. While he does criticize the philosophical tradition for unreflectively endorsing the Eleatic prejudices enshrined in language, Nietzsche suggests that he and those willing to question these prejudices may take a path less traveled. First, he points to Heraclitus as a historical counterpoint to Parmenides. Unlike Parmenides, Heraclitus accepted that the world is constantly changing, though he is still criticized for doubting the "testimony of the senses" when "it made things look permanent and unified." Nietzsche maintains that "the senses ... do not lie at all. What we *do* with the testimony of the senses, that is where the lies being, like the lie of unity, the lie of objectification, of substance, of permanence. ... 'Reason' makes us falsify the testimony of the senses. The senses are not lying when they show becoming, passing away, and change" (*TI, 'Reason' in Philosophy*, 2). Although the world remains in a constant state of becoming, our sensory apparatus is unable to fully capture all of the changes occurring around us. While we often notice changes in our environment, microscopic changes detectable by instruments are pervasive even in environments that appear static to our unaided senses.

While the senses may seem to be deceiving us by revealing certain stable complexes, Heraclitus is wrong to charge them with lying. The senses do not produce judgments and what they reveal is the result of a complex causal process. On the spatiotemporal scale humans utilize, set by our contingent evolutionary history and physiological operations, certain external complexes will register as changing while others register as static. Nietzsche maintains that the senses should not be rejected because of this seeming unreliability in the manner of the Eleatics, Heraclitus, or Plato. On the contrary, Nietzsche firmly asserts that the use of the senses is necessary for us to know anything at all: "We have science these days precisely to the extent that we have decided to *accept* the testimony of the senses,—to the extent that we have learned to sharpen them, arm them, and think them through to the end." Some disciplines are pre-scientific because they have not yet embraced empirical evidence ("metaphysics, theology, psychology, epistemology"), while others "do not have anything to do with reality" because they simply have no connection to the senses (logic and mathematics) (*TI, 'Reason' in Philosophy*, 3). While Nietzsche's suggestion that mathematics and logic have no connection to the senses may be questioned, his point is that, while these "formal science[s]" may be applied to reality as a tool, their functions and basic theorems do not rely on correspondence to any particular facet of the empirical world.

The point regarding the formal sciences of logic and mathematics is worth elaborating, because it helps shed light on Nietzsche's claim that being, unity, objectification, substance, and permanence are lies, initiated by the Eleatics and canonized by Plato. For a clear articulation of Nietzsche's point, we must turn to *Human, All Too Human*. There, he explains that logic "depends on presuppositions with which nothing in the real world corresponds, for example on the presupposition that there are identical things, that the same thing is identical at different points of time" (*HH*, 11). Mathematics shares these presuppositions. Nietzsche maintains that

> the invention of the laws of numbers was made on the basis of the error, dominant even from the earliest times, that there are identical things (but in fact nothing is identical with anything else); at least that there are things (but there is no "thing"). The assumption of plurality always presupposes the existence of *something* that occurs more than once: but precisely here error already holds sway, here already we are fabricating beings, unities which do not exist. (*HH*, 19)

Here, without expressly identifying it, Nietzsche endorses nominalism, the view that only particulars exist, and that group identity is true in name only.[22] Although some scholars have rejected reading Nietzsche as a nominalist, this reading best fits his various claims concerning identity and falsification.[23] Nietzsche's theoretical views are similar to those of many early modern nominalists, such as Locke, Berkeley, and Hume. As Berkeley (hyperbolically) notes through the character of Philo, "It is a universally received maxim, that *everything which exists, is particular*."[24] Strictly speaking, we falsify reality when we apply logic and mathematics to it, because we are imposing a group identity on intrinsically diverse phenomena. Our interpretation of the senses involves the great lie of being—of unity, objectification, substance, and permanence—precisely insofar as we treat the different as the same. This falsification occurs when we synchronically treat different individuals as members of a single group (e.g., humans), or when we treat an ongoing diachronic process as a single individual across time (e.g., counting an individual human as numerically identical across time), artificially isolating that event from the rest of the world.[25] Both of these groupings reify the existence of a mere abstraction, for example, the group "humans" is posited as an existent group to which all humans belong, or a spatiotemporal process that changes its properties across time is reified as a particular individual.[26] Logic shares in these false presuppositions because it treats events with the same schema enshrined in language and mathematics.[27]

It is the same erroneous process that also gives rise to our mistaken use of the causal paradigm (*TI*, *'Reason' in Philosophy*, 5; cf. *GS*, 110–12). Nietzsche maintains that our belief in causality is premised upon the

> basic presuppositions of the metaphysics of language—in the vernacular: the presuppositions of *reason*. It sees doers and deeds all over: it believes that will has

> causal efficacy: it believes in the "I," in the I as being, in the I as substance, and it *projects* this belief in the I-substance onto all things—this is how it *creates* the concept of "thing" in the first place. … Being is imagined into everything—*pushed under everything*—as a cause; the concept of "being" is only derived from the concept of "I." (*TI, 'Reason' in Philosophy*, 5)

This analysis of causation is elaborated more fully in *The Four Great Errors*. There Nietzsche explains that our very notion of cause comes "from the famous realm of 'inner facts,'" in particular from the mistaken belief "that our acts of will were causally efficacious" (*TI, The Four Great Errors*, 2). From the desire to ascribe moral responsibility to individuals' actions, the error of free will was propagated by primeval moralists (*TI, The Four Great Errors*, 7). The resulting "explanatory" system enshrined three false beliefs in the Western intellectual tradition: the existence of a persisting "I" or ego; that conscious thoughts causally motivate actions; and that the will is free to act, or not act, upon those motivations (*TI, The Four Great Errors*, 3). The paradigm of human willing as causally efficacious was projected upon other natural processes, in a great anthropomorphization of nature, with objects understood according to the paradigm of the supposedly persisting self: people "took the concept of being from the concept of the I, they posited 'thing' as beings in their own image, on the basis of their concept of I as cause" (*TI, The Four Great Errors*, 3). A causal explanation of a natural phenomenon designates an object or event as the cause of another object or event; the presuppositions of language isolate the cause from the effect, and posit a relationship between them. Analogously, language separates the deed from the doer, and posits a causally efficacious relationship of willing between them (cf. *GM, 'Good and Evil,' 'Good and Bad,'* 12).

Nietzsche rejects the traditional paradigm of causation by rejecting the main presupposition of enduring entities. However, he does not deny causal determinism, nor does he deny that some explanations are more accurate than others. As he says, "Morality and religion can be exhaustively accounted for by *the psychology of error*: in every single case, cause and effect are confused; or truth is confused with the effects of *believing* that something is true; or a state of consciousness is confused with its causes" (*TI, The Four Great Errors*, 6). This account is causal in nature, explaining moral and religious beliefs in terms of root causes. He also makes use of causal explanations in the case of Cornaro, who mistakenly believes that his diet is the cause of his longevity, whereas Nietzsche asserts that Cornaro's metabolism is the root cause of both his diet and longevity (*TI, The Four Great Errors*, 1).[28] Nietzsche invokes causality to explain why faulty paradigms (such as the traditional model of willing and causation) were proffered and accepted in the first place. Despite the erroneous nature of traditional paradigms, the joint desires for ascribing moral responsibility and the psychological desire for the comfort provided by familiar explanations have made the traditional paradigm dominant (*TI, The Four Great Errors*, 5). Nietzsche's own reliance on causal explanations reveals that he does not wholeheartedly reject the abstracting process involved in producing concepts or utilizing concepts in our judgments. If he did, he would be unable to offer causal explanations for types of phenomena, such as the cases of morality and religion, or cases of master and slave morality. Nietzsche does not contradict himself here. Despite his criticisms of rationality, he is engaged in a project of replacing poor interpretations with more accurate, life-affirming ones. We fall into error when we reify concepts, forgetting that they are creations, and then attribute causal efficacy to them (*TI*, *'Reason' in Philosophy*, 4, 5).

Nietzsche's treatment of morality also fundamentally relies on causal explanations, albeit ones unfamiliar to the moral tradition. Instead of focusing his account on issues of moral responsibility (such as guilt and voluntary action), Nietzsche explains putatively moral phenomena with causal explanations based on physiology. We have already seen this strategy pursued in *The Problem of Socrates*. In *Morality as Anti-Nature*, Nietzsche elaborates that there are two basic types of morality: natural morality and anti-natural morality. These two types correspond to master and slave morality from the first essay of *On the Genealogy of Morals*, respectively. Anti-natural (slave) morality is the expression of a weak physiological constitution condemned to suffer in a world of struggle and change. Weak physiological constitutions are either marked by rejecting the passions and instincts (*TI*, *Morality as Anti-Nature*, 1, 4) or by a lack of vitality that manifests itself in various ways (*TI*, *Morality as Anti-Nature*, 3). Recall that Socrates and other sages "are *types of decline*" (*TI*, *The Problem of Socrates*, 2), as well as Nietzsche's point that no objective judgment can be proffered concerning the value of life (*TI*, *Morality as Anti-Nature*, 5). Nietzsche explains that the *consensus sapientium*, that life is no good, is "the judgment of a declining, weakened, exhausted, condemned life. Morality as it has been understood so far, as it was finally summed up by Schopenhauer with the formula: 'negation of the will to life'—is the *instinct of decadence* making an imperative of itself: it says: '*be destroyed!*'" (*TI*, *Morality as Anti-Nature*, 5).

By contrast, "Every naturalism in morality—which is to say: every *healthy* morality—is governed by an instinct of life,—some rule of life is served by a determinate canon of 'should' and 'should not,' some inhibition and hostility on the path of life is removed this way" (*TI*, *Morality as Anti-Nature* 4). Strong, healthy types flourish in their environment. While the passions act as motivational stimuli that can conflict with one another, the strong bring order to their passions by spiritualizing them (*TI*, *Morality as Anti-Nature*, 1). Nietzsche explains that the process of spiritualizing the passions involves appreciating them and controlling their expression in ways conducive to an organism's overall goals (*TI*, *Morality as Anti-Nature*, 3). For the higher types, morality is recognized as a useful system of social organization that directs this process of spiritualizing the passions, analogous to how latticework will direct a vine's growth. The kind of anti-natural morality espoused by Socrates, Plato, Jesus, and Schopenhauer are simply antithetical to life; rather than shaping the passions in a productive direction, they aim to eliminate the passions, and ultimately life itself, because without the passions there can be no life. This drive to eliminate the passions is a result of the inability to spiritualize the passions, which requires power. The will of the weak and the sick is the will to nothingness, nihilism, and "man would rather will *nothingness* than *not* will at all" (*GM*, *What Is the Meaning of Ascetic Ideals?*, 28; cf. *GM*, *What Is the Meaning of Ascetic Ideals?*, 11, 28).

Given the fixation on rationality promulgated by Socrates and taken up by the Western intellectual tradition, it was to be expected that justifications would be proffered for the life-negating, anti-natural morality enshrined in that tradition. The sages of that tradition—themselves being representatives of decline—engaged in the production of fictional concepts, such as God, the soul, the afterlife, and free will. Nietzsche's criticism of moralists finds expression in his criticism of free will:

> Let us think how naïve it is to say "this is the way people *should* be!" Reality shows us an enchanting abundance of types, a lavish profusion of forms in change and at play: and some worthless idiot of a moralist sees all this and says: "no! people should be *different from the way they are*"!? ... But even when a moralist picks out a single individual and says: "this is the way *you* should be!" he is making a fool of himself. An individual is a piece of fate, from the front and from the back; an individual is one more law, one more necessity imposed on everything that is coming and going to be. To say to an individual: "change yourself" means demanding that everything change, even retroactively. (*TI*, *Morality as Anti-Nature*, 6)

We see Nietzsche's determinism at work in this passage once again. Every individual is fully determined to be who they are; the demand that even a single individual change requires that all things be different retroactively, given that all things together form a single causal nexus whose elements are codetermining. Moralists attempt to escape this conclusion by introducing the "counterfeit" notion of free will (*TI*, *The Four Great Errors*, 7). By contrast, Nietzsche and his immoralists are engaged in the great project of expunging the concept of free will from our conceptual framework.

Given such a deterministic view, one may object that the appropriate response is fatalism, and that Nietzsche's various admonishments in his writings contradict his metaphysical position. However, one may be a determinist but not a fatalist. If all things are determined, then admonishments, reactions to those admonishments, and the expense of effort in pursuit of a goal are all determined as well. Within *Twilight of the Idols* (as well as in other works) Nietzsche appears to vacillate between a total acceptance of all things and taking up a position that both approves and criticizes elements of reality.[29] He makes clear that nobody is ultimately responsible for the course the world takes, and that reality serves no ultimate purpose (*TI*, *The Four Great Errors*, 8).

Although Nietzsche's normative assessment of reality may vacillate, his criticism of the Western tradition is consistent. In light of his rejection of free will and his claim that "*there are absolutely no moral facts*," Nietzsche reinterprets the efforts of weak, anti-natural moralists as an attempt to control the stronger types. "The project of *domesticating* the human beast as well as the project of *breeding* a certain species of human have both been called 'improvements.'" Nietzsche points to the spread of Christianity in the Middle Ages as the spread of an intellectual disease that infected strong types (such as "the Teuton nobles"), making them weak (*TI*, *The 'Improvers' of Humanity*, 2). This explanation of the purpose and effects of anti-natural morality is familiar from the analysis of slave morality offered by Nietzsche the previous year in *On the Genealogy of Morality*, whose roots stretch back as far as *Human, All Too Human*.

An alternative purpose has also been pursued under the guise of morality: the breeding of castes, such as under the law of Manu. Nietzsche admires the morality of breeding for being "more reasonable," because the ultimate purpose is to produce a stable foundation for an enduring society (*TI*, *The 'Improvers' of Humanity*, 3). Interestingly, Nietzsche points to the Indian law of Manu as presenting "us with *Aryan* humanity for once, in its pure and primordial form,—we learn that the concept of 'pure blood' is anything but harmless" whereas Christianity "is the *anti-Aryan* religion par excellence: Christianity, the revaluation of all Aryan values," represents the slave revolt in morality that upends what Nietzsche considers a healthy social order (*TI*, *The 'Improvers' of Humanity*, 4). No matter the purpose of the moral system, Nietzsche notes that all codifiers and teachers of morals have given themselves the privilege of using the *pia fraus*—the holy lie—as a mechanism to ensure compliance. "Boiling this down to a formula, you could say: *all the methods* that have been used so far to try to make humanity moral have been thoroughly *immoral*" (*TI*, *The 'Improvers' of Humanity*, 5). For instance, Nietzsche regards the discourse of human rights as being founded upon a fiction. While rights may be agreed upon between parties, based on their comparative degrees of power, Nietzsche holds that postulating the existence of immutable human rights that are possessed by all people is simply a way to advance anti-natural morality. Such a view aims to increase human happiness, but the end result will be an undermining of the prerequisites for a strong, healthy society (*AOM*, 39; *D*, 112; *BGE*, 44, 62, 202, 203, 212, 265).

"Skirmishes of an Untimely Man" includes a number of disparate passages. While Nietzsche's various comments in this section are worth examining, I will here only deal with Nietzsche's treatment of the will to power and *Übermensch* in this chapter. Apart from one mention in "What I Owe the Ancients," the only places in *Twilight of the Idols* that Nietzsche mentions the will to power or the *Übermensch* are four sections of the "Skirmishes" (*TI*, *Skirmishes of an Untimely Man*, 11, 20, 37-38). These passages reveal that these concepts play a relatively minor role in Nietzsche's late thought. Both terms should be seen as succinct expressions of Nietzsche's views on natural and anti-natural morality. As Nietzsche articulated in *Morality as Anti-Nature* and *The "Improvers" of Humanity*, the strong type of individual is healthy and powerful. Being powerful means having the capacity for action, being able to translate one's will into activity, which is here dubbed "will to power." Although Nietzsche rejects the causal efficacy of conscious motivations, he proffers causal explanations of both behavior and psychological states. The feeling of power and the activity that generates it are the result of a healthy physiological constitution enforcing its will on the world.[30] The *Übermensch* is a representative of the higher, healthier, natural morality of the masters articulated in *Morality as Anti-Nature*. Such a representative contains a strong will to power. Cesare Borgia is cited as an example of the *Übermensch* for having the strength to flourish in harsh, Renaissance conditions (*TI*, *Skirmishes of an Untimely Man*, 37).

The views expressed in the penultimate section of *Twilight of the Idols*, *What I Owe the Ancients*, are also continuous with the views expressed in earlier sections of the work. Nietzsche presents a synthesis of his most important ideas, holding the pre-

Socratic Greeks up as a representative of his ideal. Here he explicitly criticizes Plato for being "a *first-rate* decadent of style" and being "so much at odds with the basic Hellenic instincts, so moralistic, so proleptically Christian." Just as Socrates is criticized at the outset of *Twilight of the Idols*, Nietzsche charges "Greek philosophy as the *decadence* of the Greek instinct" (*TI*, *What I Owe the Ancients*, 2). "Philosophers really are the decadents of the Greek world, the countermovement to the ancient, noble taste (—to the *polis*, the agonistic instinct, the value of breeding, the authority of descent)" (*TI*, *What I Owe the Ancients*, 3). Plato represents this decadence because he "is a coward in the face of reality,—*consequently* he escapes into the ideal" (*TI*, *What I Owe the Ancients*, 2).

Nietzsche identifies "Thucydides as the great summation, the final manifestation of that strong, severe, harsh objectivity that lay in the instinct of more ancient Hellenes." Contrary to the usual denigration of the sophists as cut-rate rhetoricians who do not prize truth as the highest ideal, Nietzsche holds that Thucydides "represents the most perfect expression of the *sophists' culture*, by which I mean the *realists' culture*" (*TI*, *What I Owe the Ancients*, 2; cf. *D*, 168). The prototype for Nietzsche's natural morality, the higher, stronger type of human, is none other than the ancient Hellenes of the time before Socrates:

> I saw the Greeks' strongest instinct, the will to power, I saw them tremble in the face of the tremendous force of this drive,—I saw all their institutions grow out of the preventative measures they took to protect each other against their inner *explosives*. This tremendous inner tension vented itself outwardly in terrible and ruthless hostility: the city-states tore each other apart so that the citizens in each one were able to find peace from themselves. (*TI*, *What I Owe the Ancients*, 3)

The healthy Hellenic instincts were expressed in art: "Even in their festivals and arts they only wanted to feel that they were in a *position of strength*, to *show* that they were in a position of strength: these are ways of glorifying yourself and, at times, making yourself into an object of fear" (*TI*, *What I Owe the Ancients*, 3). It turns out that Nietzsche's early identification of the Dionysian in Greek art is none other than the artistic expression of the healthy Hellenic instincts: "I was the first one to take seriously that wonderful phenomenon that bears the name 'Dionysus' and use it to understand the older, still rich, and even overflowing Hellenic instinct: one that can only be explained as an *excess* of strength" (*TI*, *What I Owe the Ancients*, 4). Socrates, Plato, and Christianity embody a physiological degeneration that "was finally summed up by Schopenhauer with the formula: 'negation of the will to life'" (*TI*, *Morality as Anti-Nature*, 5). By contrast, "The *fundamental fact* of the Hellenic instinct—its 'will to life'—expresses itself only in the Dionysian mysteries, in the psychology of the Dionysian state" (*TI*, *What I Owe the Ancients*, 4).[31]

Here Nietzsche introduces the notion of the eternal return—"the basic idea" for Nietzsche's *Zarathustra* and "the highest possible formula of affirmation (*EH*, *Z*, 1)—for its only discussion in *Twilight of the Idols*. Just like the will to power and the *Übermensch*, the eternal return represents the healthy foundation of natural morality according to Nietzsche's Roman stylistic principle of "a minimal range and a minimal number of signs achieving a maximal semiotic energy" (*TI*, *What I Owe the Ancients*, 1). The eternal return is not presented as a cosmological doctrine. It instead expresses the very will to life embodied by the ancient Hellenic instincts:

> *Eternal* life, the eternal return of life; the future promised by the past and the past consecrated to the future; the triumphal yes to life over and above all death and change; the *true* life as the overall continuation of life through procreation, through the mysteries of sexuality. ... There has to be an eternal "agony of the woman in labor" so that there can be an eternal joy of creation, so that the will to life can eternally affirm itself. The word "Dionysus" means all of this: I do not know any higher symbolism than this *Greek* symbolism of the Dionysian. It gives religious expression to the most profound instinct of life, directed towards the future of life, the eternity of life,—the pathway to life, procreation, as the *holy* path. (*TI*, *What I Owe the Ancients*, 4)

Christianity, representative of the "negation of the will to life," inverts Greek values "with its fundamental *ressentiment against* life" by making "sexuality into something unclean," by throwing "*filth* on the origin, the presupposition of life" (*TI*, *What I Owe the Ancients*, 4).

In *Twilight of the Idols*, Nietzsche expresses and synthesizes the most important insights developed throughout his philosophical writings. He connects his famous concepts of the Dionysian, the will to power, the *Übermensch*, and the eternal return with his psychology of power, health, and master morality. Opposite to this intellectual constellation of health stands its antipode: the Socratic/Platonic/Christian/Schopen hauerian rejection of the will to life, an effect of physiological degeneration and exhaustion deterministically expressed through the anti-natural morality brought to prominence by the slave revolt in morals. In an attempt to rationally justify itself, the intellectual movement of the sick posits a separate, "higher" world of Being, denigrating this world and its presuppositions (e.g., sexual reproduction, exploitation, the need for strength) to a secondary, illusory status. The senses are rejected for their constant testimony against this fictional world of being. Master morality and the activity of the healthy are undermined by the introduction of the counterfeit notion of free will, rejecting causal determinism in an effort to assign moral responsibility and linking one's fate in the "true world" to one's actions in this life.[32] Although language and conceptual thinking forces us to make use of the fictions of Being, we need not be lured into the fictitious and life-denying stance of the sick. Language and concepts may be used in the service of life, and Nietzsche ultimately invites his immoralists to revalue values once again: "With this I come back to the place that once served as my point of departure—the '*Birth of Tragedy*' was my first revaluation of all values: and now I am back on that soil, where my wants, my *abilities* grow—I, the last disciple of the philosopher Dionysus,—I, the teacher of the eternal return" (*TI*, *What I Owe the Ancients*, 5).

Notes

1 Julian Young, *Friedrich Nietzsche: A Philosophical Biography* (Cambridge: Cambridge University Press, 2010), 497.
2 By this point, Nietzsche had changed the title of his planned magnum opus from *The Will to Power* to *Revaluation of All Values. The Antichrist*, originally seen as the first part of the *Revaluation*, eventually came to constitute the entirety of the revaluation. See Young, *Friedrich Nietzsche*, chapter 26 for an overview of this change. Nietzsche refers to *The Antichrist* as "The *Revaluation of All Values*" after the table of contents in *Ecce Homo*. See also Bernd Magnus, "The Use and Abuse of *The Will to Power*," in *Reading Nietzsche*, eds. Robert C. Solomon and Kathleen Marie Higgins (Oxford: Oxford University Press, 1988), 218–35.
3 Young, *Friedrich Nietzsche*, 497.
4 On the exchanges between Nietzsche and Brandes, see Young, *Friedrich Nietzsche*, 487–89.
5 Plato, *Phaedo* in *Plato: Five Dialogues*, 2nd ed., trans G. M. A. Grube, revised by John M. Cooper (Indianapolis: Hackett Publishing Co., 2002), 97c.
6 See Plato, *Phaedo*, 96a–102a.
7 Given the relative difficulty of determining what, if any, positions were actually Socratic rather than Platonic, it is likely safer to simply discuss the views of Plato and Aristotle. However, I attribute this position to Socrates by way of Plato, keeping with Nietzsche's approach of doing the same.
8 Aristotle, *Nicomachean Ethics*, 1.7.
9 Gilles Deleuze and Félix Guattari, *What Is Philosophy?* trans. Hugh Tomlinson and Graham Burchell (New York: Columbia University Press, 1994), 2.
10 Nietzsche's influence is found in the works of numerous influential thinkers, including Sigmund Freud, Martin Heidegger, Albert Camus, Jean-Paul Sartre, Jacques Derrida, Michel Foucault, and Bernard Williams, to name but a few.
11 Barry Allen has recently argued that the Chinese tradition does not make the assumption that wisdom is merely the knowledge of certain truths. See *Vanishing into Things* (especially 223–27) for discussion.
12 Plato, *Phaedo*, 118a.
13 See the discussion of *The Four Great Errors* below for an elaboration of Nietzsche's rejection of free will.
14 For a study of Nietzsche's use of biological metaphors, see Gregory Moore, *Nietzsche, Biology and Metaphor* (Cambridge: Cambridge University Press, 2002), especially Chapter 4.
15 There is a growing consensus that Nietzsche knew of, and appreciated, the sciences of his day. See Brian Leiter, *Nietzsche on Morality*, 2nd ed. (New York: Routledge, 2015) and Gregory Moore and Thomas H. Brobjer, eds., *Nietzsche and Science* (London: Ashgate, 2004).
16 In the cultural sphere, Nietzsche identifies Euripides as representing "*aesthetic Socratism*, whose supreme law runs roughly like this: 'In order to be beautiful, everything must be reasonable'" (*BT*, 12). For Nietzsche, this shift signals the end of the Dionysian influence on theater, and the ultimate decline of what was best in the Greek instincts. See *BT*, 11–13 for elaboration.
17 Also see *D*, 18, 34, 112.

18 Nietzsche articulates this criticism in *HH*, 1–2, 223 and *D*, 1, 18, 34, 95, 112.
19 René Descartes, *Discourse on Method and Meditations on First Philosophy*, 4th ed., trans. Donald A. Cress (Indianapolis: Hackett Publishing Co., 1998), meditation two.
20 See the arguments attributed to Socrates in Plato's *Phaedo* to this effect.
21 Although Plato's *Euthyphro* does not contain a detailed discussion of the Forms, Socrates's interrogation of Euthyphro's knowledge of piety does offer a succinct articulation of the conceptual problem that the Forms are designed to address, which is the question of what makes some seemingly disparate group of phenomena properly belong to a single group by containing some property. See Plato, *Euthyphro*, 5c–d.
22 Despite my classification of Nietzsche as a nominalist, he never uses that term (as far as I am aware).
23 See Maudemarie Clark, *Nietzsche on Truth and Philosophy* (Cambridge: Cambridge University Press, 1990), 77. There, Clark explicitly rejects the reading of Nietzsche as a nominalist.
24 George Berkeley, *Three Dialogues between Hylas and Philonous*, ed. Robert Merriew Adams (Indianapolis: Hackett Publishing, 1979), 28.
25 In *The Gay Science*, 335 Nietzsche describes all actions as "altogether unique and unrepeatable."
26 See *D*, 105 where Nietzsche explicitly states that "general judgments about 'man'" concern "the bloodless abstraction 'man,' that is to say, … a fiction."
27 For other instances in Nietzsche's writing that can be read along these lines, see *The Gay Science*, 112. This point has recently been mentioned by Kent A. Peacock and Andrew Tedder, "Identity, Haecceity, and the Godzilla Problem," in *"Shut Up" he explained. Essays in Honour of Peter K. Schotch*, ed. Gillman Payette (London: College Publishers, 2016), 63–79.
28 On this point, see Brian Leiter, "Nietzsche's Theory of the Will," *Philosophers' Imprint* 7 (2007): 1–15.
29 For instance, in *What I Owe the Ancients* Nietzsche claims that his "taste which may be the opposite of tolerant is far from saying yes to everything it encounters: it does not like saying yes at all and would even prefer to say no" (*TI*, *What I Owe the Ancients*, 1).
30 This connection is also made in *Antichrist*, 2.
31 Schopenhauer's influence on Nietzsche is evident here. On the "will to life," see Arthur Schopenhauer, *The World as Will and Representation*, vol. 1, trans. Richard E. Aquila in collaboration with David Carus (New York: Pearson Longman, 2008), 54. Nietzsche's will to power is, on some level, a version of Schopenhauer's will to life. Whereas Schopenhauer concludes that the will to life ought to be rejected, Nietzsche reverses this anti-natural ethical stance, advocating for its acceptance, as is done in his interpretation of the ancient Greeks.
32 On this connection, see *On the Genealogy of Morality*, "'Good and Evil,' Good and Bad'," 14–15.

Part Two

Nietzsche and Modernist Culture

7

Peacocks and Buffalos: Nietzsche and the Problems of Modern Spectacle

Yunus Tuncel

The question of spectacle never ceased to fascinate Nietzsche, even if he wanted to leave it and its most vivid and closest example in the persona of Wagner behind him. It pursued him from his first published work to one of the last, and many of his other works reveal spontaneous eruptions of this question. What does Nietzsche mean by spectacle, *Schauspiel*, and all the other related terms he uses in his works? What are the forces at work in spectacular relations in their unique historical contexts? And why does this question occupy such a space in Nietzsche's thought?

These are some of the issues that will be explored in this chapter. I will start with Nietzsche's reflections on Greek theater, which, in its early form, is the prototypical grand spectacle. For Nietzsche, ancient Greek theater, in its origin and at its height, forms the backdrop according to which all spectacles can be assessed. This, I believe, is true even for his late writings, although there are some signs that may indicate otherwise. However, this does not mean that Nietzsche calls for a direct adaptation of Greek theater or a direct imitation of Greek culture in general, but rather a creative appropriation of its great symbolic qualities.

This chapter will also explore Nietzsche's gradually changing evaluation of Wagner and his grand spectacle at Bayreuth. Here we have Nietzsche's evaluation of a contemporary cultural formation that still exists today and that says about contemporary culture and its pathos of spectacle. After surveying some general ideas on the topic that appear in Nietzsche's other works and discussing the festive nature of spectacle-making, in the last section I present the drama of Zarathustra as Nietzsche's own grand spectacle, albeit in a symbolic form, in the post-godly epoch. Although Nietzsche was not a spectacle-maker in the strict sense, this drama stands as an example for spectacle-making next to his critical and insightful reflections on the Occidental pathos of spectacle since the ancient Greeks. Nonetheless, Nietzsche as the author of this work can be considered to be a spectacle-maker in a broad sense, or in the sense of grand spectacle, if we follow the symbolist tradition à la Mallarmé.

Tragedy as an artistic spectacle

The theme of spectacle emerges again within the context of artistic production. This is one of the themes that Nietzsche struggles with in *The Birth of Tragedy*. Here we will first make an attempt to understand, with respect to Nietzsche's interpretation of tragedy and tragic culture of ancient Greece, the notion of artistic spectacle in each of its three aspects and in their unity. What kind of a relation exists between the spectacle and the spectator? What place does the imagination have in this relationship? Once we develop an understanding of Nietzsche's notion of tragic spectacle, we are afforded a more wide-ranging idea of artistic spectacle as well as a notion of the spectacle in the broadest sense. From all of these, we will be able to repose the question as to how one relates to spectacle in general.

First, I will present the tragic spectacle and its composition. Our guiding thread here is Nietzsche's genealogy, which helps to examine forces and their configuration, that is, their interrelatedness, in a specific context. This genealogical method is implicitly at work in the early period of Nietzsche's writings, but more developed in the late period (as in *On the Genealogy of Morality*). The context here is the tragic culture and tragedy as one of its artistic spectacles. The forces that make this spectacle possible as an event are the tragic stage (chorus, satyr, actor representing a hero, a god or a character, etc.), the tragic poet who creates the spectacle, and the tragic audience as the unity of individual spectators. Tragedy is then what stands for the unity of this spectacle.

The tragic stage represents the Dionysian reality as opposed to the everyday reality and, as such, has its own unity. These two so-called realities are not rigid oppositions, but rather modalities, modes of being or dispositions; to say that I carry ecstatic disposition within me and can be ecstatic in everyday life is not, for instance, a contradiction. However, the tragic stage is a cultural formation wherein the Dionysian reality is brought to life and is given an artistic style. In this capacity, it cultivates ecstasy in an artistic context. This Dionysian reality is created and recreated in the dynamic constellation of the chorus, the satyr, and the actor. How does Nietzsche see this happen in tragedy? We will explore this now.

The tragic chorus to which Nietzsche traces the origin of tragedy is the micro-cosmic mirroring of the universal ecstasy of humankind; this universal ecstasy is brought to life in the dancing, singing, and acting of the chorus. One may reconstruct Nietzsche's claim historically as to the origin of tragedy, but what is more important, as was said earlier, is the genealogical origin of tragedy.[1] The latter pertains to the forces, at a given point or a cross-section, that are at work in tragedy. When he writes that chorus is the proto-drama for tragedy, this does not only point to the fact that there was only chorus at some point before the rise of tragedy, but, more significantly, to the fact that all forces of tragedy collapse into the chorus since it is the locus of universal ecstasy.[2] This is far from the positions that "the chorus is the "ideal spectator" or that "it represents the people in contrast to the aristocratic region of the scene," (*BT*, 56) which Nietzsche does not accept. Neither the individual poet nor the individual actor(s) can fulfill this function of "universal ecstasy." The chorus, as the moving image of dancers and singers, stands for the symbolic values of ecstasy. In other words, it has its own aesthetic and ecstatic worth in the unity of tragedy; although some parallels may be drawn to Plato's allegory of the cave here, I see an opposite tendency there. In other words, in the cave "spectators" are also drawn into the spectacle of images, but the spectacle keeps them in the dark, Whereas the Dionysian chorus elevates the spectators. The function of spectacle works in opposite directions between Greek tragic spectacle, as Nietzsche understands it, and Plato's spectacle in the cave. Furthermore, the integrity of chorus in tragedy is what Schiller calls its "ideal domain," (*BT*, 58) as Nietzsche cites him: "He regards the chorus as a living wall that tragedy constructs around itself in order to close itself off from the world of reality and to preserve its ideal domain and its poetical freedom." (*BT*, 58) It is in and through the chorus that tragedy sustains, in the language of *The Birth of Tragedy*, its Dionysian reality as opposed to the everyday reality. The satyr chorus as the chorus of primitive tragedy is part of this "ideal domain" and its Dionysian reality.

Moreover, the tragic poet is a dramatist in that he cultivates the ecstatic powers of tragedy. It is through these powers that he can transform himself into another and speak as though he were this other. Both the poet and the dramatist in one artist work together to create the tragic spectacle in which the poetic presencing in imagination (*vorhanden vorzustellen*) and the magic or ecstatic transformation (*verzauberung* or *verwandlung*) are coupled together to create the effect of presencing on stage or representing as visible (*sichtbar darzustellen*) that which is invisible. And we have already said that what is made present on stage is Dionysus and his wisdom in different shapes and via different masks. In the last year of his philosophical life, Nietzsche was still concerned with the tragic spectacle and its forces. In regard to the tragic artist, he says in a note: "The *profundity of the tragic artist* lies in this, that his aesthetic instinct surveys the more remote consequences, that he does not halt shortsightedly at what is closest at hand, that he affirms the *large-scale economy* which justifies the *terrifying*, the *evil*, the *questionable*—and more than merely justifies them" (*KSA*, 12:10[168]). It is a question of strength, feeling of power, and an ability to experience suffering as a pleasure; it is out of such a disposition that the tragic artist creates his drama and his spectacle.

We should reflect a little further on the role of images and imagination in Nietzsche. Aside from his association of the visible with the Apollonian—and this cannot be stated enough that the Apollonian and the Dionysian are equally important for the life of culture—Nietzsche has much to say on this topic despite his seeming obsession with sound and music. First, Nietzsche is critical of those who underplay the role of image in human life; those who are contemptuous of images are, in fact, contemptuous of themselves (*KSA*, 9:5[9]). Second, images play their role in our interpretative processes; they take part along with other things such as feelings (*KSA*, 9:7[29]); in image-thinking they play more of a role. Finally, in all the things we do and say, images accompany our ideals and our philosophy of the world. All creators have an image of the world and impose it on the rest, as Nietzsche observes: "The most powerful man must be the worst, inasmuch as he enforces his ideal onto all men against all their ideals and transforms them into his own image—the creator" (*KSA*, 9:7[26]). This is why ideals are almost always tied to images (*KSA*, 9:8[24]).

What the satyr and the satyr chorus are is significant for tragedy,[3] as Nietzsche observes, especially from the perspective of ecstatic dimension of the tragic worldview. For the satyr chorus, "The Greek built up the scaffolding of a fictitious *natural state* and on it placed fictitious *natural beings*. On this foundation tragedy developed" (*BT*, 58). How is it that both the tragic stage and the satyr are *natural* and *fictitious*? We will go astray here if, by *natural*, we understand something that pertains strictly to external nature; to say the least, there is no distinction between external nature and internal nature in Nietzsche's immanentism. We can then interpret *natural* within the context of his cosmology and say that the tragedy brings on stage the play of eternal creation and destruction. And the satyr, as a sensual and sexual creature between human, animal, and god, is an ecstatic play of the same cycle. This is what may be thought in the term *natural*. *Fictitious*, on the other hand, points to the fact that they are created or invented, as intended by the root of the originally used word, *fingieren*. In Nietzsche's interpretation of the role of the tragic satyr, we are back again to the binding together of ecstasy and invention or creation through cosmological principles. It is not that theater is a natural phenomenon, but rather it is in and through theater that human beings can conceptualize the natural, that is, relate to nature and cosmos in a symbiotic way, which lifts them up and enables them to affirm life. Satyrs, among other mythic figures, play that crucial role of being bridges between the human and nature.

For Nietzsche the satyr is the voice of wisdom and is expressed in this way: "The satyr, as the Dionysian chorus, lives in a religiously acknowledged reality under the sanction of myth and cult. That tragedy should begin with him, that he should be the voice of the Dionysian wisdom of tragedy, is just as strange a phenomenon for us as the general derivation of tragedy from the chorus." (*BT*, 58–59). This is strange for Nietzsche's contemporaries who are lacking in ecstatic experience and cannot, therefore, hear this voice. The general derivation of tragedy from the chorus is equally strange for them, because this derivation presupposes, whether in the historical or the genealogical sense, the absence of a distinction between the spectator and the spectacle where ecstasy is a value for all in the lived reality of universal ecstasy of all. This is what Nietzsche sees as "the most immediate effect of the Dionysian tragedy," namely "that the state and society and, quite generally, the gulfs between man and man give way to an overwhelming feeling of unity leading back to the very heart of nature" (*BT*, 59). It is in and through ecstasy and ecstatic disposition that divisions among men, whether they are those of hatred or divisions that separate them in their everyday reality, melt into universal harmony. It is from the ecstatic standpoint that their unity can be attained. Nietzsche sees this feeling of unity symbolized in the satyr and the chorus of satyrs on the tragic stage as they bring Dionysus and his wisdom to presence.

One finds the presences of Dionysus on stage not only in the satyr chorus but also in the use of masks in Greek tragedy, as Nietzsche observes: "The tradition is undisputed that Greek tragedy in its earliest form had for its sole theme the sufferings of Dionysus and that for a long time the only stage hero was Dionysus himself … that all the celebrated figures of the Greek stage—Prometheus, Oedipus, etc.—are mere masks of this original hero, Dionysus" (*BT*, 73). These masks of Dionysus, as gods or heroes, are used by the tragic actor. Acting is one of the most intense inter-human forms of ecstatic experience since the actor must be able to see himself, fully in body and soul, in the character he is making present on stage. As he recreates himself in the form of a character, he must do this in the most *natural* way in order to act well; his creativity and imagination must run parallel to his ecstasy and sense of mortality. True actors show both traits strongly and in equal measure; when there is a discrepancy, acting turns into buffoonery.[4] Nietzsche sees this ecstatic aspect of acting in the dramatic proto-phenomenon, namely, "to see oneself transformed before one's own eyes and to begin to act as if one had actually entered into another body, another character" (*BT*, 84) and calls it "magic transformation" which is the presupposition of all dramatic art.

The actor is somehow set apart from the chorus since he, as an individual actor, is the presence of Dionysus on stage in an individuated state. He is, however, related to it in a dynamic way. His ecstatic arsenal and Dionysian wisdom are nurtured by the chorus; he has a blood tie to it. An analogy, then, can be made between the relationship of an individual to cosmos and that of the actor to the chorus as the microcosmos on stage. That is to say, the chorus is where he has come from and where he will return, at least symbolically. After indicating the two phases of tragedy as chorus and then drama in relation to the absence and presence of Dionysus, Nietzsche expresses this tie as follows: "the dithyrambic chorus was assigned the task of exciting the mood of the listeners to such a Dionysian degree that, when the tragic hero appeared on the stage, they did not see the awkwardly masked human being but rather a visionary figure, born as it were from their own rapture" (*BT*, 66). Only the chorus, with its own ecstasy in song, music, and dance, could bring the spectators to their ecstasy and, thereby, help the actor perform in this ecstatic mode so that he can appear as Dionysus. To be able to see something as illusion on stage, it is necessary that one lose oneself in that illusion; in tragedy, chorus helps create the mood so that the actor can appear as an illusory figure with his own devices. Here we have a dramatic unity of ecstasy and illusion, the rapture of the chorus is coupled with the illusion created by the actor.

Language as yet another dimension of tragedy sits atop its psychic and somatic aspects in which linguistic experience forms a constellation with ecstatic and illusory experiences. The language used in tragedy, which is the most suitable for such a constellation in an artistic context, is not the direct everyday language with direct messages, but rather poetic language. It is in poetic language where ecstasy and illusion find their expression in our experiences of language. Lyric poetry, for instance, is suitable for the choral part of tragedy and for singing since, in lyric poetry, language imitates music, as Nietzsche observes. The tragic dialogue, if removed from its context, may mistakenly be identified with quotidian dialogue. It is, on the contrary, immersed in riddles, enigmas, and ambiguities, which address the imaginative, the creative, and the poetic in human beings.

To summarize what has been said so far regarding the tragic stage and to think of it in its unity, the tragic chorus cultivates and preserves itself as the domain of the Dionysian reality and, as such, retains the value of ecstasy. The satyr as an ecstatic being is the living symbol of this reality and the voice of the Dionysian wisdom either individually or as the satyr chorus. In this capacity, he may be thought as the symbolic link between the chorus and the individual actor who makes Dionysus present on stage through ecstatic and illusory effects. Whether in singing, dancing, acting, dialogue, or music, their playfulness in dramatic unity is created and recreated in the imagination and the ecstasy of the tragic poet. This is also what the German word for drama, *Schauspiel*, signifies.

The tragic poet is at once a poet and a dramatist: "At bottom, the aesthetic phenomenon is simple: let anyone have the ability to behold continually a vivid play and to live constantly surrounded by hosts of spirits, and he will be a poet; let anyone feel the urge to transform himself and to speak out of other bodies and souls, and he will be a dramatist" (*BT*, 84). He is a poet in that he can make present that which is absent in and through his imagination. He lives his fantasy world intensely, and the images he creates are as vivid as real: "For a genuine poet, metaphor is not a rhetorical figure but a vicarious image that he actually beholds in place of a concept. A character is for him not a whole he has composed out of particular traits, picked up here and there, but an obtrusively alive person before his very eyes" (*BT*, 63). Presencing is one of the significant traits of the tragic culture, which is reflected in the tragedies. It has inherited this trait from the poetic traditions of the preceding age, since it is through poetry that the powers of presencing are cultivated. Here a rich poetic imagination runs parallel to storytelling, soothe-saying, and legendary traditions. Whether it is Dionysus, heroes of the past age, the gods of an older mythic age (the Titans) or of the recent one (the Olympians), the tragic poet has the power to recreate them and make them present on stage as though they were alive.

Finally, a few words must be said on the role and position of *the tragic spectator* in the tragic spectacle, which is already discussed above to some extent. With this, we complete the circle of forces, at least, in the context we are discussing here. The claim that the spectator plays a lesser role and is a non-contributing participant, a contemporary notion of the spectator, is not acceptable from the standpoint of the tragic spectacle. Whether tragedy is interpreted as a prototypical chorus or as a distinct spectacle on stage, the role of the tragic spectator is irreducible and *equally* important to the other forces of spectacle. Just as a culture strives higher when the individuals who belong to that culture strive higher, tragic spectacle becomes richer when the spectators are rich in their imagery and symbolic experiences. Now a few remarks on the role of the spectator in the tragic spectacle.

It has already been intimated that the tragic spectacle becomes possible in the presence of spectators who are predisposed to ecstasy and for whom illusion is a value so that the Dionysian reality becomes a lived reality for them in spite of their everyday reality. Both the ecstasy and the illusion reside in the symbolic and imagery registers of the body and the soul of each spectator; the audience, as the unity of such spectators, represent a cross-section of the culture in which the symbols and the images that rise and fall in tragedy are part of the lived reality of that culture. The enigma that Oedipus is and the legends that are built around his life, the rebellious and yet philanthropic Prometheus in agony and the sufferings of Dionysus live in culture as the shared treasures of its mythology and poetry. It is from this treasure house that the tragic poet borrows, and on it that she builds, adding another room to this house.

In the cycle of recreation of culture through tragedy, the spectator is an active participant. Her position in the constellation demands that she elevate herself to ecstasy, see and feel the presence of representation of Dionysus on stage as the god himself and hear the voice of wisdom. The former is achieved through the mood created by the chorus; in this mood, the spectator reaches ecstasy with the chorus: "A public of spectators as we know it was unknown to the Greeks: in their theaters the terraced structure of concentric arcs made it possible for everybody to actually *overlook* the whole world of culture around him and to imagine, in absorbed contemplation, that he himself was a chorist" (*BT*, 63). This is not an identification of the chorus with the spectator, a position criticized by Nietzsche; their roles and positions in the constellation are distinct. However, this distinction is no objection to their ecstatic coming-together. Moreover, the spectator values illusion as illusion and lets the theatrical effect have a hold of her through his fantasy world.

An imaginative, fantasy-rich way of relating to the spectacle is expected from the spectator; such an indirect and creative relationship to what she has created is implicit in the poet's image of the world. Just as the images and symbols jostle around on stage as prefigured in the imagination of the tragedian, entering into new constellations, they do so in the body and soul of the individual spectator on a smaller scale. Insofar as the spectator is the Dionysian spectator, the audience as the unity of spectators becomes the source from which the poet and the stage derive their blood supply in order to recreate these new constellations. Together they contribute, in a dynamically ever-growing way, to the larger pool of images and symbols of the culture they belong to, which are found in its myths and legends.

However, insofar as the spectator is the woman of everyday reality, she is faced with the demands of the Dionysian reality in the tragic spectacle. The woman of everyday reality is not a subjective construct, it is a trait or a disposition; in a way, we are all part of an everyday reality. The tragic spectacle reorders the traits and refurbishes the Dionysian cosmology as the underlying trait on top of which sits the trait of everydayness. Whereas the woman of everyday reality as a trait pulls her toward believing that her reality is the only reality, the tragic spectacle shows the possibility of creating and recreating a multiplicity of realities in and through ecstasy of all. Therein the spectator sees the abyss, the nothingness of existence, that is, the destruction of all that comes to being, a horrifying thought. At this moment, art, with its illusory devices and with its play between the absence and the presence, comes to rescue (*BT*, 59, 61).

The unity of the tragic spectacle

The genealogical configuration of forces, which make up the tragic spectacle, we shall call the unity of tragic spectacle. We have above elaborated on these forces: the tragic stage, the tragic poet, and the tragic spectator. This unity of spectacle is dynamic, it rises and falls together, and its dynamic flow lies in the fluidity of the circle for which the primordial artist as the poet, the actor, and the spectator, at the same time, is emblematic. Furthermore, the richness in the creativity of the poet is a function of the richness of his culture and, therefore, of his audience and the entire spectacle: "The poet is possible only in an audience of poets … A fantasy-rich audience. This is like his material that he forms" (*KSA*, 7:16[6]). When the treasure house of a culture is rich, which is reflected in the audience of spectators and its spectacles, the poetic material becomes richer.

Wagner, Bayreuth, and Nietzsche's criticism of modern spectacle

Any discussion of spectacle in Nietzsche demands a consideration of the Nietzsche-Wagner relationship, in particular of the type of spectacle Wagner created at Bayreuth and of Nietzsche's evaluation of that contemporary spectacle: first, his expectations from and support for Wagner and his project (as reflected in *BT*, 15–25 and *RWB*), then his disappointment with them (as expressed in his writings starting with *Human, All Too Human* and more explicitly and concisely in *The Case of Wagner* and *Nietzsche Contra Wagner*). The personal problems and conflicts notwithstanding, the Wagner phenomenon, for Nietzsche, is a contemporary phenomenon par excellence. And Bayreuth is a good example for modern experience of spectacle; hence, the intensity of Nietzsche's critique.

In what follows below, I survey those aspects of the Wagnerian project that enticed Nietzsche. *The Birth of Tragedy* is not only Nietzsche's analysis of ancient Greek tragic spectacle, but also an implicit critique of contemporary experience of spectacle. This is especially so since the former lies at the root of the latter. In the last sections of the book, Nietzsche sees in German philosophy (in Kant and Schopenhauer) a reversal of Socratic optimism and a concomitant phenomenon in music, namely the revival of tragic culture in Wagner's music—that is, a return to the Dionysian origins of culture via the mythopoeic function of music.

In the opening pages of the fourth *Untimely Meditation*, *Richard Wagner in Bayreuth*, Nietzsche declares Bayreuth to be a great event. From the standpoint of the unity of spectacle, both the creator of spectacle and the spectator, in Nietzsche's words, those who accomplish the event and those who experience it, must possess greatness of spirit for an event to be great. The greatness of the spectators at Bayreuth is briefly sketched by Nietzsche, although it is hard to surmise how Nietzsche came to this conclusion, a conclusion that he did not later uphold. Wagner's greatness, however, is brought up more often than not: his knowledge of necessity, that is, his ability to make an effect, his strife and struggle (strife for power and intoxication), his talent and the scope of his knowledge and experiences, his ability to bring all of these experiences together.

What was of utmost importance to Nietzsche was Wagner's notion of *Gesamtkunstwerk*, the total artwork,[5] and his ability and persistence to bring it to life within the context of his project to reform theater and to recreate artistic spectacle in a new constellation and with a new architectonic of its forces.[6] In this sense, Bayreuth is "the spectacle of all spectacles" (*RWB*, 4). In the total art work, all forces of spectacle come together in an *optimal* way, and theater is such a focal place where they converge; hence, Nietzsche's and Wagner's interest in it.

It is important to note here that Nietzsche and Wagner had much in common in this period: philosophical interest in Schopenhauer and his metaphysics of the will, passion for music, artistic admiration of ancient Greek culture and tragedy, and the belief that modern culture and theater are decadent and must be reformed. It is from this common background that we can understand why Nietzsche was drawn to the Wagnerian project.

Before we discuss Nietzsche's interpretation of the total artwork, it is necessary to understand what, according to Nietzsche, is problematic in modern experience of spectacle (within the context of theater and its spectatorship): strangely clouded judgment (confusions, reduction of art to formulas, ideologies, etc.); ill-dissembled thirst for amusement, for distraction at any cost (to expect entertainment from spectacle at all costs, a symptom of the decline of ecstatic-Dionysian origins of theater, and to use spectacle for distraction, as a way out of modern boredom); scholarly considerations (a source of academic chatter); pomposity and affectation on the part of the performers (the megalomania of the actor as the center of all attention, the originary pious acting has fallen into oblivion); brutal greed for money on the part of the proprietors (the commercialization of artwork and spectacle, to view them solely as means to make business and money); vacuity and thoughtlessness on the part of the society that sees people only as employable or as dangerous to society and attends concerts and the theater without any sense of duty or commitment (the lack of cultivation in the general spectatorship). All these points sum up modernity, as Nietzsche writes: "All this together constitutes the musty corrupted air of our world of art today" (*RWB*, 4). More than a century later and with changes in spectacular experiences, these problems persist, and have even multiplied, in today's world.

If Nietzsche was at first close to Wagner, what made him turn away from Wagner in such a radical way? We can consider some circumstances that precipitated this rupture: (a) there were already unspoken, unrecognized differences between the two all along their friendship, (b) Nietzsche changed (his recovery from romantic pessimism, which starts with *Human, All Too Human*, and the later shift in his thought, which is articulated in the language of the eternal return, the overman and the will to power), and (c) Wagner changed (Bayreuth can be considered a turning point in Wagner's life especially from the standpoint of Wagner as a reformer of culture by way of artistic spectacle). All of these circumstances form the background of the rupture.

As his notes and letters from this period indicate, Nietzsche's disappointment with Wagner starts even before the publication of his meditation on Bayreuth, in which Nietzsche writes of Wagner in favorable terms and still supports the project for the most part. Nietzsche retrospectively considers this work a farewell to Wagner; in the 1886 Preface to *Human, All Too Human*, Part II, he says that meditation is setting oneself at a distance and *Richard Wagner in Bayreuth* is an act of homage and gratitude to his own past. One needs to read this work more deeply than usual and with thick lenses to believe it to be a farewell to Wagner. There are, however, many notes written by Nietzsche from this period that testify to his disappointment with Wagner and his project.

Nietzsche's criticism of Wagner should be placed within the context of his transvaluation of contemporary spectacle. Pessimism and romanticism still permeate our culture and spectacular experiences; effects at any price are endemic to our mass culture; ascetic idealism, though in many different forms, is still present and does manifest itself in today's spectacle; lastly, the spectacle/spectator divide that provoked young Nietzsche to reflect on ancient Greek theater but persisted within him as a philosophical question persists in our age in our relations to spectacle. It is precisely these problems that Nietzsche detected in Wagner's worldview, most of which were grounded in the old world order and the problems of Bayreuth, and in modern spectacle. Therefore, he realized that Wagner was not the artistic reformer he had believed him to be during their friendship, when he was mesmerized by the "magician." Despite Nietzsche's later bitter and harsh criticism of Wagner and his works, the Nietzsche-Wagner encounter remains, as Richard Strauss observed, one of the most interesting and illuminating encounters of the cultural and intellectual life of the nineteenth century and provides much fodder for today's thinkers to reflect on the problems of spectacle.

Artistic spectacle

Any notion of artistic spectacle in Nietzsche presupposes his notion of art and the importance he places on art and artistic creativity.[7] Although this subject cannot be dealt with here, let it suffice here to say that for Nietzsche art, in the broadest sense, pertains to all creative activity (for instance, to creation of works of art, to culture, and to one's own character) and, as such, presents models for creative activity; that all aspects of our world-interpretation—that is, culture—are created at some point and time (therefore, they can be recreated); and that art enters into constellation with other aspects of human existence such as cosmology, philosophy, science, and politics. From a spectacular point of view, artistic spectacle is the place where creativity displays itself with its acts and models, where image-symbol relationships are recreated, and where other forces of culture are still *present* although they may be mute.

Two themes pertinent to artistic spectacles, which were studied above, run through Nietzsche's works despite the vicissitudes and the seemingly contradictory remarks in his writings: the unity of spectacle (the artist, the spectacle, and the spectator) and the unity of inner forces of spectacle. Within the context of the unity of spectacle, Nietzsche considers artistic spectacle a cultural space in which the public is artistically educated. *Human, All Too Human* 167 highlights this point, but I will focus on another point in the following aphorism in which Nietzsche brings to light the importance of the parallel development of the artist and the spectator:

> *Artistic education and his following must keep in step.* Progress from one stylistic level to the next must proceed so slowly that not only the artists but the auditors

> and spectators too can participate in this progress and know exactly what is going on. Otherwise there suddenly appears that great gulf between the artist creating his works on a remote height and the public which, no longer able to attain to that height, at length disconsolately climbs back down again deeper than before. For when the artist no longer raises his public up, it swiftly sinks downwards, and it plunges the deeper and more perilously the higher a genius has borne it, like the eagle from whose claws the tortoise it has carried up into the clouds falls to its death. (*HH*, 168)

To sustain the unity of spectacle, the progress of the artist needs to advance parallel to that of the public; otherwise, the unity shatters, and the spectators are no longer in a dynamic bond with the work of art. The artist rises, so does the spectacle itself, in proportion to the rise of the audience who actively engages itself with the work of art. Although the eagle-tortoise metaphor in this aphorism points to the notion of passive spectatorship, Nietzsche's thoughts intensify on the notion of active, connected spectatorship. In short, the artist and the spectators rise and fall together; spectacle is that mirror between the two and shows where a culture is in terms of its artistic activity and its intensity.

Although Nietzsche sees an unconscious unity between the artist and the audience, this unity is subliminal and does not involve a direct education or a moral improvement of the spectators. Throughout his work, Nietzsche is critical of moralistic interpretations of artistic spectacle. In *The Birth of Tragedy*, we see this critical attitude in the way he analyzes the chorus and its role in tragedy. *In Daybreak* 240, he explicitly warns against moral interpretations of the stage: "Whoever thinks that Shakespeare's theater has a moral effect … is in error. ... It is not the guilt and its evil outcome they have at heart, Shakespeare as little as Sophocles. … The tragic poet has just as little desire to take sides *against* life with his images of life!" (*D*, 140–41).

In regards to the inner dynamics of spectacle, Nietzsche talks about symbolic issues such as the inner world of symbolism and gestures. Symbolism, whether musical or gesture symbolism, has shaped our contemporary worldviews in such a way that it has become a part of our inner world. No such symbolisms, however, are given as eternal.

> Music is, of and in itself, not so significant for our inner world, nor so profoundly exciting, that it can be said to count as the *immediate* language of feeling; but its primeval union with poetry has deposited so much symbolism into rhythmic movement, into the varying strength and volume of musical sounds, that we now *suppose* it to speak directly *to* the inner world and to come *from* the inner world. (*HH*, 215)

A long history of symbolic association between musical sounds and words, that is, the tradition of tonal art, has created a musical sentiment, which understands music wholly symbolically. Nietzsche makes a parallel remark about gesture symbolism:

> As soon as the meaning of gestures was understood, a *symbolism* of gestures could arise: I mean a sign-language of sounds could be so agreed that at first one

> produced sound *and* gesture (to which it was symbolically joined), later only the sound. (*HH*, 216)

According to Nietzsche, symbolic relationships are recreated in their epochal and sociocultural settings, although they are of primal importance in shaping the way one relates to existence or human relations in general, including spectacular relations.

What types of *affects* do artists and artistic spectacles have on their audience? This has been a recurring question for Nietzsche. In this question lies the significance of spectacle for culture. Nietzsche expresses gratitude for the artists of theater who "have given men eyes and ears to see and hear with some pleasure what each man *is* himself, experiences himself, desires himself; only they have taught us to esteem the hero that is concealed in everyday characters; only they have taught us the art of viewing ourselves as heroes" (*GS*, 78). While emphasizing the significance of spectacle, he was, at the same time, aware of the problems of spectacle; one such problem is the burdening of the spectator with sentiments. In response to Aristotle's theory of tragedy as that which arouses pity and fear, Nietzsche says, "Just look at the Greek tragic poets to see what it was that most excited their industry, their inventiveness, their competition: certainly not the attempt to overwhelm the spectator with sentiments. The Athenian went to the theater *in order to hear beautiful speeches*" (*GS*, 80). Sentimentality weakens the individual; sentimental spectacle does not allow any room for the individual spectator, because the feelings the spectators are supposed to feel are predetermined.

Nietzsche was also wary of the intoxicating effect a spectacle could have on modern audience, especially on an audience that is not tuned artistically to the spectacle. Such an intoxicating effect is like giving electric shock to a corpse:

> I know very well what sort of music and art I do *not* want—namely, the kind that tries to intoxicate the audience and to force it to the height of a moment of strong and elevated feelings. This kind is designed for those everyday souls who in the evening are not like victors on their triumphal chariots but rather like tired mules who have been whipped too much by life. (*GS*, 86)

To such an audience, art becomes an entertainment, another excuse for the weariness and sleepiness of the modern soul.

Finally, the question of disinterestedness of spectator is raised by Nietzsche as he responds to Kant. Nietzsche's point of departure in this criticism of Kantian aesthetics (in *GM*, *What Is the Meaning of Ascetic Ideals?*) lies in the artistic experience of the work of art from the artist's perspective; therefore, any notion of spectator that creates a detachment of the spectator from spectacle (the problem of impersonality) is not acceptable by Nietzsche, and not just any spectator can be the judge of aesthetics (the problem of universality). Although Nietzsche's interpretation of Kant's disinterestedness has been assessed differently by philosophers and scholars (Heidegger claims that it is misguided by Schopenhauer), the issues he raises are of significance for a theory of spectacle:

> All I wish to underline is that Kant, like all philosophers, instead of envisaging the aesthetic problem from the point of view of the artist (the creator), considered art and the beautiful purely from that of the "spectator," and unconsciously introduced the "spectator" into the concept "beautiful." It would not have been so bad if this "spectator" had at least been sufficiently familiar to the philosophers of beauty. (*GM*, *What Is the Meaning of Ascetic Ideals?*, 6)

Nietzsche introduces a parallel idea, namely that the highest place of the artistic spectacle cannot be reduced or lowered to the common denominator of the spectator, in *The Birth of Tragedy*, where he discusses the artistic freedom of the chorus by way of Schiller. Here Nietzsche, to show the high and lofty ground of artistic experience, aims at the wrong target in Kant, because Kant is not talking about the same thing; his aporia has to do with the conditions of aesthetic experience, and the disinterestedness is that of the imagination in relation to other (cognitive) faculties of the mind. Nietzsche may respond to that by saying Kant is not an artist and is not writing about aesthetic experience the way an artist would.

Spectacle as festival

Another important aspect of Nietzsche's interest in spectacle is its festive nature. In ancient Greece, like many other archaic societies, festivals occupied a significant space in the life of culture, as in competitive games (there were four major sites for such games) or in the performance of dramas (in Athens there were four drama festivals per year). And Nietzsche must have had a good knowledge of these festivals from his early studies. As Bergmann observes,[8] Nietzsche's festival ideal[9] is formed at an early stage, roughly around 1867 before his Wagner phase, and coincides with his interest in the Greek culture of competition. A bit later, Wagner and Burckhardt—one of the leading historians of festival at the time—further encourage his festival ideal. According to Burckhardt's vision, festivity captures the religious, moral, and political life of a people and constitutes the point of transition from everyday life into the world of art; it thus functions as a unifying principle. In his *Die Griechische Kulturgeschichte*, he claims that the Greek city-states used the festivity of contests to sustain a sense of Pan-Hellenic unity after the colonization of the Mediterranean.

There are several instances in Nietzsche's early works where he discusses the role of festival in ancient Greece. In *The Birth of Tragedy*, he writes not only about the Dionysian festivals of ecstatic states, but also the Apollonian festivals of rhapsody (one can even add, to the list, the festivals dedicated to other gods and goddesses, which Nietzsche does not discuss in this text). In his unpublished "Greek Music Drama," he attributes the greatness of the Greeks to their agonal festivity; one central idea here is that "genius was only realized in the act of displaying oneself in the public arena."[10]

Nietzsche's interest in the festival ideal did not subside in his later writings. In *The Gay Science*, he refers to the art of festivals as the "higher art."[11] In a note from this period the Greeks come up again, this time the terms "danger" and "festival" appear in the same sentence: "Greeks lived only in danger: in their force, calmness, and justice they revered their convalescence, their inhalation, and their festival"[12] (*KSA*, 9:7[123]). That ancient Greeks "lived in danger" or played with fire is a recurrent theme in Nietzsche's works, highlighting the intensity and the depth of Greek expressiveness; the Dionysian ecstatic expressions, the agonistic games, the festivals, the political life all point to this Greek expressiveness in which Nietzsche sees a great vitality. Finally, he regards death as festivity: "It is a festival to go from this world over to the 'dead world' and to be released from life and to become dead nature again can be felt as festival—by those wanting to die"[13] (*KSA*, 9:11[25]). Many cultures celebrate death, and the burial rites are organized as festivals. That death is part of life and can be celebrated festively just like any other aspect of life (as in funeral games) is another point Nietzsche shares with the ancients.

There are many scenes in *Zarathustra* that are presented in the spirit of a festival, including the circus-like scene in the market place in the prologue and the scene where the higher men appear in the last part of the book. Besides the fact that Zarathustra in general is a festive spirit like a troubadour and that his journey, his grand spectacle can be considered a long festival, and being with him is also portrayed as a festival: "Living on earth is worth while: one day, one festival with Zarathustra, taught me to love the earth." (*Z*, *The Drunken Song*, 1). These words are uttered by the ugliest man, the murderer of God. With the death of God, one *festival* is over, another festival is yet to start.

The pathos of spectacle after the death of god

In the sections above, I focused on artistic spectacle in Nietzsche's philosophy, which is at the center of his thought from his first book to one of his last books (Wagner, for Nietzsche, was a case study for artistic spectacle). The notion of spectacle, however, is not limited to artistic spectacle in Nietzsche. In his early writings (in the *Nachlass*), Nietzsche focuses on, for instance, the spectacle of contest in ancient Greek culture. In various texts, different forms of spectacle appear: the spectacle of history (*HL*, 3, 4 and *GM*, *What Is the Meaning of Ascetic Ideals?*, 26); the spectacle of strength, suffering and cruelty (*D*, 18, 201, 548, 558); life as a spectacle (*GS*, 301) and so on. All of these types of spectacles and others not mentioned by Nietzsche deserve special attention in a large project dealing with spectacle itself, since spectacle is the locus where something comes to the public realm and can become a part of a culture, consciously or unconsciously, depending on its affect (it lies in the intersection between value and power). And all spectacles are somehow related within an epochal context and in the light of an epochal pathos of spectacle. Here I will touch upon another type of spectacle that Nietzsche calls "great spectacle," which would prefigure all other types of spectacles. It is the spectacle of value-creation, that of self-overcoming, with which Nietzsche ends his *Genealogy*—and the drama of Zarathustra can be understood as one such great spectacle: "As the will to truth thus gains self-consciousness—there can be no doubt of that—morality will gradually *perish* now: this is the great spectacle in a hundred acts reserved for the next two centuries in Europe—the most terrible, most questionable, and perhaps also the most hopeful of all spectacles." (*GM*, *What Is the Meaning of Ascetic Ideals?*, 27).

If this epochal turning is the great event and the great spectacle, what does it say on spectacle itself? Will the pathos of spectacle also turn with the epochal turn? If so, in what direction will it turn? This question raises yet another, broader question as to what epochal shift Nietzsche refers to and what *the values* of the new epoch are. It is not too far-fetched to think that Nietzsche wrote *Zarathustra* as a sketchy (or symbolic) drama that can be recreated as a grand spectacle. The work is prefigured as a tragedy (at the end of the fourth book of *The Gay Science*), and in structure it resembles a Greek tetralogy and Wagner's Ring Cycle.[14] In addition, the work embodies, at the symbolic level, the elements of a total artwork (understood in the spirit of ancient Greek theater): it is infused with images and landscapes (the stage of Zarathustra and its visual effects); Zarathustra sings songs (*The Night Song*, *The Dancing Song*, etc.) and dances;[15] and there are other songs and dances in the drama; and finally, the music is embedded in the text (Graham Parkes has paid a particular attention to the musicality of the work for his recent translation). On the other hand, *Zarathustra* may be regarded as Nietzsche's poetic/dramatic response to Wagner, the only such response on a grand scale.

Furthermore, Zarathustra's journey displays the values of the new epoch in a great spectacle, hence the meaning of *incipit tragoedia*. In this great spectacle of Zarathustra, there are also signs as to what the new pathos of spectacle is. It can be said that the pathos of spectacle that Nietzsche implicitly or explicitly presents in his works belongs to the economy of values of the new epoch. Wagner's reform, despite its problems and in spite of Nietzsche, may belong to this epochal shift in the spectacular experiences in the West and is one of the first examples of such attempts at a reform among which can be counted many artistic and poetic movements of the last two centuries.

As for the new pathos of spectacle that Nietzsche envisions for the post-God epoch shaped by the eternal return, I see several pivotal points in his writings, all of which have been elucidated above: self-overcoming toward greatness, the relationship between spectacle and audience (on the affects of the spectacle), the Dionysian/ecstatic connectedness, and the unity and diversity of all arts. The first relates to the overhuman, the second to power and the will to power, and the third to the eternal return. To summarize: for a culture to achieve greatness, it needs great artists—philosopher-poets, who perpetually overcome themselves toward greatness, as well as their works and the spectacles of these works, so that the greatness in different artistic forms, together and separately, can imprint itself on the spectators, who also strive, in their own individual ways, to live up to what is presented to them. In this way the spectacle functions like a mirror of greatness between great values and culture according to the cycle of creation and destruction, life and death, all of which are summed up in the nucleus thought of the eternal recurrence of the same.

Spectacle symbolism

In addition to his reflections on tragedy and Bayreuth, and his vision of *Zarathustra* as a grand spectacle, Nietzsche uses the metaphor of spectacle and its variations (*Schauspiel*, *Schauspieler(in)*, *Zuschauer*, etc.) throughout his texts. As poets convey their inner world through symbols, so does Nietzsche. A grand spectacle has its multisensory *affects* on culture at its symbolic registers. A few examples from Nietzsche's texts can be given to show this *spectacular* symbolism. For example, in his discussion of history and Occidental obsession with the historical, Nietzsche refers to the science of history as *ein solches unüberschaubares Schauspiel*, "such an immense spectacle" (*HL*, 4, 77). This science has had such an impact on culture that now we view the past through its lens. Here Nietzsche plays with the word *schauen*, which cannot be carried over into English. The immensity can be associated with highest values, often invisible but present, which shape a civilization. This science of history has such a grand *affect* that it presents itself against life forces; its *truth* must persist no matter what.

A second example illustrates the symbolic relationship between spectacle and its *affects*. In Aphorism 201 of *Daybreak*, Nietzsche presents aristocratic culture as being in tune with the feeling of power and its possible *affects* or *impressions* on others: "In both cases the aristocratic *culture* breathes power, and if its customs very often demand merely the semblance of the feeling of power, the impression this game produces on the non-aristocratic, and *the spectacle of this impression*, nonetheless constantly enhance the actual feeling of superiority."[16] Here the symbolism brings to light the power relations and their *affects* in spectacle; hence, the phrase *das Schauspiel dieses Eindrucks*. In this quoted part, Nietzsche plays with the word *Spiel*, which repeats in two different contexts, first referring to power relations and then to spectacular relations as play.

In the third example I shall present, Nietzsche refers, in *Daybreak* Aphorism 558, to a "religious" spectacle, that of Buddha; clearly not an actual spectacle, but a symbolic one. Here he discusses a specific brand of vanity. It is the vanity of those who hide their virtues. Referring to this type of vanity, Nietzsche writes: "But to do this means to present the world with an ill spectacle [a literal translation is: 'to give the world not a good spectacle'],—it is a sin against taste."[17] (*D*, 558; brackets added) Here the emphasis may be on taste in spectacle.

The last example, from *The Gay Science*, Aphorism 301, highlights the multisensory aspect of spectacle: "He fancies that he is a *spectator* and *listener* who has been placed before the great visual and acoustic spectacle that is life" In German, the last part reads "das grosse Schau- und Tonspiel gestellt zu sein, welches das Leben ist."[18] Here Nietzsche plays with the word *Schauspiel* and breaks it apart as *Schau- und Tonspiel*, thereby bringing closer to what spectacle actually is. I assume the direction that he is taking is toward multisense in spectacle or what some call "synesthesia."[19] The aphorism is the broad spectrum of human experience and feeling, which he ascribes to "higher human beings."

None of the examples above refer to any concrete spectacle, but they are all analogous to grand dramatic spectacles of ancient Greece and Nietzsche's conception of spectacle inspired by them. The symbolism that is present in these examples throws together the ideas of grandiosity, affectability, taste, and synesthesia (unity of all senses).

Epilogue

Although Nietzsche was disillusioned with Wagner and his grand spectacle, and to some extent with theatrical arts due to Wagner, the importance he places on spectacle in general or on artistic spectacle does not change. One must also keep in mind that, in many ways, Nietzsche and Wagner have affinity to Symbolist movement of their times. Spectacle is one of several issues, which persists in Nietzsche's works from *The Birth of Tragedy* to *The Case of Wagner*; his pursuit of the problem of Wagner is itself a pursuit of the problem of spectacle. Why does then spectacle have a significant place in Nietzsche's thought? A broad response to this question cannot be presented here; tentatively said, however, it is in and through grand spectacle that highest values shape a culture, and it is in and through grand artistic spectacle that spectacular experiences and relations are reshaped in a specific cultural context.

Since Nietzsche's time, much has changed in the area of spectacular experiences. Not only there are new forms of spectacles such as film and television, but there are also qualitative changes in the way we have come to experience spectacle. Spectacle has entered into households, the making of spectacle has become more accessible than before, people have become more at ease with being a part of spectacle; in short, we have become more *spectacular*. Despite these changes, the questions Nietzsche poses to his contemporaries with his conception of spectacle and his analysis of tragic spectacle and Bayreuth are still valid and need to be pondered over in the light of contemporary problems and his influences on the artistic movements of the twentieth century.

Notes

1 With due credit to Nietzsche's insight into the tragic, the *unhistorical* origin of tragedy is already raised by Schiller in his essay, "On the Use of the Chorus in Tragedy," which is cited by him in section 7. Schiller writes: "The tragedy of the Greeks developed, as is well known, out of the chorus. But just as it extricated itself from it historically and time-wise, so it can also be said to have risen out of it poetically and spirit-wise, and that without those persistent witnesses and bearers of the action it would have turned into a wholly different sort of poetry." Preface to *The Bride of Messina*, trans. Charles E. Passage (New York: Frederick Ungar Publishing Co., 1962), 7.

2 The word "ecstasy" comes from the Greek word, *ekstasis*, which means to come out of an existing state; ex- for out of, histanai, to cause to stand; together "existenai."

3 This is related to, but also independent of, the fact that tragedy trilogies are accompanied by a satyr play, making them tetralogies, not to mention the fact that tragedy is said to have developed out of the cult of Dionysus to whom the satyr was a companion.

4 In modern secular stage, acting is, like everything else in the modern world, detached from its cosmological origins.
5 Wagner's first formulation of total artwork is to be found in his aesthetic writings of 1848–51, during his Feuerbachian phase influenced by his sensual materialism and evolves, in mid to late 1850s, into a more music-dominated version under the influence of Schopenhauer.
6 Wagner, *Actors and Singers*, "Bayreuth (The Playhouse)."
7 Regarding art and aesthetics in Nietzsche, I find Philip Pothen's position illuminating and consistent with Nietzsche's spirit. Pothen sees art in Nietzsche in the broadest possible sense, "as meaning a notion of activity, creativity, or organization in the most basic sense, or quite simply, Nietzschean will to power" *Nietzsche and the Fate of Art* (Burlington, VT: Ashgate, 2002), 195.
8 Peter Bergmann, *Nietzsche, The Last Antipolitical German* (Indianapolis: Indiana University Press, 1987), 60.
9 I do not know the exact number of festivals Nietzsche attended, but one festival he experienced in the company of Wagner was the Singers' Festival in Lucerne in August 1869.
10 Bergmann, *Nietzsche*, 63.
11 *GS*, 89, 144. This aphorism carries the sense of grand artistic spectacle presented as a spectacle. Our age is contrasted with that of the Greeks (without being named) in which the works of art served for such festive, grand spectacles.
12 Translation is mine.
13 Translations are mine.
14 This is studied closely by Roger Hollinrake in his *Nietzsche, Wagner, and the Philosophy of Pessimism* (London: George Allen & Unwin Ltd, 1982).
15 For this topic, see Kimerer L. LaMothe's book *Nietzsche's Dancers* (New York: Palgrave Macmillan, 2006). In the first half of the book LaMothe explores Nietzsche's use of dance as analogy, as she gives a substantial emphasis to *Zarathustra*.
16 *D*, 201: "the spectacle of this impression."
17 *D*, 558. "But this means to give the world not a good spectacle—it is a sin against taste" (translation is mine).
18 *GS*, Aphorism 301: "the great visual and acoustic spectacle that is life" (from Walter Kaufmann's translation which does not capture the word play of the original).
19 See Rainer Hanshe's essay on this topic, "Nietzsche's Synaesthetic Epistemology and the Restitution of the Holistic Human" in *Proceedings of The Becoming of Life, Nietzsche: An International Conference*, Santiago, Chile, 2010.

8

Not Another Image of Torment: Nietzsche, Eternal Recurrence, and Theatricality

Jeremy Killian

Introduction

Early in his career, Friedrich Nietzsche boldly proclaimed that "only as an aesthetic phenomenon is existence and the world eternally justified" (*BT*, 5). This justification of "existence and the world" occurred in Attic Greek tragedy and was to occur again in Wagnerian tragic opera. In *The Birth of Tragedy*, the reader understands that a "tragic" view of life made central on the Greek Dionysian stage is embodied in the proclamation of Silenus to Midas: "The very best thing is utterly beyond your reach not to have been born, not to *be*, to be *nothing*. However, the second-best thing for you is: to die soon" (*BT*, 3). These facts of life, according to the narrative of *The Birth of Tragedy*, were apprehended by Attic culture, and the Greeks—instead of using art as a kind of escape from this brutal reality—embraced and exulted in these truths at the tragic festival of Dionysus. As his thought progresses, Nietzsche seems somewhat dissatisfied with the project of justifying existence in aesthetic terms; beginning in *Human, All Too Human*, he turns toward another mode of justifying existence, a mode which will eventually take the form of the will to power embodied in the *Übermensch*. Nevertheless, Nietzsche still tells a "tragic" story of the world, insofar as that story describes a reality fundamentally hostile to human existence.

Nietzsche's change of focus is evident in his "Critical Backward Glance." In the preface to a second edition of *The Birth of Tragedy*, written in August 1886, Nietzsche does not retreat from his original thesis; instead, he characterizes the project using more nuanced terms, describing the Apollonian/Dionysiac "urges" in terms of physiological exuberance or neurosis (*BT*, *P*, 4). In the original work, Nietzsche had described these forces as arising on occasion of dream and intoxication. In the earlier description, these forces are characterized in terms of their phenomenological character,[1] while in "Critical Backward Glance," Apollo and Dionysus are described in a narrative informed by kinds of psychological descriptions of mental states Nietzsche has absorbed throughout his career. One of Nietzsche's complaints about *The Birth of Tragedy* is that it is "very convinced and therefore too arrogant to prove its assertions, mistrustful even of the *propriety* of proving things" (*BT, P, 3*). In other words, the later Nietzsche recognizes the grandiose nature of his earliest claims about tragedy. Though the mature Nietzsche still resists the sort of "proofs" for assertions offered by the natural sciences, this Nietzsche does seem to wish to offer more careful assertions about the nature of tragic response than the young and brash philologist offered.

Additionally, there is some reason to think that the mature Nietzsche has re-examined the significance of aesthetic tragedy as a justification of reality. In aphorism 313 of *The Gay Science*, he writes: "*No image of torment:* I want to follow Raphael's example and never paint another image of torment. There are enough sublime things; one does not have to seek out sublimity where it lives in sisterhood with cruelty; anyway, my ambition would find no satisfaction if I wanted to make myself a sublime torturer" (*GS*, 313).

Might Nietzsche be suggesting here that the tragic experience drawn from art is no longer a necessary feature of a justification of reality? In this chapter, though I will argue that aphorism 331 of *The Gay Science* illustrates that Nietzsche has significantly moved away from the claim that reality can be aesthetically justified as presented in *The Birth of Tragedy.* I will then examine Nietzsche's doctrine of eternal recurrence. Next, I will offer an interpretation of eternal return that presents a new justification of reality, one in which objective judgment can combat nihilism. I will further argue that, despite Nietzsche's move away from an aesthetic conception of reality, eternal recurrence is best understood in aesthetic terms, particularly in terms of "theatricality." Nietzsche conceives of life as a kind of play to be performed eternally, and I will demonstrate how this understanding of recurrence informs the psychological and moral question posed by the demon in *Gay Science* 341.

Perhaps this understanding informs how one might think about modernist aesthetics in particular. As inheritors of Nietzsche's bold vision of aesthetic creativity, modernists seem to take seriously the life-affirming quality of artistry, and though the interpretation of Nietzsche's thought I offer might undermine his earliest (and boldest) claims about tragedy's significance, I will show how art can provide a template for a particularly modern validation of life's meaning. Such a template draws upon theatrical conventions, and I believe it bolsters the conception of Nietzsche as an "artist of the self." More broadly, this reading of Nietzsche might inform a modernist view of the significance (or perhaps insignificance!) of artistic activity as a chief human endeavor.

A justification of existence

Throughout this chapter, I will be referring to a "justification of existence," so it may be fruitful for me to discuss what Nietzsche means by *justification.* Here, I draw upon the interpretative work of Daniel Came. Of the term "justification," Came remarks that it "has a self-conscious echo of the Western theological attempt to justify the ways of God to man; and it is clear that he conceives of his task of justification as a secularized version of this project of theodicy—that is as an attempt to vindicate the desirability of life in the face of suffering."[2] According to Came, *justification* refers to an account that provides a reason for living in the face of suffering, an account that is able to measure suffering in moral terms.

Nietzsche has certain misgivings about a rationalist justification of existence for at least two reasons: (1) rationalist attempts at justification rest on a "profound delusion which first appeared in the person of Socrates, namely the imperturbable belief that thought" can penetrate the "deepest abysses of being," and (2) on the periphery of science, Socratic logic of causality "curls up around itself at these limits and finally bites its own tail" (*BT*, 15). Because the art of rationality rests on faith in the wisdom of logical theory and denies the pre-theoretical as "un-examined," rational pictures of the world are always incomplete at best, and false at worst. Came takes the argument further; he writes, "If reason is not adequate to the nature of reality, then it cannot reliably assess reality's value, assuming that the value of reality is a function of reality as a whole."[3] Any rationalist' attempt to justify the ways of the universe to man will always fail.

If a justification of existence is beyond one's cognitive power to grasp, why does Nietzsche feel compelled to offer one at all? Came points out that on Nietzsche's view, though the world may never be *actually* justified through human cognitive faculties, this only matters "if we think we are in some sense *required* to align our evaluative stance vis-à-vis the world with the actual value of existence."[4] On this point, Nietzsche sees himself in opposition of Schopenhauerian nihilism; for Nietzsche, justification of existence does not have to be objective and mind-independent in order to be meaningful. On this view, a justification for existence is less of an epistemological claim, and more of a way in which one might affirm a positive attitude toward life and living. Came illustrates:

> I can be positively disposed towards all kinds of things (the taste of muffins, the smell of coffee, etc.) without supposing that my attitude reflects anything about the actual value of the object of my esteem. In such cases, my approbative attitude can be unpacked in terms of a relationship between X and me, and not in terms of the intrinsic properties of X or in terms of X's relationship to anybody else.[5]

Justification for existence, on Came's interpretation of Nietzsche, is entirely phenomenological and discussions of the objective facts-of-the-matter with respect to moral or epistemological evaluations of the world are irrelevant to an attitude whereby one might affirm life.

Is all talk of mind-independence in a Nietzschean justification for existence misguided? According to Came, such discussion is irrelevant to Nietzsche's project. Part of what I will show, however, in my later discussion of the doctrine of eternal return is that this doctrine does restore a sort of objectivity to an evaluation of the world, albeit a different sort than the traditional Western rationalist model produces. Came's model of justification works very well for the early Nietzsche; however, it must be nuanced if it is to describe the later Nietzsche's description of the world.

Images of torment

One might object to my characterization of Nietzsche's relationship to tragedy in his later work. Is there enough evidence to conclude that Nietzsche's views of tragedy have changed, and is *Gay Science* 313, a tiny and often ignored aphorism, marking a shift away from an aesthetic justification of existence toward some other justification? Two immediate questions seem apparent: (1) Perhaps aphorism 313 does not refer to tragedy at all, what good reason has one to assume that "images of torment" refers to the kind of tragic spectacle Nietzsche praises in *The Birth of Tragedy*? and (2) Even if aphorism 313 ought to be interpreted in the way that I suggest, is this enough to support the claim that Nietzsche has re-envisioned his project of reality justification? I will attempt to address these questions as follows:

Question (1) is a significant hurdle to overcome on linguistic grounds. First of all, aphorism 313 uses a German word choice that Nietzsche hardly employs in *The Birth of Tragedy*. In the aphorism, Nietzsche seems to be referring to a conception of Raphael commented on by Jacob Burckhardt in *The Cicerone: An Art Guide to Painting in Italy* (1878). Burckhardt was an acquaintance of Nietzsche's, and there is an interesting linguistic connection between Burckhardt's understanding of Raphael and Nietzsche's. In a footnote regarding the lack of images of Jesus in the Temple by Raphael, Burckhardt writes:

> We should learn much if we could discover what subjects Raphael would not paint, in spite of the wish of others, and for what reasons he rejected them. There are no *pictures of martyrdoms* [*Marterbild*] by him: the nearest approach to this is the Bearing of the Cross (the Spasimo di Sicilla) besides the early Crucifixion [emphasis mine][6]

The term Burckhardt employs to describe images of martyrs' fate, "Marterbild," is the same term Nietzsche uses in aphorism 313, which Nauckhoff translates as "images of torment." One might point out that in the aphorism, Nietzsche is not commenting on tragic art in a broad sense, but rather specifically on images depicting crucifixion of martyrs and torture of the saints.

In its strongest form, this objection relies on an assumption that Nietzsche writes in a Kantian tradition, using German terms latent with meaning and embedding understanding in the very word choice and syntax he employs.[7] While there are certainly instances of such writing in Nietzsche, in most cases, Nietzsche is not using the kind of precise language that Kant or Hegel might to communicate a philosophical point. Therefore, it may be a mistake to ascribe too much meaning to the presence or absence of a specific word. In *Human, All Too Human,* Nietzsche himself calls careful linguistic readings of his work into question. In "*Learning Many Languages*," he writes that "Learning many languages fills the memory with words instead of ideas" (*HH*, 267). Here Nietzsche places higher value on the ideas communicated through language than on the specificity with which one might use language to communicate those ideas. This statement ought to make one suspicious of linguistic analysis as a way of determining what ideas Nietzsche intends to connect. The use of the term *Marterbild* reflects Nietzsche's intellectual understanding of Raphael via Burckhardt, and this use should not be ascribed any additional import than Nietzsche's other discussion of torment or torture in *BT.*

Suppose, however, that one does take seriously the use of *Marterbild* as referring to sacred images of torment as a category distinct from other sorts of depictions of suffering. One might rightly point out that images of cruelty, torture, and torment are prevalent in Nietzsche's later work: Zarathustra suffers, and there are depictions of cruelty in *Genealogy of Morals* and *Ecce Homo.* It does not seem that Nietzsche wishes to jettison all cruel art. As this is the case, does this undermine my interpretation? Even if this is the case, I wish to suggest that for the mature Nietzsche, the problem is not that such depictions appear in powerful art; his contention is that those images are not the point of the experience. In *The Gay Science*, 313 Nietzsche sees his earlier reflections on sublimity of tragedy as a kind of *schadenfreude*, a delight in another's misfortune. However, in his notebooks Nietzsche contrasts this attitude as he describes such images of cruelty as pointing toward an appropriate disposition toward the realities those images depict:

> It appears that, broadly speaking, *a preference for questionable and terrifying things* is a symptom of strength ... it is the *heroic* spirits who say Yes to themselves in tragic cruelty: they are hard enough to experience such suffering as a *pleasure.* It is a sign of one's feeling of power and well-being how far one can acknowledge the terrifying and questionable character of things; and whether one needs some sort of "solution" at the end. The type of *artist's pessimism* is precisely the *opposite of that religio-moral pessimism* that suffers from the "corruption" of man and the riddle of existence—and by all means craves a solution, or at least hopes for a solution ... the *profundity of the tragic artist* lies in this, that his aesthetic instinct surveys the most remote consequences, that he does not halt short-sightedly at what is closest at hand, that he affirms the *large-scale economy* which justifies the *terrifying,* the *evil,* the *questionable*—and more than merely justifies them. (*KSA*, 12:10[168])

According to *The Gay Science* 313, tragic images offer the spectator sublimity, but the sublime is not sufficient as a justification of existence. Nietzsche's earlier attitudes toward tragedy are similar to Raphael's presumed religious attitude in that by offering a teleological account of suffering's value, he ascribed a solution to the tragic sufferer's problem. Nietzsche has come to recognize that what such images of cruelty offer is an opportunity for the strong to realize their greatness. The greatest humans can look at the "terrifying, the evil, and questionable," without retreating from those truths in favor of religious and quasi-religious conceptions of the "corruption of man" and the "riddle of existence." Tragic images offer a lens through which one might gaze upon the brute facts of the world, but those images represented in the tragic aesthetic moment are not sufficient to justify human existence.

Throughout Nietzsche's work he expresses a significant problem with image-making in general. Though images have the capacity to elicit feelings of sublimity, too often these images draw spectators away from reality instead of deeper into it. For example, in a musing produced during the writing of *Zarathustra*, Nietzsche remarks that "the image of an action is not/a concept of the same, but an ideal" (*KSA*, 10:12[26]). This remark, reminiscent of Plato's complaints about poetry in *Republic X*, illustrates that for Nietzsche, image-making and observing those representations might constitute a high human activity, but man is not justified to the world in terms of an ideal. In point of fact, even the young Nietzsche had described Apollonian images produced by the Greeks as "plastic" (*BT*, 2), which does not inspire confidence in the power of tragedy to justify human experience. Nietzsche generally describes Apollonian activity, the generation of images, as grounded in the impulse to organize a chaotic world into recognizable semblances; however such semblances do not accurately represent reality—rather, these semblances represent a noble attempt to "perfect dreams." Certainly, in union with spirit of Dionysus, Apollonian images can be deeply sublime, and Nietzsche praises man's capacity for image-making as courageous,[8] but this sublimity does not necessarily offer rich and reliable meaning for the spectator because of the problematic nature of images.

Given what I have offered above, I claim that the strongest reading of *The Gay Science*, 313 is that in this passage, Nietzsche is laying aside tragedy as the phenomenon whereby the world and existence might be "eternally justified." In the aphorism, he is suggesting that the sublime can be apprehended regardless of its "sisterhood with cruelty," and he adds that his ambition will find no greater satisfaction by inflicting images of suffering upon other people. One does not have to relish and inflict suffering on others, even in an aesthetic context, in order to actualize her will to power. What I will show later in this chapter is that tragedy, composed of its images of cruelty, suggests that it is possible for the strong to affirm existence, but tragedy alone does not justify existence in and of itself.

By establishing the likelihood that my interpretation of *The Gay Science* 313 is correct, I have not yet shown that Nietzsche has wholly revised his approach to justifying reality. It is possible that this aphorism does not reflect a larger shift in his overall philosophical project. In order to show that Nietzsche is, in fact, adjusting his approach, I must next address Question (2). In "An Attempt at Self-Criticism," Nietzsche writes: "I now regret very much that I did not yet have the courage (or immodesty) at that time to permit myself *a language of my very own* for such personal views and acts of daring," because he had been trying to communicate a philosophy which "fundamentally ran counter to both the spirit and taste of Kant and Schopenhauer," in Kantian and Schopenhauerian aesthetic terms (6). It does appear that the mature Nietzsche sees his analysis of tragedy as somewhat incomplete. In *The Birth of Tragedy*, Nietzsche ascribed the creation of tragedy to only Dionysus and Apollo, when there is a more fundamental force at work. He identifies this force in *Human, All Too Human* as Eris, bringer of war and strife, a god of ambition. He writes that the Greek poets were motivated to create tragedy "in order to conquer; their whole art cannot be thought of apart from contest." Tragedians in *The Birth of Tragedy* are moved to create out of a desire to represent the world aesthetically in a context of communal revelry, but the later Nietzsche recognizes that tragedians created primarily "to make oneself superior and to wish this superiority to be publicly acknowledged" (*HH*, 170). Nietzsche's discussion of the tragedians' motivations should not be understood as pejorative; the desire for conquest is a desire toward personal excellence, a kind of self-overcoming that is ultimately life-affirming. While *The Birth of Tragedy* narrative does not provide much of a motivational account as to the reasons tragedians created (other than some sort of primal urge), in the story of tragedy told in *Human, All Too Human* Nietzsche has created a palatable, and believable account of creative motivation toward a kind of power and world-overcoming. Tragedy is still a subject of Nietzsche's inquiry, but in his later work, it seems to be only a part of the picture, whereas in the early Nietzsche, it constituted the most significant activity humans could undertake. The scope of the task of justifying reality through all eternity has become larger, and it is an important feature of Nietzsche's later-developed doctrine of eternal recurrence.

The eternal return, self-affirmation, and objectivity

Only twenty-eight aphorisms after Nietzsche's assertion that he is putting aside *Materbild,* he offers a thought experiment that points toward a new mode justifying existence, a mode of justifying existence that appears removed from aesthetic depictions of suffering. In aphorism 341 in *The Gay Science,* entitled "The Heaviest Weight," Nietzsche prompts the reader to consider what she might do if,

> in some day or night, a demon were to steal into your loneliest loneliness and say to you: "This life as you now live it and have lived it you will have to live once again and innumerable times again; and there will be nothing new in it, but every pain and every thought and every joy and every thought and sigh and everything unspeakably small or great in your life must return to you, all in the same succession and sequence—even this spider and this moonlight between the trees, and even this moment and I myself. The eternal hourglass of existence is turned over again and again, and you with it, speck of dust! (*GS*, 341)

Nietzsche provides the reader with two options at this moment: either she throws herself down and gnashes her teeth, cursing the demon, or she proclaims that the demon is a god, imparting divine beauty upon her life. Nietzsche continues by asking the reader "how well disposed would you have to become to yourself to your life to *long for nothing more fervently* that to this ultimate confirmation and seal?" This aphorism is considered the first emergence on Nietzsche's doctrine of eternal recurrence, which he will refer to (at least in the context of his writing of *Thus Spoke Zarathustra)* as "the highest formula of affirmation that is all attainable" (*EH*, *Z*, 1). It is unclear exactly what the "doctrine" here is. What central teaching is Nietzsche communicating here? That the universe is fixed as an eternal, repetitive loop? That one ought to be ready to give an account of her life? That one ought to accept or reject her fate in a never-ending feedback loop?

One might read the aphorism as an exhortation to live one's life in such a way that when the demon appears one is able to praise the demon because she will have the opportunity to live as fully through all eternity. This reading does not account for two important features of Nietzsche's philosophical project: (1) Nietzsche is very suspicious of the notion of "freedom of the will," an important theme in *Genealogy of Morals* that is largely illusory and a product of the misguided approach of Western philosophy.[9] What we think of as free moral choices, Nietzsche describes as the products of the evolution of civilization. If freedom of the will is illusory, it is unlikely that Nietzsche is suggesting that a meeting with the demon might change the way that the reader would behave. (2) Paul Loeb has provided a strong argument that the moment in which the demon appears is the moment of death.[10] If he is correct, the demon would simply be offering the reader an evaluative opportunity, not a chance to change her ways. Both of these criticisms underscore the point that the best way to read *The Gay Science* 341 is as a psychological test. The demon's statement allows the reader to evaluate her attitude toward her life. Is she able to affirm her life, even the darkest, most tedious, treacherous parts, or does the knowledge that life will repeat eternally banish her to a kind of mental Sisyphean hell? Ultimately, this is a test that determines what kind of person the reader is by determining her psychological response to her life's infinite return.

Given Nietzsche's fatalism with respect to human action, and the fatalism seemingly inherent in the knowledge that human life recurs eternally, a common response to this thought experiment is, "So what?" Aaron Ridley puts the objection this way:

> And if the demon is coming to me *now*, he has presumably also been to me at precisely the same point of my life innumerable times before—and what difference has *that* made? If I passed the test I passed, if I failed I failed, and I'll go on doing whichever I did infinitely many more times, without it changing a thing. The thought of eternal recurrence, then, should be a matter of the deepest indifference. Why *care*?[11]

Ridley is echoing a sentiment Heidegger expresses in *Nietzsche: Volume 2, The Eternal Recurrence of the Same.* Loeb points out that this objection relies on a misguided understanding of the kind of fatalism inherent in the eternal return. It assumes, as Magnus puts it, that "given recurrence fatalism, what sense can be made of 'my' behavior?"[12] Loeb's reply is that even if my choices eternally recur, this does not alter the fact that they are still *my* choices. In the doctrine, I am determining my reaction to the demon's question, regardless of the fact that I have made the same choice throughout eternity.[13]

Loeb's response to the "why care?" question is certainly satisfactory, however I would like to argue that this discussion has missed an important feature of the doctrine of eternal recurrence. The doctrine of eternal recurrence is important because it represents a moment of Nietzsche's denial of nihilism and affirmation of an objective "justification of existence." In the moment in which the demon appears, the reader is able to make a value judgment that is more than just "epistemically neutral," as Came might put it. In this moment, even if it occurs at the end of life, the reader is able to make a judgment about all the preceding (and perhaps future) moments of her life, rendering all these moments justified and objectively meaningful.

Assuming the eternal return is an expression of something like an actual event one might experience,[14] the person having such an experience is now in a remarkable position of providing an actual, objective justification of the life they have lived. By "objective justification," I refer to a justification of reality that is mind-independent. How is this possible? In order to grasp this, it is important for the reader to appreciate fully what is occurring at the moment in which the demon appears. At this moment, the reader is standing, in a sense, outside of time. She is able to appreciate her whole life, "every pain and every thought and every joy and every thought and sigh and everything unspeakably small or great in your life … even this spider and this moonlight between the trees, and even this moment." The demon invites her to gaze at life in its entirety (this is especially forceful if the demon appears at the moment of death, as Loeb argues). In this instant, one observes that two selves exist. We can identify these selves thus: S1 is the temporal self, the reader living the day-to-day events of life, and S2 the meta-self, the reader, who by the machinations of the demon, is able to see and appreciate her life as a whole.

How does an awareness of the reader's two selves restore objectivity to a scheme of world-justification? If there is a moment when S2 is able to gaze over life and affirm or deny it by praising or cursing the demon, then all of S1's actions in her temporal existence become significantly meaningful to S2. S1's suffering, her failures, her successes, her boredom, and joys all matter when S2 chooses to relish or mourn her life. For S1, there is a mind, independent of her own, who ascribes value to every moment of her life. S2 determines if this life is worth living eternally, and this determination is made by examining every temporal event S1 experiences. Because S2 is an outside observer (in the case of the demon's appearance, outside of time and space), she renders judgment on S1s life, and S1 is justified in making non-relativistic moral claims about the events of her life based upon that judgment.

One might suspect that Euthyphro rears his head here. How does S2 render a judgment of S1's life that is not merely a subjective description? How does S2's position outside S1's temporal experience make a difference? The best way to answer this question is to again point out Nietzsche's deterministic views on the nature of the universe. One must appreciate Loeb's exegesis of *The Gay Science* 341 in which he argues that this aphorism must be interpreted in the context of the entire project of *The Gay Science* Book V. In the later aphorisms, Nietzsche contrasts two types of sufferers, "those who suffer from life's overfullness, and those who suffer from life's impoverishment."[15] These categories are not based upon some choice the sufferer has made; instead, these categories are descriptions of the kind of sufferer each person is. One cannot make up her mind to simply suffer from life's overflow any more than one who suffers from life's lack. Aphorism 341 should be read, then, as a description of the kind of person the reader is, not as a charge to the reader to become a certain kind of person with response to her suffering.

With this in mind, one might appreciate the objective nature of the justification of existence that the demon's visit provides to the reader. S2's evaluation of the suffering and joy S1 enjoys or endures is not capricious. Instead, it springs from the nature of S2. S2 is not empowered to be any other kind of person; either she suffers from a flourishing life or from an impoverished one. Therefore each event of S1's life is objectively explained by virtue of S2's evaluative position and unchangeable nature. The value of each event in S1's life is objectively good or bad, independent of S1's knowledge of it, because S2 is in a position to make such a judgment. Even if one does not appreciate my delineation of two selves in the moment of the demon's appearance, one might still accept this interpretation, because the reader's response to the question posed has been determined based upon her nature and is therefore a brute, objective fact.

The theatricality of recurrence

The argument I have presented here seems strangely theological, and certainly Nietzsche would not approve of some sort of theological turn in interpretation of the grounding doctrine of his later work. I have gone to a great length to demonstrate that Nietzsche no longer conceives the project of justification of existence in aesthetic terms, however here I should offer something of a caveat to that claim. As I conclude this chapter, I wish to offer a few remarks about how the eternal recurrence might be viewed as an aesthetic development in Nietzsche's thoughts, and I wish to suggest that this doctrine be best conceived in terms of theatricality. By conceiving eternal recurrence in terms of theater, one can appreciate how eternal return develops from his interest in tragedy, and this interpretative framework offers the reader what I believe to be a sound conceptual apparatus with which to grasp the choice the demon offers Nietzsche's reader in *The Gay Science* 341.

According to Paul Woodruff, theater, broadly conceived, is the "art of making human action worth watching for a measured time and space."[16] Nietzsche would likely have small qualms with this definition; however, if one accepts some form of this description of theater, she is able to quickly see the parallels that can be drawn between his conception of eternal recurrence and theatrical practice which consumed his early thought. In *The Gay Science* 341, for example, the demon invites the reader to stand outside her life as a spectator, and this outside position makes all the events that have occurred—no matter how small—significant, because time and space have become "measured." By *measured*, I mean that one is able to understand all the events in terms of the whole. This is impossible for S1 to see, but S2 is able to grasp it from her perspective as an outside observer.

If one bears in mind that life will be seen as a kind of measured event, one is able to appreciate the theatricality in Nietzsche's question. This understanding also provides the reader a meaningful way to understand what Nietzsche asks. One might imagine herself as an actor preparing to perform a role. In the role, all the lines have been written, and the action staged, before the actor steps onstage. One might suggest that all the preceding actions the actor will undertake throughout the measured time of the play are determined. What choice does a complicit actor have with respect to her actions once the play begins? Provided that the actor wishes to abide by the script and the demands of the director, she still has a choice to make; she can adopt her role with a kind of relish and affirmation, determining to make the most of all the terrible and wonderful things the play demands, or she can simply go through the motions, completing her previously choreographed steps with accuracy and precision, but no joy.

When Nietzsche rejects "images of torment" in *The Gay Science* 313, he is not denying that life, at its heart, and the most poignant artistic representations of it, is bound up with suffering. What Nietzsche is denying, however, is that representations of suffering demonstrate to us that the point of life is pain. The cruelty, hardship, and turmoil of living displayed in tragedy provide us the occasion to know ourselves and overcome ourselves, not merely by accepting the realities to which tragedy points, but by embracing those realities as we navigate them in our daily lives.

This is a lesson that Nietzsche has learned from classical theater, for classical theater puts such self-affirmation on display. In *The Gay Science* 80, he writes: "We have developed a need that we cannot satisfy in reality: to hear people in the most difficult situations speak well and at length; we are delighted when the tragic hero still finds words, reasons, eloquent gestures, and altogether intellectual brightness, where life approaches abysses and men in reality usually lose their heads and certainly linguistic felicity" (*GS*, 80). The delight the tragic spectator receives when watching the play is not a sadistic satisfaction derived from seeing someone suffer. Instead, the suffering of the tragic hero—the "images of torment"—offer the audience an occasion to observe a truly great human bear up beneath the brutality of existence in an eloquent and intellectually potent way. Amy Price claims that for Nietzsche, this is the power of tragedy: tragedy affirms the capacity of a powerful individual to expose herself to "ugly truths, learn from those truths, and live with them."[17] In light of this, one might appreciate that one who is able to bear the "greatest weight," and praise the "demon as a god" is reminiscent of the tragic hero, a person with greatness that is undaunted by the approach of life's abysses. So, although Nietzsche claims that "images of torment" are no longer necessary to justify existence, it seems clear that imagination, particularly the kind of imagination aroused in the tragic space, apprehends models of self-affirmation and discloses to the strong individual her capacity for greatness. Presumably, one who wishes to live well displays such an attitude toward her own actual suffering.

I believe that this sense of theatricality provides a window into the kind of choice the demon is presenting to the reader in *The Gay Science* 341. Though all events of S1's life are causally determined, Nietzsche is praising S2 who would take on the suffering, tedium, and glory of her life with a relish, determining to affirm and play the role she has been given with relish and gusto. Again, it should be clear that for Nietzsche, this is not a choice one can make against her nature; instead the person whose life, like Zarathustra's, is overflowing can be appreciated as one would appreciate the great actor taking on her role gloriously. Tragedy suggested this teaching to Nietzsche early on, but he has been able to actualize this truth through his realization of the inadequacy of the sublimity of images of torment.

Perhaps the interpretation that I have offered adds something to Nietzsche's assertion in the foreword to the 1886 edition, that what he had uncovered in his discourse on tragedy is "the problem of science" itself. In *The Birth of Tragedy,* Nietzsche realized that knowledge of suffering mediated through the Socratic method in the Western tradition assumes that suffering has a solution, and the key insight of *The Birth of Tragedy* is that such suffering is not solvable, and the appropriate response to this is revelry. Nietzsche's revised attitude toward reality still affirms that mirth is the appropriate response to suffering displayed in tragedy, but as the eternal recurrence illustrates, a truly great person is positively disposed toward the actual suffering of her own life. The later Nietzsche affirms that viewing tragedy is an occasion to display such greatness, but this greatness can be lived out in daily life, with an attitude of gaiety toward one's own torment, beyond the tragic theater (but with theatrical flourish!), regardless of whether or not one subjects herself to images of torment.

Notes

1 In *The Birth of Tragedy*, Nietzsche is heavily reliant on the aesthetics of Schiller. Nietzsche's conception of the "naïve" artist is directly drawn from Schiller's description of the naïve and sentimental poet in "On Naïve and Sentimental Poetry." For Schiller, the naïve poet communicates an "immediate" experience of the world in his lyric. By "immediate experience," he means that the poet communicates a feeling without mediating or qualifying that experience to the reader. For a valuable discussion of Schiller's influence on Nietzsche, the reader might consult Paul Bishop and R. H. Stephenson's article, "Nietzsche and Weimar Aesthetics," *German Life and Letters* 52 (October 1999): 412–31.

2 Daniel Came, "The Aesthetic Justification of Existence," in *A Companion to Nietzsche,* ed. Keith Ansell-Pearson (Boston: Blackwell Publishing 2006), 45.

3 Came, "The Aesthetic Justification of Existence," 46.

4 Ibid.

5 Ibid., 47.

6 Jacob Burckhardt, *The Cicerone: An Art Guide to Painting in Italy,* trans. A. H. Clough (London: T. Werner Laurie, 1979), 144a.

7 This should even be considered within the context of the aphorism itself, as Nietzsche does not consistently use the term "Marter" throughout. Instead of using a variation of the word to describe the "sublime torturer," he uses the more common term "Folterknecht." This lack of consistency should make the reader suspicious of some sort of embedded linguistic sub-text here.

8 "One seeks the image of the world/in philosophy, in which we are most free to be courageous; e.g. In which our most powerful/impulse feels free to its activity. So it will be with me too!" (*KSA*, 12:8[24]).

9 For the most specific development of this claim, the reader might consult *GM* II:7.

10 Paul S. Loeb, "The Moment of Tragic Death in Nietzsche's Dionysian Doctrine of Eternal Recurrence: An Exegesis of Aphorism 341 in *The Gay Science*," *International Studies in Philosophy* 30 (1998): 131–43.

11 Aaron Ridley, "Nietzsche's Greatest Weight," *Journal of Nietzsche Studies* 14 (1997): 20.
12 Bernd Magnus, "Eternal Recurrence," *Nietzsche-Studien 8*, 336.
13 Paul S. Loeb, "Identity and Eternal Recurrence," in *A Companion to Nietzsche* (Boston: Blackwell Publishing, 2006), 180.
14 The evidence does seem to support the claim that Nietzsche thought more of the doctrine than a mere thought experiment. In an 1881 note he writes, "My doctrine says; the task is to live in such a way that you must wish to live again—you will anyway! To whom striving is the highest feeling, let him strive; to whom rest gives the highest feeling, let him rest; to whom ordering, following, obedience give the highest feeling, let him obey. May he only become aware of what gives him the highest feeling and spare no means! Eternity is at stake!" (qtd. in Loeb, "Identity and Eternal Recurrence," 179).
15 Loeb, "The Moment of Tragic Death in Nietzsche's Dionysian Doctrine of Eternal Recurrence: An Exegesis of Aphorism 341 in *The Gay Science*," 138.
16 Paul Woodruff, *The Necessity of Theater: The Art of Watching and Being Watched* (Oxford: Oxford University Press, 2008), 38.
17 Amy Price, "Nietzsche and the Paradox of Tragedy," *British Journal of Aesthetics* 38, no. 4 (October 1998), 388.

9

The Birth of Dada, Out of the Spirit of Nihilism

Kaitlyn Creasy

Limiting our scope: Which Dada? Why Nietzsche?

Although Dada is often treated as a unified movement, it is no secret that the purposes, practices, and purported principles of those in the Dada movement varied widely and oftentimes contradict one another. The beginnings of European Dada can be firmly placed in 1916 Zürich's Cabaret Voltaire nightclub, founded by a group of artists and intellectuals fleeing the First World War and including Hugo Ball, Richard Huelsenbeck, and Tristan Tzara.[1] After shows at the Cabaret Voltaire waned in popularity, however, a Dada diaspora came to follow, leading some founders and practitioners to Berlin, some to Paris, and still others to New York and beyond. Along with this geographical distance came a widening of artistic and theoretical differences among the founders of Dada.[2] Furthermore, although Dada involved the production of artistic displays, performances, and poetry, there was also an intellectual component to the movement which found expression in the manifestos and personal writings of the Dadaists.

In this chapter, I investigate the influence of Friedrich Nietzsche on those who began Dada at the Cabaret Voltaire in Zürich, especially Hugo Ball, Richard Huelsenbeck, and Tristan Tzara. In his 1916 *Dada Manifesto*, Ball mentions Nietzsche by name; in a 1920 reflection on his time spent in Zürich, Huelsenbeck writes of himself and other members of the Dada movement that they "had all read Nietzsche … [and] learned with Nietzsche to appreciate the relativity of things and the value of unscrupulousness."[3] Tzara's pseudonym is famously thought to be a play on Nietzsche's Zarathustra, and a close reading of his manifestos finds mention of not only Nietzschean themes but Nietzschean terminology. Dadaist critiques of reason and rationality (along with the limiting nature of language and concepts), their rejection of a world of Being in favor of a world of fluxional chaos, and their assessments of morality as harmful to the individual all indicate the large extent to which the Dadaists were heirs to the destructive projects of Nietzsche.

While identifying points of Nietzschean influence on the intellectual direction of Dada, I aim also to interpret the writings of the Dadaists through a Nietzschean lens, reading these writings as engaged in that destruction of values which characterizes Nietzsche's leonine individual from *Thus Spoke Zarathustra*. Dadaists, like Nietzsche, were certainly interested in creating new values and perspectives, celebrating and affirming life, and engaging in a destruction which is at the same time creative; indeed, they recognized, like Nietzsche, that "a creator always annihilates" (*Z*, *On a Thousand and One Goals*, 29). In writings characterizing the purposes of Dada performance and writings, the Dadaists place a forceful emphasis on the need to destroy and negate previous values, and they insist on the erasure of all distinctions in value. The insistence that "there are no longer any privileged zones in human aspirations, the lower values are as much valued as the highest" leads them into an aporia of meaninglessness.[4] From out of this aporia, Dada artists aim to actively express and create new meanings, affirming life in their poems and works of art. It is my claim, however, that a particularly problematic interpretation of life—a teleological, vitalist interpretation—undermines the Dadaist aim to celebrate life as becoming, as variegated, contradictory, and chaotic. Instead, the notion of life promoted by Ball, Huelsenbeck, and Tzara is implicitly life-denying, and thus nihilistic.

Indeed, a closer look at Dada—paired with a look at those works of Nietzsche's which were most influential for Dada thinkers—reveals an interesting tendency, of which Richard Sheppard makes us aware: a desire to "affirm or at least countenance the coexistence in nature of chaos and elusive pattern," or "dynamism and fluid structure."[5] In short, while celebrating the flux and chaos of existence, Dada thinkers such as Ball and Tzara continue to entertain (1) a vitalist account of life and 2) an understanding of "nature itself [as] inherently structured" or "immanently patterned."[6] These metaphysical and teleological commitments, I argue, are nihilistic beliefs of the kind Nietzsche criticizes. Furthermore, Dadaist attachments to such beliefs are attachments which Nietzsche would likely regard as emerging from out of a need for "metaphysical consolation" (*BT*, *P*, 7). In this second way, Dadaists remain haunted by the specter of nihilism.

Similarities between Nietzsche and Dada

The similarities between Nietzsche's thought and Dadaist commitments, as well as the way these emerge as modernist responses to post-Enlightenment cultural values, have been examined by a number of scholars of modernist literature and art history. Richard Sheppard's *Modernism-Dada-Postmodernism* and Mark Pegrum's *Challenging Modernity: Dada between Modern and Postmodern* look at the ways Dada both emerged as a response to post-Enlightenment Europe and helped lay foundations for postmodern thinking in the West. Both of these works remark upon the influence that Nietzsche's critiques of culture had on the founders of Dada at the Cabaret Voltaire,[7] with Sheppard's seminal work remarking upon the profound influence of Nietzsche's critiques of rationality, the self as ego-substance, morality, and language and "[their] major initial impact during the 'high modernist' period."[8] In his work on Dada,

Pegrum remarks upon the significance of Nietzsche's death of God, characterizing it as a prophecy fulfilled as a new modernist era emerges alongside Dada and other cultural movements.[9] Furthermore, in his introduction to Huelsenbeck's *Memoirs of a Dada Drummer,* Hans Kleinschmidt argues that "Nietzsche had become the leader of a new and truly revolutionary movement, or more accurately, the spiritual leader of many intellectuals and artists,"[10] remarking that "to Ball and Huelsenbeck, Nietzsche's voice sounded like a cry to arms."[11] This cry functioned as a call to overthrow those values to which modern Europe adhered, to destroy or annihilate the values of modernity and create values anew.

The most focused account of Nietzsche's influence on a particular Dada thinker is Phillip Mann's "Ball and Nietzsche: Study of the Influence of Nietzsche's Philosophy on Hugo Ball."[12] In this study, Mann delves into Ball's unfinished doctoral thesis, *Nietzsche in Basel,* a project in which Ball seeks to offer a unified account of Nietzsche's life and thought, pinpointing the origins of his thought in the influence of various thinkers, such as Schopenhauer, Wagner, Lange, and Darwin.[13] Mann also investigates Ball's speeches, diary entries, and other writings in order to discover points of influence between Nietzsche and Ball. Ball's critical stances toward morality and reason; his theory of theater influenced by *The Birth of Tragedy*; his belief in those irrational, Dionysian forces underlying reality, which Mann characterizes as Nietzsche's "monistic irrationalism"; his attraction to Nietzsche's early understanding of "a kind of negation and destruction that is precisely the discharge of a powerful longing for holiness and salvation": all of these beliefs, according to Mann, are evidence of Nietzsche's deep influence.[14]

Given these analyses, the similarities to be found in Nietzsche's thought and in the manifestos, memoirs, and philosophies of those Dadaists who began at the Cabaret Voltaire should not be surprising. After all, Dada's famously iconoclastic stance—as anti establishment and "anti-art"—parallels Nietzsche's own iconoclasm.[15] Just as Nietzsche declares the death of God and the necessary destruction of post-Enlightenment values, the Dadaists' belief that "art is dead" leads to their attempted destruction of those artistic conventions which preceded them.[16] As announced by Hugnet:

> Dada was intent on being subversive, and in 1916 the subversive was the modern: cubism, futurism, hot jazz, everything that exasperated society. But Dada is not modern and even less modernistic; Dada is always a thing of the present.[17]

While the movement was clearly influenced by cubism (with some Dadaists even personally acquainted with Braque and Picasso) and borrowed heavily from practices of the Italian futurist movement, Dada still maintains a contrarian position toward preceding artistic movements.[18] Cubism is proclaimed to be too realistic,[19] and though futurism is acknowledged as influential, Huelsenbeck maintains that Dada is still "opposed to it."[20] Especially suspicious of representational art, Dada artists "maintained that art must be neither realistic nor idealistic" and aimed to create works of abstract act which expressed the chaotic and fluxional nature of life.[21] Expressionism, in particular, is decried as moralistic, passive, and life-denying.[22]

In order to "[battle] against all semblance of any establish art and all the formal rules it implied," the Dadaists in Zürich created performances, poems, and other works which expressed the chaotic complexity of a constantly changing world.[23] In performances at the Cabaret Voltaire, poems—often composed of nonsensical words and phrases—would be recited on stage simultaneously. Dada artists employed "tin cans and keys" in their performances to create a cacophony of sounds "until the enraged audience protested."[24] To emphasize the random, illogical nature of life, Dadaists created poems by assembling collages of random words. Tzara's description of how to "make a dadaist poem" illuminates this technique:

> Take a newspaper.
> Take a pair of scissors.
> Choose an article as long as you are planning to make your poem.
> Cut out the article.
> Then cut out each of the words that make up this article and put them in a bag.
> Shake it gently.
> Then take out the scraps one after the other in the order in which they left the bag.
> Copy conscientiously.
> The poem will be like you.[25]

Such works functioned as expressions of Dada's destructive stance toward mainstream art and modernity in general.

While it might not be surprising, then, to see Nietzsche's critical attitude reflected in an art movement which hoped to "kill art" (led by those who aimed at the "destruction of their own idols),"[26] the *extent* to which Nietzsche's demolition of post-Enlightenment values shaped the Dada movement certainly is. Indeed, in both early manifestos and later writings of those thinkers who founded Dada in Zürich, one finds not only broad similarities—a critique of rationality, for example—but near-identical critical remarks, even including Nietzschean turns of phrase. In the following section, I attend to three deep points of similarity between Nietzsche's philosophy and Dada thought in order to demonstrate the incredible influence which Nietzsche had on these thinkers (even when, as I argue, they depart from the spirit of his work).

Critiques of rationality, objectivity, and absolute knowledge

Perhaps the most obvious continuity between Nietzsche and the Dadaists is an exceedingly critical attitude toward rationality, objective truth, and disinterested knowledge in post-Enlightenment Europe. According to Nietzsche, post-Enlightenment Europe comes to a general consensus in the belief that reality is systematic and that man, in virtue of his reason, has access to objective truths (or "absolute knowledge") about reality. Of course, Nietzsche problematizes—and ultimately rejects—this view.

In *The Birth of Tragedy*, we find one of Nietzsche's most memorable early descriptions of Western culture's increasing faith in rationality and scientific inquiry in his account of the theoretical man from *The Birth of Tragedy.* According to Nietzsche, modern culture is hyperrational, and the "highest ideal" of "our whole modern world" is that of the theoretical man, who makes the acquisition of scientific knowledge his utmost priority (*BT*, 18). This man wishes to "penetrate to the ground of things and to separate true knowledge from illusion and error" and his faith in the "highest powers of [human] understanding" ensure Western culture that such a pursuit is possible (*BT*, 15). Western culture, under the ideal of the theoretical man, makes "existence appear comprehensible and thus justified" and "ascribes to [rational] knowledge and insight the power of a panacea" (*BT*, 15). In short, modern mankind attempts to fit the world into its categories of rational concepts and judgments by insisting on the existence of objective truth and then employing empirical means in order to discover such objective truth in the world.

While this critical perspective appears in Nietzsche's earliest thought, it is truly ubiquitous throughout his work. In *The Gay Science,* Nietzsche remarks upon the modern European belief that "nothing is more necessary than truth; and in relation to it, everything else has only secondary value" (*GS*, 344). The theoretical man in the post-Enlightenment West assumes that the world is both comprehensible and identically intelligible to all seekers of objective truth. This man also understands human reason as the tool by which one comes to know one's world, and believes it possible to apprehend the world disinterestedly, or objectively. In modernity, Nietzsche remarks, the "objective spirit" is praised (*BGE*, 204). Nietzsche continually problematizes this modern notion of objectivity, disputing the possibility of objective knowledge as "contemplation without interest" involving a "pure ... knowing subject" (*GM*, *What Is the Meaning of Ascetic Ideals?*, 12).[27] In *Twilight of the Idols,* Nietzsche claims that it is not only impossible for one's rational mind to take an objective, disinterested view of the world; in fact, it is partly in virtue of their rationality that human beings *misunderstand* their world. In short, by forcing the world into preexisting, rational frameworks and categories, we falsify the world (*TI, 'Reason' in Philosophy, 2, 5*).

Indeed, one of the Nietzsche's most critical condemnations of the modern rationalist worldview appears in "'Reason' in Philosophy" from *Twilight of the Idols.* Here, Nietzsche notes that when one "[invents] fables about a world 'other' than this one," one "[avenges oneself] against life with a phantasmagoria of 'another,' a 'better' life" (*TI, 'Reason' in Philosophy*, 6). In the modern scientific assumptions of (1) completely objective knowledge, (2) the effectiveness of human reason for coming to know objective truths about the universe, and (3) the comprehensibility of reality, Nietzsche locates a lingering wish and hope for a "true" world apart from the world we occupy (*GS*, 344). Given the impossibility of this way of knowing objective knowledge, the ineffectiveness of human reason, and the incomprehensibility of the universe, both modern rational ("scientific") inquiry and the world it seeks are nihilistic. An objective and objectively ascertainable world is simply a post-Enlightenment version of the "true world"—a world that does not exist—and belief in this world still requires the same faith characteristic of problematic religious traditions (*GS*, 373). Thus, insofar as science insists on the existence of a "true world" known only through scientific inquiry, the scientist is a nihilist who denies both the perspectival nature of knowledge and the world of becoming in all of its variety and richness. In short, the scientist degrades existence and "divest[s] existence of its rich ambiguity [*seines vieldeutigen Charakters*]" (*GS*, 373). The subtle deception of modern scientific nihilism makes this version of nihilism all the more dangerous, insofar as it is all the more difficult to recognize for what it is.

The Dadaists understand themselves as situated in the same hyperrational culture critiqued by Nietzsche, and they are equally critical of this cultural tendency. In 1914 reflections from *Die Flucht aus der Zeit* [*Flight Out of Time*], Hugo Ball identifies Immanuel Kant as the "archenemy" who "turned all objects of the visible world over to the understanding and to its control … reason must be accepted a priori."[28] According to Ball, Kant insists that the world is intelligible in virtue of human rationality; the authority of reason on this view is indisputable. Ball echoes Nietzsche's critique in his own, remarking upon the way in which reason "controls" those objects it attempts to apprehend; reason *limits* the world in a way that does not allow for the objects in the world to appear as they might be "in themselves." In other words, for Ball as for Nietzsche, reason is profoundly falsifying. In this same entry, in fact, Ball remarks that Nietzsche was "the first one to do away with all reason."[29]

In "Psychoanalytical Notes on Modern Art," Huelsenbeck identifies the aim of modern art as the "search for a reality outside the rational ego, something independent of any rational system, whether religious or philosophical"[30] only a few paragraphs after setting up Nietzsche's declaration of the death of God as a condition of such a search. Earlier, in *Memoirs of a Dada Drummer,* Huelsenbeck explicitly critiques objectivity and, in the context of endorsing cubist critiques of objectivity, endorses a technique of coming to know the world which "[views] an object not just from one side … while superimposing, accumulating, and thereby re-experiencing the various sides."[31] Given Huelsenbeck's deep familiarity with Nietzsche's work, one can imagine the similarity between this description and Nietzsche's perspectivism is not merely coincidental.

No Dada thinker, however, more avowedly attacks rationality than Tzara. This critique can be traced through the whole of his famous 1918 manifesto, beginning with his claim that Dada is "for continuous contradiction … recognize[s] no theory… [and] against any notion of life" which is "classified, cut into sections, channelized."[32] To be for contradiction and against theory is to disown faith in rational, logical modes of thought; yet it is Tzara's critique of what one might call a Kantian notion of life which demonstrates just how strongly Tzara was influenced by Enlightenment and post-Enlightenment thought. This first critical jab at a Kantian picture of knowledge continues through the next pages, with Tzara claiming to "[wave] the baton as the categories dance"[33] and "destroy the drawers of the brain."[34] These two reflections are undoubtedly further rebukes to Kant's notion of the categories of knowledge and his supreme faith in reason. Tzara is critical also of dishonest philosophical practices—"the system of quickly looking at the other side of a thing in order to impose your opinion indirectly is called dialectics"[35]—and interested in how we misunderstand the ways in which we come to know the world when we identify our rational facilities as our sole means of access to the "true" world, the world as it really is. Although Tzara remarks that "some people think that they can explain rationally, by thought, what they think," he insists that "there is no ultimate truth," since experience is "a product of chance and individual faculties."[36] He remarks upon his "detest [of] greasy objectivity and harmony, the science that finds everything in order." Late in the manifesto, he calls for the "abolition of logic,"[37] remarking that it is "always wrong" and "its chains kill."[38] In opposition to accounts of knowledge which prioritize rational, logical means of knowing, Tzara insists that such accounts give us an inaccurate account of our means of access to the world, by claiming that we can discern the world disinterestedly and objectively, all with the same Kantian categories, instead of recognizing that chance experience offers everyone a multitude of different perspectives on the chaotic world to which we belong. To deny the Nietzschean influence—and, notably, the influence of perspectivism—would be foolhardy.

Metaphysical critiques and the world of becoming

In this section, I offer an account of both Nietzsche's doctrine of becoming and the connection between modern man's attachment to being as substance and permanence. Thus, we may see its influence on Dada thinkers. On the way to understanding what kind of metaphysical picture Nietzsche offers, however, it is helpful to first see the kinds of metaphysics he rejects. In order to aid my case for the kind of metaphysics which Nietzsche sketches in his work, I will focus especially on his critique of (1) Being and a metaphysics of substance and (2) atomistic-mechanistic interpretations of the world. By detailing Nietzsche's critiques of these metaphysical interpretations, we will also be able to draw a point of influence between Nietzsche and Ball, through Ball's account of Lange's influence on Nietzsche in his unfinished doctoral dissertation. We will also see that Huelsenbeck and Tzara were inspired if not by Nietzsche's critique of atomism and substance metaphysics then by the positive account of reality which Nietzsche offers after rejecting what he understands to be false ones.

Nietzsche's crusade against those metaphysical interpretations that include notions of atomism and substance turns up very early in his writings, as early at least as 1873, and continues throughout both his body of work and in his unpublished notes. Here, I will establish this lifelong tendency by tracing it genealogically through the development of Nietzsche's thought. In *Philosophy in the Tragic Age of the Greeks*, Nietzsche supports Heraclitus's denial of the stability and permanence of existence, or the belief that the world "nowhere shows a tarrying, an indestructibility, a bulwark in the stream" (*PTAG*, 51). He also praises Heraclitus's genius for recognizing that any supposed stability ascribed to reality by human beings is a result or consequence of the falsifying function of human experience and language (*PTAG*, 51–52).

In *Human, All Too Human,* this tendency continues. Early in the first book, Nietzsche argues that a genealogical account of the idea of substance and being ("that all the rest of the world is one thing and motionless") reveals that "belief in unconditioned substances and in like things [*gleiche Dinge*] is … a primordial and equally ancient error of everything organic" (*HH,* 18). In short, and as Nietzsche makes clear at the end of this section, human belief in substance is a fundamental error of organic life, and "insofar as all metaphysic has concerned itself particularly with substance and with freedom of the will, it should be designated as the science that deals with the fundamental errors of mankind as if they were fundamental truths" (*HH*, 18). Metaphysics for Nietzsche, then, will not be a metaphysics of substance. Nietzsche argues that our understanding of a "very object by itself, as in essence a thing unto itself, therefore as self-existing and unchanging, in short, as a substance" reveals certain necessary features of human cognition, *not* certain features about the world (*HH*, 18).[39] In other words, the fixing of flux into stable substances is an activity of the mind which makes the world comprehensible to human beings. There is, in actuality, no such thing as a metaphysical substance (*GS*, 111).

In "'Reason' in Philosophy" from *Twilight of the Idols,* Nietzsche rejects notions of permanence, being, and substance more straightforwardly perhaps than anywhere else in the corpus: "Precisely insofar as the prejudice of reason forces us to posit unity, identity, permanence, substance, cause, thinghood, being, we see ourselves somehow caught in error, compelled into error (*TI*, *'Reason' in Philosophy*, 5). He begins this critique of substance metaphysics again with reference to Heraclitus, this time explaining in more detail that human attempts to interpret the testimony of the senses with the use of reason falsifies reality (*TI*, *'Reason' in Philosophy*, 3). Later in this section, Nietzsche goes on to explain *how* rational beings get it wrong: through the translation of the world into language, by explaining the world in the same terms we employ to explain our own first-personal experience. As Nietzsche notes, "Everywhere [reason] sees a doer and doing; it believes in will as the cause; it believes in the ego, in the ego as being, in the ego as substance, and it projects this faith in the ego-substance upon all things—only thereby does it first create the concept of 'thing'" (*TI*, *'Reason' in Philosophy*, 5). A metaphysical interpretation of the world as containing unified, discrete substances is merely a result of human beings' first-personal experience of themselves as unified egos and their mistranslation of this experience into reality. As we see also in his 1887 notes, this role for language and first-personal experience in metaphysical interpretations (which understand the world as composed of unified substances) is why Nietzsche identifies the Cartesian ego as the source of this mistaken metaphysics of substance. We see Nietzsche emphasizes this role of first-personal experience as unified through an ego-substance also in his assertion that "the concept of substance is a consequence of the concept of the subject: not the reverse! If we relinquish the soul, 'the subject,' the precondition for 'substance' in general disappears" (*KSA*, 12:10[19]).[40] According to Nietzsche, without the unity of the subject first proposed by Descartes and his *cogito,* humanity would not have internalized the concept of metaphysical substance and interpreted the world primarily by employing this concept.

Along with a metaphysics of substance (or "being"), Nietzsche also rejects atomistic interpretations of the world, according to which the world is composed of countless discrete pieces of matter called "atoms." In an excerpt from his notes entitled "*Against* the physical *atom,*" Nietzsche remarks:

> to comprehend the world, we have to be able to calculate it; to be able to calculate it, we have to have constant causes; because we find no such constant causes in actuality, we invent them for ourselves—the atoms. This is the origin of atomism.

> The calculability of the world, the expressibility of all events in formulas—is this really "comprehension?" (*KSA*, 12:7[56])

The last question, of course, is rhetorical. Just as with substance, the atomistic conception of reality is an invention and projection of human beings. What Nietzsche calls elsewhere the "atomistic hypothesis [*der atomistischen Hypothese*]" is a hypothesis "with which we humanize the world … and make the world accessible at the same time to our eye and our calculation" (*KSA*, 11:25[371]). In other words, the formation of an atomistic worldview for Nietzsche is merely a translation of reality into discrete substances—atoms—which allow us to calculate and measure our world. Yet as Nietzsche remarks in his 1887/88 notes, "There are no durable ultimate units, no atoms, no monads: here, too, 'beings' are only introduced by us (from perspective grounds of practicality and utility)" (*KSA*, 13:11[73]). This projection of an atomistic interpretation onto the world, formulated as a useful way for humans to understand the world around them, falsifies the world.[41]

Nietzsche's conclusions about metaphysics are heavily influenced by the work of Albert Lange.[42] In "Kant, Lange, Nietzsche: Critique of Knowledge," George Stack demonstrates how the rejection of substance in Nietzsche was influenced by his reading of Lange's 1866 *The History of Materialism and Criticism of its Present Meaning*.[43] Lange rejects "absolute unities"[44] and claims that the "process of expressing judgments about what we perceive is a simplification and metaphorical transformation of our immediate experience of unique particulars."[45] Both Nietzsche's rejection of a world of Being and his insistence on the falsifying nature of language can be attributed, to some extent, to Lange's influence, and this influence is especially important as we come to compare a Dadaist critique of metaphysics to Nietzsche's own.[46] Indeed, in his unfinished doctoral dissertation, Ball demonstrates an awareness of the anti-metaphysical tradition from out of which Nietzsche's thought develops in his insistence that Lange's influence on Nietzsche was equal to that of Wagner.[47] The influence of Lange shows up in Nietzsche's critique of the anthropomorphizing tendency of modernity, which shows up as "fanaticism for a teleology" or purpose and denies the true nature of the world as chaotic flux. Furthermore, it is from out of the joint influence of Lange and Darwin on Nietzsche that Ball finds Nietzsche's reason for "[seeking] to reverse this whole 'Being' philosophy, which wants to fix the world with a rational principle and concept, with the opposing 'Becoming' philosophy of Heraclitus."[48] Thus, Ball—as a founder of Dada and chief influence on Richard Huelsenbeck—was keenly aware of this key aspect of Nietzsche's anti-metaphysical thought.[49] In his attempts to situate it in Nietzsche's predecessors, Ball situates the foundations of anti-metaphysical thought in the cultural and philosophical circumstances of modernity.[50] Although we see no evidence that Huelsenbeck or Tzara were aware of the extent of Lange's influence on Nietzsche, it is clear that they, like Ball, were strongly influenced by Nietzsche's account of reality as chaotic flux, which is falsified when it is "made in the image of humanity and ordered according to humanly intelligible and acceptable notions of order."[51]

Together with his negative metaphysical remarks, Nietzsche also insists that the world is "not being, but becoming." In *Twilight of the Idols*, Nietzsche notes that "all [philosophers] believe, desperately even, in what *is*" (*TI*, *'Reason' in Philosophy*, 1). By Nietzsche's lights, however, this stubborn belief in being and substance is a mere illusion and mistake of interpretation: it is only our rational interpretation and simplification of empirical experience which gives the appearance of permanence, stability, and *being*. Indeed, "What we *make* of [the senses'] testimony is what first introduces the lie … of unity, of thinghood, of substance, of duration. … 'Reason' is what causes us to falsify the testimony of the senses. Insofar as the senses display becoming, passing away, and change, they do not lie" (*TI*, *'Reason' in Philosophy*, 2). Differently put, "Precisely insofar as the prejudice of reason forces us to posit unity, identity, permanence, substance, cause, thinghood, being, we see ourselves … compelled into error" (*TI*, *'Reason' in Philosophy*, 5). Nietzsche makes a similar point in his 1887 notes, where he remarks that "in a world of becoming, 'reality' is always only a simplification for practical ends, or a deception through the coarseness of organs, or a variation in the tempo of becoming" (*KSA*, 12:9[62]). He then goes on to tie this simplification and deception with nihilism and world-denial: "Logical world-denial and nihilation follow from the fact that we have to oppose non-being with being and that the concept 'becoming' is denied" (Ibid). Over time, humanity has come to value the stability of being over becoming; becoming, as being's opposite, is implicitly devalued on this picture. On Nietzsche's view, however, the world is a world of becoming; the denial of becoming, then, is a denial and denigration of this world and this-worldly existence.

The denial of the world of becoming and change—which, as Nietzsche makes clear, is the only world there is—in favor of some higher world of being and stability results in a nihilistic conception of the world.[52] Humanity's yearning for permanence and aversion to flux is life-denying and nihilistic because it causes human beings to feel as though the world as it actually is—in flux—is of little to no value in comparison with the unchanging world that philosophers and religious figures supposed it to be. In reality, the world is constantly in flux; it is composed only of "dynamic quanta, in a relation of tension to all other dynamic quanta [and] their essence lies in their relation to all other quanta" (*KSA*, 13:14[79]). If we deny and condemn this flux, we deny and condemn this world and this life. A non-nihilistic response instead would affirm this world and this life as it is: as a world of ceaseless becoming.

A celebration of the world as chaos, as becoming, and as forever in flux appears in nearly every Dada manifesto and writing. Perhaps nowhere does this theme appear as obviously and with as much joy as in Tzara's proclamations in his 1918 Dada Manifesto, in which he remarks that "novelty resembles life,"[53] celebrates "the purity of a cosmic, ordered *chaos*, eternal in the globule of a second without duration," and points out his "detest [of] greasy objectivity and harmony, the science that finds everything in order."[54] Indeed, not only is man's world chaotic, but so is man: how, Tzara asks, "can one expect to put order into that chaos that constitutes that infinite and shapeless variation: man."[55] In his 1920 essay "A History of Dada," Huelsenbeck's discussion of the importance of simultaneity to Dada performances and principles remarks that "simultaneity is against what has become, and for what is becoming";[56] he speaks of Dada devotion to the "movement of life" which includes a Dadaist's understanding that "he is not the same man today as tomorrow, the day after tomorrow he will perhaps be 'nothing at all,' and then he may become everything."[57] This interpretation of life as fluxional, always becoming, and of man as a microcosm of this cosmic flux, is similar to Tzara's remark that the chaos of the world is reflected in the chaos of the human being. Huelsenbeck expands on the importance of impermanence and flux for Dadaists in a 1960 essay included in Huelsenbeck's *Memoirs of a Dada Drummer*:

> In the beginning, dada stressed the fight against rational and conventional values and emphasized the uncertainty of man's existence. … But as dada went on, it directed itself against all concepts of permanence. The dadaists were interested in two main facts: shock and movement. They felt that man was in the hands of irrational creative forces. He was hopelessly wedged in between an involuntary birth and an involuntary death. … Life, as the original dada held and as the dada revival of the immediate present emphasizes, cannot be lived on the expectation of the permanent. The dadaist sides with Heraclitus against Parmenides. He began doing so long before Zen became fashionable; he sees life as change and motion. … The dadaists, more than any other people of their day, felt that life lives us as we live life. In their philosophy, life was always in flux and growing.[58]

Sheppard's work on Dada in *Modernism-Dada-Postmodernism* also illuminates the Dadaist conviction that we are situated in a world of flux and chaos. He notes how Ball describes reality as a "disorderly, conflicting totality of mainly illogical actions which stand in a strikingly antithetical relationship with one another" and a "vast series of phenomena that are in perpetual motion and conflict with one another."[59] This picture of reality, as inherently illogical, chaotic, contradictory, and fluxional, Sheppard notes, "[replaces] an anthropomorphic world of organized space in which stable, metaphysically guaranteed objects moved along predictable trajectories."[60] The parallels between this Dadaist picture of reality and Nietzsche's rejection of both the world of stable being and a world which operates according to atomistic principles is striking. It is undeniable that Nietzsche's metaphysical critiques and positive account of reality was of paramount influence in Dada thought.

The destruction and creation of values in Nietzsche and Dada

In *Modernism, Dada, Postmodernism,* Sheppard describes Dada as an "irrationalist [movement] intent on a transvaluation of all values."[61] The fact that Dadaists shared Nietzsche's critical perspective on morality as well as his aim to create new values which might overcome the old has been addressed by others. My aim here will be simply to look at specific and clear similarities between Dada and Nietzsche, so that the extent of the influence is made exceedingly clear.

From the ironic beginning of his 1918 *Dada Manifesto*—in which he claims to be "in principle … against manifestos and … also against principles"—to the end, Tzara identifies Dada as a movement which attacks conventional morality and values.[62] Tzara describes traditional morality as characterized by a hidden, complex manipulation and repression of man's instincts;[63] he claims that "morality creates atrophy, just like every plague produced by intelligence" and relates "the control of morality and logic" to an apathy and passionlessness which facilitates a slavish mindset.[64] Tzara is explicitly and pointedly critical of charity and pity, which morality has "called good," although "there is nothing good about them";[65] incredibly, Tzara even remarks that such sentiments "[destroy] health." As an alternative to damaging and repressive conventional morality which harms the individual, he suggests "dada spontaneity": "the kind of life in which everyone retains his own conditions, though respecting their individualisms, except when the need arises to defend oneself."[66]

This critique of morality is undoubtedly influenced by Nietzsche's critical engagement with traditional, Judeo-Christian values. His account of slave morality from *On the Genealogy of Morality* interprets conventional morality as emerging from out of a repression of one's instincts, and especially a repression of one's desire for power. According to this account, moral principles and judgments first functioned as a covert means for weak individuals to exert their inferior type of strength over individuals who were more powerful by calling characteristics of noble, strong individuals "bad" and characteristics of weak, suffering individuals "good." (This is the origin of what Nietzsche calls "slave morality.") In *Beyond Good and Evil,* Nietzsche describes the "Christian European" as "the almost willful degeneration and atrophy of humanity" and "a stunted, almost ridiculous type, a herd animal, something well-meaning, sickly, and mediocre" (*BGE*, 62).

Tzara's condemnations of pity and charity as destructive and harmful sentiments are preceded by Nietzsche's extensive critiques of both of these. In *Beyond Good and Evil,* Nietzsche alleges that the actions of "charitable" individuals mask hidden motivations to exert their power over others in some way: "They treat the needy like their own property, since they are helpful and charitable out of a desire for property" (*BGE*, 194). In *Dawn,* Nietzsche calls pity "a weakness, like every loss of oneself through a damaging [*schädigenden*] affect" (*D*, 134). In *Ecce Homo*, we see why pity, as a "loss of oneself," is damaging: it is a "particular case of being unable to withstand stimuli" (*EH*, *Why I Am So Wise*, 4). Pity damages the "compassionate" individual by lessening her vitality and turning her away from her ends. This same picture of pity appears in *The Antichrist,* where Nietzsche remarks that "pity stands in opposition to … emotions which augment the energy of the feeling of life [*die Energie des Lebensgefühls erhöhn*]: it has a depressive effect. One loses force [*verliert Kraft*] when one pities" (*A*, 7). Finally, in the *Twilight of the Idols,* Nietzsche connects his critique of charity and pity with slave morality and weakness more generally (*TI*, *Skirmishes of an Untimely Man*, 37). Here, Nietzsche describes the "virtues" of pity, selflessness, and love of one's neighbor as characteristics of a weak age and weak individuals. In place of such virtues, Nietzsche recommends—in innumerable places throughout his corpus—that one identify and hold those values which best facilitate one's own strength and development. As he remarks upon in *The Gay Science,* "Your virtue is the health of your soul … there is no health as such, and all attempts to define such a thing have failed miserably. Deciding what is health even for your body depends on your goal, your horizon, your powers, your impulses, your mistakes and above all on the ideals and phantasms of your soul" (*GS*, 120). In his call for a "revaluation of values" from *Beyond Good and Evil,* Nietzsche remarks upon a need for "spirits strong and original enough to provide the stimuli for opposite valuations and to revalue and invert 'eternal values'" (*BGE*, 203). The similarities between Nietzsche's critical revaluation of values and Dada's rejection of conventional morality are innumerable.

This Nietzschean influence also appears in the works of Ball and Huelsenbeck. In a diary entry from 1915, Ball insists that "the usual morality is a self-deception," remarking in the same entry upon the possibility of a restoration of morality which requires a preliminary "restoration of nature."[67] A year later, he remarks that "what we call Dada is a farce of nothingness in which all higher questions are involved; a gladiator's gesture, a play with shabby leftovers, *the death warrant of posturing morality*."[68] These critical remarks about conventional morality also appear in *Dada Fragments* from 1916, in which Ball calls for "symmetries and rhythms instead of principles" and characterizes Dada as a movement which "aims at the destruction of all generous impulses."[69] Ball's influence on Huelsenbeck in these matters is clear. In his essay "A History of Dada," Huelsenbeck claims that there is "no longer a 'thou shalt,'" that "the good is no 'better' than the bad" since there is "only a simultaneity, in values as in everything else."[70] In "Dada," written much later, Huelsenbeck describes the "new man" for which he called in previous manifestos as "a man of transcendence, by whom good and evil are no longer viewed from different standpoints," for whom "moral and immoral are the relativized components of a total personality."[71] And, as Kleinschmidt quotes in his introduction to *Memoirs of a Dada Drummer,* Huelsenbeck insists that a "dadaist knows that moral struggle is individual, man must arrive at his own decisions, his own values."[72] Although the continuity between Nietzsche's revaluation of value and Dada's revaluation of values is perhaps the most well-known point of influence, the extent of this influence—and the utter similarity of those critiques—is staggering.

Nietzsche, Dada, and nihilism

The influence of Nietzsche's work and thought on both the Dada movement generally and individual thinkers in Dada—especially Ball, Huelsenbeck, and Tzara—is extensive and undeniable. After situating these thinkers as heirs to the legacy of Nietzschean nihilism, I will step away from examining similarities between Nietzschean and Dadaist thought, and instead interpret Dada aims and principles through a Nietzschean lens. As mentioned above, Dada thinkers hoped to engage both in the destruction of modern values and the creation of new values which might enable individuals to celebrate life as fluxional chaos. The destruction of previous values leads Dada into an aporia of meaninglessness, from out of which they hope to create anew. The creation of new works, perspectives, and values in the world involves creating from out of the wellspring of life as fluxional chaos. Creative practices such as simultaneity and brutism aim to express and celebrate life *as it really is:* life as a "form-giving force" behind everyday events, a "dark vital force." In what follows, I problematize this vitalist, teleological picture of life as life-denying and nihilistic from a Nietzschean perspective. To conclude, I show how the undue attention which Dada thinkers paid to *The Birth of Tragedy*—a work in which Nietzsche puts forth an "artist's metaphysics" which is, by his own lights, dangerously life-denying—might have encouraged this conception of life.

"*Nihilismus*" in Nietzsche has many senses. Here, we will examine nihilism as "European nihilism [*Der europäische Nihilismus*]": the historical denigration of earthly or this-worldly existence by European culture, either explicitly stated or implicitly represented by particular belief systems (*KSA*, 12:2[131]). European nihilism, as not only an historical phenomenon but a *cognitive* one, involves two moments: (1) humanity's development of the belief in a meaningful world which involves *nihilistic* conceptions of truth, purpose, and value and (2) the collapse of these conceptions and, therefore, humanity's belief in a world absent of meaning.

For Nietzsche, European nihilism results from a devaluation of the highest values. When the Christian-moral longing for other possible worlds and for transcendental values which justify this-worldly human existence is undermined, European humanity is thrown into a crisis of meaning. Nietzsche describes nihilism in his notes as the conviction that our highest values cannot be defended or justified, "plus the realization that we lack the least right to posit a beyond or in-itself of things that might be divine" (*KSA*, 12:10[192]). This latter realization leads us to reject the Christian-moral hypothesis [*christliche Moral-Hypothese*] which "granted man an absolute value, as opposed to his smallness and accidental occurrence in the flux of becoming and passing away," "posited that man had knowledge of absolute values," and prevented man from "taking sides against life [and] despairing of knowledge" (*KSA*, 12:5[71]).

As European nihilism, nihilism is (1) a crisis of knowledge and our expectations for absolute, comprehensive, and objective knowledge of our world, (2) a crisis of purpose, and (3) a crisis of value. In large part, such nihilism results when human beings realize the contingency of their most fundamental beliefs about the world: a belief in truth and drive toward knowledge, a belief in some ultimate *telos* or purpose of the universe, and the adoption of traditional moral systems in the West. Humanity—once so sure of a necessary, transcendental source of meaning, value, and truth and justification for existence—despairs of this contingency. After all, European culture at the time of Nietzsche located the meaning of life in humanity's pursuits of truth, progress, and morally correct action. Once the contingency of these various values is revealed, humanity's self-understanding is seriously compromised and the world appears meaningless. Although mankind despairs in the moment of European nihilism, this moment of nihilism is, as Nietzsche remarks in notes from 1887, "ambiguous" (*KSA*, 12:9[35]). Indeed, for the creation of new values, nihilism (as "active nihilism") is a necessary transitional stage, represented by the leonine individual from *Thus Spoke Zarathustra*. One must learn to become childlike and to create new values from out of old, for to remain in an aporia of meaningless—or to seek out and adhere to nihilistic conceptions of one's world—would be to fall victim to life-denial.

The destruction and creation of values in Dada

Ball, Huelsenbeck, and Tzara occupied the same intellectual landscape as Nietzsche. By reading Nietzsche they were compelled to not only destroy old values but become active individuals, celebrate life, and create values anew. Indeed, employing Nietzschean terminology, Sheppard describes Dada as an "irrationalist [movement] intent on a transvaluation of all values."[73] In the early writings, Dada thinkers emphasize the aporia of meaninglessness in which they find themselves. Oftentimes, they embrace this meaninglessness.

In an article from 1915, Hugo Ball describes how a young European intellectual "from a bourgeois background can nowadays find no ground under his feet … he feels himself to be without protection."[74] In a diary entry from 1915, Ball notes that "what is commonly called reality is, to be exact, a puffed-up nothing" and describes a feeling of "giddy horror at the nothingness of what former generations called humanity";[75] later in this diary, Ball straightforwardly acknowledges a contemporary uncertainty about the meaning of all existence.[76] Ball's reflections on the first-personal experience of inhabiting an aporia of meaningless is followed by his representation of the meaninglessness his age as a whole experiences. In the first section of his 1917 Kandinsky lecture, Ball depicts meaninglessness as modern Europe's Nietzschean inheritance:

> God is dead. A world disintegrated. I am dynamite. … There are no more perspectives in the moral world. Up is down, down is up. The transvaluation of values came to pass. Christianity was struck down. The principles of logic, of centrality, unity, and reason were unmasked. … The meaning of the world disappeared. The purpose of the world—its reference to a supreme being who keeps the world together—disappeared. Chaos erupted. Tumult erupted. Man lost his divine countenance, became matter, chance.[77]

Ball's understanding of the age in which he lived as meaningless is echoed in a long passage from Huelsenbeck's "A History of Dada":

> Dada turns decisively away from the speculative, in a sense loses its metaphysics … . The Dadaist, as the psychological man, has brought back his gaze from the distance and considers it important to have shoes that fit and a suit without holes in it. The Dadaist is an atheist by instinct. He is no longer a metaphysician in the sense of finding a rule for the conduct of life in any theoretical principles, for him there is no longer a "thou shalt"; for him the cigarette butt and the umbrella are as exalted and as timeless as the "thing in itself" Consequently, the good is for the Dadaist no better than the bad—there is only a simultaneity, in values as in everything else. This simultaneity … has abandoned the principle of "making things better" and above all sees its goal in the destruction of everything that has gone bourgeois. Thus the Dadaist is opposed to the idea of paradise in every form. The word "improvement" is in every form unintelligible to the Dadaist.[78]

In this selection, Huelsenbeck describes Dada as a response to the meaningless world which the modern European inhabits. Yet even as Huelsenbeck harkens the death of God, that Nietzschean cultural catastrophe which leads to a crisis of meaning and value, he insists on the continued vitality of a different kind of god, a god "within ourselves as the creative power and the creative search for meaning" which enables man to identify and recognize his truest self.[79] This movement is described as the "realization of potentiality, the endless wandering toward a necessary but indefinable aim."[80] In short, after the death of God and divine sources of meaning, man must recognize that there are other "necessary" aims at which he is oriented in virtue of his nature as a creative being. Dada, as a movement, enables man to recognize this higher self and move toward this necessary goal through the production of performances, poems, and other artworks. This picture mirrors Nietzsche's perfectionist account from "Schopenhauer as Educator," in which man identifies a highest self and moves toward that self in action. In Dada, these actions especially include written expressions, performances, and the creation of artworks.

In their writings, Ball, Huelsenbeck, and Tzara alternately exhibit attitudes of profound ambivalence toward life coupled with a near-manic excitement for the senselessness of life and the creative revelation of the artistic process. In "A History of Dada," Huelsenbeck describes life as "useless, aimless, and vile" in the paragraph before he remarks that Dadaists are "devoted to the movement of life."[81] In their ambivalence to life, Dadaists believe themselves to mirror the indifference of life itself, thus celebrating life as it actually is. Indeed, Huelsenbeck remarks that "the Dadaist loves life, because he can throw it away every day; for him death is a Dadaist affair."[82] This frank and profoundly ambivalent attitude about the nature of life decries a need for metaphysical consolation, for a "Tusculum of the 'Spirit'" or "refuge for [one's] own weaknesses."[83]

Tzara's profound and famous ambivalence toward life is on full display in his "manifesto on feeble and bitter love," in which he claims that Dada "transforms itself—affirms—simultaneously says the opposite—*it doesn't matter*—screams—goes fishing," though it is also "against the future,"[84] remarking in a supplement which closes out the manifesto that "life is charming and death is charming too."[85] In his 1918 Dada Manifesto, he identifies affirmation with negation[86] and insists upon the falsity of all perspectives on life one might take, remarking he "does not consider the relative [results of philosophical questioning about life] more important than the choice between cake and cherries after dinner."[87] In a moment harkening back to the atemporal perspective occupied by the one experiencing Dionysian ecstasy in *The Birth of Tragedy*—Tzara remarks that "measured by the scale of eternity, all activity is vain"; for one who takes this perspective, life is a "poor farce, without aim or initial parturition,"[88] redeemed only by art as an expression of intoxication with life: "Dada Dada Dada, a roaring of tense colors, and interlacing of opposites and of all contradictions, grotesques, inconsistencies: LIFE."[89] This coupling of a manic desire to celebrate life with the recognition that life is useless or meaningless underpins the Dada aim to create works which affirm and express life *as it really is.*

To represent life *as it really is* for Dadaists is to express "cosmic, ordered chaos";[90] they call for an "abolition" of both "memory" and "future," instead celebrating "every god that is the immediate product of spontaneity."[91] Given a post-Nietzschean dearth of the divine, an understanding of reality as fluxional, and a lack of absolute moral principles, the Dadaist celebrates all values simultaneously, condemns progress, and advocates for the continued destruction of those nihilistic categories and concepts which plagued Europe before the death of God.[92] In his "manifesto on feeble love and bitter love," Tzara writes in praise of randomness and chaos, critiquing human faith in reason while advocating for a blurring of truths together with lies.[93] He calls on his reader in this manifesto to "scramble the meanings—scramble the ideas and all the little tropical rains of *demoralization*, disorganization, destruction, and ruckus."[94] In "Proclamation without Pretenses," Tzara remarks:

> We are in search of
> the force that is direct pure sober
> UNIQUE we are in search of NOTHING
> we affirm the VITALITY of every IN-
> STANT[95]

This Dada understanding of life as comprised of "force that is direct pure sober" is echoed by Huelsenbeck's description of beliefs to which Dada adheres: that "man was in the hands of irrational creative forces ... that life lives us as we live life" and that this "life was always in flux and growing."[96] This Dada desire to access and express the creative inner life force—that which, as Ball notes, expresses itself in the artist as "inner necessity"—does not "[aspire] to nihilism (Tzara) but to a new integration."[97] This new integration harkens back to Ball's Nietzschean fascination with "the idea of destruction which was at the same time creative":[98] a fascination with the creative expression characteristic of life itself, manifest as inner necessity in the artist, which allows for life itself to appear on the canvas, in the performance, in the poem. Such creation moves beyond destruction and toward an affirmation of an underlying form, structure, or cosmic order; indeed, Huelsenbeck remarks that the Dada thinkers' "deep longing for form and structure" manifests in "symbols of permanence" in their work.[99]

So it is that Ball celebrates Kandinsky in his 1917 lecture on the artist for recognizing a "regularity and order created not by an external and ultimately powerless force, but by the *feeling of the good*."[100] The "feeling of the good" which drives the painter and his *seemingly* anarchic process of creation is an "inner necessity" that "shapes the external, visible form of the work" and is that "on [which] everything ultimately depends: it distributes the colors, forms, and emphases."[101] Ball interprets Kandinsky's "feeling of the good" as a kind of necessity, a goal-directedness of the artist which is "the ultimate gateway that the artists ... cannot break down."[102] Ball celebrates the "inner necessity" of the artist as a manifestation of "spirit" which reveals itself through the artist and in the artwork.

This account of the positive aims and beliefs of Dadaists is critically important for understanding why the kind of "life-affirmation" in which these thinkers participate is still problematic from a late Nietzschean perspective. In *Modernism-Dada-Postmodernism*, Sheppard remarks upon Ball's early preoccupation in his doctoral thesis on Nietzsche with the notion that "nature itself [might be] inherently structured."[103] As we begin to see above, and as Sheppard argues, this notion of some inherent structure to nature is picked up by other Dadaists, Tzara and Huelsenbeck included. In 1917, Tzara insists that since art is an expression of life and "order" is "the necessary condition of the life of every organism," the expression of cosmic order is an "essential quality of art."[104] Artistic creation for Dada thinkers requires one to "know how to recognize and pick up the signs of the power [they] are awaiting."[105] To depict life *as it actually is* in Dada creations is not to express pure, fluxional chaos, but to express the hidden powers and ordering structures of life; it is to express "structure and chaos" as "two complementary aspects of a single, ungraspable reality."[106] While Sheppard connects this idea that "nature is both dynamically chaotic and yet full of elusive, shifting patterns" with late Nietzsche's notions of the Apollonian and Dionysian, it seems clearer to me that Dadaist's teleological understanding of life—a vitalist account of life as "immanently patterned"—appears much more obviously in early Nietzsche (especially in his concept of the "world-artist" in *The Birth of Tragedy*)[107]—and that such an account of life is one Nietzsche later rejects as otherworldly, life-denying, and nihilistic.

One need only to look to Nietzsche's account of life as a primordial oneness underlying reality (in virtue of the Dionysian) which is organized into structures or patterns (in virtue of the Apollonian) to see the similarities to Dada's conception of life as structure and chaos. In *The Birth of Tragedy*, Nietzsche speaks of "artistic powers which erupt from nature itself, without the meditation of any human artist, and in which nature's artistic drives attain their first, immediate satisfaction" (*BT*, 2). While Ball speaks of the inner necessity which erupts from out of the life in the artist's creation and Huelsenbeck insists that human beings are "in the hands of irrational creative forces"—that "life lives us"—so too early Nietzsche remarks that in tragedy, "man is no longer an artist, he has become a work of art: all nature's artistic power reveals itself here … here man, the noblest clay, the most previous marble, is kneaded and carved and, to the accompaniment of the chisel-blows of the Dioynsiac world-artist" (*BT*, 1). And not only does Nietzsche insist on man as an eruption of nature's creative power which has creative power of its own in virtue of its belonging to the creative primordial oneness; he also here argues that the "Dionysiac artist … become[s] entirely one with the primordial unity, with its pain and contradiction, and he produces a copy of this primordial unity as music" (*BT*, 5). In the moment of artistic creation, Nietzsche argues that the human artist "merges fully with that original artist of the world," becoming able to recognize the vital goal-directedness of life and express this hidden nature of life in works of art (*BT*, 5).

In section five of *The Birth of Tragedy*, the solution which Nietzsche finds to the tragic perspective on life, to the threat of nihilism and meaninglessness, is that "only as an aesthetic phenomenon are existence and the world eternally justified." Later, Nietzsche remarks that this answer to the question of the meaning of existence—that individuals can be "[led] back to the of nature" and experience themselves as meaningful part of the universe—allows one to experience a "metaphysical solace" in the experience and creation of artworks (*BT*, 7). This is because, as Geuss notes, that primordial oneness underlying all reality (das *Ur-Eine*) is "itself a kind of artist"; it is that "world-artist" to which Nietzsche refers. By understanding life as an "artistic game" which this world-artist "in the eternal fullness of its delight, plays with itself"—a game of "playful construction and demolition of the world" which can be likened to Heraclitus's description of a child building and destroying castles of sand on the beach. Human existence is justified, becomes meaningful, as a part of this cosmic game; through artistic creation, man becomes able to experience a small amount of the cosmic play of the world-artist, whose drive to creation (and the destruction such creation requires) drives the world and explains the order of structure in the chaos, the patterns of creation and destruction which appear. In *The Birth of Tragedy*, Nietzsche does not offer this as a metaphor for life, but as a metaphysical account which provides consolation to the individual who otherwise might have thought life meaningless.

In A*ttempt at a Self-Criticism*, however, Nietzsche offers a pointed critique of the metaphysical account offered in *The Birth of Tragedy*: it is an "arbitrary, pointless, and fantastic" "artist metaphysic" (*BT*, *P*, 5). Most importantly, though, it is life-denying and nihilistic, functioning ultimately as a "narcotic," a harmful bit of "metaphysical consolation" (*BT*, *P*, 7). This critique, I argue, is based in the mature Nietzsche's rejection of all notions of a higher purpose, no matter how secular or anti-Christian they seem. In a note from 1887, Nietzsche remarks that "the nihilistic question 'for what?' is rooted in the old habit of supposing that the goal must be put up, given, demanded from outside." According to Nietzsche, the asking of this "nihilistic question" need not only involve humanity's hope for a higher purpose to be established by some "*superhuman authority*," but also "the authority of reason … or the *social instinct* (the herd) … or *history* with an immanent spirit and a goal within, so one can entrust oneself to it" (*KSA*, 12:9[43]). Although Christianity's nihilistic ask after a transcendent justification for existence more obviously involves a devaluation of this-worldly existence *as it actually is*, Nietzsche's point here is that any attempt to find a higher purpose which justifies existence—a purpose in which human pursuits are unified and the value of these pursuits conditioned in the same way—is an attempt to locate a purpose in existence which *does not exist* in actuality. When we direct ourselves toward such a purpose or understand our lives as meaningful with reference to such a purpose, we implicitly denigrate the world as it actually is and fail to engage meaningfully with the world to which we belong. The question "for what?" already supposes that some justification must come from outside the individual purposes and goals of embodied, this-worldly life; in short, this question belies a habitual and common understanding of a "higher purpose" as that which is able to justify this-worldly existence.

Insofar as a version of this worldview is ascribed to by Dada thinkers, the life-affirmation at which Dada aims—at least as Dadaists explain it in their writings—is ultimately life-denying. Because the affirmation of life on Dada's view seems to require a commitment to a teleological, structured, and vitalist understanding of life through which the lives and creations of artists are justified, Dada thinkers repeat the same unintentional life-denial which Nietzsche criticizes in his later works. By locating the meaning of life in an arbitrary metaphysics, Dada thinkers blind themselves from recognizing the true nature of life: as Will to Power which neither aims at a necessary goal or purpose nor provides a pattern or structure which underlies reality as it is experienced. Only when one embraces life as Will to Power can one affirm life as it actually is and create values which do not deny life.

Thus, while noticing the large extent to which Dadaists were influenced by Nietzsche's critical projects—his disavowal of absolute knowledge, destruction of metaphysics, and rejection of previous values—we should also recognize that elements of the positive philosophy articulated by the Dadaists fall victim to the same critique which Nietzsche leveled against himself and his early work: namely, that their cosmological commitments continue to nihilistically seek a justification for life as it really is. Importantly, this is not to argue that all of Dada thought is nihilistic, or that Dada performances and creations cannot be life-affirming in some sense. Rather, the underlying Dada commitment to an ordered, vitalist conception of the cosmos ultimately undermines their attempts to think life beyond nihilism, and to move beyond that aporia of meaninglessness in which they find themselves.

Notes

1 Thank you to the editors of this volume for their suggested improvements to this chapter.
2 Motherwell, *The Dada Painters and Poets,* 266.
3 Richard Huelsenbeck, *Dada sieght: Eine Bilanz des Dadaismus* (Berlin: Malik Verlag, 1920), 12–13.
4 Georges Ribemont-Dessaignes, "History of Dada," in *The Dada Painters and Poets,* 103.
5 Richard Sheppard, *Modernism-Dada-Postmodernism* (Evanston, IL: Northwestern University Press, 2000), 193.
6 Sheppard, *Modernism-Dada-Postmodernism*, 192.
7 Ibid., 39–40. Mark Pegrum, *Challenging Modernity: Dada between Modern and Postmodern* (New York: Bergahn Books, 2000), 7.
8 Sheppard, *Modernism-Dada-Postmodernism*, 46, 62.
9 Pegrum, *Challenging Modernity,* 7–10. Pegrum locates the same critical response to post-Enlightenment values in Ball's 1917 lecture on Kandinsky, in which Ball echoes Nietzsche's most famous proclamation—that "Gott ist tott" (Pegrum, *Challenging Modernity,* 33).
10 Hans J. Kleinschmidt, "Introduction," in *Memoirs of a Dada Drummer*, ed. Richard Huelsenbeck (Berkeley, CA: UC Press, 1974), xl.
11 Kleinschmidt, "Introduction," xlii.
12 Phillip Mann, "Ball and Nietzsche: Study of the Influence of Nietzsche's Philosophy on Hugo Ball," *Forum for Modern Language Studies* XVI, no. 4 (1980).
13 Mann, "Ball and Nietzsche," 294/5.
14 It is worth noting here that these Nietzschean themes to which Mann points come mainly from Nietzsche's earliest published writings, such as *The Birth of Tragedy* and Nietzsche's *Untimely Meditations* (excepting a critique of morality and reason, which appear throughout Nietzsche's body of work). This will be significant as we begin to investigate the ways in which certain Dada thinkers, from a Nietzschean perspective,

ultimately remain attached to nihilistic ideals. That the earlier works are most influential for such thinkers is critical since, as we see in "Attempt at a Self-Criticism" (*BT*), Nietzsche believes he, too, remained attached to nihilistic ideals at this stage.

15 Tzara "Zurich Chronicle" in Motherwell, *The Dada Thinkers and Poets,* 242. See also Jack Flam, "Foreword" in Motherwell, *The Dada Thinkers and Poets,* xiii.
16 Tzara "Zurich Chronicle" in Motherwell, *The Dada Thinkers and Poets,* 242.
17 Georges Hugnet, "The Dada Spirit in Painting" in Motherwell, *The Dada Thinkers and Poets,* 125.
18 Huelsenbeck, "A History of Dada" in Motherwell, *The Dada Thinkers and Poets,* 25, 39–41.
19 Hugnet, "The Dada Spirit in Painting" in Motherwell, *The Dada Thinkers and Poets,* 132.
20 Huelsenbeck, "A History of Dada" in Motherwell, *The Dada Thinkers and Poets,* 25, 39–41.
21 Ibid., 24.
22 Ibid.
23 Hugnet, "The Dada Spirit in Painting" in Motherwell, *The Dada Thinkers and Poets,* 132.
24 Ibid., 131. It is worth noting that even Huelsenbeck ("A History of Dada") acknowledges that bruitism and *poème simultané* were co-opted from the futurists. It is thus worth considering to what extent early Dada was actually "opposed" to futurism, as Huelsenbeck claimed.
25 Tristan Tzara, "Dada Manifesto 1918" in Motherwell, *The Dada Painters and Poets*, 92.
26 Georges Ribemont-Dessaignes, "History of Dada," in Motherwell, *The Dada Thinkers and Poets,* 105.
27 See also *BGE,* 16.
28 Hugo Ball, *Flight Out of Time*, ed. John Elderfield (Berkeley, CA: UC Press, 1996), 11.
29 Ball, *Flight Out of Time*, 11.
30 Richard Huelsenbeck, "Psychoanalytical Notes on Modern Art" in *Memoirs of a Dada Drummer,* 159.
31 Richard Huelsenbeck, "The Case of Dada" in *Memoirs of a Dada Drummer,* 137.
32 Tristan Tzara, "Dada Manifesto 1918," in *The Dada Painters and Poets*, ed. Robert Motherwell (Cambridge, MA: Belknap Press, 1951), 76.
33 Tzara, "Dada Manifesto 1918," 78.
34 Ibid., 79.
35 Ibid.
36 Ibid.
37 Ibid., 81.
38 Ibid., 80.
39 See also *KSA*, 9:11[330], *KSA*, 9:11[156].
40 See also *KSA*, 12:9[62].
41 See this stated especially in relation to Boscovich in BVN-1882, 213.
42 Boscovich was also influential for Nietzsche in the development of these ideas.
43 George Stack, "Kant, Lange, Nietzsche: Critique of Knowledge," in *Nietzsche and Modern German Though*t, ed. Keith Ansell-Pearson. (New York: Routledge, 1991).
44 Stack, "Kant, Lange, Nietzsche: Critique of Knowledge," 38.
45 Ibid., 34.
46 Ibid.

47 Hugo Ball, "Nietzsche in Basel: Eine Streitschrift," in *Der Künstler und die Zeitkrankheit.* (Frankfurt: Surhkamp, 1984), 82.
48 Ball, "Nietzsche in Basel: Eine Streitschrift," 95.
49 The influence of Ball on Huelsenbeck cannot be overemphasized. Indeed, as Kleinschmidt remarks in his Introduction to *Memoirs of a Dada Drummer,* Huelsenbeck—six years younger than Ball and a young student when they first met in Munich in 1912—was taken with Ball, and later followed Ball to Switzerland in the fall of 1915 (Hans Kleinschmidt, "Introduction" in *Memoirs of a Dada Drummer,* xx–xxii.)
50 We see this, in part, in Pegrum's attention to Ball's claim that "the abolition of atoms in science" as one of three "causes for the chaotic disintegration of the old order of European society" (Pegrum, *Challenging Modernity,* 33).
51 Sheppard, *Modernism-Dada-Postmodernism,* 175.
52 Importantly, there is a difference between a nihilistic (or life-denying) conception of the world and nihilism proper. European nihilism follows when nihilistic conceptions collapse.
53 Tzara, "Dada Manifesto 1918" in *The Dada Painters and Poets,* 76.
54 Ibid., 78.
55 Ibid., 77.
56 Huelsenbeck, "A History of Dada" in *The Dada Painters and Poets,* 35.
57 Ibid., 43.
58 Huelsenbeck, "Psychoanalytical Notes…" in *Memoirs of a Dada Drummer,* 160/1.
59 Sheppard, *Modernism-Dada-Postmodernism,* 175–76.
60 Ibid.
61 Ibid., 172.
62 Tzara, "Dada Manifesto 1918" in *The Dada Painters and Poets,* 76.
63 Ibid.
64 Ibid., 81.
65 Ibid.
66 Ibid., 80.
67 Ball, *Flight Out of Time,* 47.
68 Ibid., 65 [emphasis mine].
69 Hugo Ball, "Dada Fragments," in *The Dada Painters and Poets*, ed. Robert Motherwell (Cambridge, MA: Belknap Press, 1951), 51.
70 Ball, "Dada Fragments," 42.
71 Huelsenbeck, "Dada" in *Memoirs of a Dada Drummer,* 140.
72 Kleinschmidt, "Introduction" in *Memoirs of a Dada Drummer,* xviii.
73 Sheppard, *Modernism-Dada-Postmodernism,* 173.
74 Hugo Ball, "Die junge Literatur in Deutschland," *Der Revoluzzer* I No. 10 (August 14, 1915): np. Cited by Sheppard, *Modernism-Dada-Postmodernism,* 174.
75 Ball, *Flight Out of Time,* 46.
76 Ibid., 120.
77 Ibid., 223.
78 Huelsenbeck, "A History of Dada" in Motherwell, *The Dada Thinkers and Poets,* 42.
79 Huelsenbeck, "Psychoanalytical Notes" in *Memoirs of a Dada Drummer,* 160.
80 Ibid.
81 Huelsenbeck, "A History of Dada" in Motherwell, *The Dada Thinkers and Poets,* 43. He also characterizes life shortly thereafter as "naive, obvious life, with its indifference towards happiness and death, joy and misery."

82 Huelsenbeck, "A History of Dada" in Motherwell, *The Dada Thinkers and Poets*, 28.
83 Ibid.
84 Tristan Tzara, "manifesto on feeble and bitter love" in Motherwell, *The Dada Thinkers and Poets,* 95 [emphasis mine].
85 Ibid.
86 Tzara, "Dada Manifesto 1918" in Motherwell, *The Dada Thinkers and Poets,* 78.
87 Ibid., 79.
88 Ibid., 80.
89 Ibid., 82.
90 Ibid., 78.
91 Ibid., 81.
92 This concern with meaninglessness as a European problem persists late into Huelsenbeck's writings. In a much later essay, Huelsenbeck remarks on the uncertainty that the modern European feels in lieu of his recognition that the meaning of life is an "uncertain proposition" (Huelsenbeck, "Psychoanalytical Notes" in *Memoirs of a Dada Drummer,* 152/3).
93 Tzara, "manifesto on feeble and bitter love" in Motherwell, *The Dada Thinkers and Poets,* 86.
94 Ibid., 91.
95 Tzara, "Proclamation without Pretenses" in Motherwell, *The Dada Thinkers and Poets,* 82.
96 Huelsenbeck, "Psychoanalytical Notes" in *Memoirs of a Dada Drummer,* 160–61.
97 Huelsenbeck, "Dada" in *Memoirs of a Dada Drummer,* 140.
98 Mann, "Ball and Nietzsche," 298.
99 Huelsenbeck, "Dada" in *Memoirs of a Dada Drummer,* 141.
100 Kandinsky, "Über die Formfrage," 157. Cited by Hugo Ball in "Kandinsky," *Flight Out of Time,* 227.
101 Ball, "Kandinsky," 227.
102 Ibid., 227.
103 Sheppard, *Modernism-Dada-Postmodernism*, 192.
104 Tristan Tzara, "Pierre Reverdy: La Voleur de Talan," I:399/64. Cited by Sheppard, *Modernism-Dada-Postmodernism,* 193.
105 Tristan Tzara, "Note on Poetry," *Seven Dada Manifestos,* 75. Cited by Sheppard, *Modernism-Dada-Postmodernism,* 194.
106 Sheppard, *Modernism-Dada-Postmodernism*, 196.
107 Ibid., 192.

10

Nietzsche's Decadent Modernism

Adrian Switzer

Decadent proto-modernism

The Salon de la Rose + Croix—an annual gathering of visual and musical artists in the Paris, home of the novelist and mystic Joséphin Péladan—was the center of artistic Decadence in the last decade of the nineteenth century.[1] Throughout the 1890s, artists such as Pierre Amédée Marcel-Béronneau, Gustave Moreau, Émile Bernard, Alphonse Osbert, Jean Delville, and Odilon Redon exhibited large format, ornately painted canvases that variously depicted Christian religious symbols with figures from Greek, Buddhist, and Egyptian mythologies. Painted in dark palettes of blues, greys, and blacks, idealized figures were often surrounded by horrific, fantastic creatures in surreal landscapes. Marcel-Béronneau's *Orpheus in Hades* (1897), which was exhibited at the sixth Salon de la Rose + Croix, is exemplary in this regard. Marcel-Béronneau's large oil painting centers around Orpheus in the underworld; the work shows Hades as a dark, cavernous space haunted on all sides by monstrous lizards, snakes and birds of prey. Among the Homeric shades at Orpheus's feet, Marcel-Béronneau places a Christ-like figure tortured in a tangle of thorns.

If Péladan's salon was the central space of Decadent art, Gustave Moreau was the movement's central figure. Moreau, in whose *atelier* Marcel-Béronneau worked upon arriving in Paris and who encouraged him to exhibit at the Salon de la Rose + Croix, showed at both the official Salon de Paris of the Académie des Beaux-Arts and in the Salon des Indépendants. It was Moreau's extensive *œuvre* from both academic and non-academic settings that helped define the Decadent aesthetic in *fin-de-siècle* Paris. As the Symbolist poet and novelist Jean Lorrain described Moreau's influence: "He has smitten a whole generation of artists, yearning today for otherworldliness and mysticism, with the dangerous love of delightful dead women, the dead women of yore called up by him in the mirror of Time."[2]

An early series of paintings of Greek myths—*Oedipus and the Sphinx* (painted 1861; exhibited 1864), *Medea and Jason* (1865), *Thracian Girl Carrying the Head of Orpheus* (1866), and so forth—introduce many of the themes and styles employed by the Decadents.[3] Combining fantastical creaturely life with idealized figural beauty, Moreau blends parts of different myths and fever-dreams in non-natural settings. Significantly, referring to himself as "the painter," Moreau describes his work as follows:

> The painter takes a man who has arrived at the grave and severe time of life, finding himself in the presence of the eternal riddle. It holds him in the close embrace of its terrible claw. ... It is the earthly chimera ... represented by this charming head of a woman, with wings presaging the ideal, but the body of a monster, a flesh-eater that rends and annihilates.[4]

Life and death; human and monster; the feminine ideal and gross flesh: in combining contrasting ideas and in reimaging ancient legends in a late-Romantic style and palette, Moreau's painting announces the Decadents' abiding interest in the beauty of unreality. That he writes of his work in the third person speaks to Moreau's proto-modern sensibility—a link between artistic description and modernism that will be explored in the first part of the present chapter.

Contrary to the critical opinion of modernism as simply a rejection of Late Romanticism, the claim, here, is that Decadence in its symbolic polysemy, its stylistic experiments with form and content and its presentist aesthetics of bodily sensation significantly sets the stage for modernism. Though focused on how the Decadent's adherence to Gautier's "*l'art pour l'art*" aestheticism prefigures the apolitics of modernist poetry, Vincent Sherry's *Modernism and the Reinvention of Decadence* shares the present work's sense: An art historical view of modernism as a decisive break from the Decadence that preceded it over-simplifies the complex aesthetic context of late-nineteenth-century Europe.[5] Accordingly, if we are to understand Nietzsche's aesthetic modernism in the same historical context, and do so by way of his reflections on decadence—the task of the second part of the present chapter—first, we must develop the concept of the latter and show what is proto-modernist in an art movement that seems otherwise hopelessly Romantic.

* * *

In the manifesto of the Rose + Croix Brotherhood, published in *Le Figaro* in 1891, Péladan defined the character of Decadent art: "It accepts all allegory, legend, mysticism and myth and even the expressive head if it is noble or the nude study if it is beautiful."[6] Further, Decadence as described by Péladan, "restore[s] the cult of the *ideal* in all its splendor, with *tradition* as its base and *beauty* as it means."[7] The art historian Jean Pierrot notes that though the Decadents never had, "a single very coherent doctrine ... shared by all," still, there were recurrent themes and forms in their works. Pierrot notes an abiding interest in "correspondences" and "double meanings" between images within a single painting and between different art forms; further, there is "the importance of music, the use of free verse, a constant concern with technical detail, philosophical idealism, [and] a predilection for the world of dream and legends."[8]

Consider, in these regards, Moreau's *The Apparition* (*L'Apparition*) (1876) as described in J. K. Huysmans's *Against Nature* (*À rebours*) (1884):

> With a gesture of horror, Salomé tries to thrust away the terrifying vision [of the Saint's decapitated head] which holds her nailed to the spot, balanced on the tips of her toes. ... A gorgerin grips her waist like a corselet, and like an outsize clasp a wondrous jewel sparkles in the cleft between her breasts; lower down, a girdle encircles her hips, hiding the upper part of her thighs, against which dangles a gigantic pendant glistening with rubies and emeralds. ... Under the brilliant rays emanating from the Precursor's head, every facet of every jewel catches fire.[9]

An embellishment of the story as told in the Gospel of Saint Mark, Moreau presents Salomé either before or after her dance for King Herod; Salomé's reward of St. John the Baptist's head hovers before her, which she either reaches out to seize upon or extends a protective arm against.[10] The "correspondences" between images, which according to Pierrot characterizes the Decadent aesthetic, is here at play in the resonances between the jewels that adorn Salomé's body, the jewel-encrusted walls in Herod's orientalized palace and the glowing eyes in the Saint's severed, radiant head. Following this logic of correspondence still further, we find in Moreau's painting of Salomé as here described by Huysmans an affinity with Flaubert's literary description of Salammbô: "Over her breast was a cluster of luminous stones, imitating in their medley of colors the scales of a muraena. Adorned with diamonds, her arms were left bare by her sleeveless tunic, spangled with red flowers against a jet-black ground."[11] As the sites and sources of reference multiply—from biblical legend to painting and from novel to novel—and as further correspondences are drawn from symbol to symbol, the elements of a Decadent work become polysemic.

The question of whether Salomé is in the painting reaching out toward or protectively raising her hand against the apparition—whether, indeed, there is a head to be seen, or, it is nothing but a figment of Salomé's overheated imagination—recalls Pierrot's point about the "double meaning" of Decadent symbols. But, the symbolism of aesthetic decadence is not merely double, it is manifold. As the art historian Pierre-Louis Mathieu notes, the scene Moreau sets in the painting is geographically and historically diverse: "The drama unfolds in the innermost recesses of a mosque, before the highly ornate niche of a mihrab housing a statue of the Buddha, whose head is surrounded by a cross-marked nimbus."[12] This is syncretism in the extreme. Moreau crowds Jewish, Christian, Buddhist, and Muslim images into Herod's ancient Roman palace.

In a different treatment of the same biblical tale—*Salomé Dancing before Herod* (1874–76)—Moreau places a lotus flower in Salomé's hand. What to make of this symbol? "Had it the phallic significance which the primordial religions of India attributed to it? Did it suggest ... a sacrifice of virginity, an exchange of blood, an impure embrace?" Continuing, Des Esseintes—the protagonist of Huysmans's *Against Nature* whose reflections on Moreau's paintings we are reproducing to show the proto-modernist practice of ekphrasis in Decadence—wonders whether "the painter had been thinking [in including the lotus bloom] of the dancer, the mortal woman, the soiled vessel ... [or of] the sepulchral rites of ancient Egypt, the solemn ceremonies of embalmment."[13]

A disembodied head that may be a reward, eagerly claimed, or a nightmarish vision to be warded off; the sanctification by God of a true believer, or a fantastical being haunting a placeless palace filled with religious wonders; a lotus flower that may symbolize the phallus, feminine virginal purity, slatternly impurity, the living, sexual body of woman or a corpse in decay before burial preparations: confronted with Moreau's paintings, Huysmans describes Des Esseintes as "puzzled [in] his brains [as to] the meaning" of these symbols.[14] Mathieu comes to much the same conclusion: "The spectator [of Moreau's Salomé *Dancing before Herod*] is disconcerted by the [*sic*] array of symbols taken from so many different religious sources."[15]

Art composed by image-to-image correspondence, which draws equally and without distinction on Eastern symbols, Greek myths, and allegories from the Bible is one where meanings multiply. In Decadence, we are faced with an art whose interpretation is interminable. It is an interpretive task made all the more endless in its practice of ekphrasis: Decadent novels interpret Decadent paintings; Decadent paintings, in turn, refer to and rework literary and religious myths, and so forth. Indeed, faced with the possibilities upon possibilities opened up by Decadent art, we might ask whether Des Esseintes's wont to decide *the* meaning of the lotus flower in Moreau's Salomé painting is not so much that the symbol signifies too much, and so signifies nothing at all. Rather, the problem might be that Huysmans's character holds to a premodern epistemology in which reference and meaning are taken to be direct and singular.

World-weary, nostalgic, and, in ways deeply anti-modern, Des Esseintes confines himself to a narrowly aestheticized world. The character's youthful hedonism, bent on pursuing ever-new experiences, has given way in middle age to a search for the perfect arrangement of his internal and external life. Des Esseintes's country estate has an air of a carefully appointed mausoleum. In turning his tired eyes on Moreau's paintings, Des Esseintes cannot help but not see what stands before him. Rather than apply the logic of correspondence from image to image—rather than follow the play of symbols Moreau has scattered across his canvas—Des Esseintes works to settle the painting's meaning so as to catalogue it as either ideal or unideal. But, an imaginative recombination of symbols as laden with significance as half-human/half-animal mythological creatures and androgynous gods that embody life, death, decay, and regeneration inaugurates a non-binary semiotics. It is a semiotics that operates in Huysmans's novel despite its main character being too degenerate—too decadent in the physiological sense of the word—to recognize the new aesthetic circumstances in which he was living.

In his retreat from the modern, cosmopolitan city to the isolated environs, meticulously decorated, of his Fontenay estate, Des Esseintes seems in search of a singular aesthetic experience. Simply, Des Esseintes would have his life be beautiful. The libraries and galleries of the estate are filled with classical works of art and literature brought from Paris. Yet, Des Esseintes takes little interest in the richness of his surroundings. Rather, he is constantly culling his collection in search of the perfect novel, poem, and painting. Upon viewing the Goyas and Rembrandts that adorn his walls, Des Esseintes feels, "a most painful thor[n] in his flesh, for unaccountable vogues had utterly spoilt ... [the] pictures for him that he once held dear"; invariably he "ended up ... discovering some hitherto imperceptible blemish, and promptly rejected" the works.[16] Des Esseintes's library, his perfumery, his flower garden and kitchen all receive similarly close scrutiny. All, in all of their varietal colors, scents, and tastes, are reduced to the minimum of his decadent search for the ideal. Assuming the role of the perfumer, Des Esseintes combines various essences to create a complex bouquet: "Ambrosia, Mitcham lavender, sweet pea ... tuberose, orange, and almond blossom."[17] Ultimately, the myriad smells "assai[l] his jaded nostrils, shaking anew his shattered nerves"; he collapses on the window ledge gasping for fresh air.[18]

"Beauty" is one name for the standard by which Huysmans's character judges art and the world. Recall, in this regard, that Péladan proclaims the Decadent aesthetic to be a search for ideal beauty. Alternately, the literary critic Arthur Symons identifies the philosophy of Huysmans's great Decadent novel as a matter of "sensation," which is the "one certainty in a world that may be [otherwise] well or ill arranged."[19] It is not an hedonic sensationalism that motivates Des Esseintes. Rather, it is a fostering of those feelings that, by his own gauge, best suit his delicate temperament. In her Deleuzian interpretation of *Against Nature*, Bryden reads the central perfume chapter of the novel in just this way. Des Esseintes's initially learned and studied experimentation with differently scented oils quickly overwhelms him as the bouquets multiply: "As he experiments [with perfumes], he enters a phase of acceleration and delirium, abandoning his punctuation, shattering the ... syntax he had labored to understand."[20] Note the ambiguity of the pronouns in this sentence: the first "he" refers to Des Esseintes, the character of the novel; the second "he" refers to Huysmans, the author of the text. Setting aside, for the moment, the modernism of this shift in reference from literary content to form, note that Des Esseintes ends the scene bathed in the natural scent of frangipani wafting in through the open window:[21] complex sensory experience gives way, finally, to a simple, soothing sensation.

While a search for ideal beauty points Decadence back to Romanticism, its preoccupation with depicting the immediacy of sensation points forward to modernism. We will return to this point, below, in considering Frederick Jameson's reading of Baudelaire's poem "*Chant d'automne*." For now, whether it is a matter of beauty or sensation, there is a singularity of conceit to Des Esseintes's decadent life. The character curates his richly aestheticized life so that lotus blossoms are made to mean *one* thing when they appear in paintings, and gilded, bejeweled tortoises that are left to wander around living rooms do so *solely* to augment the color contrast between the carpet and wallpaper.[22] Indeed, in the very air he breathes Des Esseintes's is an artificial life in which nature's myriad smells are distilled into the essence of single-note perfumes.

The perfume chapter of Huysmans's novel evinces Decadence's anticipations of modernism; equally, the same chapter shows up the aesthetic's failure fully to attain to such modernism. If, as noted, Des Esseintes ends the scene in a state of physiological repose, Huysmans's frantic prose comes to no such relief. As Bryden describes the style in which this section of the novel is written: "[The] language ... becom[es] dangerous, confronting order and exhibiting what Julia Kristeva would call ... a 'semiotic vehemence.'"[23] The conclusion of the chapter is composed as, "one hurtling, interminable sentence which occupies a whole paragraph."[24] Form outpaces content; Huysmans's syntax overruns the sensory capacities of his character. The unconventional style in which the chapter ends simply is too modern for Des Esseintes's degenerate senses. This discord between form and content, and this incompleteness is exemplary of modernist text. Huysmans is at work in this central chapter of his novel on matters of style that will preoccupy many of the poets and writers of the early twentieth century.

The art historian Moshe Barasch credits Delacroix and the chemist Michel Eugène Chevreul with overcoming the trend in early-nineteenth-century French art and art theory of differentiating between the arts—a differentiation based on the basically Hegelian principle that works are fully realized only on condition of their being generically well-defined. Recall, in this regard, Lessing's argument in the *Laocoön* (1766) that painting and sculpture as spatial arts must need to be clearly distinguished from literature and poetry, which are temporal arts. Only by unfolding sequentially, as in the passing minutes of time, can poetry accede to its fullest realization. Conversely, a painting freed from the influence of sequential narration is better than one that tries to visualize a story.[25] By the mid-nineteenth century, Barasch argues, there was, in contrast to this Lessingian and Hegelian view, a tendency "toward merging the senses and the arts," that is, a correspondence between the arts that we have already noted in Decadent painting and literature.[26]

In his 1863 essay in *Le Figaro*, "The Painter of Modern Life" (*Le Peintre de la vie moderne*), Charles Baudelaire applies the term "modern" to the synaesthetic, intermedial trend in late-nineteenth-century art. Constantin Guys's "sketch[es] of manners," which are the focus of Baudelaire's piece, that is, Guys's quickly rendered drawings and water color paintings of the fashions of contemporary bourgeois life, are located aesthetically somewhere between the "coloured engravings" of eighteenth-century Parisian fashion and Balzac's multivolume social novel *La Comédie humaine*.[27] Further, Baudelaire develops an analogy between Guys and the lead character in Poe's *The Man of the Crowd* (1845), which Baudelaire translated into French in *Nouvelles Histoires Extraordinaires* (1856). Note Baudelaire's equivocal reference to painting and literature in describing Poe's story: "Do you remember a picture (it really is a picture!), painted—or rather written—by the most powerful pen of our age, entitled *The Man of the Crowd*?"[28]

Like Poe's written/pictured character, Guys, for Baudelaire, is a modern *flâneur*: "His passion and his profession are to become one flesh with the crowd. For the perfect *flâneur* ... it is an immense joy to set up house in the heart of the multitude, amid the ebb and flow of movement, in the midst of the fugitive and the infinite."[29] Guys is an artist/non-artist who explains the world through paintings "more living than life itself,"[30] loses himself in the crowd in search of what Baudelaire asks his reader to allow him to call "modernity [*modernité*]."[31] The dualistic meaning of "modern," for Baudelaire, is "the ephemeral, the fugitive, the contingent, the half of art whose other half is the eternal and the immutable."[32] Guys as the painter of modern life "makes it his business to extract from fashion whatever element it may contain of poetry within history, to distill the eternal from the transitory."[33]

Modern, then, is something more than art that portrays impermanence. In the paradoxical phrase with which Baudelaire begins his essay, modern art is the "representation of the present [*répresentation du présent*]."[34] "Modern," as an aesthetic category, refers both to the fleeting and to the permanent; or, more generally, "modern," for Baudelaire, is not a simple historico-temporal term that marks the present in its immediate passage into the future. Rather, modernity is an altogether different order of time, one that Jean-François Lyotard describes as "obsess[ed] ... [with] periodization" because, "periodization is a way of placing events in a diachrony."[35] Modern time is not synchronous; modern time is not simply sequential: modern time is diachronically the difference *within* the present; it is the "now" that is never one with itself.

Diachronically, Guys's works depict the impermanent as well as the eternal; in representing their own discordance, they express the spirit of modernity. Still more, Guys's art is modern in rendering the im/permanence of the *flâneur* in the crowd as "sketches" of manners. In this way, the artist has brought form and content together. The ever-moving, ephemeral crowds in the London street—Guys, recall, was an illustrator for the *Illustrated London News*—are roughed-in in quick, liney pen works. In turn, there is Baudelaire's thematic writing about Guys. The "themes and obsessions," as Hiddleston puts it, of Guys's drawings and paintings correspond to the short chapters on "women, dandies, carriages, and so on" that divide Baudelaire's essay.[36] Stylistically like the art it critiques, "The Painter of Modern Life" is a intermedial exercise in art theory from which an image of modernity arises. Less an historical era than an aestheticization of time itself, modernity in the Baudelairian sense is constituted in the stylized, intermedial play between Guys' drawings and Baudelaire's formally mimetic writing about those works.

In this sense, Huysmans is like a modern writer; or, rather, in this regard his work anticipates modernism. Huysmans consistently engages in the practice of ekphrasis, that is, putting the pictorial, the painterly—the imagistic, generally—into words. As we have seen, Des Esseintes spends long sections of *Against Nature* describing Moreau's paintings.[37] Such intermedial play between literature and painting points Huysmans's work toward the modern. But, in writing about art in a persistently Romantic voice, with winding, multi-clause sentences full of ornate descriptions and florid adjectives, the intermediality of Huysmans's writing is unidirectional. Huysmans ornaments his prose in borrowed painterly forms. Thus, he makes ekphrasis into a merely decorative means of adorning his writing. Arguably, the same can be said of Moreau's paintings: they endow their pictorial symbols with a seeming significance borrowed from biblical and mythological sources.

Whether identified with an open, truly intermedial ekphrasis or a coincidental and thus reflexive interplay between form and content, Baudelairian modernism is a critical and aesthetic step beyond the painterly prose of Huysmans's novel, and beyond Moreau's literarily symbolic paintings. Writing about Velásquez's *Las Meninas*, Foucault describes its (early) modernism at the beginning of *The Order of Things* in just these same terms. In contrast to Huysmans's literary account of Des Esseintes's puzzlements over *the* meaning of Moreau's Salomé paintings, Foucault's remarks are multiple and multiplying according to a truly modern ekphrasis: "The relation of language to painting is an infinite relation. It is not that words are imperfect, or that, when confronted by the visible, they prove insuperably inadequate. Neither can be reduced to the other's terms: it is in vain that we say what we see; what we see never resides in what we say."[38] The art critical task of modernity, as Foucault explains, is "to keep the relation of language to vision open [and] to treat their incompatibility as a starting-point for speech instead of as an obstacle to be avoided."[39]

The Order of Things ends as it begins: with a long meditation on the early modernism of *Las Meninas*. Here, Foucault is more programmatic about the historical place and significance of Velásquez's painting in conclusion than in the Preface: *Las Meninas* stands at the "threshold between Classicism and modernity," a "threshold" that is crossed definitively, "when words ceas[e] to intersect with representations."[40] Continuing, Foucault locates the final break with representational language, and thus the crossing of the classical historical threshold into modernity, with Nietzsche's late-nineteenth-century philological "openin[ing] up" of language. In Nietzsche's philosophy, Foucault finds the "enigmatic multipl[ying]" of signs and meanings that inaugurates the properly modern work of art and its critical reception in a modern aesthetic theory.[41]

Nietzsche's decadent modernism

The first of Nietzsche's texts to be translated into French was "Richard Wagner in Bayreuth" (1876)—the fourth of the *Untimely Meditations*. The French translation by Marie Baumgartner appeared to little acclaim a year after the piece was published in German; it found a small reading audience only among a group of Wagnerians in Francophone Switzerland.[42] Throughout the essay, Nietzsche pairs the topics of decadence and modernity. Specifically, Nietzsche contrasts Wagner's singular, revolutionary vision of tragedy with the decadence of the modern theater and the degeneracy of its audience. In re-centering the theater around Bayreuth, Wagner also undertakes the task of reforming his contemporary audience: "It is quite impossible to produce the highest and purest effect of which the art of theatre is capable without at the same time effecting innovations everywhere, in morality and politics, in education and society" (*KSA*, 1:448).

Modern persons are decadent, which is to say, they are physiologically degenerate. A sign of that degeneracy is the poor state of their art: "The relationship of our arts to life is a symbol of the degeneration of this life ... [O]ur theater is a disgrace to those who maintain and frequent it" (*DS*, 4). Though modern cultural decay is of nearly epidemic proportion, still, its epidemiology must be outlined from a special perspective. Hence, Nietzsche's completion of his study at Bayreuth in the summer of 1876 and at the inaugural opening of the festival. From the particular vantage of that time and place, "common" and "everyday" modern decadence was made "conspicuous" to Nietzsche's critical eye—or, perhaps, to his discerning nose.

Decadence can be understood in both an aesthetic and a physiological sense—and we will develop presently how these different modes of the same concept relate to one another. Wagner's new tragic theater overcomes aesthetic decadence. In turn, Nietzsche, as what Ahern calls a "cultural physician"[43] diagnoses the symptoms of physiological decadence and prescribes a healthy regimen of Wagnerian art: "Already [it] is making the art-centers of modern man tremble; whenever the breath of his spirit has wafted into these gardens, everything withered and ready to fall there has been shaken" (*RWB*, 10). Soon, it will seem to those who hear Wagner—or, to those who breathe in the air of his music—that "a curtain has been raised on the future" and the "ill odor" that has clung to popular theater has finally wafted away (*RWB*, 10).

The synaesthetics of music that clears the stale air of traditional theater recalls the pungency of Des Esseintes's perfumery in Huysmans's *Against Nature*. Similarly, Nietzsche follows the Decadents in situating artworks across the different senses in describing Wagner's music as a visualization of the audible and an orchestration of the visible: "His art always conducts [Wagner] along this twofold path, from a world as audible spectacle into a world as a visible spectacle enigmatically related to it, and the reverse" (*RWB*, 7). Indebted as all this is to the Decadent aesthetics of immediate sensation and intermedial synaesthesia, Nietzsche casts decadence in the negative; further, he invokes Wagner's multisensorial art *against* the modernist tendencies of the movement: the *Gesamtkunstwerk* is held out as the last bulwark against modern ruin.

To make sense of how contrary conclusions could be drawn from the same evidence—of Wagner as the hero of decadent modernism and of Wagner as the savior from decadent modernism—it will help to develop some of the conceptual complexities of decadence as an aesthetic and medico-scientific term. In an aesthetic register, "decadent" applied, as we have seen, to a range of different artists, artistic forms, and practices. Anticipating, in ways, later performance art practices, "decadence" also applied to an aesthetics of everyday life. The figure of the dandy, described by Baudelaire in "The Painter of Modern Life" as "cultivating the idea of beauty in their own persons,"[44] translates the decadent aesthetic into a way of life. Or, rather, the line between art and life is blurred by the dandy in that Huysmans based Des Esseintes on the Comte Robert de Montesquiou who was an aesthete famous for his ornate home décor and flamboyant fashion sense; Montesquiou, in turn, was an author and poet of various Decadent literary works.

The lived embodiment of the Decadent aesthetic in the person of the dandy points up the physiological sense of the concept. Living by an acute, refined sensibility—a heightened attention to taste, touch, sound and smell—the dandy is a connoisseur. In his medico-scientific history of the notion of *dégénérescence* in mid- to late-nineteenth-century France, Pick quotes the following from an 1886 issue of *Le Décadent* (the main art journal of the movement): "Society disintegrates under the corrosive action of a deliquescent civilization weighed down by refinement of appetites, of sensations, of taste, of luxury, of pleasures."[45] Aesthetic decadence is associated with social disintegration and a degenerate refinement of the senses. But, this is *dégénérescence* in a positive sense in challenging the otherwise rampant spread of post-Revolutionary petty bourgeoism: Dandyism was to be a form of sociocultural critique; Decadence was to be its critically lived philosophy.

The same constellation of concepts and terms—aesthetic decadence, cultural decay, physiological degeneracy—appears in the negative in the scientific treatises of the day. The pathologization of various, interrelated conditions grouped under the heading of "degeneracy" authorized the confinement and treatment of those who suffered from the ailment. Pick focuses through the central chapters of his history on Bénédict Morel's *Traité des dégénérescences physiques, intellectuelles et morales de l'espèce humaine* (1857), which catalogued "hernias, goiters ... stunted growth, cranial deviations, deaf and dumbness, blindness, albinism, club-feet ... tuberculosis, rickets and sterility" all under the heading of "degeneracy."[46] From Morel's association of decadence with a wide array of diseases and malformities, doctors and psychologists began to practice medicine as a modern curative science aimed at returning patients to a state of normalcy. What the Decadent artist and dandy celebrated in the name of a particular modernism, namely, a non-utilitarian, creative anti-capitalism,[47] Morel and early modern doctors pathologized in the individual and collective social body in the name of a normatively proper bourgeois citizenry.

In 1876 at Bayreuth, Nietzsche, whose health was just beginning to deteriorate, invokes the concept of decadence to account for Wagner's counter-modernism. While the aesthetic sense of the term is operative in "Richard Wagner in Bayreuth"—Nietzsche cites the "morbidly luxuriant forms and techniques" of certain contemporary artworks (*RWB*, 2); and Wagner's tenure in Paris, which kept him in company with Baudelaire and other Decadent artists, had only just ended—primarily, Nietzsche has the physiological sense of "decadent" in mind. This is because of the historical tenor of the meditation. Above, we noted the seeming forward-looking, future tense of Nietzsche's paean to Wagner: as with the "curtain" that Wagner raises on the future of theater, so his music "speaks ... to individual[s] ... of the future" (*RWB*, 10). But, the futurity of Nietzsche's vision of Wagner is decidedly past-oriented. Throughout the essay, as in *The Birth of Tragedy* (1872), Wagner's musical theater is rooted in and redeems the promise of ancient Greek tragedy. The Bayreuthian present and the possible Wagnerian future are restorative expressions of the ancient past. In conclusion, in asking where in contemporary society a Brünnhilde or a Siegfried is who is free and fearless enough to stand up in the twilight of the gods, Nietzsche looks to a past future wherein Wagner appears "not [as a] seer of the future," but as an "interpreter and transfigurer of the past" (*RWB*, 11).

Seemingly future-looking while really historically minded as Nietzsche is in the fourth *Untimely Meditation*, decadence cannot but operate for him only in its physiological register. By contrast, aesthetic decadence is presentist; it is so, particularly when referred to the body in the immediacy of sense-experience. In reflecting on Baudelaire's poem "*Chant d'automne*," Jameson puts plainly this bodily presentism: "The referent of [Baudelaire's poem] is ... the body itself, or better still, the bodily sensorium"; or, even more simply, "sensation."[48] What is properly modernist in the poem is Baudelaire's combination of perceptual language—the sound, in this case, of firewood being chopped in a courtyard; its "dreary thud [*choc monotone*]" on the cobblestones—with the "opacity of the body," that is, the persistence of reference and the suggestion of meaning even in the mute immediacy of bodily sensation. Continuing, Jameson writes, "language ... always seeks to transform that scandalous and irreducible content [of bodily sensation] back into something like meaning. Modernism will then be a renewed effort to do just that."[49] In taking on the nearly impossible task of translating bodily sensations into meaningful language, Baudelaire inaugurates the project of modernism—and does so, in Jameson's terms, through a metaphorical and metonymic play of symbols made to stand for the immediacy of the senses.[50]

Physiological decadence, by contrast, is past-oriented. The degeneracy of certain peoples is a consequence of their heritage. As Pick recounts, Philippe Buchez, among other mid-nineteenth-century French medical practitioners, produced a vast literature showing *dégénérescence* to be an organically inherited condition.[51] Here, for instance, is Théodule Ribot describing hereditary degeneracy in his 1875 text *Heredity*: "In France, ... there are causes ... which tend ultimately to lower the race. ... The descendants of [degenerates] go on degenerating, and the result for the community is debasement."[52] The figure of the cretin, as portrayed in Balzac's novel *The Country Doctor* (1833), exemplifies in the popular imagination what in the scientific literature was termed the "degenerate." In both cases, real and literary, the disease is biological and passed down through bloodlines. Early in the novel, Balzac writes, "Marriages among these unfortunate creatures are not forbidden by law ... [s]o cretinism was in a fair way to spread" all over the country from a few isolated cases.[53]

Similarly, it is the historical tenor of Nietzsche's 1876 meditation on the past future of Wagner's music that leads him to miss the presentist aesthetics of decadence. Nietzsche's historicism narrows his understanding of "decadent" to its scientific, physiological sense of an organic, heritable degeneracy. For example, in Section 6 of the essay Nietzsche invokes the biological scientific view of humans as degenerate according to basic laws of nature (RWB, 6). Implicitly, the critical force of Nietzsche's objections to modern decadence is borrowed from the negative, pathological evaluation of the same in the scientific literature of the day. The ruin wrought by "modern man" on Germany's roots in ancient Greece parallels the scientific literature's pathologization of physiological degeneracy as a generationally inherited threat to communal health. Nietzsche thus trades on those moments of true insight in the essay into the complexities of the concepts of decadence and modernity for the force of a cultural critique of the present borrowed from a past-oriented, natural/biological idea of degeneracy.

In "Literary History and Literary Modernity" Paul de Man raises similar questions against the second of Nietzsche's *Untimely Meditations*: "On the uses and disadvantages of history for life" (1874). The text, de Man argues, is "a good example of the complications that ensue when a genuine impulse toward modernity collides with the demands of a historical consciousness."[54] As in "Richard Wagner in Bayreuth," "modern" in the second *Untimely Meditation* primarily refers in the negative to the degenerate state of Nietzsche's German contemporaries; and, this is in contrast to the "*inexpressibly richer and more vital culture*" of the ancient Greeks (*RWB*, 4). Still, another sense of modernity operates in the second *Untimely Meditation*. It is a "more dynamic" and "far-reaching" sense of "modern" than the mere equivalent of contemporary degeneracy; it is "what Nietzsche [in the essay] calls 'life.'"[55] "Modern" in the sense of "life," and Nietzsche's efforts to develop a critical concept of (modern) life, "complicat[es]" the argument of the essay; "modern" in the sense of "life" renders problematic what de Man calls the "historical consciousness" of the meditation.[56]

Nietzsche associates life, not as a biological term but as a mode of existence and experience—as what de Man calls an "ontological" concept[57]—with the ability to forget; or, what is the same put in the converse: "It is impossible to live ... without forgetting" (*HL*, 1). In the concept of life as forgetting, Nietzsche has "capture[d] the authentic spirit of modernity."[58] This is because, as de Man continues, "modernity exists in the form of a desire to wipe out whatever came earlier, in the hope of reaching at last a point that could be called a true present."[59] Here is Nietzsche's "genuine impulse toward modernity" in a positive sense of the term. The state of forgetfulness that Nietzsche recommends to the too historical, and thus enervated, German people is like the Baudelarian *flânuûr*'s "kaleidescopic" consciousness, which mirror-like reflects without being impressed upon by its ever-present environs.[60]

De Man's question, and it is one we asked of the fourth *Untimely Meditation*, is whether Nietzsche avails himself of the full sense of "modern" operative in his text: "Can [Nietzsche] free his own thought from historical prerogatives ... [can] his own text approach the condition of modernity it advocates?"[61] Simply, no. More fully, the modern, diachronic sense of the present requires just what Nietzsche argues must be forgotten: the temporal horizon of the past (and future) in which the present is situated. The present is fleeting only relative to history as a mass of past presents—each of which and all together show up the impermanence of the now. As de Man puts the point, generally, the modern experience of the present as a passing phenomenon "makes the past irrevocable and unforgettable."[62] To advocate for the forgetting of the past, as Nietzsche does, and this in the service of reinvigorating his contemporary culture—in the service, that is, of making Germany vitally modern—is to mistake the modern present. The modern present is inherently diachronic: it is always other than itself, whether relative to its past and future, or relative to a permanency that contrasts with its fleeting inconstancy. A present bound on both sides by a forgetting of what it is not is a present reduced to synchronic time—it is a present that is lifelessly unmodern.

Further, de Man shows how Nietzsche's idea of a generative, lively present is modeled after his idea of human existence as "an uninterrupted pastness that *lives* from its own denial and destruction."[63] To be modern in the positive sense is to be presentist; but more, it is to be productively presentist. The modern present is a time rife with creative potential. Constantin Guys, for Baudelaire, held himself in the potent present of modern London, and through his innovative style produced thousands of drawings and sketches.[64] Similarly, Nietzsche would have his contemporaries live in a creative present free from a too-well-remembered, moribund past. Yet, Nietzsche defines such a present by critical historicism in the second *Untimely Meditation*, and by cultural historicism in the fourth. On de Man's reading, Nietzsche at this point in his intellectual life cannot but imagine the potency of the present as like a process of past generation.[65]

Decadent art is a symptom of a degenerate heritage; that it was the predominant art in Europe near the turn of the twentieth century called, to Nietzsche, for a cultural critique of the modern-to-come in the name of the ancient past. Yet, a positive, though undeveloped, sense of decadence also operates in "Richard Wagner in Bayreuth"—just as "life" functions in a double sense in the second *Untimely Meditation*. At times, Nietzsche is able to envision an aesthetically transformed and creative modernity, and to do so in terms of decadence. What keeps Nietzsche from exercising "decadent" and "modern" in their full, non-dialectical potential is his historicism: a charge similar to the one Nietzsche raises against himself in the "Attempt at Self-Criticism" (1886). It is the historian's voice that speaks in *The Birth of Tragedy*; it is a "grav[e] and dialectical[ly] ill-humor[ed]" voice unable to express the question it really had in hand (*B*, *P*, 3). That question is the question of modernity. That Nietzsche here frames his failure to ask it as a matter of form and style means, too, that it is the question of aesthetic modernism: "It should have sung, this 'new soul'—and not spoken! What I had to say then—too bad that I did not dare say it as a poet" (*B*, *P*, 3). We will return to the modern question of style, below, in reading *The Case of Wagner* (1888).

The question of modernity cannot be raised apart from that of decadence—a non-dialectical hermeneutic that has guided the present study. Told in terms of art and cultural history, the reason for this interdependence is because the Decadents immediately preceded and anticipated modernist experiments with intra- and intermedial ekphrasis, symbolic polysemy and a presentist aesthetics of sensation. Pierrot concludes his art history of Decadence by tracing its influence on twentieth-century French Surrealism,[66] and Sherry presents both Ezra Pound and T. S. Eliot's modernist poetry as carrying on key decadent aesthetic themes.[67] In terms of the ontology of concepts, decadence and modernism operate non-dialectically according to similar logics. Both concepts signify a non-synchronous temporality; and both stand for and function as unprecedented, non-natural modes of productivity in a diachronic present. As the paintings of Moreau, the novels of Huysmans, and art theory of Baudelaire exemplify, the concepts of decadence and modernity operate together in plural and productive ways—at least in those works, whether artistic or theoretical, that allow for the interplay of their full significance.

Implicitly, Nietzsche in his early works seems aware of the conceptual interrelatedness of the decadent and the modern: he consistently pairs the two in leveling his cultural critique against the then current state of Germany. Further, Nietzsche seems aware that decadence is an artistic mode of presentist creativity, just as is the concept of the modern in its positive valence. Nietzsche seems to grasp this in writing to and about Wagner: the *artiste exemplaire* of French Decadence and, as founder of Bayreuth, the complete artist who would create the future of German art and culture. That Nietzsche misses the complex ontology of the concept of the modern, and the polysemic significance of decadence, is, we have argued, a consequence of his historicism, that is, that the Wagnerian future was to be a rebirth of Greek antiquity.

An "historical consciousness," as de Man puts it, of the modern present cannot but model the potent force of that present after a kind of biological, hereditary generation. What Nietzsche misses in the early works, and what he comes to realize by the end of his intellectual life—in *Ecce Homo* and *The Case of Wagner*—is that by drawing decadence to the foreground of a non-historical aesthetic theory he is able to exercise the creative, modern force of the concept. It is to these late works that we turn, now, in conclusion.

* * *

Though "Richard Wagner in Bayreuth" made only a faint impression on French intellectual and cultural life, Nietzsche's philosophical influence in late-nineteenth-century France grew by indirect means. The historian Hyppolite Taine and the writer Jean Burdeau corresponded with Nietzsche in 1888 about further French translations of his work[68]—Burdeau being one of the translators and disseminators of Schopenhauer's work in French throughout the 1870s and 1880s.[69] Further, some Lycée professors were including Nietzsche's work in excerpt as early as 1889. The Symbolist poet and novelist Alfred Jarry recalls that at Rennes his philosophy professor Benjamin Bourdon included passages from Nietzsche in the course readings.[70] Two publication events in 1891 and 1892, respectively, drew out these undercurrents of Nietzschean influence on *fin-de-siècle* French art and culture. First, a French translation of *The Case of Wagner* was published; the book was followed the next year by a series of articles in the French scholarly press.[71]

Nietzsche announces the ahistoricism of *The Case of Wagner* from the first page of the book; and, he frames the task at hand as a matter of decadence:

> What does a philosopher demand of himself, first and last? To overcome his time in himself, to become "timeless." With what must he therefore engage in hardest combat? With whatever marks him as the child of his time. Well, then! I am, no less than Wagner, a child of this time; that is, a decadent. (*CW*, *P*)

Continuing, Nietzsche names decadence as the concept that "preoccupied" him more than any other cultural and philosophical problem (*CW*, *P*). Put otherwise, in decadence Nietzsche confronted the problem of modernity—and in Wagner, the problem of modern art. The musician who hates but can listen to no other music than Wagner's and the philosopher who would be modern by the only possible means, namely, by being a Wagnerian: Nietzsche understands both perfectly well in that they describe his own musical taste and his own philosophy (*CW*, *P*).

Decadence and modernity run together throughout *The Case of Wagner*. If Nietzsche's prefatory comment rings untrue that nothing has preoccupied him so much as decadence, it is fairly said of this late work, and of *Ecce Homo*. The latter book begins with a de-naturalized vision of maternal and paternal descent: "This dual descent ... both from the highest and the lowest rung on the ladder of life, at the same time a decadent and a beginning ... perhaps distinguishes me" (*EH*, *Why I Am So Wise*, 1); or, more plainly, "apart from the fact that I am a decadent, I am also the opposite" (*EH*, *Why I Am So Wise*, 2). The equivocal tone of Nietzsche's autobiographical identification with and distance from decadence signals the complex significance of the concept in his last book. Similarly, in *The Case of Wagner* decadence appears variously and shifts in its use between positive and negative registers. So, Wagner's music transforms Schopenhauer's decadent pessimism into a creative impulse (*CW*, 6); further, Wagner is an exemplary modern artist because of the decadence of his music (*CW*, 5). Continuing, Nietzsche invokes literary decadence directly (CW, 7), centers decadent modernism in Paris (*CW*, 9), and in the epilogue cites decadence and symbolism in his discussion of modern art (*CW*, *Epilogue*).

Decadence in something closer to its full, complex significance is able to operate in this way because the text is free from the historicism of Nietzsche's early works. No historical reconstruction or justification of Wagner's works is offered; no mention is made of the promise of Ancient Greek tragedy to overcome the history of theater. Indeed, the mythic grounding of Wagner's operas, which was much celebrated by Nietzsche in his early studies, comes up in *The Case of Wagner* for comedic derision. Nietzsche removes Parsifal from his otherworldly airs and reveals an everyday theology student with a secondary school education; similarly, when stripped of their "heroic skin," Wagner's heroine's become "indistinguishable from Madame Bovary" (*CW*, 9). In this way, Wagner's work is revealed to be about the problems that preoccupy "the little decadents of Paris," that is, "entirely modern, entirely metropolitan problems" (*CW*, 9).

Rather than situating Wagner in an historically reconstructed context, Nietzsche instead engages Wagner's operas at the level of the works themselves. In so doing, Nietzsche anticipates autonomous art criticism and becomes a properly modern aesthetician. Questions of style, composition, and the interplay between form and content dominate the short book: the partial theory of music on offer in *The Case of Wagner* is in these regards proto-autonomist. Nietzsche argues for the importance of the color of musical tone and contrasts melody and harmony—advocating for a disharmonic music like what Wagner "dared" to create (*CW*, 6). Melody, by contrast, appeals to the masses; melody plays on the audience's passions and panders to popularity. Overly melodic works, then, are stylistically unmodern in deriving their aesthetic value from something other than their form and composition.[72]

Similarly, Nietzsche is critical of Wagner's operas as works of "redemption." The moralism of innocents redeeming the lives of sinners, as is the case in *Tannhäuser*, or, chaste youths redeeming the reputations of fallen women, as in *Parsifal* (*CW*, 3)—or, even, of Wagner redeeming himself as an artist in the *Der Ring des Niebelungen* (*CW*, 3)—mark the works as decadently, lifelessly degenerate. This is because the operas borrow their force from something other than the aesthetic dictates of musical composition, namely, from Christian doctrine and ancient Aryan mythology. In one-to-one correspondence, every part of Wagner's late operas stand for a redemptive moral lesson; and, each, to this extent, is negatively decadent in being dependent upon concepts and forms borrowed from non-aesthetic sources. That the final line of *Parsifal* is "redemption for the redeemer!" announces the opera's negative decadence (*CW*, *Postscript*): Wagner's art, in the end, devolves into mere didacticism.[73]

Moore and Paré are right to refuse the title of autonomism to Nietzsche's late aesthetic theory: after all, it fails to critique artworks solely by aesthetic standards of form, style, technique, genre, and so forth.[74] The extra-aesthetic concept that persists into Nietzsche's late theory is the concept of life, which, as we have seen, is made to stand in for the concept of the modern in a positive, creative sense. What makes *Parsifal* a decadent work in a negative sense is its sickening, weakening reliance upon something other than its own aesthetic standards, that is, its handling of changes in time signature, its tonalities and atonalities, its harmonics, and so forth. Here, we are reminded of Huysmans's and Moreau's respective decadence. Like the Decadent novelist and painter whose company he kept during his time in Paris, so Wagner limits the intermedial play of symbols between text and music to run only in one direction from allegory and moralism to art. In trying to vivify his decadent music by borrowing from Teutonic myth and lore, Wagner enervates his late works of their intra-aesthetic vitality—a Nietzschean critique of the works that conflates the language of (modern) aesthetic autonomism with the metaphorics of "modern" as "life."

The other side of the same conceptual coin, so to speak, also has currency in Nietzsche's late study of Wagner. In "dwell[ing] on the question of style" in section 7 of book, Nietzsche asks what the sign is of literary decadence: "Life no longer dwells in the whole. The word becomes sovereign and leaps out of the sentence, the sentence reaches out and obscures the meaning of the page, the page gains life at the expense of the whole" (*CW*, 2). "Life" in this passage comes close to an autonomous aesthetic category—specifically, in the fit and interplay between the parts and whole of a work. Wagner's positive decadence, which is to say, his modernism in a creative, productive sense, consists in the way his works handle this part/whole compositionality. Beginning from what Nietzsche calls a "hallucination … of gestures," Wagner "gains small units … he animates these, severs them, and makes them visible" (*CW*, 7). In sum, "Wagner is admirable and gracious … in the invention of the smallest, in spinning out details"; he is, Nietzsche claims, "our greatest miniaturist in music" (*CW*, 7). What of the grandeur and excess of Wagnerian opera as *Gesamtkunstwerk*? It is the whole of the parts encompassed in what Nietzsche calls Wagner's "dramatic style" (*CW*, 7); it is what, more familiarly, from the history of music we call his debt to and development of nineteenth-century grand opera.

Freed from the confining constraints of the historicism of *The Birth of Tragedy* and the *Untimely Meditations*, the complex ontology of the concepts of decadence and modernity gives shape to Nietzsche's aesthetic theory in his late, last works. Hence, the ambiguity of Nietzsche's various appeals to the concepts in *The Case of Wagner* and *Ecce Homo*; hence, too, the ambivalence with which Nietzsche identifies himself—and Wagner—both as and as not decadents and moderns. In turn, and in properly modernist fashion, we can put the same autonomist aesthetic questions to Nietzsche that he puts to Wagner. In so doing, we measure the form and content of Nietzsche's theory by the same aesthetic standard. What of Nietzsche's handling of the parts and whole of his aesthetic theory? What of its style, which once was aphoristic, but in the end resorts to a kind of undecorated, confessional prose? Do other extra-aesthetic concepts like "life" and "(natural) creation" figure into Nietzsche's late critical aesthetic theory? To the extent that we can answer these questions positively, to that extent Nietzsche is modernist—and his aesthetic theory is fully autonomist. To the extent that we can answer the same questions negatively, then to that extent Nietzsche remains a decadent—a conclusion he reached, self-revealingly, about himself in his last works. That Nietzsche could do no more than anticipate autonomism in aesthetic theory—that he could be no more than a decadent modernist—attests above all to the prevalence and influence of the concept of decadence at what Foucault identifies as the Nietzschean threshold to modernity.

Notes

1 Vivien Greene, ed. *Mystical Symbolism: The Salon de la Rose + Croix in Paris, 1892-1897* (New York: Guggenheim Museum Publications, 2017), 58.
2 Pierre-Louis Mathieu, *Gustave Moreau: Complete Edition of the Finished Paintings, Watercolours and Drawings* (Oxford: Phaidon, 1977), 255.
3 Odilon Redon recounts his first encounter with Moreau's *Oedipus and the Sphinx* at the 1864 Salon as follows: "How the work beguiled me! For years I retained the memory of that initial impression, and it may have acted so strongly upon me as to give me the strength to pursue a lonely path"—a solitary "path" that yet "paralleled" Moreau's own (Mathieu, *Gustave Moreau,* 84). If there is unity to Decadence as an art movement, Redon's description of it might be most fitting: a group of solitary artists moving in parallel with one another following the lead of Moreau.
4 Mathieu *Gustave Moreau*, 84.
5 Vincent Sherry, *Modernism and the Reinvention of Decadence* (New York: Cambridge University Press, 2014), 22.
6 Michelle Facos, *Symbolist Art in Context* (Berkeley, CA: University of California Press, 2009), 174.
7 Facos, *Symbolist Art in Context*, 175.
8 Jean Pierrot, *The Decadent Imagination, 1880-1900*, trans. D. Coltman (Chicago: University of Chicago Press, 1981), 6.
9 J. K. Huysmans, *Against Nature*, trans. R. Baldick (New York: Penguin, 2003), 67–68.
10 Facos, *Symbolist Art in Context*, 61.
11 Gustave Flaubert, *Salammbô*, trans. A. J. Krailsheimer (New York: Penguin, 1977), 52.
12 Mathieu, *Gustave Moreau,* 124.
13 Huysmans, *Against Nature,* 66–67.
14 Ibid.
15 Mathieu, *Gustave Moreau,* 124.
16 Huysmans, *Against Nature,* 109.
17 Ibid., 124.
18 Ibid., 129.
19 Arthur Symons, *The Symbolist Movement in Literature*, ed. M. Creasy (Manchester, UK: Carcanet Press, 2014), 206.
20 Mary Bryden, "The Odorous Text: A Deleuzian Approach to Huysmans," *The Romanic Review* 100, no. 3 (2009): 274.
21 Huysmans, *Against Nature,* 129.
22 Ibid., 54–55.
23 Mary Bryden, "The Odorous Text," 274.
24 Ibid.
25 G. E. Lessing, *Laocoön: An Essay on the Limits of Painting and Poetry. Classic and Romantic German Aesthetics*, ed. J. M. Bernstein (New York: Cambridge University Press, 2003), 52–53.
26 In 1839, Chevreul published the scientific treatise *De la loi du contraste simultane des couleurs*, which set the precedent for subsequent nineteenth-century color studies. In the text, Chevreul establishes a physiological *rapprochement* between sound and color. The harmony of beautifully ordered colors, Chevreul argues, is analogous to

the harmony of beautifully ordered sounds. In turn, Delacroix drew on aspects of the sciences of sight and sound to form a kind of musical painting: "If painting is to express the intangible, it is music rather than any of the other arts ... that becomes [its] main model." Delacroix maintained a close correspondence with Chopin, and credited the composer's work with conveying to him the *feeling* for "counterpoint and harmony." The Decadents in the last decades of the nineteenth century continued this trend of combining the visual arts with music: for example, Félix Vallotton's woodblock prints of Wagner, which were exhibited in the 1892 Salon de Rose + Croix, attest to the great influence the German composer had on the French painters of the era. (Cf. Moshe Barasch, *Modern Theories of Art, 1: From Winckelmann to Baudelaire* (New York: New York University Press, 1990), 201).

27 Charles Baudelaire, "The Painter of Modern Life," in *Baudelaire: Selected Writings on Art and Literature*, trans. P. E. Charvet (New York: Penguin, 1972), 394.

28 Baudelaire, "The Painter of Modern Life," 397.

29 Ibid., 399.

30 Ibid., 400.

31 Ibid., 402.

32 Ibid., 403.

33 Ibid., 402.

34 Ibid., 391.

35 Jean-François Lyotard, "Rewriting Modernity," in *The Inhuman: Reflections on Time*, trans. G. Bennington and R. Bowlby (Stanford: Stanford University Press, 1991), 25.

36 J. A. Hiddleston, *Baudelaire and the Art of Memory* (New York: Oxford University Press, 1999), 219.

37 In later works—*Là-bas* and *Trois Primitifs*—Huysmans drops the voice of his characters to write in the first person about the works of Grünewald. In the Karlsruhe Christ, which depicts Christ as the "Redeemer of the doss house" and "the God of the morgue," Huysmans discerns "gleams of light filtered from the ulcerous head; a superhuman radiance illuminat[ing] the gangrened flesh and the tortured features": that most sacred and ideal of subjects here treated with stark, brutal realism. Cf. J. K. Huysmans, "Two Essays on Grünewald," in *Grünewald: The Paintings*, ed. E. Ruhmer (Oxford: Phaidon Press, 1958), 9.

38 Michel Foucault, *The Order of Things: An Archaeology of the Human Sciences*, trans. A. Sheridan (New York: Routledge, 2002), 10.

39 Foucault, *The Order of Things*, 10.

40 Ibid., 331.

41 Ibid., 332.

42 Forth suggests that Nietzsche's essay did not receive wider attention because it was not carried in *La Revue wagnérienne*: the main organ, at the time, of French-language Wagner studies and scholarship. The journal did not carry Baumgartner's translation, Forth speculates, because its cofounder Houston Stewart Chamberlain's disliked Nietzsche: an animosity born of their shared time together at Bayreuth (C. E. Forth, "Nietzsche, Decadence, and Regeneration in France, 1891-95," *Journal of the History of Ideas* 54, no. 1 (1993): 101).

43 D. R. Ahern, *Nietzsche as Cultural Physician* (University Park, PA: The Pennsylvania State University Press, 1995), 3.

44 Baudelaire, "The Painter of Modern Life," 419. The literary origins of the dandy predate Baudelaire's "The Painter of Modern Life" by a generation: Cf. Balzac's

Traité de la vie élégante (1830) and Jules Barbey d'Aurevilly's biographical study *Du dandysme et de George Brummell* (1845).
45 Daniel Pick, *Faces of Degeneration: A European Disorder, 1848-1918* (New York: Cambridge University Press, 1989), 41–42.
46 Pick, *Faces of Degeneration,* 50.
47 Michel Lemaire, *Le dandysme de Baudelaire à Mallarmé* (Montreal: University of Montreal Press, 1978), 25ff.
48 Frederick Jameson, "Baudelaire as Modernist and Postmodernist: The Dissolution of the Referent and the Artificial 'Sublime,'" *The Modernist Papers* (New York: Verso 2007), 227.
49 Jameson, "Baudelaire as Modernist and Postmodernist," 229.
50 Ibid.
51 Pike, *Faces of Degeneration,* 66.
52 Ibid., 41.
53 Ibid., 46.
54 Paul de Man, "Literary History and Literary Modernity," in *Blindness and Insight: Essays in the Rhetoric of Contemporary Criticism* (Minneapolis: University of Minnesota Press, 1983), 145.
55 de Man, "Literary History and Literary Modernity," 146.
56 Ibid.
57 Ibid.
58 Ibid., 147.
59 Ibid., 148.
60 Baudelaire, "The Painter of Modern Life," 400.
61 de Man, "Literary History and Literary Modernity," 148.
62 Ibid.
63 Ibid.; emphasis added.
64 Baudelaire, "The Painter of Modern Life," 412.
65 de Man, "Literary History and Literary Modernity," 150.
66 Pierrot, *The Decadent Imagination, 1880-1900,* 256ff.
67 Sherry, *Modernism and the Reinvention of Decadence,* 175ff. The connection between Eliot's modernist poetry and French Decadence is direct. As Frank Kermode recounts, "For his formation as a poet the most important moment [in Eliot's early career] ... was his coming, in 1908, upon Arthur Symons' book *The Symbolist Movement in Poetry* (1899)." Symons's book, Kermode continues, "[was] originally entitled *The Decadent Movement in Poetry,*" but was retitled after "Decadent" "ceased to be fashionable after the Oscar Wilde trials" (Frank Kermode, "Introduction," in *The Waste Land and Other Poems* (New York: Penguin, 1998), viii).
68 Forth, "Nietzsche, Decadence, and Regeneration in France, 1891-95," 102n.19.
69 Pierrot identifies Schopenhauer as the main philosophical influence on Decadence. Though *The World as Will and Representation* (1818) did not appear in French translation until 1886, various other of Schopenhauer's works were available in the 1870s, together with secondary studies of his philosophy: for example, Paul Challemel-Lacour's "*Un Bouddhiste contmporain en Allemagne*" (1870) and Théodule Ribot's *La Philosophie de Schopenhauer* (1874). From Schopenhauer's particular interpretation of Kant's transcendental idealism, the Decadents developed an anti-realist worldview which made of objects mere ideas. From Schopenhauer's pessimism, the Decadents understood human existence to be "subject to the

pitiless necessities of a physical, physiological and social determinism." Finally, like Schopenhauer, they held that "religious faith" was nothing other than a "nostalgic memory" and love to be nothing but, "an unconscious subjection to an instinct aimed solely at the survival of the species" (Pierrot, *The Decadent Imagination, 1880-1900,* 56–57).

70 Forth, "Nietzsche, Decadence, and Regeneration in France, 1891-95," 102n.19.

71 In early 1892, Téodor de Wyzewa published "Frédéric Nietzsche: le dernier métaphysicien" in the journal *La Revue bleue*. Wyzewa's article was reductively critical of Nietzsche's philosophy as a species of nihilistic pessimism. Never in the history of human thought, Wyzewa claimed, had a greater "destroyer" of culture and society appeared than Nietzsche. In response, and in defense of Nietzsche, Halévy and Gregh published an article titled, simply, "Frédéric Nietzsche" in the Spring issue of *Le Banquet*. The article constructs a positive Nietzschean philosophy, and does so in terms of decadence and Wagner. Between "Richard Wagner in Bayreuth" and *The Case of Wagner*—the two texts by Nietzsche then available in French translation—Halévy and Gregh trace Nietzsche's development from a typical Wagnerian decadent to a critic of the same in the name of modern life and culture (Forth, "Nietzsche, Decadence, and Regeneration in France, 1891-95," 104–05).

72 While it is possible to read this section of the text ironically, as Moore and Paré do, and this because the praise Nietzsche heaps on Bizet's *Carmen* at the beginning of *The Case of Wagner* would suggest his valuing melody over harmony, such a reading misses the first- to third-person shift in voice in the text. Bizet's melodic work is good for Nietzsche, given his particular physiology: "Every time I heard *Carmen*, I seemed to myself more of a philosopher ... so patient do I become, so happy ... so settled" (*KSA*, 6:15). By contrast, for Nietzsche in the third-person Wagner's music provides a case study in modern—or, at least, proto-modern—aesthetic theory (M. Moore and R. P. Paré, "'*Not Mere Music*': Nietzsche and the Problem of Moral Content in Music," in *Sound Figures of Modernity: German Music and Philosophy*, eds. J. Hermand and G. Richter (Madison, WI: The University of Wisconsin Press, 2006), 136).

73 Moore and Paré read Nietzsche's particular distaste for *Parsifal* as a matter of its asceticism: "Nietzsche argues that art must be life-affirming ... [t]hus the ascetic ideals in Parsifal are antithetical" to his aesthetic theory—so, Nietzsche concludes against Wagner's opera as decadent. This all follows, however, only on a narrow construal of the conceptual significance—of the conceptual ontology—of decadence. Behind an interpretation of Nietzsche's aesthetic theory as valuing works that are life-enhancing and devaluing works that are enervating is a reductively physiological understanding of decadence. Above, we argued, with de Man, for a different conception of "life" in Nietzsche than the strictly biological. A sense of "life," instead, that signaled the potency and creativity available in the modern present. Moore and Paré, by contrast, operate only with a biological sense of "life"—one that is either served by healthy art or disserved by decadent art. So, they miss the modernism of Nietzsche's aesthetics. That modernism, we have argued, derives in part from the concept of decadence in its full aesthetic and physiological significance (Moore and Paré, "'*Not Mere Music*': Nietzsche and the Problem of Moral Content in Music," 129).

74 Ibid.

11

Nietzsche's Relation with Psychoanalysis: From Freud to Surrealist Modernism, Bataille, and Lacan

Tim Themi

Introduction

Nietzsche and Freud are important influences in the development of cultural modernism. Laura Winkiel sees their influence, along with that of Darwin and Marx, as part of a crisis of reason in modernism, where irrationality, instinctual violence, exploitation, and purposeless chance are discovered to have much more prevalence than previously hoped.[1] Perhaps the most telling example of this combined Nietzsche-Freud influence is that of dissident surrealist philosopher Georges Bataille, one of the first interwar French authors to undergo his own analysis ("with Dr. Borel" in 1927), who even applied its results at the end of his erotic novella *Story of the Eye* (1928), before going on to found French Nietzscheanism through the journal *Acéphale* and College of Sociology (1936–39), having earlier in 1923 experienced Nietzsche as "decisive."[2] Further to all this is that Bataille would become a subterranean influence on Lacan, the famous French Freudian, with his notion of *heterology* as a science of the real conceived of as impossible to acknowledge, and inassimilable to our socio-symbolic constructs—not without a "*jouissance* [enjoyment] of transgression" that links up in an erotics our sexuality with death.[3] What this chapter will first discuss is the prior influence of Nietzsche's philosophy on the founders of psychoanalysis themselves, namely Freud and his earliest collaborators in the Germanophone context, east of the Rhine. By discussing Nietzsche's relation with, and influence on, psychoanalysis itself, the aim here is to throw further light on how their combined influence impacts the cultural modernism of which surrealism was part, which Bataille was engaged with as a kind of Freudo-Nietzschean practitioner and critic—whose consequence was in a sense the discourse of Lacan, the analyst initially no stranger to surrealism itself, just as surrealism was equally no stranger to Freud.[4]

The Germanphone context: Nietzsche and Freud

In his seminal 1980 work *Freud and Nietzsche*, Paul-Laurent Assoun notes "a strange contemporaneity" between Nietzsche and Freud, only twelve years apart in age—where Nietzsche publishes his greatest works and finally achieves recognition at "the end of the 1880s, at the moment of the birth of psychoanalysis."[5] But the strangeness comes from the seeming ambivalence Freud has toward reading Nietzsche: at times expressing "an excess of interest" in the philosopher who "represents a nobility inaccessible," who might "find the words for many things which remain mute within"; while at other times expressing a defensive resistance to the sheer number of places pointed out where Nietzsche had "intuitively anticipated" psychoanalytic findings—being later prepared "to forgo all claims to priority in the many instances."[6] Part of what Assoun suggests is at stake in this cautious distance, mixed with admiration, kept by Freud is his ambition to found psychoanalysis as a science, rather than a clinically applied philosophy. For philosophy being associated, here, with a "world-view (*weltanschauung*)" that leaps from facts to values means that Nietzsche's "anticipatory divinations," from insights into his own pathology, would stand opposed to Freud's project. As Assoun puts it, Freud does not want to sacrifice "the 'pain' of scientific labor, which has authenticated Nietzsche's intuitions"—echoing Freud's 1925 article, "An Autobiographical Study," which calls Nietzsche, after Schopenhauer, "another philosopher whose guesses and intuitions often agree in the most astonishing way with the laborious findings of psychoanalysis."[7] But as Alan Bass notes, the idea that Nietzsche's project came from insight into his own pathology, projected out as ideology with "guesses and intuitions," overlooks how Nietzsche's insights stemmed from "his critique of metaphysics." Bass cites Paul Ricoeur's study which famously conjoined Nietzsche, Freud, and Marx as the three "masters of suspicion" to note that Nietzsche's results also stemmed from his beginning "as a philologist who then extended the method of historical, linguistic interpretation over the whole of philosophy," to make "interpretation a manifestation of the will to power."[8]

Freud's distancing comments also tend to overlook his own need for introspection when it came to his clinic—daring initially "to attach importance," Lacan notes, "to the antinomies of his childhood," "neurotic problems," and "dreams," knowing "he would only make progress in the analysis of the neuroses if he analyzed himself"—along with overlooking the perpetual incompleteness of his ambition to establish his findings on the slippery slopes of the unconscious as a hard science.[9] But this difference (as resistance) between himself and Nietzsche also comes out in the more *passive* relation to the moral law, with its Judeo-Christian origins, maintained by Freud—as compared to the transformative incitements of Nietzsche's ethics, calling for nothing less than a *revaluation of all values*.[10] For Nietzsche based the latter on a genealogical critique of Christian Platonism that traces it to its *Hebraic*, as well as Hellenic, roots—having felt so keenly that the Sovereign Good of Western metaphysics, and the Law it enshrined, was a wrong turn that left us alienated from natural instincts. This for Nietzsche was the "denaturalizing" of our "natural values" pertaining to biologically inherited instincts for sex, aggression, and will to power[11]—through an "ascetic ideal" that discourages the proper flourishing of culture such that instead, paradoxically, through crude negations and excessive *denial* of natural enjoyments, "pleasure is felt and *sought* in ill-constitutedness, decay, pain, mischance" (*GM*, *What Is the Meaning of Ascetic Ideals?*, 11). And whether this decay is through the demand for confession, renunciation, or "self-flagellation" (*GM*, *What Is the Meaning of Ascetic Ideals?*, 11) of late-Judaism or the Christian Middle-Ages—residues of which remained in Freud's clinic—or the reversed "late-capitalist" imperative now to *enjoy* consumerism blindly, perversely, until it hurts—here is the ascetic ideal that, nevertheless, links the Freudian *superego* of the "internalization or turning inwards" of violence to the Nietzschean "bad conscience" (*GM*, *'Guilt,' 'Bad Conscience,' and the Like,* 16): which is further linked in a Lacano-Nietzschean way by Alenka Zupančič who notes "Lacan's reading of the superego law in terms of the 'imperative of enjoyment,'" and that "Nietzsche recognizes this mode of enjoyment in the whole history of Christianity."[12]

When it comes to this dialectic of "perversion and asceticism," Sylvia Ons observes that "Nietzsche anticipated psychoanalysis when he pointed out the connection between the two" in speaking of "ascetic voluptuousness," and the "lascivious nature of asceticism"—as if "the operation performed by Freud in the clinic were parallel and related to that performed by Nietzsche in philosophy."[13] But there are moments here where Freud halts before tracking his own critique of superegoic Christianity back to denaturalizing Judaic Law, protesting that a simple "head cold" suffices to cure him "of such desires" for any concomitant Nietzschean intoxication, seeing only "death-wish" which, Assoun notes, "is what stops Freud at the gates of the temple of Dionysos"—as the "Jewish atheist" who resists the genealogical affirmation that with the church in Greece and Rome, "Israel triumphed with its vengeance over all the most noble ideals"—such that while "every return to Nietzsche" is "replacing a repressive Superego" with *will to power*, "drunk with innocence," "psychoanalysis obstinately summons back the condition of desire from the side of the [Judaic] Law."[14]

While acknowledging these moments where this *difference* between Freud and Nietzsche comes to the fore, it nevertheless remains of interest to observe the moments of the opposite effect taking place—where, perhaps, the *influence* of Nietzsche seems to encourage Freud to take a more active stance in his appraisal of the *status quo ante* of the general field of ethics. There is, for instance, the Vienna Wednesday Seminars of 1908, where Nietzsche's thought is actively discussed and presented on, while Freud responds with his usual admixtures of praise and resistance, and even wild analysis in speculating of Nietzsche about "maternal fixation," a "paternal complex," "Christ as an adolescent fantasy," and "narcissism" linked to "homosexual tendencies."[15] This ties into Freud's idea that Nietzsche's findings were the result of introspection projected or universalized out onto the world, transforming thereby an "is" into an "ought" which disqualifies his psychology from the status of science and renders him of all things, unable to free himself of the will to play theologian—simply by virtue of intervening philosophically into the moral sphere.[16] But where else, if not from facts, should our thinkers base their values on?—Errors? This is what Nietzsche saw as the blunder of Western religious metaphysics, with its imaginarized notion of the Good mistaken as real, amounting to "a level of ignorance at which even the concept of the real, the distinction between the real and the imaginary, is lacking" (*TI*, *The 'Improvers' of Humanity*, 1). It can even strike as a bit of amateur Humean philosophy by Freud, here, to suggest it *follows* from the fact that an "ought" cannot be deductively inferred from an "is" that one therefore *ought not* infer one's "oughts" in some other viable way from appraisals of facts, lest they fall prey to theology.[17]

Earlier in 1908, however, despite such positivist quibbles about sticking to facts and avoiding any judgments of value, Freud comes out with his article "'Civilized' Sexual Morality and Modern Nervous Illness," where he can be found *actively condemning* the intimidating effect of our religious mores on libidinal development, noting "the harmful suppression of the sexual life of civilized peoples (or classes) through the 'civilized' sexual morality prevalent in them"—such that when the libido did emerge it was irreparably damaged, with people who "would have been more healthy" being "less good" falling now as "victims to neurosis," becoming the "well-behaved weaklings who later become lost in the great mass of people that tends to follow, unwittingly."[18] This invokes Nietzsche's lament that "Christianity gave Eros poison to drink," such that "he did not die of it but degenerated—into a vice" (*BGE*, 168), a move determined not only by the later Judaic priests who provided the soil upon which Christianity could grow, but also by the later intervention of the Platonic Socrates into the *original* flourishing of *Hellenismos*: what Lacan calls its "fertile period" of the "sixth and fifth centuries" which were "overflowing with intellectual creativity," where "we find ourselves at the historic climax of a particularly active era."[19]

Here in our philosophical prime, in what for Nietzsche is *not* a coincidence, "the symbols of sex" were also "venerable as such" (*KSA*, 12:8[3]; *TI*, *What I Owe the Ancients*, 4), which accords with Freud's idea that our relation to libido "lays down the pattern" for our "other modes of reacting to life."[20] The succeeding paradigm shift toward negation, however, suggests to Nietzsche that whereas "the Sophists were Greeks," "when Socrates and Plato took up the cause of virtue and justice, they were *Jews* or I know not what" (*KSA*, 13:14[147])—speaking to their combined *denaturalizing* intervention that meant a demonizing ignorance of the most basic "prerequisite of our life," which "threw *filth* on the beginning" (*TI*, *What I Owe the Ancients*, 4).[21] But we see Freud take up this countenance of lament and reform also in his 1925 article "Resistances to Psychoanalysis," where, without referencing Judaism, but for noting anti-Semitism as readying him for the isolating resistances psychoanalysis encounters, he *recommends* "more play given to truthfulness" in our relation to libido, with repression "replaced by a better and securer procedure" and a "reduction in strictness" relative to our inherited moral codes—a recommendation that can be indeed be read as a program for a *revaluation* of values.[22]

Later in 1925, Freud pens a letter to the Jewish press center in Zurich where he professes to standing "as far apart from the Jewish religion as from all other religions," having "no part in them emotionally" except as "a subject of scientific interest"—although not without adding that, nevertheless, he "always had a strong feeling of solidarity" with his fellow Jewish people which he encouraged in his children, having "all remained in the Jewish denomination."[23] But perhaps the most revealing place where what is at stake in this repetition of difference *within* the influence of the philhellenic Nietzsche on the Hebraic Freud is where Lacan discerns a "strange Christocentrism" in Freud's treatment of the Judeo-Christian thematic that is "odd to find."[24] This is where Freud posits two Mosses, the first of whom was murdered by his followers, harking back to the murder of the primal father-ruler of the Paleolithic hordes we are said to have lived in, and echoing forward to the murder of Jesus alleged to bring this complex to light to redeem us of the repressed guilt, enabling us to accede to the renunciation demanded by his Law. Lacan finds this odd not just because of the scant evidence, finding the primal Father really a symptomatic "fantasy" of omnipotence "caused" by the repressive operation of the Law, but also because of Freud's usual condemnation of the unrealistic nature of Christian Law—having rebuked the demand to "love thy neighbor as thyself" in finding that "the historical spectacle of a humanity that chose it as its ideal is quite unconvincing, when that ideal is measured against actual accomplishments."[25] But armed with his primal father thesis, Freud proceeds to make the striking claim that Nietzsche's *Übermensch* [overman] was not a transformative figure "from the future," as Nietzsche hoped, but rather a projected fantasy of this primal Father figure "at the very beginning of the history of mankind." This is odd because Nietzsche's model for the *Übermensch* is often the really existing educated Greek and Roman nobles of Antiquity, along with figures like Goethe and Beethoven closer to Nietzsche's present—as has been pointed out, for instance, by Brian Leiter.[26] Nevertheless, there is again a moment where Freud *could* be read as acknowledging the force of Nietzsche's critique of the entire trajectory of Judeo-Christian Law, where Freud notes that the "harmony in the cultivation of intellectual and physical activity" that was "achieved by the Greek" was "denied to the Jews"—although not without adding that in choosing to value the spiritual over the physical, the Jews at least chose "the worthier alternative," clinging to a denaturalizing God-Father figure despite the misfortunes they continued to suffer, according to what for Nietzsche was ultimately an "idiotic formula" of "obedience" (*A*, 26), concocted by "priests."[27]

Nietzsche would disagree with the claim that to value spirit over body is to choose the best of the two, finding this the kind of impossible choice that leads precisely to our civilization's discontents—as the intellect becomes infused with symptoms of repression and continually distorted, overwhelmed in its cognitive claims. In any case, here we can see where there is the *influence* of Nietzsche on psychoanalysis, and where there is a residue of *resistance that leads to a difference*: Nietzsche's project demands an intellectual affirmation of the real of the bodily drives and a transformation of the alienating Law that unduly prohibits it; whereas Freud at times, by comparison, remains locked in the Schopenhauerian pessimism of *eschewing* the desiring will from fear that it entails much risk and leads to no good, staying closer to the Hebraic Law of confession, castration, and renunciation. This is evident in the response to Freud of those of his collaborators such as Otto Rank, who, as Assoun notes, saw himself as being to Freud what Nietzsche was to Schopenhauer regarding negation versus affirmation of the will.[28] And Nietzsche notes of Schopenhauer that "as soon as the thing-in-itself was no longer 'God' for him, he had to see it as bad, stupid, and absolutely reprehensible" (*KSA*, 12:9[42]); he "treated sexuality as a personal enemy" (*GM*, *What Is the Meaning of Ascetic Ideals?*, 7), and "revenges himself on all things" by "branding them" with "the image of his torture" (*GS*, 370). But it is of interest also to track this relation of influence-*and*-difference forward in time and west of the Rhine, into the milieu of the cultural modernism that the Freudian Lacan shared with the Nietzschean Bataille[29]—whose valuable participation in and confrontation with the modernist *surrealist* art indebted to the techniques of Freud comes, I will suggest, from being embedded with the combined influence of *both* Nietzsche and Freud.

The Francophone context: Bataille, modernism, surrealism, Lacan

In one of the first works to begin the task of reading Nietzsche and Lacan in light of each other, Zupančič suggests that Nietzsche himself is modernist when claiming "to break the history of mankind in two"—remaking 1888 as "year I" for the "new calendar" demanded by the completion of *Antichrist:* "the first book of the *Revaluation of all Values*" (*TI, P*).[30] Together with his "bombastic" style which can also strike "as quite modernistic or, rather, as avant-garde," Zupančič compares him here to the painter Kazimir Malevich, who, with his work *Black Square*, claimed to have introduced "the first new form that was ever created," "a new object in reality," with the "painting-surface as object."[31] Although Zupančič concedes that Nietzsche's own tastes in art can still seem "conservative" from this perspective, Nietzsche's idea for the revaluation of values entailed a radical *re*-naturalizing of our drives in a manner akin to *pre*-Platonic cultures, which is something he already saw threatening to emerge in the various historical figures he endorsed to overturn the Christian-Platonic Sovereign Good that lasted "almost two millennia" with, figuratively speaking, "not a single new god" (*A*, 19). And it is here that we can form a comparison with Bataille's surrealism, which points to an analogy with the Renaissance project that Nietzsche admired and wanted to extend, but in an expressly Freudo-Nietzschean way, I suggest, that again conjoins surrealism with the incitements of modernism to start all over, again and anew.[32]

It is in his 1948 Club Maintenant presentation, "The Surrealist Religion," where Bataille suggests that just as the Renaissance involved the Middle Ages feeling they had strayed too far from antiquity, seeking "to find again in Greece and Rome a mode of existence that had been lost"—surrealism seeks to revitalize by going back to "primitive society," where "the quest for primitive culture represents the principal, most decisive and vital, aspect and meaning of surrealism, if not its precise definition."[33] But surrealism's method for this is a Freudian investment of dreams and encouragement to *automatic writing*, Bataille notes—in an earlier 1945 article reviewing a work by surrealist founder André Breton—describing automatic writing as a "type of thought, analogous to dream, which is not subordinated to the control of reason" but governed by "chance."[34] This is precisely the technique that Freud deployed as "the fundamental rule of psycho-analysis": *free-association*—"which lays it down that whatever comes into one's head must be reported without criticizing it," depicted in *The Interpretation of Dreams* as the "relaxation of the watch upon the gates of reason" by the "adoption of an attitude of uncritical self-observation"—to which Freud adds: "I myself can do so very completely, by the help of writing down my ideas as they occur to me."[35]

In another 1948 article on "Surrealism," Bataille even quotes Breton in similar terms describing "automatism" as the "real functioning" and "dictation of thought in the absence of all control exercised by reason and outside all aesthetic or moral considerations."[36] But with this "free poetic release," Bataille notes, what emerges is "as difficult to bear as it is decisive and virilely sovereign," and so "the difficulty which remained was to affirm the value of what was finally released within the shadow."[37] This is where Bataille's expressly Nietzschean current comes to the fore, seeking to revitalize the present through *affirmation* of the real of the drive in its own archaic sovereignty, by overcoming what he called "the dualist evolution" in his 1948 *Theory of Religion* text—where the sacred or divine "appears linked to purity," cleansed of "animal intimacy," and redefined as *opposite* to anything earthly, animal, bodily, sensuous: with the latter relegated to the status of fallen, if not sin, or hell.[38]

Bataille will intervene on such puritanism with a Nietzschean return of Dionysus, knowledge of which is no doubt extended through Freud's focus on the infantile subsistence of the polymorphous libido and its partial drives: from the oral to the anal and genital in its active-passive palpitations and regressive pulls—but not by also losing the demand for *positive* affirmation of this normally unconscious terrain. Such affirmation again comes of Nietzsche's preference for Dionysos to the opposition of *the Crucified* (*EH, Why I am a Destiny*, 9; *KSA*, 13:14[89]): that is, from being *pro* instead of "anti-nature" castrating in morality (*TI, Morality as Anti-Nature*)—preventing the analysis from regressing to a Christian confessional practice of renunciation and negation for adaptation to the status quo.[39] It enables restoration of the *erotic* aspect of religious being, of the divine animality originally implicit of all the sacred: where even as late as Ancient Greece, Bataille recalls, "animality deeply stamps the gods"[40]—enabling a communication of *experience* through the rituals of myth that form the bonds for a community, a community of the real, where, Bataille hopes, "the state of passion, the state of unleashing which was unconscious in the primitive mind, can become lucid."[41]

Armed with this new lucidity, stemming from renewed openness to our animal immediacy, here is where we can imagine a modernist reconfiguring of the usual relations of taboo-*and*-transgression beyond the Western metaphysical tradition of the dualist Good, which ever since Socrates and Plato, as Nietzsche saw, sets up the spirit as a pure space from which to prohibit outright our earthly, bodily animality and condemn it as "false" precisely on account of what makes it *real*: namely "death, change, age, as well as procreation and growth" (*TI, 'Reason' in Philosophy*, 1). But we can see the influence to *re*-structure prohibition also in the Freudian Lacan, who was "a silent presence," Roudinesco notes, "at the secret activities of *Acéphale*"—the secret Nietzschean society founded by Bataille—with the gatherings of Bataille's other prewar groups, *Contre-Attaque* and the College of Sociology, also "held in his apartment."[42] For Lacan's *Ethics Seminar* speaks of those societies that "live very well" with transgression built *into* laws, who rather than "promoting their universal application," "prosper as a result of the transgression of these maxims" to allow periodic outlets for the primitive drive—all of which Lacan can contrast with the ruminations of St. Paul who feels an "excessive, hyperbolic," "desire for death" as a result of his universalized taboo on animality: "the Law which causes sin" paradoxically built up by the demand to repress without respite.[43]

Then Lacan notes how our own societies still do not know what to do with their *jouissance*, as the destructive aspects of the drive tend to explode blindly in what "seems to us to be an inexplicable accident" or "resurgence of savagery," through such horrors as mass-marketed industrialized war—leading us down a "race to destruction" ironically forged by "*Western moralism*" itself.[44] But here again we can see the influence of Bataille's notion of ruinous, non-productive, or non-utilitarian *expenditure* in *The Accursed Share*, which seeks to "lift the curse" placed on the *gift* of the drive by capitalist society emerging from Christianity without knowing how to structure its waste, hellbent only on *accumulation* of profits.[45] The aim is to *lift the curse* by reconfiguring a space where this wasteful, destructive aspect can be affirmed in a sublimated manner, what Lacan calls a "retreat from goods" and the "competition for goods" through an "open destruction of goods," like the "ritual ceremonies" of "potlatch" of primitive societies past—enabling a "maintenance and discipline of desire" by *transgression* of taboos normally governing the everyday, workaday, "ethical register of utilitarianism," but done "consciously and in a controlled way."[46] Lacan here is building on Bataille's tracing of this *correlation* of "organised transgression together with the taboo" to the "oral teaching" of the anthropologist Marcel Mauss, with Bataille noting fellow surrealist and cofounder of the College of Sociology, Roger Caillois, to have definitively taken this insight up—with Caillois, in turn, describing an "intellectual osmosis" with Bataille that made it difficult to distinguish their respective contributions to the work they "pursued in common."[47]

Part of what Bataille also wants to do with this organized transgression is place surrealism among the modernist practices that enable our drive's proper release. By *not* "subordinating it to anything" or forcing "a superior end to it," it becomes "the prerogative of surrealism to free the activity of the mind from such servitude"—thus liberating our drives from "rationalism" through a "poetic liberty" that was traditionally linked to "myths and the rituals connected to them."[48] Bataille sees surrealism restoring this *sovereignty* when its "words, no longer striving to serve some useful purpose, set themselves free and so unleash the image of *free existence*," bestowed "in the instant": the seizure of which "cannot differ from ecstasy." Bataille adds to this that "reciprocally one must define ecstasy as the seizure of the instant"—citing Breton's depicting of this as "a vertiginous descent into ourselves," a "perpetual promenading across forbidden zones."[49] So it is through these forbidden zones we are led in surrealism *beyond* the narrowing reductive realms of utilitarian accumulation and production, enabling the ruinous expenditure that also defines for Lacan the death-drive as "*jouissance* of transgression."[50] No more significant program for the arts can be imagined: For by enabling space for this *jouissance*, the death-drive is less so the death-wish that Freud feared, and more a sublimated *jouissance* of the real giving us the communal release we need to maintain a precarious psycho-sexual balance—gifting us access to the primitive animality left behind through human taboos purposed for work, granting poetic space for transgression of these taboos that places us now in the more primitive, archaic realm of myth.[51]

This high-value Bataille bestowed on surrealism for this transgressive liberty it possessed can come as a shock, given the very public falling out he initially had with Breton. But Bataille's dispute with Breton and surrealism was in some ways short-lived, and, as Michael Richardson notes, "emphasized by writers associated with post-structuralism" who sought to see Bataille "as a precursor of 'postmodernism'" by dissociating him "from contamination with surrealism."[52] Bataille's postwar *Writings on Surrealism*, however—the collection translated by Richardson here discussed—demonstrate that there was a clear rapprochement forming particularly after the war, with Bataille even noting: "Breton later wrote (in 1947) that I was 'one of the few men in life I have found worth taking the trouble of getting to know.'"[53] This is despite the fact that before the war, Bataille puts together the art journal *Documents* which contained contributions from "most of the surrealists with whom Breton had fallen out in 1929."[54] As one of the latter, Bataille came to express regret for the polemics with Breton which he committed to print, seeing them as a case of mutual misrecognition and lamenting, "how much better silence on both sides would have been."[55] But what was at stake for Bataille at the time can very much be seen as a Freudo-Nietzschean critique of any residue of idealism in the surrealist branch of modernism, preferring the *counter*-idealist move of *de*-sublimation: what Dennis Hollier called the "inscription of perversion," as *truth*—to the Icarian move of flight or *transposition* toward the light Bataille initially took to constitute "the idealist plot" of Breton, who in turn dismissed Bataille as an "obsessive," an "excremental philosopher."[56]

We can see how Bataille's critique of Icarian idealism bears the classic trace of Nietzsche's influence from, for instance, Nietzsche's critique of Plato's idea of the Good, placed "as the supreme concept," for representing the "higher swindle" and ideal of "a coward in the face of reality" (*TI*, *What I Owe the Ancients*, 2). Nietzsche famously contrasts Plato's idealism with Thucydides's "realist culture," his "strong, stern, hard matter-of-factness" (*TI*, *What I Owe the Ancients*, 2)—and we can sense a similar countenance in Bataille's contrasting of the "formless," "heterogeneous," and "base materialism" with the idealism he thought he found in Breton, taking his cue also "from Freud" to extract "raw phenomena," "excluding all idealism," by "direct interpretation."[57]

But in tackling here the question of Bataille's modernism, which, as Raymond Spiteri puts it, entails a critique of "idealism implicit in conventional accounts of modernism," Spiteri notes also ambivalence in Bataille's own literature which has moments where he himself uses "transposition" as a defensive escape from the "base material" of the real: for example, when he sees the priest's eye, or eye of the pure and frigid Marcel, in the vagina of the licentious Simone, or "God" in the vagina of the prostitute *Madame Edwarda*.[58] These *surreal* manifestations, however, can also be thought to go the other way, as I have argued elsewhere in a sustained manner concerning Bataille's *Story of the Eye*, where "God" or its corollary in the form of the internalized, puritanical "super-ego" (super-*I*; super-*eye*)—"the eye of the conscience," as Bataille calls it, what Nietzsche calls "bad conscience" as an "evil eye" for our "natural inclinations" (*GM*, *'Guilt,' 'Bad Conscience,' and the Like*, 24)—is, rather, *lowered* into the base materialism of the formless, placed in the heterogeneous orifice of the transgressive "whore" as a way to reopen the closed, narrowly fixated taboo-structure idealized by Christianity.[59] We find, moreover, this "back-and-forth movement" of high-*and*-low, "from refuse to ideal, and from ideal to refuse," affirmed as a whole already in *Documents*[60]—where Bataille seeks not so much to privilege lows to the exclusion of highs but affirm the whole cycle: which speaks to Nietzsche's critique of the Good as being part of his *active* will to affirm the eternal return as the *being* of becoming, as both the same and a repetition of difference.[61]

This return of difference is what might normally be a return of the repressed death-wish, monstrous perversion, or crippling symptom, if viewed through a narrowing Freudian lens devoid of any Nietzsche, halting at the Schopenhauerian stage of pessimism about the will—preferring through renunciation and resignation the risk of neurosis and nihilism to the chance entailed of affirming the drive *in* the real.[62] And what Bataille ultimately wants to do is refocus the eternal return of Nietzsche, and the return of the repressed of Freud, onto a periodic cycle between high-*and*-low reconstituted as between the human *and* animal side of us—coordinated between the times for human taboos placed on animality for purposes of work and accumulation, and times for transgression of these normally operating taboos to re-access our "low" animality and discharge or expend our energies.

Whatever the initial misrecognition in placing Breton as fixated on the "high" in this cycle, who in turn misplaced Bataille as fixated on "lows," Breton's rapprochement with Bataille after *Documents* (1929–31) began for the *Contre-Attaque* group founded by Caillois (1935), to reconcile surrealism with activism in response to the rise of fascism and betrayal of the revolution by communism—subsequent to the collapse of the bourgeois center, exposed as the corruption which could not hold. But so as to outdo fascism's reclaiming of the power of *affect*: something which led to accusations of "sur-fascism" and the splitting of the surrealists from *Contre-Attaque* (1936)[63]—Bataille and Callois took their more directly Nietzschean inspiration to found the journal (and secret society) *Acéphale* and the College of Sociology to explore the sacred. Here is where they begin referring to themselves as "ferociously religious," in line with Nietzsche's declaration of being the "last disciple of the philosopher Dionysus"—with his vision for "eternal recurrence," saying "Yes to life beyond death and change" (*TI*, *What I Owe the Ancients*, 4–5), acting as inspiration for their symbolic *acephalic* ("headless") figure illustrated by fellow (ex)-surrealist André Masson: Of which, Bataille proclaims, "Superman and *acephalic* man are bound with a brilliance equal to the position of time as imperative object and explosive liberty of life," where Dionysos is the "symbol of the will to power" and "the destructive exuberance of life"—and "time becomes the object of ecstasy," which "appears as the 'eternal return.'"[64]

With the collapse of these movements in the onset of war, Bataille was accused of mystic-priest idealism this time: echoing his earlier critique of Breton as a "religious windbag"—by the wartime surrealist group during Breton's exile in response to Bataille's *atheological* works founded on the sovereign *jouissance* of Nietzsche's word: "God is dead."[65] But with Breton's return at the cessation of war, Bataille's *Writings on*

Surrealism between 1945 and 1951 confirm the thesis of their being minimal difference between the two—despite Bataille at one point referring to himself as "the enemy from within" in light of past polemics—as subsequently they worked together on surrealist publications, with Bataille providing the positive analyses here discussed, and on a surrealist exhibition on the topic of "Myth," with Bataille contributing his important text on *The Absence of Myth*.[66]

Conclusion

"The Absence of Myth" is an important text for understanding the modernism implicit of surrealism, and Bataille's intervention into as a Freudo-Nietzschean practitioner and critic, which again sheds further light on the initial relation between Nietzsche and psychoanalysis, as has all along been the aim of this chapter. Here, then, by way of conclusion, we can recapitulate on how in order to revitalize our profane world in the order of things, which for Bataille has been "reduced to the nothingness of things" and strangled by the myth that it is *absent* of myth: the "coldest, the purest, the only *true* myth"[67]—Bataille hoped in surrealist art to go back into our natural-animal, primitive-archaic roots so as to leap forward and begin again in the present with something radically *new*. And this is a project we can more fully comprehend, here, in conclusion, by enumerating some of its key consequences not just for a new aesthetics but also for a new ethics: an ethics of culture that entails both a new erotics and a new ontology—all along the path of forging this new, potentially ameliorated society.[68]

The consequences of Bataille's project for a new *aesthetics* would be that the taboos normally placed on our inner-animality can give way in the arts to a structured transgression enabling us to *enjoy* our lost animal-sensual side—a sublimated space for what Lacan calls "*jouissance* of transgression" or "*jouissance* of the real."[69] And rather than this being the potential sado-masochistic crippling or impoverishing of the organism alluded to by Lacan when following Freud, it is through a mytho-poetics something much closer to the experience of "Dionysian ecstasy" first discerned by Nietzsche in *The Birth of Tragedy*, where the early Greeks could overcome the mental restrictions of "fear and pity" to experience tragic wisdom in a cathartic, orgiastic release: to go "*beyond* pity and terror," Nietzsche cries, and "*realise in oneself* the eternal joy of becoming"—"which also encompasses *joy in destruction*" (*TI*, *What I Owe the Ancients*, 5).[70]

This 1888 concluding of *Twilight of the Idols* above repeats Nietzsche's earliest conviction of his 1872 *Birth of Tragedy* on tragic catharsis as a joyous, sensuous, Dionysian affirmation much to the contrary of Aristotle's "medical or moral," "pathological discharge" of "pity and fear" (*BT*, 22). For the beauty implicit in Nietzsche's returned-as-affirmed sensuality is also what acts as lure for us to face, and even affirm, the harshest, most difficult, and amoral truths of the real—a premise also of Lacan's praise for the magnificence of *pre*-Platonic tragic art.[71] This lure to affirmation thus is what makes possible a *newethics*—built on the increasing lucidity of how our normally unconscious, animal-desiring drives manifest in us, which means we can ethically respond more appropriately on balance as we learn more about the difficulties and conditions of our *jouissance*. This is something that can be delivered through art when augmented by a philosophy and psychoanalysis replenished with the combined Nietzsche-Freud influence—to teach us to privilege and produce the types of art that facilitate this affirming ethical process: based not just on self-knowledge of the drives but also on a more active, positive self-relation to them, which does *not* at all eschew *experience*.

Thus, in order for this ethics to be more sustainable, which can still demand the work of understanding a work of art—as well as the complexities of the mind—what is required also is the preservation of a space for a new *erotics*, which would mean that few motivational deficits occur because the libidinal demand, once it is no longer artificially resisted, is an implacably constant, energy source fueling our thoughts and acts whether we acknowledge *it* or not. In Nietzschean terms Dionysos, in the sexual sense of "the psychology of the orgy" he uncovers, must remain as prerequisite for Apollo, as set out in his first book *The Birth of Tragedy* which he later dubbed, in *Twilight of the Idols*: "my first revaluation of values" (*TI*, *What I Owe the Ancients*, 5). For without Dionysos as premise we get not the lucid, formal clarity of Apollo but the hyper-moral rationalism of the Socratism and Platonism that Nietzsche saw as *hostile* to "the instincts" (*TI*, *The Problem of Socrates*, 11; *BT*, 13), which ultimately leads to the denaturalizing neuroses of Christianity and the monstrous perversions, or mediocre nihilisms, of capitalism.[72] Dionysos here instead means we are not just producing "knowledge" of the real, or using knowledge to produce facile consumer goods which tap the real while denying it: what Lacan calls "the service of goods" which "colonize" the Freudian Thing with delusional "imaginary schemes" or "fantasm" of object *a*[73]—but enabling rather a deepest satisfaction of the drives beyond normal mores, through the periodic rotations enjoining taboo-*with*-transgression, or rational accumulation *with gifts* of potlatch-type expenditure.

Such a properly coordinated rotation between taboos that enable rational accumulation, and transgressions that enable potlach expenditure, is what is absent from our "modern" today, always on the hunt for commercial profit wherever any expenditure takes place: its emphasis thus *still* on accumulation rather than the drive in its glorious destruction and waste as *gift*, consciously sublimated into something divine *beyond* any reductively pre-given, utilitarian purpose. Attic tragedy provides a superlative example of this, transferring unwanted physical destructions to psychological simulation which can indeed have positive physical consequences as we return to the world renewed with the Dionysian wisdom, deftly veiled in an alluring way through the beautifying formal function of Apollo. In this way a culture of modernism can create new structured transitions between a politics of taboo and an aesthetics of transgression in a philosophically guided way that minimizes excessive disturbances in either domain—whether in the form of a neurotics of ossified, fixated taboo or a perversion of wild and wayward transgression, which ultimately stems from the same lack *in* the real.

And so, lastly, to stabilize this structure, what is also required, as well as entailed, is a new *ontology*: one that preserves a clear distinction between the time for work, governed by taboo and the *symbolic* relation to the real, by equitable politics and rational conceptual clarity—and the time for aesthetics, which returns to the *imaginary* manifestation of the real but consciously through transgression and the erotic return of animality, what Bataille saw as "poetic and divine though animal."[74] This ontology is tripartite and deflationary so as to never again allow the formation of an Icarian dualist religion, caught in the bellows of an imaginary mislabeled as real in a way that distorts the symbolic to the point of disfunction. But this ontology of "the imaginary, the symbolic, and the real," extracted from Lacan, is also, as Louis Saas notes, one of the "expressions of an essentially modernist sensibility" of Lacan's own, which should come as no surprise given how, "in Paris, Lacan frequented the surrealists and other avant-garde groups," and "maintained a lively interest in the latest developments in philosophy, literature, and the human sciences"—while "his second marriage was to the film actress Sylvia Maklès, estranged wife of his friend Georges Bataille, infamous for his writings on the necessity of transgression in both sexuality and religion."[75]

In conclusion, then, what these findings all serve to demonstrate is how *re*-reading Nietzsche and psychoanalysis back together, where they began in the late-nineteenth-century Germanophone context, is beneficial both for psychoanalysis and philosophy *and* for culture and the arts in general. For by tracing this combined heritage from its source in Nietzsche and Freud, forward to the twentieth-century Francophone context of modernism and surrealism where we find together the mostly Nietzschean Bataille and mostly Freudian Lacan: across a span of time and place traditionally thought to be that of modernism itself—we find exemplified by the surrealist modernism that Bataille-and-Lacan were ensconced in, as Freudo-Nietzschean practitioners of the symbolic-and-imaginary modes of the real, a backward movement that enables us to leap radically forward with a new aesthetics, ethics, erotics, and ontology. Here we can finally find in the act the restored Nietzsche-Freud relation that is especially important insofar as the motivation is what Lacan calls a "love of truth" as well as a "recognition of realities"[76]—enabling *affirmation* where the aim is to better navigate the realm of *jouissance*, through a properly structured relation to the drive in the relation of culture to nature and art to work: to continually begin again and anew until resistance to the whole cycle of eternal return between human and animal, high and low, is minimized such that disturbances are contained, as we improve in our trained abilities to stay with the venture of *revaluation*—into the *new*.

> I call Christianity the *one* great curse … the *one* immortal blemish of mankind … And one calculates *time* from the *dies nefastus* [unlucky day] on which this fatality arose—from the *first* day of Christianity!—*Why not rather from its last?—From today?*—Revaluation of all values!
>
> —Nietzsche, September 30, 1888 (*A*, 62)

Notes

1 Winkiel, *Modernism: The Basics* (New York: Routledge, 2017), 65–66.

2 Bataille, "Autobiographical Note (1958)," *October* 36 (1986): 106–08. For Bataille as one of the first "French Nietzscheans" and authors with "experience of the analyst's

couch," see Elizabeth Roudinesco, *Jacques Lacan: Outline of a Life, History of a System of Thought*, trans. B. Bray (New York: Columbia, 1997), 132–34, 131, 121.

3 In discussing Sade, Bataille paradoxically calls heterology a science of the heterogeneous "outside the reach of scientific knowledge, which by definition is only applicable to homogeneous elements." Lacan depicts the *jouissance* of transgression as to "trample sacred laws underfoot" in *Seminar VII* in terms of Sade, and in terms of masochism in his *Seminar XXIII* on James Joyce, noting that "*jouissance* of the real includes masochism" as "the main share of the *jouissance* endued by the real." For Bataille's links with Lacan, see Roudinesco, *Jacques Lacan*, 135-8. Lacan left his first wife to marry Bataille's, raising their daughter as his own. Bataille, "The Use Value of D.A.F. de Sade," in *Visions of Excess: Selected Writings*, trans. A. Stoekl (Minneapolis: Minnesota, 1985), 97. Lacan, *Seminar VII, The Ethics of Psychoanalysis*, trans. D. Porter (New York: Norton, 1991), 195, 197–203; *Seminar XXIII, The Sinthome*, trans. A. Price (Cambridge, UK: Polity, 2016), 63.

4 Roudinesco notes that Lacan contributed to the surrealist journal *Minotaure* and "his doctoral dissertation was greeted by them as an event." Hal Foster notes that Lacan "was a young associate of the surrealists in the early 1930s" who referred to them "in the unveiling of man's relationship with the symbolic," but also how "surrealism appears to be illustrative of Freudian notions" but can also "anticipate" or "contradict them," like "actual instances of 'objective chance' (to use the surrealist term)." Roudinesco, *Jacques Lacan*, 136. Foster, *Prosthetic Gods* (Cambridge, MA: MIT Press, 2004), 246, 419, 227.

5 Assoun, *Freud and Nietzsche*, trans. R. Collier (London: Continuum, 2007), 3–4.

6 Freud, "Letter to Ludwig Binswanger"; *Correspondence, 1927-1939*; "Letter to Fleiss"; and *Minutes of the Vienna Psychoanalytic Society*; all cited in Assoun, *Freud and Nietzsche*, 21, xxiv, 20, 7–8. Freud, "On the History of the Psychoanalytic Movement," in *The Standard Edition of the Complete Psychological Works of Sigmund Freud*, trans. J. Strachey (London: Vintage, 2001), 14:15–16.

7 Assoun, *Freud and Nietzsche*, xxix–xxx, 10, 37. Freud, "An Autobiographical Study," in *Standard Edition*, 20:59-60.

8 Bass, *Interpretation and Difference: The Strangeness of Care* (Stanford: Stanford Press, 2006), 2.

9 The harshness of the positivist ideological tradition on Freud's claim to scientific status is seen in interviews by Todd Dufresne. Among them, Frank Sulloway suggests some of the "self-analysis" made "a causal agent of Freud's originality" came from his awareness of developments in sexology then read into his analysis and clinic. Lacan, *Seminar I, Freud's Papers on Technique, 1953-1954*, trans. J. Forrester (New York: Norton, 1991), 2. Dufresne, *Against Freud: Critics Talk Back* (Stanford: Stanford Press, 2007), 55–56.

10 Nietzsche, *Ecce Homo*, "Destiny," 1, in *On the Genealogy of Morals /Ecce Homo*, trans. W. Kaufmann and R. J. Hollingdale (New York: Vintage, 1989). Henceforth GM and EH.

11 For denaturalizing's Platonic and Hebraic origins and modern formations, see Nietzsche, *Sämtliche Werke: Kritische Studienausgabe in 15 Einzelbänden*, ed. G. Colli, M. Montinari (Berlin: De Gruyter, 1988), 12:9[86], 12:9[107], 12:10[46–7], 12:10[80], 12:10[194], 13:14[111]; henceforth KSA; English translations from Nietzsche, *The Will to Power*, trans. Hollingdale Kaufmann (New York: Vintage, 1968), 299, 37, 292, 203, 298, 430; henceforth WP. Nietzsche, *The Antichrist*, 24–26, in *Twilight of the Idols /The Antichrist*, trans. Hollingdale (London: Penguin, 1990); henceforth TI and A.

12 For Lacan and Nietzsche links via the superego acting as ascetic ideal and nihilism, see Tim Themi, *Lacan's Ethics and Nietzsche's Critique of Platonism* (Albany: SUNY, 2014), 36–37, 53, 107, 140, 142, 178, 195, 216, 223. Freud, "Analysis Terminable and Interminable," in *Standard Edition*, 23:244. Zupančič, *The Shortest Shadow: Nietzsche's Philosophy of the Two* (Cambridge, MA: MIT Press, 2003), 50, 53, 81.
13 Ons, "Nietzsche, Freud, Lacan," in *Lacan: The Silent Partners*, ed. S. Žižek (New York: Verso, 2006), 85.
14 Assoun, *Freud and Nietzsche*, 27–29, xxiv, xxvii, xxxix.
15 Assoun, *Freud and Nietzsche*, 9.
16 Ibid., 6–11, 186.
17 Nietzsche saw *reducing* values to "truth" as continuing the faith that "God is truth, that truth is *divine*," an altered *expression* of "the ascetic ideal" (*GM*, *What Is the Meaning of Acestic Ideals?*, 24–25, 27). Sensing that science "never creates values" (*GM*, *What is the Meaning of Ascetic Ideals?*, 25), he reserves this for "*genuine philosophers*" acting as "*commanders and legislators*." For explanation of both Nietzsche's defending of "idealists against positivists" in *Beyond Good and Evil* and *Gay Science*, and his defending of "positivists against idealists" in *TI*, see Themi, *Lacan's Ethics and Nietzsche's*, 117–23. Hume's treatment of the "is-ought" or "fact-value" dynamic is in *A Treatise of Human Nature* (London: Penguin, 1986), III:1.1. Nietzsche, *Beyond Good and Evil*, trans. Kaufmann (New York: Vintage, 1989), 211; *The Gay Science*, trans. Kaufmann (New York: Vintage, 1974). Henceforth BGE and GS.
18 Freud, "'Civilized' Sexual Morality and Modern Nervous Illness," in *Standard Edition*, 9:185, 191, 197.
19 Lacan, *Seminar VIII, Transference*, trans. B. Fink (Cambridge, UK: Polity, 2015), 70.
20 Freud, "'Civilized' Sexual Morality," 9:198.
21 Nietzsche bemoans the ensuing loss of "all the scientific methods," of "natural science in concert with mathematics and mechanics," "the *sense for facts*," and "art of reading well," replaced by the Hebraic "art of holy lying" which "is not lacking in Plato" (A 59, 44, 55).
22 Freud, "Resistances to Psychoanalysis," in *Standard Edition*, 19:220, 222.
23 Freud, "Letter to the Editor of the *Jewish Press Centre in Zurich*," in *Standard Edition*, 19:291.
24 Lacan, *Seminar XVII, The Other Side of Psychoanalysis*, trans. R. Grigg (New York: Norton, 2007), 176.
25 Lacan later calls Freud's Oedipal primal father and Moses thesis a "cock-and-bull story" making "absolutely no sense," a "Darwinian buffoonery" of repressed murder returning "via mnesic transmission through chromosomes." For discussion of Lacan's critique through a Nietzschean prism, see Themi, *Lacan's Ethics and Nietzsche's*, 97–105. Lacan, *Seminar XVII*, 129; *Seminar VII*, 193; *Seminar XVII*, 111, 114, 112, 115.
26 Freud, *Group Psychology and the Analysis of the Ego*, in *Standard Edition*, 18:123. Leiter, *Nietzsche on Morality* (New York: Routledge, 2002), 122.
27 Freud, *Moses and Monotheism*, in *Standard Edition*, 23:115.
28 Otto Gross, Alfred Adler, Carl Jung, and Wilhelm Reich also used what Assoun calls Nietzsche as "a referent in the disagreement." Assoun, *Freud and Nietzsche*, 34, 32, 202n.
29 Roudinesco notes that Lacan read Nietzsche keenly when breaking from his family's religion, writing "a brilliant eulogy of Nietzsche's thought" for his brother to deliver

at their Catholic college, earning their wrath. The brother nevertheless went on to become a monk, while Lacan gravitated more to Freud. Bataille, conversely, all but declares himself as Nietzsche's sole heir, proclaiming: "I am the only one who thinks of himself not as a commentator of Nietzsche but as being the same as he." Roudinesco, *Jacques Lacan*, 13–14. Bataille, *The Accursed Share, Volume III: Sovereignty*, trans. R. Hurley (New York: Zone, 1993), 367.

30 Zupančič, *Shortest Shadow,* 5, 26.

31 Ibid., 5–6.

32 Robert Gooding-Williams notes that modernism is "not simply a period concept" but "a break in an otherwise continuous sequence," such as Nietzsche's creation of "*new* values" from the death of God connecting them to "revaluation of those Christian-platonic values." Gooding-Williams also notes that Habermas links Nietzsche to "aesthetic modernism" as "a precursor to surrealism" and postmodernism's rejection of "the Enlightenment." Nietzsche deems the *Renaissance* "the last great cultural harvest Europe had to bring home," restoring "noble values" through "*revaluation of Christian values*," but destroyed by the Reformation when "a German monk, Luther, went to Rome" (A 61); see also A 59 and GM I:16. Gooding-Williams, "Nietzsche's Pursuit of Modernism," *New German Critique* 41 (1987): 98–99, 96.

33 Bataille, "The Surrealist Religion," in *The Absence of Myth: Writings on Surrealism*, trans. M. Richardson (London: Verso, 2006), 71.

34 Bataille, "Surrealism and How It Differs from Existentialism," in *Writings on Surrealism*, 57, 62.

35 Freud, "The Dynamics of Transference"; *Interpretation of Dreams*; in *Standard Edition*, 12:107, 4:103.

36 Bataille, "Surrealism," in *Writings on Surrealism*, 55.

37 Bataille, "Surrealism and How It Differs from Existentialism," 65.

38 Bataille also tracks the *original* sacred's declension to "sin" and "evil"—built on a "contempt for animals" which "are now disgusting"—in his 1957 *Eroticism*. Bataille, *Theory of Religion*, trans. Hurley (New York: Zone, 1992), 69, 71–72; *Eroticism*, trans. M. Dalwood (London: Penguin, 2001), 126–27, 136–37.

39 Chloë Taylor cites "three critiques of confession" in Foucault which could be "critiques of psychoanalysis." Lacan's critique of "adaptation" in "ego-psychology" is also known. Taylor, *The Culture of Confession from Augustine to Foucault: A Genealogy of the 'Confessing Animal'* (New York: Routledge, 2009), 119. Dylan Evans, *An Introductory Dictionary of Lacanian Psychoanalysis* (London: Routledge, 2005), 4–5.

40 Bataille, *Lascaux, or the Birth of Art*, trans. A. Wainhouse (New York: Skira, 1955), 123.

41 Bataille, "The Surrealist Religion," 81.

42 Roudinesco, *Jacques Lacan*, 136.

43 Lacan is applying Freud's 1915 article "Repression," which notes how beyond "conscious influence" repressed material "proliferates in the dark" into "extreme forms of expression" which are "deceptive" due to "damming-up." Freud, "Repression," in *Standard Edition*, 14:149. Lacan, *Seminar VII*, 78, 83–84, 170.

44 Lacan, *Seminar VII*, 235; *Seminar I*, 277.

45 Bataille, *Accursed Share, Volume I: Consumption*, trans. Hurley (New York: Zone, 1991), 9.

46 Lacan, *Seminar VII*, 235, 216.
47 Bataille, *Eroticism*, 65. Mauss, *The Gift*, trans. W. Halls (New York: Norton, 2000). Caillois, *Man and the Sacred*, trans. M. Barash (Chicago: Illinois Press, 2001), 15.
48 Bataille, "Surrealism and How It Differs from Existentialism," 65.
49 Ibid., 66–67.
50 Lacan, *Seminar VII*, 195.
51 Lacan cites Aristophanes where "the id gets the upper hand, pulls on the boots of language" for "sexual needs most especially," which is "powerful stuff"—as in "*The Clouds*" where *it* "makes fun of Euripides and Socrates." Lacan, *Seminar V, Formations of the Unconscious*, trans. Grigg (Cambridge, UK: Polity, 2017), 122.
52 Richardson, *Georges Bataille* (London: Routledge, 1994), 4; "Introduction," in Bataille, *Writings on Surrealism*, 1.
53 Bataille, "Surrealism from Day to Day," in *Writings on Surrealism*, 41.
54 Richardson, "Introduction," 4.
55 Bataille, "Notes on the Publishing of 'Un Cadavre,'" in *Writings on Surrealism*, 32.
56 Hollier, *Against Architecture: The Writings of Georges Bataille*, trans. B. Wing (Cambridge, MA: MIT, 1992), 108. Allan Stoekl, "Introduction," in Bataille, *Visions of Excess*, xi. Bataille, "Surrealism from Day to Day," 41.
57 Bataille, "Formless"; "Base Materialism and Gnosticism"; "The Use Value of D.A.F. de Sade"; and "Materialism"; in *Visions of Excess*, 31, 45, 94–99, 15–16. But for that on Sade, the articles first appeared in *Documents* among others tackling similar themes of "low" versus "high."
58 Spiteri, "Georges Bataille and the Limits of Modernism," *Emaj: Online Journal of Art* 4 (2009): 1, 11, 21–22. Bataille, *Story of the Eye*, trans. J. Neugroschal (London: Penguin, 2001), 76; *Madame Edwarda*, in *My Mother, Madame Edwarda, The Dead Man*, trans. A. Wainhouse (London: Marion Boyars, 2003), 150.
59 The evidence is the immolation of all the metaphoric *substitutes* for the eye in the novella: often with urine, particularly "the eggs." See Themi, "Lacan, Barthes, Bataille, and the Meaning of the Eye—or Gaze," *Undecidable Unconscious: Journal of Deconstruction and Psychoanalysis* 3 (2016): 102, 105, 107, 110, 113.
60 Bataille, "Rotten Sun," in *Visions of Excess*, 20–21.
61 Deleuze saw return connected to "diversity and its reproduction, of difference and its repetition," as a principal of "the will to power." Jared Russell connects this clinically to perspectival flows of interpretation, "to neutralize *ressentiment*." Deleuze, *Nietzsche and Philosophy*, trans. H. Tomlinson (New York: Columbia Press, 1983), 49. Russell, *Nietzsche and the Clinic* (London: Karnac, 2017), 9–11, 22–23.
62 Deleuze calls this stage two "*reactive* nihilism," where ideals produced through negation of life are removed but not the negativity that caused them. A third stage is "*passive nihilism*," where new ideals are secreted to preserve negative life in a state "close to zero"—with this whole trajectory taking us "From God to God's murderer, from God's murder to the last man." Deleuze, *Nietzsche and Philosophy*, 148–51.
63 Spiteri notes Bataille's complaint in response was where "surrealism merely pacified revolt, channelling discontent into the artistic and poetic practices that the bourgeoisie tolerated, despite the occasional scandal." Stoekl, "Introduction," xviii. Spiteri, "Surrealism and its Discontents: Georges Bataille, Georges Ribemont-Dessaignes, and the 1929 Crisis of Surrealism," *French History and Civilization* 4 (2011): 154.

64 Bataille, "The Sacred Conspiracy (1936)"; "Nietzschean Chronicle (1937)"; and "Propositions (1937)"; in *Visions of Excess*, 179, 206, 200. These articles initially appeared in *Acéphale*.
65 Richardson notes the attack on Bataille in the 1943 "childish tract, *Nom de Dieu*," following publication of Bataille's *Inner-Experience*, where, in the section "Critique of Dogmatic Servitude (and of Mysticism)," he writes: "God, even without a form or mode ... is a stop in the movement that brings us to the most obscure apprehension of the *unknown*"—adding that by freeing this from "confession" he is justified abandoning "the word 'mystical.'" Richardson, "Introduction," 11. Bataille, *Inner-Experience*, trans. S. Kendall (Albany: SUNY, 2014), 10, 215–6n.
66 Bataille, "On the Subject of Slumbers"; "The Absence of Myth"; in *Writings on Surrealism*, 48–49.
67 Bataille, "Absence of Myth," 48.
68 In his 1948 "Surrealist Religion," Bataille suggests when surrealism "has an influence over industry and over the whole of human activities, these human activities will have been profoundly changed," in ways "we could not have predicted." In a 1946 article for surrealist journal *Troisième Convoi*, he invokes this "affirmation of the hope of breaking the solitude" and that while its "books are in order on the shelves" and its "paintings adorn the walls," "the *great surrealism* is beginning." Bataille, "Surrealist Religion," 88; "Subject of Slumbers," 49.
69 Lacan notes that the fault-line separating "*jouissance* and desire" is "where anxiety is produced." Lacan, *Seminar VII*, 195; *Seminar XXIII*, 63; *Seminar X, Anxiety*, trans. Price (Cambridge: Polity, 2014), 182.
70 This *joy*, Richard Boothby notes, is death-drive unbinding us from "the ego," which Lacan calls a "'resistance to the elusive process of becoming, to the variations of desire,'" and is why there is "a paradoxical identity between the death drive and the realisation of a fuller vitality." Boothby, *Freud as Philosopher: Metapsychology after Lacan* (New York: Routledge, 2001), 144, 150–51.
71 Lacan notes that "Nietzsche put his finger on it" in sensing "Socrates' profound incompetence every time he broaches the topic of tragedy," which, with Plato's *enthusiasm* for Socrates, creates "the longest transference ... history has ever known." For Nietzsche and Lacan's praise of tragic art and critique of Aristotle's catharsis, see Themi, *Lacan's Ethics and Nietzsche's*, 41–63. Lacan, *Seminar VIII*, 81–82, 7.
72 For how Bataille's use of Max Weber details how capitalist transgressions have "more in common with the *disturbed* transgressions of the Christian age than they do with those sacred of the Hellenic," see Themi, "Bataille and the Erotics of the Real," *Parrhesia: Journal of Critical Philosophy* 24 (2015): 323–28.
73 Lacan notes the "small *a*" (*autre*-other) to be "substitute for big A," which "is the real Other" that is "involved in *jouissance*," which objectified desire only concerns "elliptically and off to one side." Lacan, *Seminar VII*, 303, 324, 99; *Seminar XVII*, 50; *Seminar X*, 182, 160–61.
74 Kevin Kennedy suggests politics and art are equally important to Bataille, linked respectively to "the necessity to fight oppression and exploitation," and "the necessity to leave all necessity behind." Bataille, *Eroticism*, 153. Kennedy, *Towards an Aesthetics of Sovereignty* (Bethesda: Academia, 2014), 275.
75 Saas follows Clement Greenberg to define modernism post-Kantianly as questioning internal forms of time and space and thus "the very structure of reality," suggesting Lacan was able to "supplement Freud's concepts" to "bring them into conformity

with these modernist concerns, while at the same time enriching modernism." Sass, "Lacan: The Mind of the Modernist," *Continental Philosophy Review* (2015) 48: 409–11. Greenberg, "Modernist Painting," in *The New Art: A Critical Anthology*, ed. Gregory Battcock (New York: Dutton, 1973).

76 Lacan follows the later Freud's key 1937 article in defining "the analytic relation" as such. Lacan, *Seminar XVII*, 165. Freud, "Analysis Terminable and Interminable," in *Standard Edition*, 23: 209–53.

12

Nietzsche, Jung, and Modern Militancy

Ritske Rensma

Introduction

Jung lived in a time of crisis. He was confronted with the atrocities of two world wars, spent his final years in the climate of the cold war, and was hugely concerned about mankind's inability to find solutions to the recurrences of mass conflict he was forced to witness in his lifetime. It should come as no surprise, then, that Jung wrote extensively about the possible causes of war and conflict. A central notion which he defended throughout his career was that the roots of war are to be found in the human psyche, in what he called our "warlike instincts," which we will never be able to eradicate:

> Anything that disappears from your psychological inventory is apt to turn up in the guise of a hostile neighbour, who will inevitably arouse your anger and make you aggressive. It is surely better to know that your worst enemy is right there in your own heart. Man's war-like instincts are ineradicable—therefore a state of perfect peace is unthinkable.[1]

It was these instincts which Jung saw as lying at the root of both world wars. According to him, these instincts "bubble up" to the surface whenever they have been repressed for too long a time, and if no way is found to integrate such forces into consciousness, the results can be catastrophic. In this chapter I will argue that Jung developed and fine-tuned his ideas about this topic through a dialogue with the ideas of philosopher Friedrich Nietzsche. As I pointed out in an earlier article concerning Nietzsche's influence on Jung,[2] Jung was fascinated by Nietzsche:

> From the time he first became gripped by Nietzsche's ideas as a student in Basel to his days as a leading figure in the psychoanalytic movement, Jung read, and increasingly developed, his own thought in a dialogue with the work of Nietzsche. As the following quote from *Memories, Dreams, Reflections* reveals, Jung even went as far as to connect Nietzsche to what he saw as the central task underlying his life's work:
>
> > The meaning of my existence is that life has addressed a question to me. That is a supra-personal task, which I accompany only by effort and with difficulty.

> Perhaps it is a question which preoccupied my ancestors, and which they could not answer? Could that be why I am so impressed by the problem on which Nietzsche foundered: the Dionysian side of life, to which the Christian seems to have lost the way?[3]

In this chapter, which serves as a more in-depth follow-up to my earlier article about Jung and Nietzsche, I will show that Nietzsche had a particularly strong influence on Jung's thinking about war and conflict. I will also show how Jung's ideas on this topic changed over time, culminating in a final theoretical position which revolves around the concept of the archetypal shadow. In order to sketch this development on Jung's part in a clear and coherent manner, I will divide this chapter into three sections, each of which will deal with a different time period from Jung's career:

Phase 1: the early years

In order to examine Jung's early ideas about the psychological roots of war we will look at the article "Role of the Unconscious" from 1918,[4] which is the most clear and complete text about this topic from phase 1.

Phase 2: the Wotan years

In the 1930s Jung goes through a phase in which he refers to the part of the psyche he associates with war and violence by the term "archetype of Wotan." In order to examine the core ideas of this phase we will look at two key texts from this time period: the short article "Wotan" from 1936[5] and the transcription of the seminar Jung gave on Nietzsche's *Thus Spoke Zarathustra* in 1934.[6]

Phase 3: the shadow years

From the early 1940s onwards Jung stops using the term "archetype of Wotan" in his texts about war and violence and begins using the term "archetype of the shadow" instead. In order to examine this final developmental stage we will look at the article "Fight with the Shadow" from 1946.[7]

To simplify the task of discussing this development, I will refer to the stages outlined above as phase 1, phase 2, and phase 3. The "dividing line" that I will use to demarcate between these phases is the term "archetype of Wotan," which Jung only uses in phase 2. Phase 1 is thus defined as lasting up until the point where he begins to use this term, which he does for the first time in the seminar on *Zarathustra* in 1934; phase 2 is thus defined as lasting from 1934 until he starts to use the term "archetypal shadow" instead (the earliest text I have found in which this term is present is from 1943[8]). Phase 3, lastly, is defined as everything after the end of phase 2 (1943–61). Because I have only a limited amount of words at my disposal to discuss this rather complicated topic, I will assume that the reader already has a basic knowledge of Jung's theoretical framework.[9] For an overview of the basic facts of Jung's interest in Nietzsche—as opposed to the topic of this chapter, which deals with outlining where in Jung's theoretical framework we can pinpoint Nietzsche's influence—I ask the reader to refer my earlier article about this topic.[10]

Phase 1: The early years

As I already explained above, the text from phase 1 in which Jung elaborates most clearly on his ideas about war and violence is the article "Role of the Unconscious" from 1918, published in an English translation in *The Collected Works of C.G. Jung* volume 10. Since this is also the only text from phase 1 in which he makes an explicit connection between this topic and the ideas of Nietzsche, it is this text that we will focus on to analyze Jung's early ideas about the psychological roots of war.

Role of the Unconscious (from here on abbreviated as *ROU)* is not an article which deals specifically with the topic of the psychological roots of war. It seems to have been written primarily to put forward the core ideas of Jung's theoretical framework to a general audience, with a strong emphasis on making his differences with Freud clear. Jung wrote it at the end of the First World War, however, and for that reason it should come as no surprise that the topic of war was heavily on his mind. The middle part of the article, then, deals almost entirely with offering possible psychological explanations for the calamities that had just swept across Europe. Jung begins this part of the chapter by reflecting on what he calls here the "barbaric," "dark," "primitive," and "animalistic" dimension of the psyche (Jung uses all these terms as synonyms in *ROU*). His core observation about the origins of this part of the psyche is that it is the residue of our evolutionary history, which, as Jung observes, is marked by a very long period of "primitive" prehistory and only a comparatively short period of "cultured" history. For this reason, the "primitive" part of the psyche exerts a much stronger influence on our behavior than the "cultured" part, according to Jung:

> A mere fifty generations ago many of us in Europe were no better than primitives. The layer of culture, this pleasing patina, must therefore be quite extraordinarily thin in comparison with the powerfully developed layers of the primitive psyche.[11]

As influential and powerful as this part of the psyche is, however, it has nevertheless been repressed by Western culture for a very long time according to Jung. Showing quite clearly the influence of Nietzsche, Jung associates this repression with the values of Christianity. Nietzsche himself repeatedly wrote that Christianity represses the instincts; it is at war with the primitive, bodily self. Some of the most explicit of the passages in which Nietzsche makes this point can be found in *The Antichrist,* for example, in this one:

> Christianity has taken the side of everything weak, base, ill-constituted, it has made an ideal out of opposition to the preservative instincts of strong life; it has depraved the reason even of the intellectually strongest natures by teaching men to feel the supreme values of intellectuality as sinful, as misleading, as temptations. (*A*, 5)[12]

Jung shares this observation. Christianity, as Jung writes in *ROU*, "split the Germanic barbarian into an upper and a lower half, and enabled him, by repressing the dark side, domesticate the brighter half and fit it for civilization."[13] But the more this dark, animalistic, "inner barbarian" is repressed, the more the unconscious seeks to correct this one-sided attitude by activating the primitive aspects of the self. This, according to Jung, is what the unconscious does time and again: it offers what he calls a *compensation* to the attitudes and values of our consciousness once these become too narrow and restrictive. Because Western culture was unable to integrate such a "primitive" compensation in an appropriate manner during the years leading up to the First World War, the results were catastrophic. War and violence ensued, on a global scale:

> By being repressed into the unconscious, the source from which it originated, the animal in us only becomes more beastlike, and that is no doubt the reason why no religion is so defiled with the spilling of innocent blood as Christianity, and why the world has never seen a bloodier war than the war of the Christian nations. The repressed animal bursts forth in its most savage form when it comes to the surface, and in the process of destroying itself leads to international suicide.[14]

This, then, is Jung's core observation about the psychological roots of war in phase 1: that the one-sidedness of Christian culture led to an unconscious compensation consisting of primitive archetypal content, which in turn led to the violence and frenzy of the First World War. Because *ROU* deals so extensively with this topic, it is an excellent text to look at if one is interested in Jung's early ideas about the war. What *ROU* also makes clear, however, is that a connection exists between Jung's ideas about the primitive, "barbaric" part of the psyche and the ideas of Nietzsche. On this topic Jung does not elaborate very much in *ROU*, writing only the following:

> This annoying peculiarity of the barbarian was apparent also to Nietzsche—no doubt from personal experience[15]

What Jung means with this rather vague statement is never made entirely clear in *ROU*, as there are no further references to Nietzsche in its pages. In order to make sense of it, we have to look at two texts from what I have defined in the introduction as phase 2: the transcription of the seminar Jung gave on Nietzsche's *Thus Spoke Zarathustra* in 1934 and the article *Wotan* from 1936.

Phase 2: The Wotan years

As I explained in the introduction, Jung makes an important change to his ideas about war in phase 2. He now begins to identify a particular archetype of the collective unconscious with war, violence, and conflict—the archetype he calls in this phase the "archetype of Wotan." Jung took inspiration from Germanic mythology when naming this new archetype: Wotan (also transcribed as "Woden") is the name of the Germanic supreme God, the equivalent of the Norse God Odin. Wotan was associated primarily with war and fury, which goes a long way toward explaining why Jung decided to use this name for the archetype he associated with the roots of war. Jung himself described Wotan as follows:

> He is the god of storm and frenzy, the unleasher of passions and the lust of battle; moreover he is a superlative magician and artist in illusion who is versed in all secrets of an occult nature.[16]

The way Jung describes the archetype of Wotan in phase 2 is highly similar to what he had to say about the primitive part of the psyche in *ROU.* The best paper to establish this is his short article *Wotan*, published in an English translation in *The Collected Works of C.G. Jung* volume 10. In this article, written by Jung in 1936, Jung repeatedly refers to the archetype of Wotan as the "dark" part of the psyche, which is the exact same metaphor he also used in *ROU* to describe the primitive part of the psyche. Another key similarity to *ROU* is that he states that the archetype of Wotan was repressed during the Christian era, and that it is now becoming dominant again because of the psychological mechanism of compensation. He also very explicitly makes a connection to violence and primitivity again. Throughout the *Wotan* essay, Jung repeatedly claims that the Wotan archetype is what is behind the uprush of violence which was visible in Europe at that time. In *ROU,* written in 1918, Jung focused on the psychological disturbances in his patients at the end of the First World War. Now, writing in 1936, Jung claims to see the same kind of disturbances behind the Hitler movement. The archetype of Wotan, according to Jung, is what has got hold of the German people:

> We have seen him come to life in the German Youth Movement, and right at the beginning the blood of several sheep was shed in honour of his resurrection. Armed with rucksack and lute, blond youths, and sometimes girls as well, were to be seen as restless wanderers on every road from the North Cape to Sicily, faithful votaries of the roving god. Later, towards the end of the Weimar Republic, the wandering role was taken over by the thousands of unemployed, who were to be met with everywhere on their aimless journeys. By 1933 they wandered no longer, but marched in their hundreds of thousands. The Hitler movement literally brought the whole of Germany to its feet, from five-year-olds to veterans, and produced the spectacle of a nation migrating from one place to another. Wotan the wanderer was on the move.[17]

In order to explain why the archetype of Wotan is still so powerful, Jung uses the same kind of "evolutionary" reasoning he also employed in *ROU:* the longer a particular part of the psyche has been dominant in our evolutionary history, the stronger its force, no matter how much cultural baggage is put on top of it to repress it. In *Wotan* Jung phrases this idea as follows:

> Archetypes are like riverbeds which dry up when the water deserts them, but which it can find again at any time. An archetype is like an old watercourse along

> which the water of life has flowed for centuries, digging a deep channel for itself. The longer it has flowed in this channel the more likely it is that sooner or later the water will return to its old bed. The life of the individual as a member of society and particularly as part of the State may be regulated like a canal, but the life of nations is a great rushing river which is utterly beyond human control, in the hands of One who has always been stronger than men.[18]

These similarities between *ROU* and the *Wotan* article point to the conclusion that Jung used the archetype of Wotan to refer to the same part of the psyche he called the "primitive psyche" in *ROU.* As we have seen, Jung made a connection in *ROU* between this primitive part of the psyche and Nietzsche, but failed to make clear what this connection exactly entailed. In the texts from phase 2 in which Jung discusses the archetype of Wotan, however, we find ample information to help us make sense of it. Nietzsche, as Jung claims in these texts, was among the first in Europe in whom the archetype of Wotan was constellated. Whereas he mentioned Nietzsche only in passing in phase 1, he now gives Nietzsche center stage. In his *Wotan* article he elaborates explicitly on Nietzsche and his connection to the archetype of Wotan, making much of the frequent references to the power of wind in Nietzsche's *Thus Spoke Zarathustra.* He claims that these are an indication that Nietzsche is gripped by the Wotan archetype, which Jung also associates very strongly with wind:

> Nietzsche's case is certainly a peculiar one. He had no knowledge of Germanic literature; he discovered the "cultural Philistine"; and the announcement that "God is dead" led to Zarathustra's meeting with an unknown god in unexpected form, who approached him sometimes as an enemy and sometimes disguised as Zarathustra himself. Zarathustra, too, was a soothsayer, a magician, and the storm-wind:
>
> > And like a wind shall I come to blow among them, and with my spirit shall take away the breath of their spirit; thus my future wills it. Truly, a strong wind is Zarathustra to all that are low; and this counsel he gives to his enemies and to all that spit and spew: "Beware of spitting against the wind." (Z, *On the Rabble*)
>
> And when Zarathustra dreamed that he was guardian of the graves in the "lone mountain fortress of death," and was making a mighty effort to open the gates, suddenly
>
> > a roaring wind tore the gates asunder; whistling, shrieking, and keening, it cast a black coffin before me. And amid the roaring and whistling and shrieking the coffin burst open and spouted a thousand peals of laughter. (*Z*, *The Soothsayer*)[19]

In *Wotan* Jung uses the term *ergriffenheit* to refer to someone becoming gripped by the Wotan archetype,[20] and claims that Nietzsche was one of the first people in Europe to experience such a thing. As the quote above already makes clear, there is one work by Nietzsche which Jung feels was especially relevant when trying to understand Nietzsche's relationship to the Wotan archetype: *Thus Spoke Zarathustra.* This work was of such importance to Jung that he devoted an entire seminar to it, which ran between 1934 and 1939. The transcripts of this seminar have been published and are an excellent source to one who wants to understand Jung's interpretation of Nietzsche.[21] The essence of this interpretation is what I have already outlined above: that Nietzsche was gripped by a particular archetype of the unconscious, the archetype of Wotan. As Jung puts it in the seminar:

> It is Wotan who gets him, the old wind God breaking forth, the god of inspiration, of madness, of intoxication and wildness, the god of the Berserkers, those wild people who run amok.[22]

The enormous energy apparent in Zarathustra, the strong language, the appeal to heroic action, to new beginnings, to the creation of a new form of life: all of this, according to Jung, is an expression of Nietzsche's attempt to deal with the uprush of the Wotan archetype in his psyche. Jung also makes much of the more violent passages in *Zarathustra,* and puts these forward as evidence of Nietzsche's *ergriffenheit* by the Wotan archetype. Passages he quotes in this regard are, for example:

> And he who hath to be a creator in good and evil, verily, he hath first to be a destroyer, and break values in pieces. (*Z*, *On Self-Overcoming*)[23]

And elsewhere:

> Let your spirit and your virtue be devoted to the sense of the earth, my brethren: let the value of everything be determined anew by you! Therefore shall ye be fighters! Therefore shall ye be creators. (*Z*, *On the Bestowing Virtue*, 2)[24]

Examples of such "militant" ideas are to be found in other works by Nietzsche as well. Nietzsche frequently glorified war and aggression, for example, in the following aphorism from *The Gay Science:*

> I welcome all signs that a more virile, warlike age is about to begin, which will restore honor to courage above all. For this age shall prepare the way for one yet higher, and it shall gather the strength that this higher age will require someday—the age that will carry heroism into the search for knowledge and that will *wage wars* for the sake of ideas and their consequences. (*GS*, 283)[25]

And elsewhere in the same aphorism:

> For believe me: the secret for harvesting from existence the greatest fruitfulness and the greatest enjoyment is to *live dangerously!* Build your cities on the slopes of Vesuvius! Send your ships into uncharted seas! Live at war with your peers and yourselves! Be robbers and conquerors as long as you cannot be rulers and possessors, you seekers of knowledge! (*GS*, 283)[26]

Nietzsche himself, as Jung claims in the seminar, was not aware of the fact that this aggressive side of his nature was something that came from outside himself—that was the result of a specific archetype of the collective unconscious rising to consciousness. This, according to Jung, was one of Nietzsche's greatest mistakes—he constantly claimed that he was unique, and *identified* with the contents of the collective unconscious that lay at the root of his creative ideas. This is also true in regards to the archetype of Wotan: Nietzsche simply assumed that his aggressiveness and warlike nature were an innate aspect of his own character. In *Ecce Homo,* he makes this especially clear:

> Another thing is war. I am naturally warlike. Attacking is one of my instincts. Being *able* to be an enemy, being an enemy—these require a strong nature, perhaps; in any case every strong nature presupposes them. (*EH*, *Why I Am So Wise*, 7)[27]

Jung, however, doesn't read Nietzsche's aggressiveness as an individual character trait at all, but as a symptom of a wider, collective phenomenon: the coming to consciousness of the Wotan archetype in individuals all over Europe. This is how he explains the violent nature of the time in which he lived. As he puts it in the seminar:

> Now old Wotan is in the center of Europe; you can see all the psychological symptoms which he personifies, including his romantic character of the sorcerer, the god of mysteries-all that is living again. … Fascism in Italy is old Wotan again; it is all Germanic blood down there.[28]

We can now finally begin to make sense of the fact that Jung was so interested in Nietzsche. Nietzsche, Jung felt, helped him to understand the age in which he lived—an age characterized by an outbreak of violence on a massive scale. Since Nietzsche was "gripped" by the same archetype which later led to an outbreak of this violence on a massive scale, studying the great man's writings was a way to understand the psychological roots of this phenomenon:

> Perhaps I am the only one who takes the trouble to go so much into the detail of Zarathustra—far too much, some people may think. So nobody actually realises to what extent he was connected with the unconscious and therefore with the fate of Europe in general.[29]

Jung's thinking about the psychological roots of war, however, did not stop in the 1930s. As is the case with many of Jung's core concepts, he continued to refine his ideas about it, arriving at a final theoretical position only after the end of another time of intense violence: the Second World War. It is to that final theoretical position that we will now turn. In order to examine it, we will look at what I consider to be the most important text Jung wrote about war in the final phase of his career: the short article *Fight with the Shadow* (from here on abbreviated as *Fight),* which Jung originally delivered as a speech in 1946 for BBC radio.

Phase 3: The shadow years

Jung begins *Fight* by making the same observation he also makes in phase 1 and phase 2: that an uprush of compensatory, instinctual material was present in the psyche of the European people as early as the 1910s and was responsible for the century's abundant cases of war and violence. As he himself puts it:

> As early as 1918, I noticed peculiar disturbances in the unconscious of my German patients which could not be ascribed to their personal psychology. Such non-personal phenomena always manifest themselves in dreams as mythological motifs that are also to be found in legends and fairytales throughout the world. I have called these mythological motifs *archetypes:* that is, typical modes or forms in which these collective phenomena are experienced. There was a disturbance of the collective unconscious in every single one of my German patients. One can explain these disorders causally, but such an explanation is apt to be unsatisfactory, as it is easier to understand archetypes by their aim rather than by their causality. The archetypes I had observed expressed primitivity, violence, and cruelty.[30]

From the outset, then, it is clear that *Fight* is strongly related to the key themes of the first two phases. Jung even makes a particular reference to *Role of the Unconscious,* stating that he wrote in 1918 about "peculiar disturbances in the unconscious of my German patients which could not be ascribed to their personal psychology." The rest of the article is equally consistent in terms of its central themes. Where we see a remarkable difference between *Fight* and the first two phases, however, is in the terminology Jung uses. As we have seen, Jung made frequent references to the archetype of Wotan in phase 2. This terminology, however, is not present in *Fight,* nor is it present in any other text from phase 3. Instead, Jung now uses the concept of the *shadow* to explain the forces which were unleashed during the two world wars:

> Like the rest of the world, [the Germans] did not understand wherein Hitler's significance lay, that he symbolized something in every individual. He was the most prodigious personification of all human inferiorities. He was an utterly incapable, unadapted, irresponsible, psychopathic personality, full of empty, infantile fantasies, but cursed with the keen intuition of a rat or a guttersnipe. He represented the shadow, the inferior part of everybody's personality, in an overwhelming degree, and this was another reason why they fell for him.[31]

In order to understand this concept properly, it is crucial to realize that Jung used the term "shadow" in two different ways, making a distinction between the *personal* shadow and the *archetypal* shadow. Jungian analyst Daryl Sharp defines the personal shadow as follows: "[It] is composed for the most part of repressed desires and uncivilized impulses, morally inferior motives, childish fantasies and resentments, etc.—all those things about oneself one is not proud of. These unacknowledged personal characteristics are often experienced in others through the mechanism of projection."[32] The personal shadow, then, consists entirely of contents from what Jung called the personal unconscious, as everything that is associated with it has become unconscious through the mechanism of repression and has therefore become unconscious during the individual's lifetime. For this reason, there is nothing innate or archetypal about the personal shadow. In his later years, however, Jung began to contrast the personal shadow with the *archetypal* shadow (see for example *Aion* par. 19[33]). In contrast to the personal shadow, the archetypal shadow is innate. It is the same in everyone, and consists of content *not* acquired during an individual's lifetime. Instead, it is made up of content that was acquired over the course of mankind's evolutionary history.

Although Jung doesn't mention which version of the shadow concept he is talking about in *Fight*—confusingly, he merely uses the term "shadow" without any kind of prefix—there is more than enough evidence that it is the archetypal shadow he is talking about. To begin with, Jung stresses time and again that the unconscious material he is discussing in this article is innate and therefore archetypal. I have already quoted him above, for example, as writing the following:

> As early as 1918, I noticed peculiar disturbances in the unconscious of my German patients which could not be ascribed to their personal psychology. Such non-personal phenomena always manifest themselves in dreams as mythological motifs that are also to be found in legends and fairytales throughout the world. I have called these mythological motifs *archetypes*.[34]

As Jung makes clear in this quote, the content of the compensatory of uprush of instinctual unconscious material he observed as early as 1918 could not be ascribed to the "personal psychology" of his patients. In short: it did not stem from the personal unconscious, but from the collective unconscious, the content of which is innate and archetypal.

Another hint that it is the archetypal shadow Jung is talking about in *Fight* is related to the fact that an entire group of people is confronted with this specific unconscious manifestation. As Ann Casement points out in her introduction to the concept of the shadow in *The Handbook of Jungian Psychology*,[35] the personal shadow is a compensation for a certain one-sidedness in the life of the individual; the archetypal shadow, however, is constellated in response to a certain one-sidedness in the cultural life of an entire group of people. It is quite clear that Jung is talking about the latter kind of compensation in *Fight,* as he is not analyzing the psychological dynamics of a single individual in this text—rather, he is looking at the dynamics of the psyche of the entire people of Europe, with a special focus on the Germans. Although he does single out Hitler in particular, he makes it quite clear that Hitler was only a mouthpiece—he gave voice to psychological disturbances that were present in every single one of his followers.

As I already stated above, apart from the terminology, no core ideas have changed in phase 3 about war and violence. The archetypal shadow is the term Jung now uses to describe the exact same phenomenon which he explained by using the term "archetype of Wotan" in phase 2. Is it the case, then, that these two terms are synonyms? Do both the archetype of Wotan and the archetype of the Shadow refer to the same archetypal part of the psyche? Even though Jung never explicitly explains that this is the case, I believe that it is very much possible to establish that this is true. One way to do this is by examining the mythological symbols Jung associated with these two archetypes. When discussing the archetypal shadow in phase 3 of his career, for example, Jung frequently stated that the Christian figure of the devil was a manifestation of this particular archetype.[36] In phase 2, Jung said exactly the same about the archetype of Wotan.[37] On top of the fact that the mythic figures he associated with these two archetypes are the same, we should also note that the phenomenon Jung tried to explain by means of these concepts are the same. In phase 2, for example, Jung uses the term "archetype of Wotan" to explain the success of Hitler at the end of the 1930s; in phase 3 he explains the success of Hitler by using the term archetypal shadow. To me, this means that concluding that the archetype of Wotan and the archetype of the shadow were synonyms for Jung is entirely justified.

So why did Jung stop using the term archetype of Wotan in phase 3? For myself, I have come to conclude that this change of terminology is probably related to the fact that calling Wotan an archetype can give rise to the belief that one subscribes to the notion of a racial unconscious. Wotan, needless to say, is a mythic figure found only in Germanic culture, which means that it makes very little sense to say that he is innate, unless one is of the opinion that there is a Germanic racial unconscious with innate material only to be found in Germanic people. Although Jung flirted with ideas of this nature, most Jung scholars have concluded that he abandoned such ideas in the 1940s and did not make them a part of his final theoretical position. What I think Jung concluded in phase 3 is that Wotan is not an archetype, but what is known in Jungian psychology as an archetypal image—a specific cultural manifestation of a collective innate structure. It is the innate structure which is inherited and to be found in every individual; the cultural manifestations the archetype gives rise to, however, are specific only to a certain group of people. By using the more general term archetypal shadow for the innate psychological structure, it becomes much clearer that there is no room for race-specific innate components in Jung's theoretical framework. That Jung would want to stress this after the atrocities of the Nazi regime should come as no surprise. Needless to say, the idea that there is a difference between the Germanic psyche and the psyche of other races was something that the Nazis not only flirted with, but turned into the bedrock of their elitist, race-based philosophy.

Conclusion

This fear of being accused of being a Nazi sympathizer perhaps also explains why Jung stops making as many references to the ideas of Nietzsche in phase 3. As we have seen, such references are abundantly present in phase 2, with Jung even devoting an entire seminar to *Thus Spoke Zarathustra*. In phase 3, however, the references to Nietzsche become much less frequent and elaborate. After the end of the Second World War Nietzsche had become a controversial figure: his concept of the *übermensch* had been popular among the Nazi party elite, which they connected with great enthusiasm to their own pseudo-scientific theories about the general superiority of the Aryan race. Whether such connections between Nietzsche and Nazism are justified is a hotly debated topic, of course, although it is certainly true that Nietzsche himself did sometimes write things that could be interpreted as having some overlap with Nazi thought, writing for example the following in his notebook in 1884:

> To gain that tremendous energy of greatness in order to shape the man of the future through breeding and, on the other hand, the annihilation of millions of failures, and not to perish of the suffering one creates, though nothing like it has ever existed! (*KSA*, 11:25[335])[38]

Jung, then, perhaps thought it wiser to stop explaining his own ideas by comparing them to Nietzsche. Nevertheless, I do think that the information provided in this chapter lends strong support to the notion that Jung's final theoretical position on war and violence was inspired by Nietzsche. What I hope to have shown clearly and persuasively is that the ideas Jung put forward about the archetype of the shadow in phase 3 stand quite firmly at the end of a long line of development, which began with *Role of the Unconscious* in phase 1 and continued with the seminar on *Zarathustra* and the *Wotan* article in phase 2. Since Jung drew quite openly on Nietzsche's ideas in these first two phases, it follows logically that the theoretical position he defends in phase 3 represents the outcome of his dialogue with Nietzsche's work.

I think seeing this development clearly is important for several reasons. For one, it shows us how important a historical approach is when reading Jung's work. He made important and drastic changes to both his ideas and terminology over time, which means one should be careful when combining ideas from texts from different time periods. It also sheds new light on his concept of the shadow, illuminating how important the difference between the personal and archetypal shadow is and showing very clearly how central the concept of the archetypal shadow is to Jung's final theoretical take on war and conflict. Lastly, I think this development also makes overwhelmingly clear how important Nietzsche was to Jung. Most importantly, it shows to which Jungian concept we should turn if we want to know where we can see Nietzsche's influence most strongly. As I hope to have shown in this chapter there is substantial evidence that this concept is the archetypal shadow.

Notes

1 An earlier version of this text was published in *Depth Insights*, Issue 6, Fall 2014. C. G. Jung, "Fight with the Shadow," in *The Collected Works of C.G. Jung Volume 10* (Princeton: Princeton University Press, 1946), par. 456.

2 R. Rensma, "Jung's Reception of Friedrich Nietzsche: A Roadmap for the Uninitiated," *Depth Insights*, no. 3 (2012).

3 C. G. Jung, *Memories, Dreams, Reflections* (New York: Random House, 1965 [1961]), 350.

4 C. G. Jung, "The Role of the Unconscious," in *The Collected Works of C.G. Jung Volume 10* (Princeton: Princeton University Press, 1918).
5 C. G. Jung, "Wotan," in *The Collected Works of C.G. Jung Volume 10* (Princeton: Princeton University Press, 1936).
6 C. G. Jung, *Nietzsche's Zarathustra: Notes of the Seminar Given in 1934-1939* (Princeton: Princeton University Press, 1988 [1934]).
7 Jung, "Fight with the Shadow."
8 C. G. Jung, "On the Psychology of the Unconscious," in *The Collected Works of C.G. Jung Volume 7* (Princeton: Princeton University Press, 1943), par. 154.
9 For an overview of Jung's most important ideas, including a discussion of how these developed over time, see chapter two of Ritske Rensma, *The Innateness of Myth: A New Interpretation of Joseph Campbell's Reception of C.G. Jung* (London: Bloomsbury, 2010).
10 Rensma, "Jung's Reception of Friedrich Nietzsche: A Roadmap for the Uninitiated."
11 Jung, "The Role of the Unconscious," par. 16.
12 Friedrich Nietzsche, *Twilight of the Idols & the Antichrist*, trans. R. J. Hollingdale (Harmondsworth: Penguin, 1971).
13 Jung, "The Role of the Unconscious," par. 16.
14 Ibid., par. 32.
15 Ibid., par. 19.
16 Jung, "Wotan," par. 375.
17 Ibid., par. 374.
18 Ibid., par. 395.
19 Ibid., par. 376.
20 Ibid., par. 386.
21 Jung, *Nietzsche's Zarathustra: Notes of the Seminar Given in 1934-1939*. For a more in-depth discussion of the seminar see: Rensma, "Jung's Reception of Friedrich Nietzsche: A Roadmap for the Uninitiated."
22 Jung, *Nietzsche's Zarathustra: Notes of the Seminar Given in 1934-1939*, Vol. 2, 1227.
23 Ibid., Vol. 2, 1214.
24 Ibid., Vol. 2, 815.
25 Friedrich Nietzsche, *The Gay Science: With a Prelude in Rhymes and an Appendix of Songs*, trans. Walter Kaufmann (New York: Vintage Books, 1974), 228.
26 Nietzsche, *The Gay Science*.
27 *Ecce Homo: How to Become What You Are*, trans. Duncan Large (Oxford: Oxford University Press, 2009), 15.
28 Jung, *Nietzsche's Zarathustra: Notes of the Seminar Given in 1934-1939*, Vol. 2, 813.
29 Ibid., 1518.
30 Jung, "Fight with the Shadow," par. 447.
31 Ibid., par. 454.
32 Daryl Sharp, *Jung Lexicon— a Primer of Terms and Concepts* (Toronto: Inner City Books, 1991), 123.
33 C. G. Jung, *Aion— The Collected Works of C.G. Jung Volume 9 part 2* (Princeton: Princeton University Press, 1952).
34 Jung, "The Role of the Unconscious," par. 447.
35 Ann Casement, "The Shadow," in *The Handbook of Jungian Psychology*, ed. Renos K. Papadopoulos (New York and London: Routledge, 2006).
36 Jung, "On the Psychology of the Unconscious," par. 143.
37 Jung, "Wotan," par. 374.

13

Streams of Becoming: Nietzsche, Physiology, and Literary Modernism

Jill Marsden

The isolation of the individual ought not to deceive us: something flows on underneath individuals.

—Nietzsche (*KSA*, 11:26[231])

Although it impinges on virtually everything that he writes, Nietzsche's thinking of becoming is never elaborated in comprehensive terms. Silently and anarchically, the energy of becoming pulses through his writings, a dark and vagrant current upon which so much of his philosophy is buoyed. From his first acquaintance with the serenity of ancient Greek art, Nietzsche had the suspicion that something rippled underneath the orderly and implacable Hellenic world. In *The Birth of Tragedy* he suggests that Apollonian delight in restraint, exemplified by the imposing columns and statues and rigid political structure of the Doric state, could only be understood as a permanent military encampment against the rush (*Rausch*) of the Dionysian (*BT*, 4). In his later writings on will to power the world is envisaged as a "sea of forces flowing and rushing together, eternally changing, eternally flooding back, with tremendous years of recurrence, with an ebb and flood of its forms" (*KSA*, 11:38 [12]). Eternally fluent, becoming resists channeling into structures of enquiry, by definition unavailable for scrutiny as an object of thought.

In what follows, I would like to draw some connections between Nietzsche's philosophy of becoming and modernist experiments with narrative in the early-twentieth-century novel. Although the thematic influence of Nietzsche's philosophy on modernist writers is well documented (Thomas Mann, Herman Hesse, D. H. Lawrence), the relevance of his work to innovations in literary form is less immediately obvious. Nietzsche's reflections on the novel as an art form are sparse in comparison to his meditations on drama and music and his remarks on the prose fiction of his contemporaries are often disparaging. As Henry Staten has commented, "It is an astounding fact that Nietzsche, prophet of modernity, substantially ignores the dominant literary form of the modern age."[1] While it is true that Nietzsche's appreciation of art and culture is contoured by his engagement with ancient Greek tragedy rather than prose fiction, it is the aim of this chapter to show how Nietzsche's deliberations on "becoming" and the "physiology of art" (both of which are developed in his thinking about tragedy) prepare the way for modernist innovation in narrative form. I shall argue that in order to understand the pertinence of Nietzsche's philosophy for literary modernism it is essential to grasp the far-reaching implications of his critique of the "will to truth." This accent on the value of truth not only clarifies Nietzsche's rejection of the naturalist novel in his own time, it also serves to illuminate what it means to consider "becoming" in aesthetic rather than ontological and moral terms.

In the first part of the discussion I will outline the key elements of Nietzsche's philosophy of becoming, looking in particular at its significance as an aesthetic phenomenon. In the second part of the chapter I will explore these ideas in relation to various aspects of modernist "stream-of-consciousness" narration, including interior monologue and free indirect style. With reference to examples from works by James Joyce, Virginia Woolf, and William Faulkner, my aim will be to show how modernist experiments to represent states of consciousness instantiate Nietzsche's philosophy of becoming. Most importantly, with this Nietzschean inflection it is possible to see how modernist writing is the materialization of an embodied mode of thinking, itself a transvaluation of the idea of the "literary."

Nietzsche's philosophy of becoming

There is a thrill in reading Nietzsche which stems from a sense of trespass upon unfamiliar and forbidden terrain. In place of a model of rational enquiry dominated by Enlightenment values, Nietzsche proposes an alternative mission for philosophy, a "seeking after everything strange and questionable in existence, all that has hitherto been excommunicated by morality" (*EH*, *P*, 3). According to Nietzsche, "becoming" is the most elusive phenomenon in the history of the Western philosophical tradition and the one that has been most systematically exiled. From the early Greeks to the rationalists and beyond, "being" has been equated with stability, constancy, and immutability, whereas "becoming" has been defined as its impermanent and imperfect counterpart, aligned with all those processes that stand as objections to knowledge of "what is": "death, change, age, as well as procreation and growth" (*TI*, *'Reason' in Philosophy*, 1). These ontological values are also moral ones; the unchanging ideal is a symbol of the "Good," of "God," the hallmark of the "True." Nietzsche claims that the will to truth is fundamentally a desire for "a world of the constant" and that change is seen as incompatible with happiness which "can be guaranteed only by being." Moreover, it is the body that is held morally accountable for our uncertainties and confusions: "The senses deceive, reason corrects the errors; consequently, one concluded, reason is the road to the constant; the least sensual ideas must be closest to the 'true world.'" This fundamental faith in true being is at its core a wholly life-negating one because it denies the value of the dizzying world of dreams and desires, the throbs of passion and stings of disappointment: "The world as it ought to be exists; this world, in which we live, is in error—this world of ours ought not to exist." In sum, Nietzsche asserts that "belief in what has being is only a consequence: the real *primum mobile* is disbelief in becoming, mistrust of becoming, the low valuation of all that becomes—" (*KSA*, 12:9[60]).

There is a topsy-turvy logic to this "condemnation of and discontent with becoming" for it proceeds from an essentially delusional projection of an ethereal, unchanging realm (*KSA*, 12:7[54]). This privileging of being over becoming reaches back to the tragic age of the Greeks, epitomized by the fateful triumph of Parmenidean and Platonic thinking over the heretical wisdom of Heraclitus. Nietzsche caricatures "Parmenides' prayer" as the bizarre plea for *certainty* in an otherwise mythical age, an ardent longing for the "rigor mortis" of the coldest, emptiest concept of all, the concept of being: "Take away everything that comes-to-be, everything lush, colourful, blossoming, illusory, everything that charms and is alive" (*PTAG*, 11). "Becoming" is the watchword for all that is sumptuous and burgeoning, seductive and beguiling. Outlawed by Judeo-Christian morality, it is the insidious threat of the profligate and irrepressible, the stir beneath the surface of our metaphysical systems, the fantasy of our conceptual edifices sweeping majestically away downstream. To Anaxagoras Nietzsche attributes the view that becoming "is not a moral but an aesthetic phenomenon" (*PTAG*, 19), a fortuitous phrase encapsulating all that is associated with plenitude and excess, with all manner of abundance. It also serves as a reminder that within ancient Greek thinking human existence is seen as imperfect: "How can anything pass away which has a right to be?" (*PTAG*, 4). The "spirit of revenge" finds existence a punishment: "'Oh, where is redemption from the stream of things and from the punishment 'existence'? Thus madness preached" (*TSZ, On Redemption, 11*). This is the "madness" of the ancient Greeks for whom existence is cursed by the painful disfiguration of becoming: existence "is not justified but expiates itself forever through its passing" (*PTAG*, 4).

Against this moral background, the quest to see becoming as an aesthetic phenomenon preoccupies Nietzsche from his earliest writings on tragedy and the Greek music drama, where he identifies becoming with the tonal subground of music and language and the vital energies of a multiplicity of rapturous states. On such a view, "becoming" defies representation: it is non-mimetic, impulse without image and unavailable as an object of contemplation. This aesthetic context is important because Nietzsche never deviates from the view that "our intellect has not been made for the conception of becoming" (*KSA*, 9:11[153]). Becoming is something that is "felt" as tragic pathos, rather than "known" by consciousness. According to Nietzsche, it is in tragic experience that one comes "*to realize in oneself* the eternal joy of becoming—that joy which also encompasses *joy in destruction*" (*TI, What I Owe to the Ancients*, 5). In *The Birth of Tragedy*, Nietzsche endeavors to choreograph the genesis of this tragic feeling in terms of the interplay of "Apollonian" and "Dionysian" physiological forces, "artistic energies" of dream and intoxication which burst forth from nature "without the mediation of the human artist" (*BT*, 2). In characterizing the Apollonian and Dionysian in this way, Nietzsche resists the classical conception of art as mimesis by refusing to distinguish art from nature, simultaneously rejecting the classical conception of the artist as the originator of art. Moreover, in giving expression to the "eternal joy of becoming" in dynamic and libidinal terms, he undermines the Kantian and Schopenhauerian language of appearance and truth that he periodically employs in *The Birth of Tragedy* when articulating the Apollonian/Dionysian relation. In many ways, *The Birth of Tragedy* represents both the problem of thinking about becoming in ontological terms and its alternative. Once the metaphysical terminology of *The Birth of Tragedy* is set aside, it is possible to appreciate the Apollonian and Dionysian as conditions differing in their "tempo" rather than their quality, in particular a difference in their physiological rush (*KSA*, 13:14[46]). In their dynamic interaction, Apollonian and Dionysian constitute the "innocent" play of "coming-to-be and passing away, structuring and destroying," without any moral ascription (*PTAG*, 7).

When considered within the context of his deliberations on becoming it is clear why Nietzsche should repudiate a kind of naturalism that operates with an uncritical view of the "truth" of nature. In *Twilight of the Idols* he claims that from an artistic point of view, nature is no "model"; the aim of art is to "exaggerate" and "distort" (*TI*, *Skirmishes of an Untimely Man*, 7). Nietzsche's dismissive attitude to writers such as the Goncourt brothers and Émile Zola has to be understood within the ambit of his critique of purely mimetic art, an art bound by the (Platonic) desire to be "true" to reality: "To study 'from nature' seems to me a bad sign: it betrays subjection, weakness, fatalism—this lying in the dust before *petit faits* [petty facts] is unworthy of a *complete* artist. Seeing *what is*—that pertains to a different species of spirit, the *anti-artistic*, the prosaic" (*TI*, *Skirmishes of an Untimely Man*, 7). In Nietzsche's estimation the truth imperative belies an instinct of weakness which is fundamentally slavish and reactive; the enthusiasm for "*la vérité vraie*" is above all a demand for the world of the "constant" once again: "the *need* for a faith, a support, backbone, something to fall back on" (*GS*, 347).

No doubt there is an element of caricature in this portrait of the naturalist novel. Nevertheless, for Nietzsche an art form that purports to represent "what is" remains subordinate to a *moralized reality*. By contrast, Nietzsche envisages within Greek tragedy the possibility of a supreme transfiguration of all that "is": "Affirmation of life even in its strangest and sternest problems, the will to life rejoicing in its own inexhaustibility through the *sacrifice* of its highest types—*that* is what I called Dionysian" (*TI*, *What I Owe to the Ancients*, 5, 110). Contra the view that Nietzsche values tragedy for its presentation of the aristocratic-heroic type,[2] it is in the overcoming of such figures that one comes "*to realize in oneself* the eternal joy of becoming—that joy which also encompasses *joy in destruction*" (Ibid.). The art of tragedy is the dark celebration of human squandering, the ecstatic sacrifice of the anthropic ideal.

Nietzsche's philosophy of becoming is charged by these strange imperatives to overflow and exceed, by these impulses of life outlawed by morality. The illegibility of becoming within the history of Western thinking owes much to the logical structure of its language. Becoming has always been equated with the world of appearances, opposed negatively to the truth of what is: "What is, does not become; what becomes, is not" (*TI*, *'Reason' in Philosophy*, 1). As a function of representation, negation is a logical operation: to say that becoming "is not" is to render it void of positive value. Yet considered aesthetically this "non-being" of becoming has darker connotations, hinting at mysterious trajectories and clandestine but precise modes in which becoming eludes capture within conceptual thought. It is this "wild" becoming that has yet to be registered in philosophy.

To understand why aesthetic becoming should continually recede from view, even after loss of faith in the realm of transcendent truth, it is important to consider the value that "truth" has in the phenomenal realm. In "How the 'true world' finally became a myth" in *Twilight of the Idols* Nietzsche accounts for the gradual decline of a Platonic-metaphysical horizon of truth in terms of the history of the nihilistic devaluation of "this world" in favor of a suprasensible beyond. When this process reaches its historically self-conscious moment ("the death of God"), the world as such begins to hemorrhage meaning: "We have abolished the true world. Which world remains? The apparent world perhaps? But no! With the true world we have also abolished the apparent world." Without the horizon of the true to give measure to appearance, a world that is "true for *us*" has to be constructed because "*knowledge* and *becoming* exclude one another" (*KSA*, 12:9[89]); "in a world where there is no being, a certain calculable world of identical cases must first be created through appearance: a tempo at which observation and comparison are possible" (*KSA*, 13:14[93]). As Nietzsche comments at length in the note numbered 569 of *The Will to Power*, the apparent world is a world trimmed according to the practical needs of the human animal. In four points given below, this basic position is elaborated.

1. For there to be communication "something has to be firm, simplified, capable of precision": consequently, "the fuzziness and chaos of sense impressions, are, as it were, logicized."
2. The "reality" of the phenomenal world lies in the continual recurrence of "identical, familiar, related things."
3. The antithesis of the phenomenal world is not the true world but the "formless unformulable world of the chaos of sensations—*another kind* of phenomenal world, a kind 'unknowable' for us."
4. Questions about the nature of "things in themselves" apart from our means of apprehending them are idle. How could we even know if "things" exist since "thingness" was first created by us: "The question is whether there could not be many other ways of creating such an *apparent* world" (*KSA*, 12:9[106]).

The need to communicate coherently accounts for the construction of a regular and knowable world. Words function as concepts—generalizations which have to fit countless more or less similar yet never identical cases. Over time, the metaphorical function of language is forgotten, the "fuzziness and chaos of sense impressions" is clarified into concepts, and the creative stream is "petrified" (*TL*, 1). We forget that words are abstract entities which arrest the fluidity they describe and behave as if they represent some extralinguistic reality: "Truths are illusions that we have forgotten are illusions" (*TL*, 1). Since a world in a state of becoming could not be comprehended or known (*KSA*, 11:36[23]), there is a certain inevitability to this way of normalizing experience. Nietzsche insists that "in a world of *becoming*, 'reality' is always only a *simplification* for practical ends, or a *deception* through the coarseness of organs, or a variation in the *tempo* of becoming" (*KSA*, 12:9[62]). The human animal is not sufficiently refined to see the absolute flux of existence. Indeed, Nietzsche attributes to Heraclitus the view that "it is the fault of your myopia, not of the nature of things, if you see land somewhere in the ocean of coming-to-be and passing away" (*PTAG*, 5). Names are deployed for things as though they persistently endured "yet even the stream into which you step a second time is not the one you stepped into before" (Ibid.) If it is thanks to the "coarseness" of our perceptual organs that we apprehend the world in terms of "being," the implication is that we sense becoming at a particularly slow "tempo." In short, it would seem that for Nietzsche a language for becoming is a logical impossibility, its perception a physiological one.

However, Nietzsche raises the prospect of there being "many other ways of creating" an apparent world (*KSA*, 12:9[106]). Given our physical limitations it is difficult to see how this could be realized but here it is to be remembered that the construction of the world into regular, separate and identifiable "items" of knowledge is first of all a creative act. Truth is not something found but is fabricated, "an *active determining—not* a becoming conscious of something in itself fixed and determined" (*KSA*, 12:9[91]). The human only lives with any repose by forgetting this primary drive to create. In other words, the problem is not simply blunted sensitivity but a stunted capability to imagine the new. For Nietzsche, the will to truth is "the impotence of the will to create" (*KSA*, 12:9[60]). The belief that the world as it ought to be really exists is a "belief of the unproductive who do *not desire to create a world* as it ought to be" (Ibid.). Once life-negating values have been incorporated in a culture they are cultivated by the prevailing ideas which serve as their nutriments; our ideas *of* the body shape the body's capacity *for* ideas. For example, Nietzsche claims that the concepts of "reality" and "being" are actually taken from our "feeling of the 'subject'" (*KSA*, 12:9[98]), the irony being that our categories of reason are of a *sensual* origin, derived from the empirical world (Ibid.). In fact, we believe so firmly in the unity of the subject "that for its sake we imagine 'truth,' 'reality,' 'substantiality' in general" (*KSA*, 12:10[19]).

To counter the dominant belief that "what is" cannot be otherwise, Nietzsche proposes that philosophy return to the swamp of the exiled and much maligned senses. He contends that compared to consciousness or the "soul," the phenomenon of the body is the "richer, clearer, more tangible phenomenon" (*KSA*, 12:5[56]). Moreover, if we take the body and physiology as our starting point for thinking we are able to appreciate "how living unities continually arise and die and how the 'subject' is not eternal," indeed, "that a fluctuating assessment of the limits of power is part of life" (*KSA*, 11:40[21]). This focus on the varying power differentials of the body attenuates the hold that the "subject" has on thinking and highlights the contingency of norms that seem unquestionably given. Ridiculing the "absurd overestimation of consciousness" (*KSA*, 13:14[146]), particularly the presumption that the ego is the "cause of all deeds" (*KSA*, 12:9[98]), Nietzsche dismisses the preoccupation with subjectivity as a mere idiosyncrasy of the human species.

This profound shift of attention from consciousness to the body does not represent a simple, precritical materialism; on the contrary, it is a revaluation of the powers of becoming that have been "interpreted" by consciousness hitherto. In the 1886 Preface to *The Gay Science*, Nietzsche poses the question of whether physiological needs have always been disguised under the cloaks of the objective, ideal, and purely spiritual and whether "philosophy has not been merely an interpretation of the body and a *misunderstanding of the body*" (*GS*, *P*, 2). In this context, he expresses gratitude for his ill health for granting him insight into the relationship between thought and physiological drives. Provocatively, he claims that it is thanks to his continual pain—including a "sensation close to sea-sickness," "semi-paralysis" making it difficult to speak, and bouts of vomiting lasting for days—that he has been able to make "the most instructive experiments in the intellectual and moral domain" (*KGB*, January 1880, III.1:1). As Pierre Klossowski has suggested, "by examining the alternations in his own valetudinary states" Nietzsche is able to interpret "the body" in terms of the fortuitous encounter of impulses which come and go and "which are *moral* only insofar as the declarations and judgements of the self re-create in language a property that is in itself inconsistent and hence empty."[3] In fact, Nietzsche suggests that the phenomenon of the body offers a ground for thinking which is *transpersonal*, stretching far beyond the psychology of the subject. The human body is that "in which the most distant and most recent past of all organic development again becomes living and corporeal, through which and over and beyond which a tremendous inaudible stream seems to flow" (*KSA*, 11:36[35]). Considered thus, the body offers the prospect of a thinking of becoming which is not predetermined by a thinking of being nor constrained by the temporal limits of an individual human life. Importantly, this is a material thinking of becoming that does not have a subject distinct from itself: "Becoming as invention, willing, self-denial, overcoming of oneself: no subject but an action, a positing, creative, no 'causes and effects'" (*KSA*, 12:7[54]).

This recourse to physiology clears the way for a very different vocabulary of tides and tempos, offering the prospect of thinking of action without agency: creative willing and invention beyond the self.

> If we give up the effective subject, we also give up the object upon which effects are produced. Duration, identity with itself, being are inherent neither in that which is called subject nor in that which is called object: they are complexes of events apparently durable in comparison with other complexes—e.g., through the difference in tempo of the event (rest-motion, firm-loose: opposites that do not exist in themselves and that actually express only *variations in degree* that from a certain perspective appear to be opposites). (*KSA*, 12:9[91])

To give up the active subject is to relinquish oppositional thinking in favor of apprehending complexes of events in terms of "differences in tempo" and "variations in degree" (Ibid.). Slipping free of its moorings in ontology, becoming silently seeps through the boundaries that hitherto shored up mutual discontinuities in dualisms and hierarchies. To think becoming aesthetically is to think physiologically, to share Nietzsche's sacred hymn to wild becoming: the embrace of "everything that comes-to-be, everything lush, colourful, blossoming, illusory, everything that charms and is alive" (*PTAG*, 11).

Modernist streams

Outlawed by morality but glimpsed fleetingly in the tragic art of the ancient Greeks, the wild becoming of Nietzsche's philosophy resurfaces in a number of tracts of experimental modernist prose in the early twentieth century. At first glance, this proposed alignment between Nietzsche's philosophy and literary modernism may appear implausible given that the latter is most frequently typified by subjectivist motifs. It is generally acknowledged that around the turn of the twentieth century novelists increasingly located "reality" in the "private, subjective consciousness of individual selves, unable to communicate their experience to others."[4] The inward gaze of the self-contemplative subject is epitomized in "stream-of-consciousness" narration which aims to represent the "continuous flow of thought and sensation in the human mind."[5] As a form of narration which evokes the moment-to-moment emergence of thoughts and emotions, there is a spontaneity and fluidity to stream of consciousness that it will be our purpose to explore; nevertheless, the Platonic image of thought as "the soul's silent dialogue with itself" is not easily shaken off. Julia Kristeva goes so far as to suggest that "interior monologue" is "the most indomitable way in which an entire civilization conceives itself as identity, as organized chaos, and finally as transcendence."[6] Such concentration of this potentially uninhibited flow within the interior realm would seem to emphatically re-entrench the values that Nietzsche submits to critique, primarily the anchoring of becoming to a subject.

In light of these arguments, why insist on the importance of Nietzsche for understanding literary modernism? It is because of these reactive views and not in spite of them that Nietzsche's philosophy is so essential. Nietzsche's critique of values enables us to appreciate the extent to which most approaches to modernism continue to operate with models of thinking and narrative that are underpinned by the "will to truth." As previously discussed, the attempt to represent "what is" is morally motivated: the conviction is that the "constant" will not deceive us, the true is the good (God). However, this is based upon a more fundamental untruth, the collective "deception" perpetuated by our coarse organs. We have forgotten the fundamentally metaphorical nature of our concepts and have come to put our faith in the value of "true facts": knowledge that is stable, ideas that are common. Most commentators on modernist fiction tend to appeal to abstract concepts of the "self" and its narrative codes, imbuing their analyses with idealist values which inhibit exploration of experiments in conveying consciousness in the moment of its becoming.

For example, in his recent work *The Value of the Novel* (2015), Peter Boxhall proposes that "if art has a value, a purpose, then we are led to imagine also that the artwork, defined by its formal features, has some sort of relationship to the world which simply is."[7] Such a view remains closely bound to a mimetic notion of art, the truth of representation and the idea of value as "the good" which a phenomenon serves: in Boxhall's words, "the artwork is judged by its capacity to represent the world truly, to find a form in which to give expression to a pre-existing set of realities" (Ibid.). These ideas about art and truth have a long lineage and are underwritten by a fundamentally Platonic privileging of being. While the distinctions between "form and content" and "art and matter" that frame the argument are inclined to blur,[8] the initial pairings serve to consolidate oppositional thinking. Identities which differ from one another by means of contrariety imply a shared prior unity as their mediating "ground." It will suffice to recall how in *The Birth of Tragedy*, Nietzsche introduces the Apollonian and Dionysian as primary physiological energies ("art forces of nature"), bypassing the logic of identity from the outset. If one takes physiology and the body as a guide for thinking, the questions that one asks are no longer of the order of how things simply "are."

Taking the body as a guiding thread seems to demand a more oblique access to art, focusing on the finer detail of how varying effects come to be rather than on "what" these effects are. However, it is not enough to simply shift attention to formal considerations. For example, when Robert Humphrey declares that "the problem of form for the stream-of-consciousness novelist is the problem of how order is imposed on disorder,"[9] he has in mind the author's task of rendering the "chaos" of experience sufficiently coherent for the reader while remaining convincingly chaotic as a representation of consciousness. While this is an interesting technical question, like much literary thinking this understanding of modernist writing remains implicitly theological, the idea being that "matter" is molded or shaped from without in accordance with an extrinsic principle. By contrast, for Nietzsche becoming is irreducible to the form of the concept. Becoming signifies proliferating luxuriance, primary plenitude, an inherent tendency to overflow bounds. In resisting the *a priori* assumptions of metaphysical thinking, Nietzsche conceives form in non-idealist terms as originating *within* the material flows of becoming.

> One is an artist at the cost of regarding that which all non-artists call "form" as *content*, as "the matter itself." To be sure, then one belongs in a *topsy-turvy world*: for henceforth content becomes something merely formal—our life included. (*KSA*, 13:11[3])

It is to be recalled here that as a figure for "form" or restraint, the Apollonian is fully physiological. "Form" is not to be distinguished from "content" or "matter," as fundamentally different in kind or as emanating from an extrinsic source, be it human or divine. Moreover, style is ineluctably material, matter no longer being conceived in logical opposition to form or spirit. Nietzsche asserts that the sense of every style is to "*communicate* a state, an inner tension of pathos through signs, including the tempo of these signs" (*EH*, *Why I Write Such Good Books*, 4). The vocabulary of tempo is one of pulse and pace, mood as measure. Nietzsche insists that "every style is *good* which actually communicates an inner state, which makes no mistake as to the tempo of the signs, as to the *gestures*—all rules of phrasing are art of gesture" (Ibid.). Communication of an intense affect then is not simply an issue of the signs employed but a matter of their tempo, their deep stylistic feel. This "matter" is inherently physiological because phrasing is entirely an "art of gesture," a configuration of sensory value (*EH*, *Why I*

Write Such Good Books, 4): "One never communicates thoughts: one communicates movements, mimic signs, which we then trace back to thoughts" (*KSA*, 13:14[119]).

Seen in this light, the tempo of a narrative is an encoding of its kinesthetic rhythm, its affective movement or libidinal pulse. Style is wholly unique insofar as it is a manifestation of a particular physiology, a point Nietzsche makes with typical loftiness: "Considering that the multiplicity of inner states is in my case extraordinary, there exists in my case the possibility of many styles" (*EH*, *Why I Write Such Good Books*, 4). In this sense, the tempo of the signs makes manifest what lies outside of communication understood as the everyday code of signification. If we attend to Nietzsche's physiology of art, it is possible to address modernist narration in terms of different bodily tempos: *streams of becoming* rather than streams of consciousness. To illustrate this, I will now consider examples of streams of becoming in three classic modernist texts: interior monologue in James Joyce's *Ulysses* (1922), free indirect style in Virginia Woolf's *Mrs Dalloway* (1925) and a hybrid form of stream of consciousness in William Faulkner's *The Sound and the Fury* (1929). In each case, the energy of the narrative style conducts the reader to the dark places beyond psychology.

Interior monologue is defined by Dorrit Cohn in terms of "reference to the thinking self in the first person" and to the "narrated moment (which is also the moment of locution) in the present tense."[10] This form of narrative unfolds in unpredictable, often meandering streams, taking shape only in the process of its telling. The archetypical example is the "Penelope" section of Joyce's *Ulysses*, Molly Bloom's long, barely punctuated set of musings as she lies in bed thinking of lovers past and present. Given that in her private thoughts Molly does not need to clarify any of the deictic expressions that she employs, there are moments of inevitable ambiguity. For example, the monologue begins with the use of a third-person masculine pronoun which is undetermined by an antecedent: "Yes because he never did a thing like that before as ask to get his breakfast in bed with a couple of eggs since the city arms hotel when he used to be pretending to be laid up with a sick voice."[11] Molly's monologue "begins" *in medias res*. Both chronology and signification are disturbed by her withheld antecedents for the reader can infer only from earlier chapters that the first "he" is Leopold, her husband. Although interior monologue might seem self-contained, it is actually only the illusion of the "I" as a point of stability that creates this impression. Molly's monologue is traversed by a movement that is wholly exterior, a stream of becoming that is never mediated by a relation with an "inner" consciousness. It is ironic that critics such as Kristeva see interior monologue as a narrative that supports "Western man's state of 'interiority'"[12] when the case seems to be entirely the reverse. The concept of the self-regarding subject is brought to these experimental texts by the critic, not found there. The only rational support for this notion is found in the Platonic narratives of identity that determine the "being" of becoming in the first place.

In spite of the illusion that Molly is the source or underlying ground to these streams of becoming, it is only the incessant gathering and dispersing of carnal memories and erotic fantasies, drifting thoughts and idle musings, which "produce" her as a subject of desire. Just as waves heave and break, Molly's sentences convey the sway and roll of the life of the mind.

> I laughed Im not a horse or an ass am I I suppose he was thinking of his father I wonder is he awake thinking of me or dreaming am I in it who gave him that flower he said he bought he smelt of some kind of drink not whisky or stout[13]

Visually the text suggests the ceaseless passage of thoughts. The omission of the standard punctuation that would frame discrete sentences simultaneously propels the reader forward in the rush of cascading talk and backward in the bid to recover the sense of lost signs. This is significant because we tend to think of flow as steady and continuous, in narrative terms as a movement onward or forward. Although Nietzsche frequently deploys the metaphor of the stream or river to evoke becoming, it is important to decouple the notion of becoming from the image of steady flow, particularly unidirectional flow. If the death of god signifies the decisive severing of becoming from teleology, it must also represent liberation from chronology: "Becoming must be explained without recourse to final intentions … the present must absolutely not be justified by reference to a future, nor the past by reference to the present" (*KSA*, 13:11[72]). Although most narratives deviate from seriality insofar as the chronology of a story is often at odds with the time of the telling, within the narrative frame there is still a strong sense of semantic and semiotic progression, mediated by the development of a subject accountable for its action.

This concept of narrative, underpinned by moral values, exerts a certain hold on critical reading. For example, Derek Attridge notes the ubiquity of the metaphor of "flow" in critical commentaries on Joyce's final chapter of *Ulysses* but he raises questions about how Joyce's "sense of an unstoppable onward movement" has been achieved.[14] Arguing that "once the missing punctuation and other typographical absences have been made good, the language of this episode is relatively conventional,"[15] Attridge contends that the flowing effect relies on the visual effects of the unpunctuated prose and "has nothing to do with the continuities of unexpressed thought."[16] The wildness of the writing is quickly caged by the claim that continuity is a feature "which belongs to the printing not the thinking."[17] The underlying assumption here is that thinking is an ideal, abstract activity that it is the role of art to represent. The Platonic notion of the soul's silent dialogue with itself underscores the larger argument too, that what we are missing are the syntactic articulations that we imagine Molly to be using as she speaks silently to herself. What this particular analysis disallows is the suggestion that thinking itself is a material force, something that materializes as literature. So long as the will to truth dictates the critical vocabulary of reading it is "physically" impossible to perceive the anarchic flow of "wild becoming," writing freed from the constraint of the sentence as a containing unit ("'units' are nowhere present in the nature of becoming" (*KSA*, 13:11[73])). Critics are right to observe that readers of Molly's monologue respond visually to the absence of punctuation but this is itself a bodily response. According to Nietzsche, art speaks to a "kind of subtle flexibility of the body," exciting fine hints of the rapturous state which gives rise to art (*KSA*, 13:14[119]). There is a thrill in the communication of this tempo of becoming, a stimulation that is physically transformative. One "still hears with one's muscles," Nietzsche tells us; "one even reads with one's muscles" (Ibid.). Molly Bloom's stream of becoming is not simply an undoing of narrative norms; it summons us back to the "tremendous inaudible stream" flowing through and beyond the body, eroding the habits of perception sedimented in the self.

In contrast to interior monologue, free indirect style is a form of stream of consciousness which evokes first-person idioms in third-person voice, dispensing with a subject of enunciation. The interior life of characters who do not "utter" their thoughts is rendered imaginatively available within a prose style liberated from speakers and intentions. In the early pages of *Mrs Dalloway*, Virginia Woolf weaves between limited third-person narration and free indirect style to evoke something of the inner thoughts of the society hostess, Clarissa Dalloway as she walks through London one June morning, reflecting on friends, acquaintances, and the incidental sights and sounds of the street:

> Somehow in the streets of London, on the ebb and flow of things, here, there, she survived, Peter survived, lived in each other, she being part, she was positive, of the trees at home; of the house there, ugly, rambling all to bits and pieces as it was; part of people she had never met.[18]

In terms of tempo the novel embodies the "ebb and flow of *things*" (my emphasis) rather than the self-contained thoughts and actions of individual characters. This is achieved in a number of ways but Joseph Boone singles out Woolf's use of free indirect style for giving "the text an overall homogeneity of tone and syntax" while moving seamlessly between different consciousnesses.[19] For example, in the skywriting scene in the early pages of *Mrs Dalloway*, the narrative thread drifts from one consciousness to another as different characters attempt to interpret the vapor trail letters of an airplane over Regent's Park. A fleeting moment or two of a character's reflections are caught before the narrative moves on, migrating between past and present, between "inner" and "outer" worlds. In this way the narrative seems to catch the "the sensation of seeing and feeling the very stream of life"[20] without ever coming to rest within the sanctuary of a single mind.

The ebb and flow of things is also suggested by the digressive phrasing of Woolf's clauses, stippled with liberal commas and semicolons which constantly amplify detail and add nuance. Such excesses call to mind Nietzsche's characterization of becoming as the vibrancy of everything that comes-to-be: lush, colored, blossoming, illusory. Although like *Ulysses* the narrative frame of *Mrs Dalloway* occupies the span of just one day, its forward motion is constantly blown off course by syntax which blooms and proliferates. Woolf records in her diary her excitement at discovering a new form for a new novel: "Suppose one thing should open out of another ... doesn't that give the looseness & lightness I want: doesn't that get closer & keep form & speed, & enclose everything, everything?"[21] Fleeting ideas put forth shoots and blossom into life in the midst of sentences. At the same time, the reader is propelled along by the boundless present participles which mirror Nietzsche's predilection for continuous nouns of action.

> "But, thank you, Lucy, oh, thank you," said Mrs Dalloway, and thank you, thank you, she went on saying (sitting down on the sofa with her dress over her knees, her scissors, her silks), thank you, thank you, she went on saying in gratitude to her servants generally for helping her to be like this, to be what she wanted, gentle, generous hearted. Her servants liked her. And then this dress of hers—where was the tear? And now her needle to be threaded. This was a favourite dress, one of Sally Parker's, the last almost she ever made, alas, for Sally had now retired, lived at Ealing, and if I ever have a moment, thought Clarissa (but never would she have a moment any more), I shall go and see her at Ealing.[22]

As the beginning of this passage indicates, Woolf uses parentheses to layer the sentence, sometimes conveying simultaneity of action (as indicated by the description of her sitting with her sewing things), sometimes to mark the simultaneity of proposing and rescinding an action (the plan to see Sally Parker). The narrative seems to open out rather than to advance, slipping surreptitiously between inner and outer points of view. Since in free indirect style pronouns are no longer points of location for speech it is difficult to distinguish between the thoughts that a character has from the thoughts that a text has "about" a character. Does Clarissa feel assured that her servants like her or are we told this with more authority by the "narrative voice"? Is it Clarissa who knows that she will never get a moment to see Sally? By using syntax in an anti-syntactical way, the usual distinction between "objective" and "subjective" spheres is undone. Instead of seeing the novel in terms of the "personal becoming" of its characters, free indirect style compels a more profound thinking of the stream of life. Once again, it seems possible to read modernist narration as a realization of Nietzsche's philosophy of becoming.

As Jacques Rancière has commented, in free indirect style the imperfect tense is used "not as a temporal marker of the past but as a modal suspension of the difference between reality and content of consciousness."[23] This is significant because Woolf's *Mrs Dalloway* concerns itself with the constraints of being determined as a subject by chronological time. The nihilistic condemnation of "this world," which Nietzsche's Zarathustra calls "the spirit of revenge," is epitomized by "the will's antipathy towards time and its 'it was'" (*Z*, *On Redemption*). According to Gilles Deleuze, "Far from being a psychological trait the spirit of revenge is the principle on which our whole psychology depends."[24] Owing to the mistrust of becoming at the heart of Platonism, human finitude is seen as an imperfect state, the phrase "it was," serving as a reminder to the human being that his existence is essentially "an imperfect tense that can never become a perfect one" (*HL*, 1). To liberate becoming from its moral and ontological determinations it is imperative to move beyond the "spirit of revenge": the idea that existence is a punishment that expiates itself through its passing. To justify existence as an aesthetic phenomenon—the goal of *The Birth of Tragedy*—is to liberate the human from moral time. If it is possible to think becoming aesthetically, it is possible to move from the time of accountability, the baneful "it was," to the joy of eternal becoming. Woolf's novel may well be about the strictures of time but the tempo of the writing carries us away from the world of subjects in waves of impersonal becoming.

In comparison to Woolf and Joyce, William Faulkner makes the most radical experiment with stream-of-consciousness narrative in the first part of his classic novel, *The Sound and the Fury*. Narrated from the perspective of a character who has no sense of time, the first part of the text gives access to the inner world of the mentally impaired Benjy Compson, who recounts fragments of episodes in no discernible order from across the course of the thirty-three years of his life. The jumble of moments is difficult to synthesize, not least because of the absence of chronology as a "ground" for the narrative. The problem is made more acute by Benjy's lack of introspection. For example, the novel opens with Benjy's account of men "hitting" in the "pasture" but it is only as the narrative progresses that the reader is able to discern that a game of golf is being played:

> Through the fence, between the curling flower spaces, I could see them hitting. They were coming toward where the flag was and I went along the fence. … They took the flag out, and they were hitting. Then they put the flag back and they went to the table and he hit and the other hit.[25]

Benjy's sentences are excessively syndetic with almost no subordination, few adverbs, and minimal information about how or why things happen. There is no indication that he grasps that the object of golf is to hit the ball, an impression created by his failure to draw inferences of cause and effect. When describing being fed at mealtimes he reports events without ascribing agents ("the spoon came up … the bowl went away");[26] for Benjy there is no "doer" behind the "deed." Indeed, the narrative seems to support Nietzsche's view that the duality of cause and effect "probably never exists" and that in truth we are confronted by a continuum and a flux "out of which we isolate a couple of pieces" (*GS*, 112). The fundamental coordinates of human agency are oddly lacking in Benjy's case.

As far as stream-of-consciousness narration is concerned it seems problematic to designate Benjy's account as interior monologue. The character's experiences are given in past tense and although Faulkner uses italics to mark temporal shifts, these seldom clarify the context within which Benjy "speaks." Moreover, while the (often hostile) words of others are also reported in this section of the novel, Benjy offers no reaction to the things that are said nor does he make reflective comments of an emotional kind. For this reason, some commentators have identified this chapter as the representation of "extreme objectivity, a condition quite impossible to the ordinary conscious mind."[27] Donald Kartiganer argues that having "no mind"[28] and being "an idiot"[29] Benjy is "actually perception prior to consciousness, prior to the 'intelligent' view of experience"[30] and thus he is truly at one with essential reality. While this "impersonal" account may appear to accord with the idea of "streams of becoming," it must be conceded that Kartiganer's reading is premised on the model of a humanity which Benjy "lacks." Since Benjy is regarded as subhuman, lacking an ability to intelligently discriminate between things, his perception is equated with a mindless gaping at "reality as a succession of objects."[31] To this end the values of subjectivity remain the reference point for reading the narrative stream.

This focus on the privative underscores the hold that normative values have on critical reading. Instead of dwelling on the absence of temporal location as a stable ground, we might consider how the narrative has its own unique tempo. Benjy's aesthetic horizon is one of flows, not of mutually exclusive subjects and objects. When describing the act of running indoors, he does not relate the event in terms of change in location but in terms of change in light and temperature: "We ran up the steps and out of the bright cold, into the dark cold."[32] In thrall to a way of thinking which privileges being, we pass over all of the minute differences in the flow of becoming and identify coherent and constant objects. Yet in many respects, Benjy's world is much fuller than one might imagine. He sees the "curling flower spaces" when he looks through the fence, assigning shape and movement to places between things. He sees and touches "the dark place on the wall like a door only it wasn't a door," a place which only comes when the light is switched on.[33] Recalling Nietzsche's remark that "thingness" was first created by us, Benjy's narrative seems to answer the question of "whether there could not be many other ways" of creating the phenomenal world (*KSA*, 12:9[106]). Faulkner's text weakens the claims of "normal" experience by showing a way of navigating the world which has not been trampled into being by the hoof-prints of the herd. The provisional nature of "reality"—its simplification for practical ends—is made all the more acute when we are compelled to inhabit a different way of seeing and feeling, when we are bemused and enthralled by affects that are not our own.

When writing has the power to move the reader, when it enlivens the senses, stirs the affects, the body that responds to the text is a subtly transformed one. Newly perceiving, this body creates new meaning. Nietzsche's philosophy of becoming is about physical transformation, the vital creativity of the body, its carnal rhythms and blood music. The artist does more than merely simulate physical pulsations or inner tensions when communicating an inner state. The imperative is to re-stimulate this sensation in the recipient, to communicate the art-creating state. This is why Nietzsche's reflections on art and literature are so much more concerned with the conditions of art than its products.

> Art reminds us of states of animal vigor; it is on the one hand an excess and overflow of blooming physicality into the world of images and desires; on the other, an excitation of the animal functions through the images and desires of intensified life;—an enhancement of the feeling of life, a stimulant to it. (*KSA*, 12:9[102])

Because the effect of works of art is to excite the state that creates art, artistic encounters tend to lead their recipients back to the body rather than beyond it.

We recall Nietzsche's assertion that "our intellect has not been made for the conception of becoming." In reading works of literary modernism through Nietzsche's philosophy it has been possible to see how becoming materializes as art. Writing becomes a way of thinking, a process that can only be comprehended as a transformative bodily action. "Thought" is not commensurate with "theory" but theory has become the default position of thought in a scholarly context. In reading modernist literature through Nietzsche's philosophy, one becomes aware of the extent to which the dominant literary values are moral ones. While it may be readily conceded that novels both criticize and perpetuate dominant social norms, the extent to which the concepts of narrative are premised on a moralized reality has been scarcely acknowledged.

Thought depends on a "culture," on nutriments which will cultivate it. We need to build on Nietzsche's realization that the living body is the medium of thought. Becoming "escapes" apprehension by our coarse organs but it is "felt" in the experiments of the modernists. Nietzsche's philosophy enables us to understand modernist literature as an embodied mode of thinking, a manifestation of blooming physicality into the world of signs. The effect is a vitalizing one, moving the reader, arousing the senses. The intellect is not equipped to grasp the concept of becoming but the body is the guiding thread to its realization in art. This is the most profound legacy of Nietzsche's philosophy for understanding modernism. Beyond all the thematic influences of Nietzsche's philosophy on individual writers, his thinking impacts on the deep core of literature, insinuating its wayward rhythms into art.

Notes

1 Henry Staten, "Dionysus Lost and Found: Literary Genres in the Political Thought of Nietzsche and Lukács," in *Nietzsche, Philosophy and the Arts*, ed. Salim Kemal, Ivan Gaskell and Daniel W. Conway (Cambridge: Cambridge University Press, 1998), 239–56, 249.
2 See Staten, "Dionysus Lost and Found," 242–48.
3 Pierre Klossowski, Nietzsche and the Vicious Circle (London: Athlone,1997), 30.
4 David Lodge, *The Art of Fiction* (London: Penguin, 1992), 42.
5 Lodge, *The Art of Fiction.*
6 Julia Kristeva, *Desire in Language: A Semiotic Approach to Literature and Art* (Oxford: Basil Blackwell, 1981), 90.
7 Peter Boxhall, *The Value of the Novel* (Cambridge: Cambridge University Press, 2015), 12.
8 See Boxhall, *The Value of the Novel*, 13.
9 Robert Humphrey, *Stream of Consciousness in the Modern Novel* (Berkeley and Los Angeles: University of California Press, 1954), 85.
10 Dorrit Cohn, *Transparent Minds: Narrative Modes for Representing Consciousness in Fiction* (Princeton: Princeton University Press, 1978), 13.
11 James Joyce, *Ulysses* (Penguin: London, 1968), 659.
12 Kristeva, *Desire in Language: A Semiotic Approach to Literature and Art*, 90.
13 James Joyce, *Ulysses*, 662.
14 Derek Attridge, *Joyce Effects: Language, Theory, and History* (Cambridge: Cambridge University Press, 2000), 98.
15 Attridge, *Joyce Effects: Language, Theory, and History*, 95.
16 Ibid., 99.
17 Ibid., 100.
18 Virginia Woolf, *Mrs Dalloway* (Penguin: London, 1925), 11.

19 Joseph Boone, *Libidinal Currents: Sexuality and the Shaping of Modernism* (Chicago and London: The University of Chicago Press, 1998), 179.
20 Robin Majumdar and Allen McLaurin, *Virginia Woolf: The Critical Heritage* (London: Routledge & Kegan Paul, 1975), 164.
21 Virginia Woolf *The Diary of Virginia Woolf Volume II 1920-1924,* ed. Anne Olivier Bell and Andrew McNeillie (London: The Hogarth Press 1978), 13.
22 Virginia Woolf, *Mrs Dalloway*, 44.
23 Jacques Rancière, *Mute Speech*, trans. James Swenson (New York: Columbia University Press, 2011), 122.
24 Gilles Deleuze, *Nietzsche and Philosophy*, trans. Hugh Tomlinson (London: The Athlone Press, 1983), 32.
25 William Faulkner, *The Sound and the Fury* (New York: W. W. Norton and Company, 2014), 3.
26 Faulkner, *The Sound and the Fury*, 17.
27 Donald Kartiganer, "*The Sound and the Fury* and Faulkner's Quest for Form," *ELH* 37, no. 4 (December 1970): 620.
28 Kartiganer, "*The Sound and the Fury* and Faulkner's Quest for Form," 622.
29 Ibid., 621.
30 Ibid.
31 Ibid.
32 Faulkner, *The Sound and the Fury*, 5.
33 Ibid., 41.

14

And Death Shall Have No Dominion: Dylan Thomas, Friedrich Nietzsche, and Tragic Joy

James Luchte

> *What is great in man is that he is a bridge and not an end: what can be loved in man is that he is an* overture *and a* going under.
>
> —Nietzsche, *Thus Spoke Zarathustra, Zarathustra's Prologue,* 4

Nietzsche's death in 1900 was a global event, an exclamation point for a defiant call for cultural transfiguration to which philosophers, poets, artists, musicians, and politicians responded with various forms of ongoing rebellion. In his *Thus Spoke Zarathustra*, he had spurred his listeners to make death a festival, perhaps the joyous wakes of the Welsh coffin or the American south. This is exactly what happened for Nietzsche—though it was a festival which precipitated myriad cultural and political explosions across the world since the turn of the twentieth century. With its forbidden exposure of the death of an exhausted civilization, the "Nietzsche event" cleared the ground for a new topography of culture, one to be inhabited by the protagonists of cultural, and sometimes, political revolution. Pound, T. S. Eliot, Yeats, Auden, Joyce, Stravinsky, Dostoyevsky, Dadaism, surrealism, psychoanalysis, to name a few: modernism in music, poetry, art, and literature—and religion and politics—displaced the irredeemable motifs of traditionalist culture which no longer had any credibility in the wake of the new dispensation.

With his deconstruction of Christian Platonism (romanticism) and his conjuration of the rebirth of tragic poetry, Nietzsche reinstates musicality, eroticism, and the terrible truth of death at the heart of poetry and culture (East and West). He shattered the lifeless, empty shells of the Apollonian forms of the past (the "Old Law Tablets"), setting free a new musicality which would, in and of itself, give birth to new images, a new *mythos* for a tragic age. Dylan Thomas encountered this new Nietzschean topography of modernism as a found object, as the Child, in the "metamorphosis of the spirit" of *Thus Spoke Zarathustra*, who innocently embraces a world born of rebellion. Leslie Lavigne details this relationship in *Nietzschean Elements in the Poetry of Dylan Thomas*, writing: "In his expression of the Nietzschean concepts of eternal recurrence and the *Übermensch*, Thomas followed in the path of Yeats, a path that bears many similarities to that of Blake."[1]

Modernism provided the breathing room for creative innovation, vast experimentation, eccentricity, exploration of different existential possibilities for a life lived in the face of mortality. Thomas's profound act of defiance against the toxic culture of traditional hypocrisy was born from his own sense of tragic freedom and joy. His poetic work is a symptom of the dynamic cultural revolution already occurring in the wake of the "Nietzsche event," one accelerated by the European and global descent into the maelstrom of the First World War, the Great Depression, and the rise of Hitler. Thomas embraced the contours of the new world, expressing his own historicity through the artistic juxtaposition of the contradictions in which he was fatefully embedded. Yet, far from being an aloof romanticist, we will disclose—through a more rigorous reading of his work—the engaged radical core of Thomas's artistic project and way of life.

Dylan Thomas in exile

Dylan Thomas's path toward modernist English poetry was laid bare when he was a child. He was not taught the Welsh language *deliberately*—a decision taken by his father David John Thomas, a head teacher of English literature and an *un-forked* poet.[2] David, who was himself bilingual and taught Welsh lessons in his own home, inundated his son Dylan with sounds and books of English words, introducing him to the great works of English literature, including modernist poetry, psychology, and philosophy. Thomas began to write poetry as a child—the "Rimbaud of Cwmdonkin Drive"[3]—and quickly began to edit his high school's literary journal. Already involved in advanced intellectual, artistic, and poetological questions and endeavors, Thomas, before the age of twenty, filled up notebooks with works which would, all in all, constitute around half of his poetic output—not counting his prose, screenplays, radio plays, and short stories. Indeed, he showed no interest in other subjects, recognizing very early that he would be a poet and writer.

Dylan Thomas left school at sixteen and began to work as a reporter. He fashioned journals and wrote poetry, and, after three years, published his first collection, *Eighteen Poems*, in 1933. This event paradoxically assured his exile from an "easy" life in quasi-traditionalist Wales. With his success, he began to roam the streets, pubs, and salons of London, coming into contact with the state of the art of modernist poetics. Of course, just as quickly, he would return to Wales, for as he said in a letter, "Cities are death."[4] His nomadic, uneasy existence as a poet—and one in the English language—continued throughout his life, as he was caught in a web between Wales, London, and later America. It was the utter lack of employment opportunities in Wales—especially as a poet—and his refusal to even consider another vocation—that gave birth to his permanent exile. If one wished to be a modern poet, one had to be in London or America—surely not in Wales (unless one could make one's lucre elsewhere). Landing work with the BBC was later a great boon for Dylan Thomas, who contributed an

English-speaking Welsh perspective to the public corporation's offerings. Under the neocolonial thumb of British culture, the Welsh public and cultural spheres were and still are dominated by England and its media corporations, publishing houses, and academic institutions.

It is not clear if this was David Johnson's intention, but he is known to have been proud that his son had produced lyrical poetry and work of international significance. Nevertheless, he merely opened the door for Thomas, who went through willingly, single-mindedly working to create his own mytho-poetic world through the articulation of his lyrical, psychological, and philosophical orientations and sensibilities. But, while his orientations were often centered around the tragic and brutal character of existence, of mortality, it was his longing for the Welsh landscape and its intimacy with nature which provided him with a sense of tragic joy, of the power of life (the concern of the physically weak), of the force of the "green fuse."[5] Indeed, Dylan Thomas acted as the Welsh druidic bard in his artistic channeling of the voices of his people,[6] his wife, children, and lifeworld, of the wind, the raging moon and the sea. His father may have sought to make it "easy" for his son by giving him the language of the oppressor, but he could take away neither the accent of his voice nor his perennial feelings of homelessness from Wales necessitated by his extravagant exile.

Though his own life ended in the contradiction of his tragic existence, dead in New York in 1953, Dylan Thomas has been welcomed home in contemporary Wales, his legacy evidenced by the 2014 celebration of the centenary of his birth. He is a celebrated son of a Wales that has enshrined bilingualism in its National Parliament. "Too English for the Welsh, Too Welsh for the English,"[7] Dylan Thomas died trying to escape the double bind of his predicament, though, as tragic, and intentionally so, he burned himself out through the ecstatic character of his lifestyle, his bohemian *ethos*—his own festival of tragic joy. Some would wish, as we will see, to bring sobriety to our view of Dylan Thomas, to pick his bones clean of any flesh, and to put to sleep or expunge his most riotous effects upon the youth (and patronizingly insulting adolescence in the process). On the contrary, however, it is precisely his eccentric rebellion that matters most about him as a tragic poet—especially one who also produced great works. That he is human, flawed, suffering, but also joyful and ecstatic, a creature of flesh and intoxication—and dying untimely—this makes him tragic in a way that allows people to empathize with him in the first instance. The rebellion of youth may be "embarrassing" for those who have acquiesced to the nihilism of otherworldly hopes, but such denial of the tragic character of existence and fleeting possibility of joy is only a regretful revenge against the force of life, one provoked by the imminence of the night.

The womb of war: in the wake of Dylan Thomas

From out of the abyss of innumerable deaths, Dylan Thomas will be remembered and will continue to be a thread in the tapestry of the modernist cultural revolution—and in its indefinite postmodern dispensation. His voice resonates in recordings, films, through his work and in those he influenced—in literature, film, art, poetry, or philosophy. We still experience the mass effect he had on the incipient American "culture industry,"[8] its poetry and popular music, and recognize his place in the pantheonic myths of popular culture. As with Leni Bruce or Allen Ginsberg and the Beat Generation, Thomas's life and art fused to conjure forth a cultural event, enshrined in an enduring myth of the tragic poet, of the pagan Bard. After all, we live in a time when a popular musician, Bob Dylan (who changed his surname from Zimmerman in tribute to Dylan Thomas) has won a Nobel Prize in literature.[9]

Dylan Thomas has nevertheless had an uneasy relationship to academic discourse since his work, as Goodby suggests, "rests on and highlights crucial fault lines within and between British, Welsh, Anglo-Welsh and English poetry"—an "identity crisis" met with silence.[10] Yet, while he claims that a rigorous tracing of Thomas's impact upon subsequent poetry will force us to rethink the meaning of twentieth-century poetry, he joins with others in denouncing the "Dylan Thomas myth," which he claims Thomas himself created as a "vehicle for his literary ambitions."[11] Those who seek to dismantle the myth of Dylan Thomas, however—since they say it is "embarrassing" or "distracting"—fail to understand the philosophical significance of myth and the artistic intentions and mythical habitations of the lyric poet. Indeed, Goodby suggests that the dilemma posed by Dylan Thomas concerns "categorization," which hardly seems to relate to a myth-making that was common among the modernists—and an essential feature of their claim to social and cultural relevance as poets. A philosophical examination of poetry must be sensitive to the poetic as a modality for the expression of truth and myth as the texture or habitation of language.

With Nietzsche's proclamation of the "death of God," the traditionalist myth was displaced by a new dispensation of *mythos* disseminated by the poets of a new modernist era. Mythical *poiesis* lays out the ground upon which we will subsequently dwell, just as the poetic naming of nature (*phusis*) eventually lead to the detailed examination of the regions demarcated by language (*poiesis*).[12] In this light, while a tracing of the enormous effect of Dylan Thomas upon twentieth- and twenty-first-century poetry is welcome, a more nuanced consideration is needed that explores the mythological impulse of the early twentieth century among modernists and the avant-garde. We must avoid contamination from the vivisectionist tendencies of the "analytic revolution" of Russell and the Vienna Circle when dealing with the lifeworld of a lyric poet, who in the Nietzschean vein of the early twentieth century sought to turn himself into a work of tragic art.[13] After all, Nietzsche himself disseminated a complex *mythos* of himself through his arch-mythological work *Thus Spoke Zarathustra* among other works. He writes, for instance, in his poem "Sils-Maria":

Still I sit, waiting, waiting,—for nothing, beyond
Good and evil, close to the brilliant light,
Close to the shadow, only a game, completely sea,
Midday, and time without destination.
There, suddenly, my friend! One became two
—And Zarathustra came to me. (*KSA*, 9:4[145])

Thus Spoke Zarathustra infected the literary and popular cultures of the world shortly before and after Nietzsche's death. As I have alluded, the "Nietzsche fevers" of European nations, Japan, China, Russia, and America made his death a global event, a festival of awakening from the repression, stagnation, and monotony of traditionalist cultures.[14] Modernist poetry in the Anglosphere woke up during this intellectual and cultural earthquake, with Pound, Eliot, and Yeats seeking to either create new mythologies or subvert and displace the old. Nietzsche and Dylan Thomas, each anticipating the mass culture in which we live, sought to create a myth which would act as a habitation or dwelling for the new age. Recalling the mythologies surrounding Pythagoras or Empedocles (or the other poet philosophers at the incipience of Western thought), Nietzsche and Thomas created a mythology which displayed their fundamental philosophical notions and concomitant ways of life. Such *mythoi* serve not only as a storehouse, but also as an active trope of dissemination in the general economy of mortal existence.[15] In other words, "Nietzsche" is no longer the clean bones in a coffin, but a "womb of war," a place of contestation and indication that we have taken up into our language and culture. Such an elevation, as it is the case with all famous artists, has a profound cultural significance as one name is chosen to persist to the exclusion of myriad others.

Or, perhaps, Nietzsche has not been chosen, but has chosen us, has placed questions before us that we cannot answer—that he has given us glimpses of ecstasy and joy, that have remained forbidden.

Dylan Thomas was such a global, tragic event, and he has also been elevated to remembrance, again, not merely by institutions, but as one who has chosen us, who continues to ask us questions about the most urgent concerns for a mortal being. Dylan Thomas writes for the mortal being and seeks to give expression to the voices of all that is, including the voices of the natural world around him, the sea, the gulls, wind, rain, and laughter—all the sounds one usually expects to hear in his native Wales.

The spirit of Dylan Thomas, the drunken poet who died young (but perhaps at the right time) is still celebrated by the Welsh in the pubs, streets, and festivals by those who share the poet's quest for tragic joy. Others will always find the legend unsavory or even disreputable—yet, we must not only, again, remember the artistic function of myth, but also be honest about the "womb of war" that is Dylan Thomas. In this context, the myth is meant to create a dwelling for the contradictions of mortal existence, expressed through the controversial perspectives of Dylan Thomas. Death, the tragic, is central to the myth, surely. Yet, for Thomas, the tragic or Dionysian perspective is not merely concerned with death or with the consolations of intoxication, but also with rebirth, recreation, and erotic joy—of the persistence of the community and remembrance of the voices of the dead.

The myth is the symbolic means by which we not only remember Dylan Thomas, but also know his type: it provides us with a clue of what we may expect from such a figure. The weapons Thomas deployed in the "womb of war" were paradox, polysemy, laughter, scorn—love and hate—as well as honesty in the wake of the brutality and terror of mortal existence. But, Thomas does not suggest that one must acquiesce to this monstrous site—on the contrary, he incites us to rebel against the horror of existence, to rage (often mockingly) against the dying of the light and the hypocrisy and hideousness of Western culture. This is the mischievous spirit of human freedom that Thomas celebrates in his poem "And death shall have no dominion." This poem, which is often read (un-ironically) at Christian funerals is just such an example of Thomas's rebellious and subversive temperament and gives us a feel for not only his destructive attitude toward tradition, but also his revaluation (creation, recreation, destruction, construction) of life, and of his poetic dissemination of the sacred intimacy of life.

And Death Shall Hold No Dominion

We will begin by simply reading the poem, followed by the more surprising task of decoding its meaning. For the poem is in fact a site of contestation, and its meaning and affiliation have been contested since its publication in 1933—not to mention its continuing array of effects as a preserved and living thread of poetic and philosophical culture. There can be many readings of this poem, which I will provisionally describe as Devout Christian,[16] Neo-Romantic,[17] Blakean,[18] Pagan,[19] and Nietzschean.[20] While there will be overlapping aspects to these heuristic positions, a deeper understanding of Thomas's own poetic methodology will provide a pathway for a navigation of the meaning and purpose of the poem itself. We begin our meditation by reading "And death shall have no dominion," published in 1933 when Thomas was nineteen years old.

And Death Shall Have No Dominion

And death shall have no dominion.
Dead men naked they shall be one
With the man in the wind and the west moon;
When their bones are picked clean and the clean bones gone,
They shall have stars at elbow and foot;
Though they go mad they shall be sane,
Though they sink through the sea they shall rise again;
Though lovers be lost love shall not;
And death shall have no dominion.

And death shall have no dominion.
Under the windings of the sea
They lying long shall not die windily;
Twisting on racks when sinews give way,
Strapped to a wheel, yet they shall not break;
Faith in their hands shall snap in two,
And the unicorn evils run them through;
Split all ends up they shan't crack;
And death shall have no dominion.

And death shall have no dominion.
No more may gulls cry at their ears
Or waves break loud on the seashores;
Where blew a flower may a flower no more
Lift its head to the blows of the rain;
Though they be mad and dead as nails,
Heads of the characters hammer through daisies;
Break in the sun till the sun breaks down,
And death shall have no dominion.[21]

In each of the many possible readings of this poem (and there are indefinite iterations)—Devout Christian, Neo-Romantic, Blakean, Pagan, and Nietzschean—that which is thematized are myriad senses of "immortality"—or, perhaps better, "eternity." Prior to an in-depth reading of the poem, a rough sketch of each of these perspectives will suffice.

The case for the Devout Christian reading is the title of the poem which is derived from St. Paul's *Letter to the Romans*, an exhortation to the Christians and Christ-curious pagans of Rome to embrace faith in God, imitation of his son Jesus Christ, belief in his resurrection, and action in accordance to the law. Paul wanted to downplay "works" in the pagan sense (idolatry), but emphasized Hebrew law and the notion that affinity with the resurrection of Christ would provide the basis by which one could receive grace. Death held no dominion over Jesus Christ and if we behave accordingly and are given grace, we may too evade the dominion of death. Such a literal, sequentialist reading also gives us a look at those who disobeyed or were fated to have their eyes and ears closed off to God by God himself. From this perspective, the poem is merely a reiteration of Christian orthodoxy, written by an allegedly devout poet, imbued with the sensibilities of the Welsh chapel culture.

A neo-romantic reading, moreover, would also emphasize, as the British and German romantics had done, the divine comedy of existence and the overcoming of the ugliness of tragedy and death in beauty, whether in nature or in God. Less axiomatic and ecclesiastical than the devout, the concern remains a life after death, and the situatedness of "eternity" in otherworldly hopes. The realm of life is that of tragic fragmentation, Schlegel reflected in his *Lucinde*, but Christian love will allow us to escape from our tragic predicament.

It should be immediately noted, in this connection, however, that Dylan Thomas expressed, at this time, a "theoretical hatred" for the romantics, as noted in his letter to Pamela Hansford Johnson in 1933.[22] Thomas would incite us to embrace the tragedy and the joy that is disclosed with it, to have the courage to acknowledge the singularity of tragic existence—not seeking to escape, but to affirm the agonistic suspense of the moment. Nevertheless, there remains an uncritical and ubiquitous attribution of romanticism to Dylan Thomas, on the all-too-superficial grounds that he dares to mention nature.

Blake, for his part, would bring us back to our senses, to our flesh, to ugliness and joy amid a life that is to be lived in the moment. He turns the tables upon the devout Christian, emphasizing the alleged energy of evil and the rebellious character of life. We could, with ease, map Blake's "Marriage of Heaven and Hell"[23] upon Thomas's poem—though Blake's Spinozistic pantheism (just as the resurrection of Jesus Christ) is not assured by Thomas on a first reading. A more resolutely pagan notion of the rebirth of nature would also be amenable to Thomas's schema and could perhaps provide a different perspective on the second stanza, one casting into relief the defiant suffering of the damned under the tortures of the inquisitor—and not merely the Christian fancy of the eternal punishment of sinners in hell.

Each of these first four readings would seem intent on prioritizing an interpretation of "eternity" as a persistence of being beyond death or to set forth a perspective that nullifies the terror and brutality of mortal existence—in redemption, in another Apollonian dream. But, is this the true meaning of the poem? Is it merely the result of juvenilia, of a childish wish to nullify the tragic double bind? One could ask, moreover, if any notion of personal survival after death can be consistent with the tragic.

In this way, two other Nietzschean readings become possible: first, his early tragic pessimism in *The Birth of Tragedy*, which narrates the drama of Dionysus fated to annihilation and rebirth as an eternally recurring force of nature. Such a view leaves not a trace of the singular, but still provides a notion of the prolific character of life. A second Nietzschean reading would come from *Thus Spoke Zarathustra* in which eternity becomes the joy of the absolute singular, fated to recur eternally as this singular life—a parodic, laughing narrative which *in truth* states the singular is all and one, a *terrible truth*, hidden in the Trojan Horse of a pseudo-eschatology, in the nihilistic garments of disseminators of otherworldly hopes, the prophets of sleep and the old law tablets.

Does "And death shall have no dominion" reflect any of these interpretive strands? Is it seeking to tell us that death is somehow unreal or irrelevant—or, is it seeking a revaluation of values in which eternity is resituated into *these-worldly* hopes and possibilities, into love and hate, sorrow and joy *in this life* and not in some world to come? For Nietzsche, what is at stake is *affirmation itself* versus a nihilism that finds *guilt* in the radical temporality of mortal existence. Such a judgment of guilt upon existence ironically subverts the very possibility of a sense of eternity, of freedom, and the innocence of life.

In order to be in a position to decide, we must undertake another reading of the poem, transcending the naive and literal readings—or the all-too-woolly religious readings honing in on any scent of spirituality so as to neutralize a rebellious voice with a deathbed conversion. In the following, the "momentary peace of the poem" will be cast into fragmentation through a reading based upon a self-description by Dylan Thomas of his poetic methodology in a letter to Henry Treece in 1938. He writes:

> A poem by myself needs a host of images, because its center is a host of images. I make one image,—though "make" is not the word; I let, perhaps, an image be made emotionally in me and then apply to it what intellectual & critical forces I possess—let it breed another, let that image contradict the first, make, of the third image bred out of the other two together, a fourth contradictory image, and let

> them all, within any imposed formal limits, conflict. Each image holds within it the seed of its own destruction, and my dialectical method, as I understand it, is a constant building up and breaking down of the images that come out of the central seed, which is itself destructive and constructive at the same time.
>
> Reading back over that, I agree it looks preciously like nonsense. To say that I "let" images breed and conflict is to deny my critical part in the business. But what I want to try to explain—and it's necessarily vague to me—is that the life in any poem of mine cannot move concentrically round a central image; the life must come out of the center; an image must be born and die in another; and any sequence of my images must be a sequence of creations, recreations, destructions, contradictions. ... Out of the inevitable conflict of images—inevitable, because of the creative, recreative, destructive and contradictory nature of the motivating center, the womb of war—I try to make that momentary peace which is a poem. I do not want a poem of mine to be, nor can it be, a circular piece of experience placed nearly outside the living stream of time from which it came; a poem of mine is, or should be, a watertight section of the stream that is flowing all ways; all warring images within it should be reconciled for that small stop of time.[24]

Out of the womb of war, the central seed of poetic conflict—as with the counterpoint of music or the *logos* of the early Greeks (the poet philosophers of flux)[25]—the life of a Dylan Thomas poem arises as an embedded linguistic complex of contradictory images, each containing the "seed of its own destruction." The center builds up and breaks down images that arise with the death of conflicting images. Thomas conjures forth an image (first stanza), then a second that stands in conflict with the first (second stanza), a third image bred out of the two (third stanza), and in this case (since it has only three stanzas) "let them all, within any imposed formal limits, conflict." Reminiscent of Eisenstein's cinema of juxtaposition, this process, enacted via what Thomas calls a "dialectical method," is focused upon the counterpunctal double bind of existence, of the musicality of life (as per modernist poetics) in which the poem is a "small stop of time," a fleeting peace, traced from the universal jurisdiction of strife (Heraclitus).

Thomas's reference to "dialectical method," moreover, especially together with "seeds of its own destruction," will call to mind not only Hegel's *Science of Logic* in which he commands us to "Think contradiction!,"[26] but also Marx's prophecy that capitalism contains the seeds of its own destruction.[27] This latter reference, in terms of the "unity of opposites," would also bring into play Hegel's Master-Slave dialectic in the *Phenomenology of Spirit*,[28] and thus, the question of freedom in relation to Death as the Master. This would provide another, kindred interpretation of the specificity of Thomas's modernist meaning and let them all, within any imposed formal limits, conflict. It would also suggest that within the overall context of Nietzschean rebellion, a Marxian thread to our reading would also be pertinent. Let us see how this insight plays itself out in the poem, when using Thomas's own technique.

First image—stanza one

The stanza, as with the other two, has nine lines (a multiple of three) and begins and ends with the refrain "And death shall have no dominion." The first image, often linked by Christian or Blakean readers to Heaven, sets out a scenario of grace, the focus of St. Paul's *Letter to the Romans*. As it is conjured, we see the dead, naked joined with "man in the wind" and the "west moon," their "bones picked clean," but stars at "elbow and foot." But, while the mad will be redeemed ("shall be sane") along with those who have drowned ("shall rise again"), it is strange that "lovers be lost, though love shall not." Thomas's complex image, however, seems to have little resonance with the imagery and artifices of St. Paul and is thus an unlikely statement of Christian orthodoxy—if not for its affirmation of Love, a notion shared by Christian *mythopoiesis*. We could perhaps regard some aspects of the image to be of Blakean, pagan, or occult significance. But, we must ask: why will the lovers be lost, when all else seems to be redeemed? From the devout perspective, carnal lovers have been traditionally equated with transgressors, with sexuality which is a corruption of the "ideal of Love." Such an emphasis upon this line would also open the necessity of alternative Nietzschean and Bataillean[29] readings of this poem, ostensibly about "immortality."

Before we decide the meaning of this image and why it contains the seeds of its own destruction, let us move onto the next, contradictory, image, cast into relief in the second stanza.

Second image—stanza two

The second stanza begins and ends, again, with the refrain, "And death shall have no dominion." The second image brings us under the winding sea where the dead "shall not die windily"—drowned, they will not be killed by the sea, nor will they be granted last words. They will twist on racks, their sinews giving way, strapped to a wheel, yet they shall not break. Faith will break in two in their hands, and even though they are tortured, they will not crack. This image presents a conflicting, if ironic, sense of immortality, susceptible of a Blakean or Nietzschean interpretation. The devout Christian reading regards this second stanza as Hell, and specifically in the sense of eternal punishment. Yet, if this is Hell, it does not celebrate God's justice, but the eternal resistance of the transgressors and lovers against the torturers—and the refusal of the "devils" to acquiesce to faith in otherworldly nihilism.

If we juxtapose these images, we note a contradiction in the doctrine of immortality, in which there remains permanent opposition, and immortality for each and all, regardless of either the doctrine of faith or the strictures of the law. Such celebration of resistance lends itself to Blakean, Nietzschean, or Marxian readings, as Thomas's poem is setting forth a heretical parody of the Pauline advocacy of resurrection in Jesus Christ. How could one, after all, advocate a religion of love and redemption that celebrates such eternal vengeance? The cruel hypocrisy of totalitarian love smacks of narcissism, greed, and sadism—and seems to have prompted Thomas to take the side of the underdog, of the lovers, among whom he found his poetic lifeworld.

With the stark contradiction standing before us, threatening the very binary structure of innocence and guilt, of redemption and resurrection, we turn to the third stanza.

Third image—stanza three

The third stanza begins and ends, again, finally, with the refrain, "And death shall have no dominion." We will regard this last stanza, as it does not yet meet the quaternary indicated in his statement on method, as that which not only holds both of the previous images together, but also as that contradiction which allows us to view the entirety of the contradictory situation of "immortality." The stanza itself is divided in itself. We are first given the image of desolation, silence: the absence of the sounds of gulls, of waves of the sea, where a flower can no longer hold its head up to the rain. But, this image is quickly juxtaposed to another with a conflicting sense, a differing possibility for silence and desolation: though "mad and dead as nails," the "heads of the characters hammer through daisies"; break upon the sun until the "sun breaks down." As if the dead themselves assure continued life, Thomas imagines heads hammering through daisies and breaking like waves upon a mortal sun. Contrary to the obsession of St. Paul upon the bodily brand of personal resurrection, we are shown a different priority for the dead, who share the task of enabling new life, as an insurrection against nothingness in which death provides an impetus for new creation. This resonates with the Blakean or pagan reading, a pantheist vision which stands in direct conflict with the binary of guilt and innocence. Such realities are inexplicable for Thomas and the third stanza could be called "beyond heaven and hell, toward a new life."

On the surface, Thomas sets forth an ambiguous, seemingly indecipherable account of immortality—but, with our reading, we can begin to dismantle the traditional schema laid out in the letter of Paul. The masters and the slaves of immortality stand in contradiction, but, at the end of the day, it will be the slaves, the transgressors, who, associated with the "lovers," will supply the energy for the recreation of new life. Indeed, from a Nietzschean perspective, the real contradiction would be between the *life-denying* and *life-affirming*, who, in this schema, would correspond to the first and second images of Thomas's poem, respectively. Those who would follow Paul to death will not affirm the sublimity of the creation itself, regarded by them as merely the testing ground of God's wrath, and not as his gift.

A Nietzschean reading, for its part, would not be concerned with the continuation of life in a romantic sense, but would be concerned with *this* life and the tragic joy which one desires will eternally recur. Thomas thematizes the tragic struggle of life ("sun breaks down," "lovers be lost"), exposing his distance from the Christian interpretation of his own work. As mortals, we are equal before death, regardless of who happens to end up as either sinners or saints. While death itself spurs new life, the location of eternity becomes the singular life of a mortal hanging over the abyss of an ultimately tragic situation, one of brutality and terror. Through this Nietzschean lens,

Thomas would prioritize *this-worldly* existence, remaining true to the lovers and the earth, expressed across the topography of his lyrical poetic world. As Thomas writes in "In my craft or sullen art":

> In my craft or sullen art
> Exercised in the still night
> When only the moon rages
> And the lovers lie abed
> With all their griefs in their arms,
> I labour by singing light
> Not for ambition or bread
> Or the strut and trade of charms
> On the ivory stages
> But for the common wages
> Of their most secret heart.
> Not for the proud man apart
> From the raging moon I write
> On these spindrift pages
> Nor for the towering dead
> With their nightingales and psalms
> But for the lovers, their arms
> Round the griefs of the ages,
> Who pay no praise or wages
> Nor heed my craft or art.[30]

Thomas's "And death shall have no dominion" also sings for the lovers, of the fleeting temporality of mortal love, of lovers who are lost with the disintegration of the specious moment. Yet, he contends that death's sorrow is no reason to take vengeance upon life.

The meaning of Dylan Thomas

From the foregoing readings we have sketched a perspective that places Dylan Thomas at odds with Pauline Christianity. Indeed, we can safely say that he is not a Christian and does not share the castigation of sexuality—vis-a-vis its "unicorn evils."[31] What is at stake is his message, or in Nietzsche's sense, his revaluation of values that hammers against a traditional culture which he seeks to radically transform. Such a message, after all, contributes to the activating sense of his poetry in contemporary Welsh culture and beyond. Thomas was a modernist, we will remember, and on the cusp of his poetic lyrical world stood his post-Darwinistic, post-Einsteinian, post-Freudian, and decidedly antiestablishment personality and worldview.

Such a joyful and Dionysian sense of remembrance still attends Dylan Thomas in the popular engagement of poetic associations, festivals, and institutions devoted to his literary engagement. It should be emphasized that Dylan Thomas's contribution to the modernist poetic protect was *the rebirth of poetry as spoken word*. Revived from its death and stagnation upon the silent page, poetry, and the musical voice, as with Edith Sitwell, infused the singular perspective of a poet with the power of communication and mass effect. Poetry became an agent of change in a culture dominated by the suffocating monotony of a staid Mandarin academic caste and a tired ecclesiastical regime of limited appeal. Poetry disseminates not only a message of contestation, but also a divergent way of life outside of the strictures of traditional *mores*. Poetry was the only voice of resistance in a decadent culture, one which orchestrated not only the bonfire of innocents in the First World War, but also enabled fascist atavisms to provoke a second conflagration. It is the poets who sing of these tragedies, condemning these negligent outrages, giving voice to the masses of faceless suffering and reminding us of our freedom to resist the seemingly inevitable.

With the ascendance of Dylan Thomas as an Icon of culture, there are, we have seen, attempts to turn the rebellious poet into a plaster saint, even a near-Christian (as if, amid a constant state of manufactured forgetfulness, Christianity can still be considered something unproblematic). Rowan Williams, the former Archbishop of Canterbury, for instance, in his article "Myth-busting: Rowan Williams on Dylan Thomas,"[32] ends with evidence from Welsh poet Vernon Watkins to the effect that Dylan Thomas lived a Christian life. Such a statement, of course, sounds like a rear-guard defense of a moribund church as it refuses to truly meditate upon the reasons for Dylan Thomas's rebellion against Christianity. He followed the pathway carved out by his Nietzschean father—though in his own manner—and, in his letters, Thomas explicitly—and mockingly—attacked the churchgoers and the anti-erotic St Paul:

> Thank God it's dark. Now I can't see the people outside. I might be in a world of my own, owing nothing but the seeds of hate to all the dark passers scuttling to the rub-a-dub-dub in the bebatted belfries of the stinking churches, scuttling homewards again or out on their half-frustrated amatory expeditions after the sin of love has been emphasised by St Paul and his pimply apostles.[33]

Nevertheless, Williams, like a carrion bird sniffing out scents of "spirituality" in the druidic Thomas, applies his own "angelic magic" to his reputation, descrying his echo of and appeal to adolescents and his celebration of tragic joy as "embarrassing." Inexplicably, and not even with an inkling of our contemporary post-Christian, secular culture, he claims it is "patronizing" to remember Thomas as a "doomed Dionysus." Williams contends Thomas must instead be regarded as a great, though troubled poet, whom we must ultimately regard as a cautionary tale. He turns Dylan Thomas from a bohemian subversive into a Christian morality play—forgetting Dionysus as a symbol of tragic rebirth.

Seeking to close off any Pagan or Nietzschean (read modernist) interpretation of Thomas, Williams seeks to rub out those aspects of Thomas's character which do not conform to his "churchy" perspective, insulting Dylan Thomas and his admirers (regardless of age) from the self-appointed ground of an alleged seriousness, sobriety, and virtue. Yet, we would be more truthful to discern Dylan Thomas as a "devil" (in the Blakean sense) and his work as a poetically housed existential philosophy, a poetics of mortality.

Modernist poetics played its part in the birth of contemporary popular culture, and Dylan Thomas, having penetrated to the heart of the culture industry, was one of the first deaths of the celebrity culture. His own mythology, surrounding the themes of death, eroticism, and the drunken, tragico-comedic poet—and, remembrance of a still easy child, playing in freedom—became stamped upon the new culture, provoking its own poetic wake in the rebellion of the Beat poets, especially Allen Ginsberg. The latter, having written *Howl*,[34] in the two years following Thomas's death, was put on trial for obscenity, a watershed case he won on October 3, 1957. Poetry had become dangerous, a threat to public morals and the youth, but unlike Socrates, Ginsberg, a gay, Jewish communist, held the day in a ruling that lead to the full-scale demolition of censorship laws. This rarely discussed event gave others such as Burroughs and Henry Miller (belatedly) access to the mass market as well as opening up a free space for film, literature, music theater—and personal freedom.

Dylan Thomas's poetic—albeit tragic—rebellion did not go unnoticed—he had forked his way into the heart of mass, popular, and academic culture. Living with an intensity that many would never dare, he sought to enact a cultural revolution before his self-prophesied demise. This evokes the vertiginous freedom at the heart of Nietzsche's eternal recurrence of the same and life conceived as an artwork, a self-given mytho-poetic destiny amid the fate of mortality. There is clearly an extensive resonance between Nietzsche and Dylan Thomas. At the same time, however, it would be mistaken to merely consider Dylan Thomas as somehow a derivation of Nietzsche. Just as it is the case with W. B. Yeats, the Nietzschean dimension of Thomas's work lies more in the "Nietzsche event," of the antiestablishment *opening* attendant upon his name. In a similar, though much more profound, manner than the Ginsberg's obscenity trial, the Nietzschean opening resonated with revolutionary political and cultural movements, contributing, for instance, to the *zeitgeist* which overthrew of the Chinese monarchy in 1911.[35]

Dylan Thomas was also such an 'event,' but despite his artistic kinship with Nietzsche, he remains original and differently aligned in terms of his political and cultural orientations. Thomas's reference to Marxian terminology was no accident, something he repeated (and joked about) on stage during his final tour of McCarthyite America, shortly before his death.[36] While Nietzsche inspired him as an artist, Thomas did not see that as an obstacle to having markedly leftist political leanings. After all, did not Nietzsche himself ask us: this is my way, what is yours? But, in agreement with Nietzsche, he sought a less realist—or merely atheistic—interpretation of the mortal significance of tragic existence.

In the end "And Death Shall Have No Dominion" sets before us a spiritual crossroads. We are left with a clever poetic repetition of the motif of "pushing up daisies." Beyond this, we have only a nameless apprehension of the singularity of life. Yet, what is it or who is it that is unsatisfied by a single, mortal life? That which is thrown into relief by Thomas are the lovers, the daisy, *this* life itself—even as they are fatally haunted by the shadow of death. He enacts a revaluation of values: from the narcissism and greed of those demanding personal resurrection to the gratitude of the *nunc stans* and the joy of the carpe diem.

All in all, in a final consideration of the trials and tribulations of the Dylan Thomas myth—and of his reputation more generally as an artist and as a persistent target of moral surveillance—it would be fitting to end by simply stating that there is no dishonor in dying young, just as there is no honor in merely living to be old. That which is essential, Nietzsche remarked, is the creator—the child finding the world in its innocence. In this light, let us end with the first stanza of "Vision and Prayer" by Dylan Thomas.

Who
Are you
Who is born
In the next room
So loud to my own
That I can hear the womb
Opening and the dark run
Over the ghost and the dropped son
Behind the wall thin as a wren's bone ?
In the birth bloody room unknown
To the burn and turn of time
And the heart print of man
Bows no baptism
But dark alone
Blessing on
The wild
Child.[37]

Notes

1 Leslie Lavigne, *Nietzschean elements in the poetry of Dylan Thomas*, Master's thesis, Concordia University, 1987. It is somewhat shocking that this work is the only text which undertakes any extensive investigation of the affinity of Dylan Thomas and Friedrich Nietzsche. While he does not cite Thomas's explicit reference to Nietzsche in his letter to Pamela Hansford Johnson of 1933, Lavigne presents a compelling case for a Nietzschean Thomas, even if he did not find the evidence for a direct link.
2 Walford Davies, *Dylan Thomas* (University of Wales Press, 2014).
3 Theodore Dalrymple, "The Rimbaud of Cwmdonkin Drive: Dylan Thomas, the last true bohemian," *City Journal* (Winter, 2015).

4 Dylan Thomas, *Dylan Thomas: Collected Letters*, "Letter to Richard Church," June 22, 1936.
5 Dylan Thomas, "The Force that Through the Green Fuse," in *The Collected Poems of Dylan Thomas: The Centenary Edition* (London: Weidenfeld & Nicolson, 2016), 43.
6 Kate Crockett, Mwy na Bardd—Bywyd a Gwaith Dylan Thomas, Cyhoeddiadau Barddas, 2014. In this book, Crockett seeks to nullify the divide between Dylan Thomas and the Welsh language by discussing his work in Welsh translation and its relationship to Wales and many of its people.
7 Bryony Wood, "A Celebration of Dylan Thomas, *Cardiff Times*, October 27, 2014.
8 Theodore Adorno, *The Culture Industry: Selected Essays on Mass Culture* (London: Routledge, 2001).
9 Hannah Ellis-Petersen and Alison Flood, "Bob Dylan wins Nobel Prize in Literature," *Guardian*, October 13, 2016.
10 John Goodby, *The Poetry of Dylan Thomas: Under the Spelling Wall* (Liverpool University Press, 2013).
11 Such a castigation of the Dylan Thomas myth seems to be inspired by an analytic methodology strictly at odds with the poetological spirit of Dylan Thomas and the meaning of his myth-making.
12 James Luchte, *Mortal Thought: Hölderlin and Philosophy* (London: Bloomsbury Publishing, 2016).
13 James Luchte, *Pythagoras and the Doctrine of Transmigration* (London: Bloomsbury Publishing, 2008).
14 James Luchte, "Daggers and Spears: Lu Xun and Nietzsche on Cultural Revolution," in *Nietzsche and Chinese Thought* (New York: The Agonist, Spring, 2016).
15 James Luchte, "Prometheus Dismembered: Bataille on Van Gogh," in *Van Gogh Among the Philosophers: Painting, Thinking, Being* (Lexington Books, 2017).
16 John Logan, "Dylan Thomas and the Ark of Art," *Renascence* XII (1960): 59–66; David Larsen, *The Company of the Creative: A Christian Reader's Guide to Great Literature* (Kregel, 2000).
17 Amos Wilder, *The New Voice: Religion, Literature, Hermeneutics* (Wipf and Stock Publishers, 2013).
18 William T. Moynihan, *The Art and Craft of Dylan Thomas* (Cornell University Press, 1966). See also Hyman H. Kleinman, *The Religious Sonnets of Dylan Thomas: A Study in Imagery and Meaning* (University of California Press, 1963).
19 Hans Meyerhoff, "The Violence of Dylan Thomas," *The New Republic*, July 11, 1955, 17–19, a review of *Adventures in the Skin Trade and Other Stories*.
20 Lavigne, *Nietzschean Elements in the Poetry of Dylan Thomas*.
21 Dylan Thomas, "And Death Shall Have No Dominion," in *The Collected Poems of Dylan Thomas: The Centenary Edition* (London: Weidenfeld & Nicolson, 2016), 23.
22 Dylan Thomas, *Dylan Thomas: Collected Letters*, "Letter to Pamela Hansford Johnson," December 25, 1933 (London: Hatchette, 2014).
23 William Blake, *William Blake: The Complete Poems*, "The Marriage of Heaven and Hell" (London: Penguin, 1977), 180–95.
24 Dylan Thomas, *Dylan Thomas: Collected Letters*, "Letter to Henry Treece," March 23, 1938. The quotation from this letter is necessary for the purposes of the argument in this chapter.

25 James Luchte, *Early Greek Thought: Before the Dawn* (London: Bloomsbury Publishing, 2011).
26 GWF Hegel, *The Science of Logic*, trans. A. V. Miller (Atlantic Highlands: Humanities Press), 431–43.
27 Karl Marx, "Address to the Central Committee of the Communist League" (1850), *Delphi Collected Works of Karl Marx*, Delphi Classics, 2016.
28 G. W. F. Hegel, *Phenomenology of Spirit*, trans. A. V. Miller (Oxford University Press, 1976).
29 Georges Bataille, *Erotism: Death and Sensuality* (Ingram, 2001).
30 Dylan Thomas, "In My Craft Or Sullen Art," in *The Collected Poems of Dylan Thomas: The Centenary Edition* (London: Weidenfeld & Nicolson, 2016), 176.
31 The unicorn is a Christological symbol of purity, symbolized in virginity.
32 Rowan Williams, "Myth-busting: Rowan Williams on Dylan Thomas," *New Statesman*, August 1, 2014.
33 Dylan Thomas, *Dylan Thomas: Collected Letters*, "Letter to Pamela Hansford Johnson," April 15, 1934. This letter should be read more widely to ascertain Thomas's radical cultural and political sentiments.
34 Allen Ginsberg, *Howl* (New York: Penguin, 2015).
35 Cf. Luchte, "Daggers and Spears: Lu Xun and Nietzsche on Cultural Revolution."
36 Dylan Thomas at the "Cinema 16" symposium "Poetry and the Film" held in New York in October 28, 1953, mentioned the dialectic in relationship to poetry and film, "One images makes another in the ordinary dialectic process," joking that it would fall to him mention "dialectic," a repetition of his 1938 letter to Henry Treece.
37 Thomas, "Vision and Prayer," in *The Collected Poems of Dylan Thomas: The Centenary Edition* (London: W&N, 2014), 154, © The Dylan Thomas Trust. This quotation is necessary for the purposes of the argument in this chapter.

15

Responding to the Crisis of Philosophy in Modernity: From Nietzsche's Perspectivism to Musil's Essayism

Sebastian Hüsch

If one reflects on the influence Friedrich Nietzsche had on twentieth-century literature, it is almost inevitable that Robert Musil and his novel *The Man Without Qualities* will come to mind, all the more so within the framework of a book series focusing on modernism. In this respect, Musil can be considered as doubly emblematic: as an author largely inspired and influenced by Nietzsche, and as one of the most eminent modernist writers.[1] Thus, I do not run too much of a risk by proposing to link Musil's thought to Nietzsche's and to relate both to the epistemological challenges imposed upon modernity. In the present chapter, I will argue that Musil builds upon Nietzsche's perspectivism to develop a genuine way of dealing with the crisis of philosophical knowledge, as well as the fragilization of possibilities of human self-affirmation (*Selbstvergewisserungsmöglichkeiten*) that modernism is confronted with. Musil's reflections will result in a philosophical methodology he calls "essayism," which shares Nietzsche's insight concerning the contingency of all human knowledge and the dissolution of truth into multiple perspectives, but broadens the horizon of possibilities emerging form this multiperspectivity. The focus of the present chapter is thus not to establish an inventory of traces of Nietzschean thought in Musil's writings (this has largely been done already[2]), but rather to undertake a comparison of two philosophical methods and their capacity to cope with the epistemological challenges of Modernity. This *mise en parallèle* will show how Robert Musil takes up some of Nietzsche's most important epistemological and methodological insights to creatively adopt and transform them according to his philosophical needs of conceptualization and representation. Musil's innovative reinterpretation of Nietzsche's perspectivism will eloquently illustrate the great potential Nietzsche's thought had for modernist thinkers.

I will begin by outlining what I consider to be some of the crucial aspects of Nietzsche's perspectivism with a special focus on elements that become relevant for a comparison with Musil's essayism. I will then present and analyze Musil's essayism as a genuine philosophical approach which is based upon epistemological foundations erected by Nietzsche, but goes beyond Nietzsche in some fundamental respects.

Nietzsche's epistemological perspectivism

As a starting point for apprehending Nietzsche's epistemological perspectivism, I would like to use a quotation from Giorgio Colli that summarizes very well a result characteristic of Nietzsche's method: "In the mine ('*Bergwerk*') of this thinker," Colli notes, "we can find every kind of metal. Nietzsche has said everything and its contrary."[3] This provocative characterization of Nietzsche's writings does not seem inappropriate. It would be misleading, however, to attribute apparent contradictions in Nietzsche's writing to his lack of coherent argumentation, as has been suggested by Walter Bröcker.[4] I would, quite on the contrary, argue that apparent contradictions in Nietzsche's writing are oftentimes precisely the result of what Nietzsche himself has baptized *perspectivism*,[5] perspectivism being a major factor in Nietzsche's destruction of the global "perspective beyond perspectives" traditional philosophy aspired to. With Nietzsche "Truth" shatters into a multitude of "truths" that are not oriented toward any common reference point.

Perspectivism and truth

If Nietzsche is sometimes credited with having brought forth *perspectivism* as a philosophical method, it should be kept in mind that reflections on perspectivity can already be found in the work of Leibniz, who observes in his *Monadology* that reality changes depending on the perspective from which it is regarded.[6] A similar consciousness of perspectivity is also the starting point of Nietzsche's perspectivism, but in the latter, it is radicalized in a way that makes it emblematic for the crisis of philosophical knowledge in modernity. This radicalization of perspectivity is linked to two major claims. First, Nietzsche emphasizes that we are irremediably attached to our human perspective. In this sense, he states in an eloquent and provocative image in *Human All Too Human*: "We behold all things through the human head and cannot cut off this head" (*HH*, 29).[7] In other words: not only is our perception of reality always attached to our human head perspective, which we take for paradigmatic, but we can also never get beyond this perspective even if we are conscious about our perspectivic perception. The second claim is based upon the first but has more far-reaching consequences. According to Nietzsche, there is in fact no reference point that could give us a hint as to whether or not one perspective is more valid than another:

> Even this costs [Man] effort: to admit to himself that the insect or the bird perceives a completely different world than man does, and that the question which of the two world-perceptions is more right is a completely senseless one, since it could be decided only by the criterion of the right perception, i.e., by a standard which does not exist. (*TL*)[8]

Nietzsche's perspectivism is thus not only an impactful modification of the idea of perspectivity, but brings forth a fundamentally new worldview. The decisive difference between the conscious perspectivity introduced by Leibniz and Nietzsche's perspectivism is that Nietzsche, unlike Leibniz, does not assume that the different perspectives that modify the way things are perceived actually refer to something *beyond* these perspectives. For Nietzsche, it is an illusion to think that individual perspectives provide insight into different aspects of an objective reality. Indeed, for Nietzsche, there is no such "real" reality, there are *only* perspectives, that is, interpretations. In a famous note, he claims explicitly and with insistence: "It is precisely facts that do not exist, only interpretations" (*KSA*, 12:7[60]).[9] According to Nietzsche's radically new premise, we have to abandon the idea of a—be it only theoretical—"true" or "objective" reality which would lie beyond perspectivity. This essentially requires us, in fact, to turn away from what the Platonic-Christian tradition has continuously intended to accomplish over the course of more than 2000 years (and what was naturally still implied in Leibniz's remark): Philosophy aimed to see the world as it "really" is, that is, behind and beyond contingent perspectives. This is a fundamental aspect in Nietzsche's epistemological positioning: He does not claim that, for whatever epistemological, metaphysical, or anthropological reasons, the access to such a truth or to a more "authentic," perfect, and eternal "backworld" ("*Hinterwelt*") (*HH*, 21) is *blocked*, but instead tells us nothing less than that a reality beyond perspectives simply *does not exist*.

If Volker Gerhardt argues that Nietzsche's conception is not all that revolutionary, as in the *Critique of Pure Reason* Kant had already emphasized the fact that human knowledge is insurmountably attached to our subjective perspective,[10] I would argue that the main point in Nietzsche's perspectivism is that he is not only *subjectivizing* knowledge as does Kant, but he is *individualizing* it. No one can get beyond their perspectives which are distinct and individual, whereas the idea of an *Erkenntnissubjekt* maintains the idea of some kind of universality of subjective knowledge. Nietzsche dismisses the traditional as well as the Kantian position and shifts from the aspiration to *know* to the possibility (and necessity) to *interpret*: "Inasmuch as the word 'knowledge' has any meaning at all, the world is knowable: but it is variously *interpretable*; it has no meaning behind it, but countless meanings. 'Perspectivism.'"[11]

Perspectivism is to be understood as a conscious play with perspectives: If we cannot get beyond our human perspective, we can nonetheless take advantage of our awareness of the insurmountable perspectivity by multiplying our perspectives by *consciously* adopting various perspectives instead of adopting them unknowingly. In fact, Nietzsche's perspectivism *demands* from us to do so, and even to learn to *methodically multiply* our perspectives as a main requirement for attaining knowledge. Ideally, we learn the art of seeing ourselves "under [our] perspectival forms, and *solely* in these" (*GS*, 374).[12] If Nietzsche himself highlights the word "solely," this means that, in his eyes, we have to give up the vain hope of overcoming our perspectival representations and getting closer to an "objective" truth, to a truth beyond perspectivity. If we remain attached to the aspiration to reach a truth beyond interpretation, we will fall into what Nietzsche calls, more or less synonymously, "lie" (*Lüge*), "appearance" (*Erscheinung*), or "error" (*Irrtum*). In *Ecce Homo* he notes that "thus far the lie has been called truth" (*EH*, *Why I Am a Destiny*, 1); and in his notebook, he writes: "*Truth is the kind of error* without which a particular kind of living creature could not live" (*KSA*, 11:34[253]).[13]

whereas in his early essay *On Truth and Lie* he explains that "true" means "to lie according to an established convention" (*TL*).

If Nietzsche calls lie what is considered by convention to be the truth—although it may be, as he puts it, a lie that is inevitable for survival—the question has to be asked as to whether, according to Nietzsche, there is any such a thing as the truth and what the term "truth" would have to refer to if it were to have any meaning at all. If we take into account the reflections developed above, Nietzsche would be obliged to answer this question affirmatively, because otherwise denouncing lies would be meaningless. Nietzsche does not seem to suggest that there is no truth, as he uses this term not only in his destruction of the traditional conceptions of truth, but also with a positive connotation and even emphatically. Thus he notes at the end of his first *Untimely Meditation* that it "is always time" and "in the present time ... more than ever" to "tell ... the truth" (*DS*, 12);[14] and, in another passage: "We are making an attempt with the truth! Perhaps humanity shall perish from it" which he ends with a hard to translate "Wohlan"! ("Let us try"; *KSA*, 11:25[305]; my translation).

In fact, one could get the impression that Nietzsche is somehow struggling in his reflections on truth. On the one hand, he unambiguously rejects the classical concept of truth based on correspondence, but on the other hand he does not establish a clearly defined or circumscribed alternative concept which would be based on perspectivity and perspectivism. One important problem is certainly that Nietzsche uses the same term "truth" to refer to two fundamentally different understandings of it, between which he continually switches without forewarning.[15]

I would partially agree with Danto's reading of the issue. Danto argues that Nietzsche has the merit to have discovered a new concept of truth, but that he was not fully—or not at all—aware of this and probably also not patient enough to systematically develop it.[16] The revolution is not only that Nietzsche depotentializes the concept of truth by transposing it from the beyond (transcendence) to the beneath (immanence), thus leaving behind the belief in objectivity as the representation of an absolute and binding truth about "objective" being,[17] but what is even more important is the idea that truth cannot be considered as something that *is* and thus can be discovered, but that it is something that is *created*.

As said earlier, Nietzsche rejects explicitly and repeatedly the idea of a backworld understood as a world of eternal present. This criticism accordingly implies that no truth can legitimately refer to such a backworld, and that truth itself is submitted to the process of becoming and perishing.[18] To adopt the perspective of perspectivism implies furthermore that even the idea of a truth from the perspective of the human head which cannot be cut off (at least not without losing the most fundamental condition of the possibility of knowing) has to be nuanced. If Nietzsche speaks of the human head perspective, this is somewhat problematic as it could imply a truth that is attainable in precisely the same way for *all* human heads. This is not, as we have seen, what Nietzsche claims. Rather, every single head of every single human being has its genuine perspective and thus its genuine truths (or lies and errors).

Even if one assumes that Nietzsche did not have full awareness of all the implications concerning his "discovery" of a new concept of truth, he was perfectly lucid as to the contingency of each and every individual perspective, which is forged by the things we have to deal with in our everyday life. To make his point Nietzsche uses the image of the craft: "Every craft makes crooked" he writes in *The Gay Science*:

> Look at the friends of your youth again, after they have taken possession of their speciality (*Wissenschaft*). … Above every craft, even one with a golden floor, is also a leaden ceiling that presses and presses on the soul until it becomes strangely and crookedly pressed. There is nothing to do about this. Don't think you can evade such crippling through same educational artifice. One pays dearly for any kind of *mastery* on earth, where perhaps one pays too dearly for everything; one is master of one's trade at the price of also being its victim. (*GS*, 366)

We all "suffer" from a selective perception that is shaped by our profession or craft; and Nietzsche explicitly speaks of *any* kind of mastery (be is spiritual or manual) and he makes clear that he is also fully aware of the *déformation professionnelle* and historical contingency which are *his own* as well as of his incapability to overcome them, even with perspectivism. This is to be understood as a hint at the fact that his own philosophy—like any philosophy—took its shape under the influence of numerous contingent factors and in contact with philosophies that had been developed before him and by his contemporaries, implying that if he had been in touch with other philosophies at another time and place, his own philosophy would have been something entirely different from what it is. In a letter to Lou von Salomé he writes:

> First, one has difficulties to emancipate oneself from one's *chains*, and then one has still to *emancipate* oneself from this emancipation! Each and every one of us has to face this chain disease in one way or another, even after having broken these chains. (*KGB*, August 1882, III.5:293; my translation)

Nietzsche was thus perfectly conscious of the fact that even the awareness of one's own distortions is not sufficient to allow us to overcome them. It is strictly impossible to attain undistorted knowledge, as the emancipation from an emancipation must itself be overcome by a new emancipation from the thus-reached emancipation and so on ad infinitum. However, once we are conscious of our inability to escape from this constellation, we still have the possibility to "improve" our standpoint as Nietzsche suggests in *On the Geneaology of Morality*:

> [T]he more affects we are able to put into words about a thing, the *more* eyes, various eyes we are able to use for the same thing, the more complete will be our "concept" of the thing, our "objectivity." (*GM*, *What Is the Meaning of Ascetic Ideals?*, 12)[19]

If there is no non-contingent perspective within our reach, perspectivistic philosophizing can at least allow for the multiplication of perspectives and thus help us attain "better" knowledge of the phenomena, as the change of perspectives leads to more of a multifaceted view. In the end, this multiplication of perspectives even allows for the term "objectivity," be it in quotation marks. The quotation marks being the hint that the thus-reached objectivity is not to be confounded with the objectivity traditional philosophy aspired for.[20] There still remains an insurmountable qualitative gap between the kind of knowledge that can be attained through multiplying one's perspectives and knowledge in the Platonic-Christian tradition. The objectivity to be reached by multiplying perspectives is not to be understood as the anticipation of one definite truth but rather as the addition of an infinite number of contingent "truths" insofar as perspectivism is not even capable of erecting *as an ideal* the aspiration to get closer to a transcendent universal truth as was done by Friedrich Schlegel, for instance.[21] The kind of objectivity that can be attained is always of limited validity—it remains subject to the contingency of perspective and to interpretation.

It is clear from what has been said that this appreciation of the epistemological constellation is also to be applied to Nietzsche's own philosophy. His truths are "perspectivic" (*perspektivisch*) and "perspectivistic" (*perspektivistisch*) truths, and thus just as subject to contingency as any truth brought forth by Man. This is a crucial point, as Nietzsche's style is often very apodictic, and can put the reader at risk of forgetting to relativize Nietzsche's claims in the light of his methodological perspectivism.[22] His "truths," however emphatically he puts them forth, are always to be thought before the backdrop of his own *déformation professionnelle* and thus never to be assimilated to the dogmatic concept of truth he sees represented in the philosophical tradition. One might nevertheless ask if Nietzsche really succeeded in keeping this distinction intact or if he does not succumb to the temptation to make claims that are incompatible with his own—contingent—*Erkenntnissituation*, that is, the consciousness of the perspectivity of his knowledge. However, it is certain that he was at least at times conscious about this precarious situation, as is illustrated by the following reflection from the *Twilight of the Idols*. This quote is very explicit about what would be needed to "know" in an eminent sense:

> In order even to approach the problem of the value of life, a man would need to be placed outside life, and moreover know it as well as one, as many, as all in fact, who have lived it. These are reasons enough to prove to us that this problem is an inaccessible one to us. (*TI*, *Morality as Anti-Nature*)

Nietzsche thus illustrates that truths must fulfill the exigencies of methodological perspectivism, and that these truths must result from the creative performance of a concrete and contingent individual seeking knowledge.[23]

In light of what has been argued thus far, what can be taken away is that it is indeed perspectivism which is the major source of the appearance of contradiction in Nietzsche's works, which can explain why Nietzsche seems to have said everything and its contrary.[24] If truth cannot be *found* but rather has to be *created*, as Nietzsche claims, then different descriptions can coexist which may seem contradictory or incompatible. However, for Nietzsche, contradiction is a marginal problem insofar as he explicitly refutes the logic upon which is based the traditional understanding of truth; for him the main aspect of truth is the creative act of *interpretation* or *description*.

The individualization of truth(s) claimed by Nietzsche, however, raises the question of how to communicate knowledge within the framework of this conception of truth. If truth is individualized, and if truth depends on individual qualities and experiences, it is difficult to imagine how such a perspectivistic truth could be communicated (on the side of the author) and understood (on the side of the reader). As a matter of fact, Nietzsche's suggestion to multiply perspectives leads to a multiplication of possible interpretations, as the multiperspectivity that is expressed through his writings finds its methodological counterpart in a reader who multiplies these perspectives in the act of reading. This is why Bernd Bräutigam spoke of a concept of truth in which the movement of thought begun by Nietzsche is passed on to the reader ad infinitum.[25] These difficulties show how fundamental it is to reflect on what it may mean to *understand Nietzsche*—which is the focus of the present volume—as well as what it may mean to influence (for Nietzsche) or to be influenced (by Nietzsche). With regard to the influence Nietzsche could have, he himself gave a brief sketch of his "ideal" reader:

> It is not at all necessary, not even *desirable* to take my side. … On the contrary, it would seem to me that a dose of curiosity, like when looking at an exotic plant, with a certain ironic resistance, would be an incomparably *more intelligent* position with regards to me. (*KSB*, III.5:1075; my translation)

Nietzsche makes clear that the reader he is looking for is not the enthusiastic admirer but the skeptical, ironic, and reflective reader who does not hesitate to contradict him. If he seeks to influence his reader, then this is not to be understood as any kind of discipleship. Nietzsche's oftentimes provocative positions are provocative precisely to stimulate contradiction, not to call for acknowledgment and adherence. I would suggest that Musil's stance with regard to Nietzsche could very well be understood as that of a "good reader" in Nietzsche's sense—which consequently also implies the possibility to deviate from and to go beyond Nietzsche. Being influenced by Nietzsche means thus for Musil to be an independent thinker.

In the following, I would like to illustrate my claim that Musil is in a way an accomplished reader of Nietzsche and that Nietzsche's influence on Musil is most fruitful precisely when he goes beyond Nietzsche: in the development of his own philosophical method, his *essayism*. Musil's essayism can be considered as an adaptation of perspectivistic thinking to the modernist setting, given that Nietzsche's multifaceted methodological approach seems to be perfectly apt to come to terms with and to circumscribe a world that has lost its center and unity. Georg Lukacs has very eloquently summed up some of the essential traits of the modern world, which are reflected in the setting in Robert Musil's novel and which perfectly illustrate the challenge modernism is confronted with:

> Our world has become infinitely large and each of its corners is richer in gifts and dangers than the world of the Greeks, but such wealth cancels out the positive meaning—the totality—upon which their life was based. For totality as the formative prime reality of every individual phenomenon implies that something closed within itself can be completed.[26]

It is precisely the precarity of positive meaning in a world of infinite possibilities referred to by Lukacs, with which Musil's essayism tries cope. To do so, Musil builds upon Nietzsche's perspectivism which is in a certain way both the cause of the loss of totality and a method to confront it. However, Musil's essayism is a genuine undertaking which gives his approach an orientation that leads away from Nietzsche's perspectivism and toward a new horizon of (possible) meaning.

Robert Musil's essayism as a philosophical method

I would like to start this second part with two quotes from Robert Musil's notebooks (1899–1904) which are directly linked to Nietzsche's perspectivism and illustrate simultaneously the fascination Musil had for Nietzsche and Musil's critical distance:

> What is characteristic is that [Nietzsche] says: this could be like this and that like that. And upon this one could build this and upon that that. In short: he speaks of numerous possibilities, numerous combinations, without showing the development of a single one of them.[27]

This remark is further developed in the following reflection:

> But it is evident that it is only then that one can judge the value of an idea, or even that one can see with whom one is dealing. There is nothing vivid in this manner—the brain fantasizes. In this case at least it is Nietzsche's +++ brain—but there are people for whom this way of doing things is unbearable, a life apart. See Nietzsche. What a fiasco as soon as one tries to find a system in him, except that of the spiritual arbitrariness of the wise.[28]

The reader can sense how Musil feels attracted to Nietzsche's perspectivism, but how on the other hand, he feels that it remains somewhat unaccomplished. According to him, Nietzsche names multiple possibilities and combinations, but because he does not follow-up on them something essential is lacking: the setting which would allow one to appreciate the value of these possibilities and combinations in their impactfulness as they unfold. Musil relativizes his criticism by highlighting Nietzsche's intellectual capacities which partly compensate for this lack of development. But in thus relativizing his criticism, Musil targets all the more the Nietzsche-epigones who cannot claim for themselves a comparable "+++ brain" and reveal themselves to be the kind of followers who ignore the wish expressed by Nietzsche that people should face his writings with distance and ironic resistance.

I would also like to draw attention to another aspect that shines through in the given quotations as it links Musil's criticism of Nietzsche's perspectivism to an anticipation of his own philosophical method. Musil refers to the danger of wanting to find a philosophical system in Nietzsche. The systemic[29] approach would lead to a *fiasco* as

Musil emphatically puts it. This rejection of systemic thought is picked up explicitly in *The Man Without Qualities* where Musil ascribes the following reflection to Ulrich, the main character: "He was no philosopher. Philosophers are despots who have no armies to command, so they subject the world to their tyranny by locking it up in a system of thought."[30]

Both the previously quoted short notes from his diary and the reflection from *The Man Without Qualities* allow the reader to situate Musil's essayism methodologically as a kind of enhanced perspectivism. The lack of development Musil observes for Nietzsche's perspectivism constitutes a starting point for developing his own methodology which will attempt to provide a remedy to the shortcomings of simply sketching possibilities and combinations. However, this remedy will also have to provide a framework other than in the form of the traditional philosophical system. To put it differently: the epistemological insight into the insurmountable perspectivity of knowledge has to find its formal reflection in a particular philosophical *style*.[31] Musil's answer to this challenge is, as I will argue, the form of the novel. *The Man Without Qualities* can be understood as his attempt to develop some of the multiple possibilities and combinations perspectivism brings forth. This means, to make this claim explicitly, that *The Man Without Qualities* is the result of a *philosophical choice of method* and thus, in an eminent sense, *philosophy as literature*. This claim will be the common thread in the following reflections which will try to illustrate to what extent the literary framework Musil creates allows him to put into practice his philosophical essayism as a method derived from perspectivism.

Musil finds in the literary text—in the quite particular shape it takes in *The Man Without Qualities*—the framework that is needed to face the challenge of developing possibilities without shutting them up in a system. It is eloquent with regard to the choice of the form of the novel that we find in Musil's notes a quote from Friedrich Schlegel originally published in the *Athenäumsfragmente*: "Novels are the Socratic dialogues of our time. Practical wisdom fled from school wisdom into this liberal form."[32] *The Man Without Qualities* represents precisely in the Schlegelian sense a "liberal" form of philosophizing which avoids the dangers of hermeticism and dogmatism inherent in the philosophical system and opens up an experimental space in which possibilities find the room for development without any pretense beyond the limited claim of validity within the framework of perspectivism—or "essayism" to use Musil's own term.[33] The creation of a literary reality as a space for evolution can be considered as the major distinction with regard to the fragmentary style through which Nietzsche primarily puts into practice his perspectivism.[34] It is Nietzsche's great merit to have brought into play possible perspectives and combinations and the possibility (or necessity) of multiple interpretations against traditional, univocal, and systemic philosophizing aspiring to ultimate justifications. Musil takes up the epistemological principles established by Nietzsche and builds upon them within the textual framework of the literary text which he uses as a laboratory in which he can on an at-trial basis develop these possibilities and combinations. The essayism at play in his novel is in this sense to be understood as applied perspectivism which brings forth insights that are relevant for life practice, the literary framework providing the space not only, as said above, to bring up ideas and to see how they evolve, but also to provide the room and possibility to (tentatively) relativize, criticize, and refute them. As Hans-Joachim Pieper pertinently observes, Musil succeeds in accomplishing "in a literary way what would always fail in a theoretical approach: the relativist perspectivism is in its turn perspectivistically relativized."[35]

If Musil goes beyond Nietzsche in this respect, he also subtly rectifies Nietzsche in yet another fundamental aspect: As we have seen, Nietzsche repeatedly reiterates his criticism of epistemology and metaphysics in the occidental tradition and in particular of the claim of a supra-sensible "backworld," his polemics culminating in the rejection of anything that goes beyond immanence.

As Musil diverges sensibly from Nietzsche on this question, it is insightful to see how Musil positions himself concerning transcendence. In an ambivalent way, his novel suggests if not the existence of a transcendent backworld, at least the possibility (and the desirability) of perspectives that go beyond mere immanence; and it is undeniable that in *The Man Without Qualities,* Musil aims at a perspective on life clearly different from Nietzsche's: He does not only, with Nietzsche, relativize the claim of reason,[36] but he also brings explicitly into focus the reflection on the possibility of a reconciliation between reason and mysticism which is the essence of his postulate of an "other condition."[37] In his quest for this other condition the main character Ulrich appears in an ambivalent way as a "God-seeker" (*Gottsuchender*). Ulrich clearly rejects the framework of the traditional Christian worldview and its problematic metaphysical premises already clearly indicated by Nietzsche, but he seeks a perspective of religiosity and meaning compatible with his epistemological skepticism. The difficulty of this undertaking is illustrated in the paradoxical formula Musil uses in his notes for the novel, where he characterizes his book as "religious under the premises of the Unbeliever,"[38] the issue at stake being the conceptual compatibility of mysticism and the demands of intellectual integrity as expressed in a passage where Ulrich first emphasizes his interest in the "holy life,"[39] just to add: "I am studying the road to holiness to see if it might also be possible to drive a car on it!"[40] Accordingly, Ulrich's stance on this issue remains ambivalent throughout the entire novel, and this ambivalence is highlighted through a narrative procedure in which the attraction that mysticism exercises on Ulrich is always counterbalanced by some kind of relativization, as the following reflection illustrates:

> There have been more than a few such essayists, masters of the inner hovering life but there would be no point in naming them. Their domain lies between religion and knowledge, between example and doctrine, between *amor intellectualis* and poetry; they are saints with and without religion, and sometimes they are also simply men on an adventure who have gone astray.[41]

The (positive) claim that there are certain extraordinary characters with a great proximity to both religion and knowledge finds its immediate relativization in the concluding assertion according to which it might just as well be the case that, in the end, these masters merely lost their way while on an adventure: The testimony of their mystic experience is thus immediately ironically relativized.

If the clear reference and affinity to the divine and to the hope linked to the possibility of an "other condition" could imply that Musil's thought is a step back compared to Nietzsche's fundamental immanentism, in that Musil seems to reintroduce an admittedly difficult to seize sort of transcendence at least as a *possibility*, using a vocabulary associated with the *Hinterwelter* (religion, mystic experience, divine, etc.), one could as well argue that Musil's perspective can be considered as a step forward. It was Nietzsche's main point that the desire to get beyond our world signifies a profound overestimation of the reach of human reason and can only result in shipwreck. Against the claim of the divinity of reason held by traditional metaphysics, Nietzsche insists on its limitation to the realm of immanence.[42] However, by restricting the realm of human reason to immanence and assuming the supposed backworld as an illegitimate claim, Nietzsche exposes his argumentation to the objection that his rejection of the *possibility* of a backworld cannot be justified. As Nietzsche restricts the realm of human reason to immanence, he can legitimately only exclude the possibility of *knowing* whatsoever about such a hypothetical backworld, but he cannot exclude that something beyond immanence exists.[43]

Musil uses precisely this breach to reintroduce transcendence, but only *as a possibility*, thus taking care to remain epistemologically on safe ground. Here, the literary form plays a crucial role, as it is the framework of the novel that provides the methodological backdrop before which Musil can take up the challenge to develop the question of transcendence in the mode of possibility. As said earlier, we can consider *The Man Without Qualities* as both a refuge and a reflective playing field where Musil can apply rules different from those of the *Schulphilosophie* and develop all the possibilities and combinations made possible by literary fiction. At the same time, this framework gives him the possibility to simultaneously unfold philosophical insight and its critique (*Erkenntnis* and *Erkenntniskritik*), as the ironic stance underlying the narration as a whole undermines the reality constituted within the novel, and thus increases possibilization: The possibility that the literary fiction represents with regard to the external reality is thus newly possibilized from within the novel and, most importantly, this double possibilization is held present through the ironic undercurrent that characterizes the novel as a whole.

In transposing the literary text into the mode of irony, Musil establishes a methodological framework which maintains all philosophical utterances, claims, and positions in the realm of possibility and thus prevents the risk of falling into a stance similar to that adopted by Nietzsche who, as says Dirk von Petersdorff polemically, "makes prophetic statements and judges everything and everyone."[44] Where Nietzsche admittedly philosophizes with the hammer and openly aims at the destruction of the occidental philosophical and religious tradition, Musil wraps his philosophical reflections, be they constructive or deconstructive, carefully into a literary framework full of conditional tenses and irony, where even doubts and reservations are put forward conditionally, only to be ironically relativized immediately after.

In fact, one of the most impactful differences between Nietzsche and Musil appears to be Musil's methodological use of a different kind of irony. Nietzsche uses irony mainly in two contexts. First, to show his insight into and approval of the ironic character of the world;[45] and second, he uses irony as a kind of antidote against his own propensity for exaggeration. Musil's irony, on the contrary, is first and foremost construed as a genuine epistemological mode which serves as the basis for the process of accessing knowledge and for which the novel is the condition of the possibility of its realization. Irony plays a double role in this context: First, it allows Musil to develop his project of a hypothetical philosophy, a philosophy that responds to the sense of possibility which implies that everything could also be different; and second, irony establishes a realm within which what is said hints at what cannot be said because it is ineffable, which is crucial for the possibility to develop the idea of an "other condition."

In the same sense that irony has a different function in Nietzsche and Musil, the conditional tense serves *in fine* different purposes, even if there are shared elements. Nietzsche uses the conditional mainly to reveal epistemological blindness linked to traditional metaphysical thought[46] but also to identify possibilities and combinations. In *The Man Without Qualities*, the conditional tense is mainly used to relativize any positive statement as all could just as well be otherwise ("*Möglichkeitssinn*"). If their use of the conditional tense is comparable in that both Nietzsche and Musil use it as an expression of their epistemological perspectivism, what distinguishes Musil's use is that he has recourse to the *Konjunktiv* to provide the ambivalent foundation of his conscious and tentative utopism, thus creating a new horizon for the construction of philosophy as possibility.

With his scrupulous methodology Musil succeeds thus in going beyond Nietzsche by reopening the door to transcendence as a possibility. If there is, as Nietzsche claims, no way for human reason to go beyond immanence, Nietzsche clearly overstreches the reach of his own criticism when he implies in his attacks against Platonism and Christianism that there *cannot* be such a thing as a *Hinterwelt*. It is precisely here that Musil deviates from Nietzsche.[47] Musil can follow Nietzsche effortlessly with regard to the skepticism the latter expresses concerning traditional metaphysics, but he does not have to content himself with mere immanent perspectives. His philosophy ironically brings into play different insights and philosophical positions which neither he nor his readers are able to classify as "true" or "false" unambiguously and with certainty. Musil agrees with the diagnostic that traditional metaphysics overestimates the reach of human reason, but he only dismisses the claim metaphysics makes with regard to knowledge. He does not dismiss the possibility of going beyond immanence, but preserves transcendence as a possibility, negatively and ironically.

Conclusion

To conclude, I would like to stress that Musil indeed succeeds in putting into practice what he found missing in Nietzsche's writings: Within the framework of his famous novel, Musil not only sketches different possibilities and combinations but he gives them room to develop a reality according to the inner logic of the literary—and ironic—text. It is essentially for epistemological reasons that Musil has recourse to the literary text. The literary text provides a veritable laboratory which contains countless possibilities—theoretical possibilities but also practical possibilities, that is, possibilities of existing. These possibilities benefit from the literary setting as they do not have to be represented as philosophical postulates, but instead they take shape as literary and ironic suggestions, thus circumnavigating the problem Nietzsche is confronted with: the problem of a stance that goes too far in its criticism of human reason, insofar as it actually claims what reason, within its new limits, cannot claim. By transposing the philosophical discourse into ironic and literary language, Musil can develop his criticism all the while respecting the boundaries of reason he circumscribes and accepts for his own enterprise. He thus avoids the temptation that philosophical discourse often succumbs to, which is to draw the limitations of reason from without. Irony enables Musil to reveal the boundaries of reason from within, not the least in perspectivizing Nietzsche's perspectivism. As it is, Musil is as coherent as Nietzsche when it comes to identifying the deficiencies of traditional philosophical thought, but he is perhaps even more coherent than Nietzsche when it comes to developing his philosophical method according to the insight into the deficiencies of philosophy and the limitations of human reason. This is why he does not have to dogmatically reject concepts of transcendence but can maintain them as a possibility.

As a last remark, I would like to hint at one aspect that emerges from what has been developed above: If Nietzsche insists on his proximity to Heraclitus, one can also find Heraclitian elements in Musil's methodology. For Musil, reflection is always to be understood as reflection in the making; and the choice of the form of the novel can definitely be attributed to Musil's effort to conserve the vividness of reflection in that the literary text remains in an eminent sense unfinished and open and calls for the reader to complete it.[48] The literary text can thus never be considered as definitely accomplished. And just as nobody can step in the same river twice, no reader can read the same book twice; the book will necessarily have changed at least in some minor, but often even in major aspects. As for Musil the aspect of becoming is so primordial, it is hardly surprising that he struggled with concluding his novel, theoretically, as well as practically. It is very eloquent that Musil noted in his diaries: "Ideally, I would stop at the end of a page, in the middle of a sentence with a comma."[49] Musil felt seduced by the perspective of undermining the illusion of a possible ending by just having his novel fade out. Ironically, this is also what finally really happened, not because *Musil* decided to do so, but *fate*: Musil died with his novel unfinished—and as the legend goes, while working on it—and leaves us thus a voluminous fragment that ironically and tragically confirms Lukacs's observation with regard to the impossibility of completion as distinctive for Modernity.

Notes

1 The *Musil-Forum*, the journal dedicated to the study of Musil's work, explicitly refers to modernism in its subtitle: *Studien zur Literatur der klassischen Moderne* (Berlin: De Gruyter, 1975-).
2 See for instance Roberto Olmi, "Musil und Nietzsche," *Musil-Forum* 7 (1981): 119–29, Hans-Joachim Pieper, *Musils Philosophie. Essayismus und Dichtung im*

Spannungsfeld der Theorien Nietzsches und Machs (Würzburg: Königshausen und Neumann, 2002), and in particular Charlotte Dressler-Brumme, *Nietzsches Philosophie in Musils Roman "Der Mann ohne Eigenschaften"* (Frankfurt/Main: Athenäum, 1987).

3 Giorgio Colli, *Nach Nietzsche* (Frankfurt/Main: Europäische Verlagsanstalt, 1980), 209; my translation). In his study on Nietzsche's perspectivism, Kai-Michael Hingst gives an account of a number of contradicting statements made by Nietzsche. See Hingst, *Perspektivismus und Pragmatismus. Ein Vergleich auf der Grundlage der Wahrheitsbegriffe und der Religionsphilosophien von Nietzsche und James* (Würzburg: Königshausen und Neumann, 1998). However, in his interpretation, Hingst shows a tendency to almost systematically dissolve these contradictions, which is methodologically problematic.

4 See Walter Bröcker, "Nietzsches Narrentum," *Nietzsche-Studien* 1 (1972): 138–46.

5 *KSA*, 12:7[60]. If Nietzsche uses this term mainly in the context of epistemological reflections—and, thus, as a theoretical tool to determine the human capacities in terms of knowledge—Nietzsche's perspectivism also has a practical dimension as a method of inquiry; when used as the latter, perspectivism causes the same phenomenon to appear entirely different—and also contradictory—as a function of the perspective adopted.

6 See Gottfried Wilhelm Leibniz, *Monadology and Other Philosophical Writings*, trans. Robert Latta (Oxford: Clarendon Press, 1898), 248 [57].

7 Quoted from Friedrich Nietzsche, *Human, All Too Human. A Book for Free Spirits* (Cambridge: Cambridge University Press, 1996).

8 Quoted from Friedrich Nietzsche: *On Rhetoric and Language* (Oxford: Oxford University Press, 1989). Rodion Ebbinghausen refers to this difference by saying that Nietzsche opposes a "subjective perspectivism" to Leibniz' "objective perspectivism." See R. Ebbinghausen, *Die Genealogie der europäischen Krisis in der Perspektive der Interpretationsphilosophie Nietzsches und der transzendentalen Philosophie Husserl* (Würzburg: Königshausen und Neumann, 2010), 224. See also J. Figl, Johann, *Interpretation als philosophisches Prinzip: Friedrich Nietzsches universale Theorie der Auslegung im späten Nachlaß* (Berlin: De Gruyter, 1982), 106.

9 (*KSA*, 12:7[60]). See also Volker Gerhardt, "Die Perspektive des Perspektivismus," *Nietzsche-Studien* 18 (1989): 260–81.

10 Gerhardt, « Perspektiven des Perspektivismus, » 263ff.

11 *KSA*, 12:7[60].

12 Quoted from Friedrich Nietzsche, *The Gay Science* (Cambridge: Cambridge University Press, 2001).

13 *KSA*, 11:34[253].

14 Quoted from Friedrich Nietzsche, *Untimely Meditations* (Cambridge: Cambridge University Press, 2007).

15 Nietzsche seems to have been aware of this problem as his use of quotations marks suggests, which he sometimes places to identify the—in his eyes—erroneous concept of truth. However, as Bröcker has shown, Nietzsche does not stick strictly to this way of differentiating the two understandings of truth. See Bröcker, "Nietzsches Narrentum," 139–40.

16 See Arthur C. Danto, *Nietzsche as Philosopher* (New York: Macmillan, 1965), 79–80.

17 See Friedrich Kaulbach, *Philosophie des Perspektivismus. 1. Teil: Wahrheit und Perspektive bei Kant, Hegel und Nietzsche* (Tübingen: J.B.C. Mohr, 1990), 1.

18 On this issue, see also Konrad Hilpert, "Die Überwindung der objektiven Gültigkeit. Ein Versuch zur Rekonstruktion des Denkansatzes Nietzsches," *Nietzsche-Studien* 9 (1980): 91–121.

19 Quoted from *On the Genealogy of Morality* (Cambridge: Cambridge University Press, 2007).

20 Volker Gerhardt, however, questions the epistemological gain of this multiperspectivism as he emphasizes that there is no valid criterion that could back up the claim that the perspective of multiperspectivity is superior to other perspectives (see Gerhardt, "Die Perspektive des Perspektivismus," 272). If Gerhardt stresses that there is no *theoretical* reason to privilege one perspective to another, he admits, that there could be *practical* reasons to do so (see ibid.).

21 See on Schlegel's idea of an infinite approximation *ex negativo* of the Absolute Manfred Frank, *"Unendliche Annäherung." Die Anfänge der philosophischen Frühromantik* (Frankfurt/Main: Suhrkamp, 1997), *The Foundations of Early German Romanticism* (Albany: State University of New York, 2004).

22 One could think of apodictic claims such as the following: "But my truth is *frightful*: for thus far the lie has been called truth.—*Revaluation of all Values*: that is my formula for an act of the highest examination on the part of mankind, which has become flesh and genius in me. My lot decrees that I must be the first *decent* man, to know that I stand opposed to the falseness of millennia. ... I was the first to *discover* the truth in that I was the first to sense the lie as lie" (*EH, Why I Am a Destiny*, 1).

23 If for Nietzsche, the traditional concept of truth is also to be considered as the result of such an act of creation, the fundamental deficiency of this concept is that it is unaware of the creative process at its origin, but is instead taken for determinate and immutable.

24 Such an interpretation has the advantage that it undertakes a shift which would transfer the ambiguous and contradictory character from Nietzsche's thought to the phenomena he tries to grasp. This is also what is suggested by Werner Stegmaier (see W. Stegmaier, "Nietzsches Philosophie der Kunst und seine Kunst der Philosophie. Zur aktuellen Forschung und Forschungsmethodik," *Nietzsche-Studien* 34 [2008], 348–74, here 353).

25 Bernd Bräutigam, "Verwegene Kunststücke. Nietzsches ironischer Perspektivismus als schriftstellerisches Verfahren," *Nietzsche-Studien* 6 (1977): 45–63, here 59.

26 Georg Lukacs, *The Theory of The Novel. A Historico-Philosophical Essay on the Forms of Great Epic Literature* (London: The Merlin Press, 1971), 34.

27 Robert Musil, *Die Tagebücher* (Reinbek bei Hamburg: Rowohlt, 1983), 12; my translation). There is a similar remark from 1899 (see ibid., 50). It is hardly surprising that these different reflections on Nietzsche have been linked by different authors to the novel *The Man Without Qualities*. See for instance David S. Luft, *Robert Musil and the Crisis of European Culture 1880-1942* (Berkeley: University of California Press, 1980), 41; Pieper, *Musils Philosophie*, 150.

28 Ibid. (my translation).

29 I use the adjective "systemic" in distinction from "systematic" to refer to a thought which aims at philosophical systems. Musil's approach avoids the traps of philosophical systems all the while being systematic.

30 MwQ 272. This remark certainly reminds the reader of Nietzsche, who notes in *Twilight of the Idols*: "I distrust all systematisers, and avoid them. The will to a system, shows a lack of honesty" (*TI, Morality as Anti-Nature*, 26).

31 On philosophical style as a mark of the choice of philosophical method, see Gilles Gaston Granger, *Essai d'une philosophie de style* (Paris: A. Colin, 1968) et *Invitation à la lecture de Wittgenstein* (Aix-en-Provence: Alinea, 1990) and Manfred Frank, "Du style et de la signification. Wittgenstein, Musil et les premiers romantiques, in *Hommage à Musil*," ed. Marie-Louise Roth et al. (Bern: Peter Lang, 1995), 63–110.

32 Friedrich Schlegel, *Kritische Friedrich-Schlegel-Ausgabe* 2 (Paderborn: Schöningh, 1967, 149; my translation); and Robert Musil, *Gesammelte Werke in 3 Bänden*, vol. 3 (Reinbek bei Hamburg: Rowohlt, 1957), 722.

33 See MwQ 267. Musil's novel has indeed significant affinities with Schlegel's "transcendental poetry." See Sebastian Hüsch, *Möglichkeit und Wirklichkeit. Eine vergleichende Studie zu Soren Kierkegaards "Entweder-Oder" und Roberrt Musils "Mann ohne Eigenschaften"* (Stuttgart: Ibidem, 2004), 296ff.; see also Manfred Frank, "Du style et de la signification"; Michael Jakob, "Möglichkeitssinn und die Philosophie der Möglichkeit," in *Robert Musil: Essayismus und Ironie*, ed. Gudrun Brokoph-Mauch (Tübingen: Francke, 1992), 13–24.

34 On the fragment as a form of philosophical expression see the edited volume by Lucien Dällenbach and Christiaan L. Hart Nibbrig (ed.), *Fragment und Totalität* (Frankfurt/Main: Suhrkamp, 1984) and in particular the chapter by Manfred Frank, "Das 'fragmentarische Universum' der Romantik" (ibid., 212–24). On literary modality see Andreas Horn, *Literarische Modalität. Das Erleben von Wirklichkeit, Möglichkeit und Notwendigkeit in der Literatur* (Heidelberg: Winter, 1981), 18ff.

35 Pieper, *Musils Philosophie*, 150; my translation; italics H.-J.P.) Structurally, there is a parallel to Friedrich Schlegel's claim that reflection has to be brought to hover ("*schweben*"). See Friedrich Schlegel, *Kritische Friedrich-Schlegel-Ausgabe* 2 (Paderborn: Schöningh, 1967), 182. One could argue that this leads to an infinite regression (as has done Kierkegaard), but I would suggest considering this idea of hovering rather as a guarantor for a reflection that remains dynamic and non-dogmatic.

36 See for instance Musil's guiding principle, "the principle of the insufficient cause" which constructs ironically a kind of negative causality in which is most likely to happen what has "no good or sufficient reason" (MwQ 140/MoE 134). See on Musil's principle of the insufficient cause Jacques Bouveresse, "Nichts geschieht mit Grund: das 'Prinzip des unzureichenden Grundes,'" in *Hommage à Musil*, 111–43.

37 See MoE, 1254. See on the "other condition" Frederick G. Peters, *Robert Musil. Master of the Hovering Life. A Study of the Major Fiction* (New York: Columbia University Press, 1978), 10; Renate von Heydebrand, *Die Reflexionen Ulrichs in Robert Musils Roman "der Mann ohne Eigenschaften." Ihr Zusammenhang mit dem zeitgenössischen Denken* (Münster: Adchendorff, 1966), 159ff.; Schöne (1961), 212f.; Jacques Bouveresse, *La voix de l'âme et les Chemins de l'esprit* (Paris: Seuil, 2001), 71.

38 Robert Musil, *Der Mann ohne Eigenschaften*, in *Gesammelte Werke in 9 Bänden*, vol. 5 (Reinbek bei Hamburg: Rowohlt, 1980) 1940 ("religiös unter den Voraussetzungen der Ungläubigen"; my translation).

39 MwQ 815.

40 Ibid.

41 MwQ 273. See also von Heydebrand, *Die Reflexionen Ulrichs*, 160.

42 See *TL*, 246.

43 In an analogous manner, Gottfried Gabriel objects to Nietzsche's criticism of logics according to which philosophical concepts would transform reality into something

fake ("*Fälschung*"): "It would only make sense to speak of 'fake' if there was an access to reality as such so that the fake could be exposed (*entlarvt*) as fake, which is precisely what Nietzsche contests" (Gottfried Gabriel, *Logik und Rhetorik der Erkenntnis. Zum Verhältnis von wissenschaftlicher und Ästhetischer Weltauffassung* (Paderborn: Schöningh, 1997, 42; my translation).

44 Dirk von Petersdorff, "Nietzsche und die Romantische Ironie," in *Antike und Romantik bei Nietzsche*, ed. Volker Gerhardt and Renate Reschke (Berlin: Akademie-Verlag, 2004), 28–43, here 39; my translation). Petersdorff adds that there are still today many admirers of Nietzsche who seem blind to these weaknesses (see ibid.).

45 See Behler (1997): Ernst Behler, *Ironie et modernité* (Paris: Presses universitaires de France, 1997), 284 and 305.

46 One characteristic rhetorical figure in this context can be found for instance in *The Gay Science*, where Nietzsche notes: "What? The final aim of science should be to give man as much pleasure and as little displeasure as possible? But what if pleasure and displeasure are so intertwined that..." (*GS*, 12).

47 In fact, as a "good reader" of Nietzsche, Musil also deviates in a number of other points, but I only take into consideration here his particularity with regard to knowledge in the above sketched context.

48 See Wolfgang Iser, "Der Lesevorgang," in *Rezeptionsästhetik. Theorie und Praxis*, ed. Rainer Warning (Munich: Fink), 253–76.

49 Oskar Maurus Fontana, "Erinnerungen an Robert Musil," in *Robert Musil. Leben, Werk, Wirkung*, ed. Karl Dinklage (Reinbek bei Hamburg: Rowohlt, 1960), 324–44, here 336; my translation).

16

Mann > Modernism < Nietzsche

Bill McDonald

> *Nietzsche, the philosopher and writer, was a phenomenon of vast cultural scope and complexity, a veritable résumé of the European spirit.**
>
> —Thomas Mann, *Nietzsche in Light of Recent Events*

The story of Thomas Mann and Friedrich Nietzsche has been told many times, and with great skill and insight. A complete German-English literature review would take up the space allotted to me for this chapter, and a comprehensive account of Nietzsche's presence in Mann's *oeuvre* a book far longer than this one.[1] So I gratefully acknowledge the many readers who have already illuminated this famous relationship, and hope to retell the story in a way that highlights their findings, and my own thoughts, in the web of European modernism.

Nietzsche was the central thinker and arguably the central personality undergirding Mann's art from his earliest ventures into short fiction. He read and reread Nietzsche continuously over the sixty years of his artistic life. His copy of the collected works is repeatedly annotated in his handwriting as it evolved—or devolved—across those decades. It's hard to name another major artist who had such a sustained, productive and, in part, self-serving relationship with the philosopher. It's always the case, of course, that any writer's themes arise from "the times," and that quotation or reference doesn't automatically establish major influence.[2] Sources often overlap and interconnect, especially for writers as tradition-conscious as Mann.[3] Having said that, their long connection seems indisputable. He wrote about Nietzsche directly in two essays, major sections of a long non-fiction book, over a hundred letters and diary entries, and, most important, in literally all his fiction, from the early stories of the 1890s right through to *The Confessions of Felix Krull, Part I* in 1955; all of it bears the imprint of Mann's fertile entanglement with Nietzsche's thought and life. Further, from the beginning Mann's view of his great predecessor was complex, ambivalent. He oscillated between assimilation and adulation on the one hand and critique, sometimes even derision, on the other. At different points, different facets of that complexity shaped his understanding of Nietzsche, always in accordance with the demands of whatever writing project was at hand.

That entanglement includes the ways in which Mann identified and manipulated Nietzsche-inflected modernist themes and practices. First among these was the importance of autobiography and "psychology," broadly defined, for philosophy and fiction, and the aestheticism and perspectivism which those enabled. Nietzsche, like Freud, often began with self-observation before moving outwards, and Mann followed suit. In addition, Mann consistently saw Nietzsche's life as an afflicted, tragic one—a frail constitution, chronic illness, hyper self-consciousness, overburdened isolation, unwanted and unrecognized heroism—with direct, and rather self-aggrandizing, parallels in his own life. He extended those parallels into his fictions. Nietzsche's suffering, in both body and spirit, seemed to Mann perpetual, and of a piece with his philosophy. This view produced both an Aristotelian "reverence and pity [*Erbarmen*]" for Nietzsche, and, it seems, for himself.[4] Second, and nearly as important, were the consequences of being transitional, or "late" figures. Mann saw himself creating fictions at the end of a long, arguably exhausted realist tradition, and Nietzsche saw himself philosophizing after the heyday and decline of German idealism. Two modernist methods in particular proved most powerful for Mann in dramatizing "lateness": montage and parody. Mann found both in Nietzsche's writings, but shaped them to his specific artistic needs.[5] He proved to be a master of literary montage, compiling complex, varietal layers of reference in constructing many characters, and equally a master of parody across its full range: comic, satiric, and tragic.[6] Both these subjects, as we shall see, involved a related third theme: a specific understanding of "decadence."

Death in Venice (1911) and *Doctor Faustus* (1947) are Mann's *Kunstlerroman* most closely associated with Nietzsche. The exploration of *The Birth of Tragedy*'s aestheticism in "Death in Venice" has received the most critical attention, followed closely by the Faust novel. In both, tragic parody links the Dionysian to the demonic, either via repression that enables a highly regarded, ascetic art but at the cost of its practitioner's life, or the deliberate choice of syphilitic infection as the only way for a belated artist to achieve creativity in a dead-end aesthetic culture. Brothels offer only dark parodies of love, and a late artist can only parody his predecessors.[7] Because these two have been written about so often and so well I've chosen two different but representative fictional examples among the dozens available to illuminate our subject: the early tale "Der Bajazzo" (1895 draft; published 1897) as a study of psychology, aestheticism, and decadence by a writer just beginning his career; the character of Peeperkorn in *The Magic Mountain* (1924), arguably Mann's most surprising and inventive exploration of Nietzsche and modernism via the use of montage and comic parody. With "Der Bajazzo" I'll include a few comments on Mann's pertinent non-fiction writings during the Great War. I'll close with a reprise of his 1947 essay-lecture "Nietzsche in the Light of Recent Events," itself a capstone and recapitulation of Mann's relationship with his formative predecessor.

* * *

Improving our style means improving our ideas, and nothing else.

—(*HH*, 131)

Thomas Mann was thirteen when Nietzsche collapsed in the Piazza Carlo Alberto in Turin, and was twenty-five when he died; Nietzsche for him was at once a ghostly contemporary and an enlivening historical figure. By 1895, and perhaps earlier, Mann had encountered Nietzsche's writing, most probably *Beyond Good and Evil* in a heavily annotated edition that belonged to his elder brother Heinrich (1871–1950).[8] Beginning in 1896 with *Morgenröte* he collected the volumes of Nietzsche's complete works as they appeared. Unlike his solitary epiphany, at sixteen, with Wagner's *Lohengrin* or his revelatory reading of Schopenhauer in his early twenties, a reading that he dramatized in his breakout novel *Buddenbrooks*, Mann's early relationship with Nietzsche's life and thought was shared with, even mediated by, his brother. In their home city of Lübeck, and then again in Italy where the brothers spent several unfettered and intense months together in 1897, Nietzsche's work was a major topic of their conversations.[9] Heinrich later wrote that his generation felt as though Nietzsche was speaking directly to them, and his younger brother shared that feeling. Nietzsche was the alpha star in Mann's *Dreigestirn*, joining Schopenhauer and Wagner as the beacons in his "destined" career as an artist.[10]

It is easy to imagine the impact of Nietzsche's cutting, aphoristic style on a late-nineteenth-century young reader schooled to burgher politeness, and to closed systems of thought and belief. "His all-probing, all-dissolving style taught the whole of Europe, Germany included, how to write, how to criticize, how to be radical."[11] What such readers took from Nietzsche was, first, a fresh understanding of the age, and the artistic possibilities for portraying human experience that followed from it. Nietzsche's writings bristled with hundreds of aphorisms, diatribes, incisive paragraphs on the artist, the age, Romanticism, Germany and the Germans, genius, pessimism, disgust: all topics that resonated deeply with our fledgling writer. And Nietzsche's *Schwere*, his demanding strenuousness and ascetic devotion to his calling, also resonated with Mann, anxious to put his traditional *Bildungsbürger* work ethic in the service of a higher purpose.[12] The youthful Mann's Nietzsche was first and foremost a master of critique; he exposed not only the shallowness and hypocrisy of burgher culture, but the collapse of Romanticism and metaphysics in both art and philosophy that together led to the "decadence" of the modern. By "decadence" Nietzsche signifies personal weakness of mind and will combine with the sense, fully conscious or intuited, that one's decaying cultural heritage no longer provides sustaining meaning. Decadence also involves parody: the great passions of the heroic age are long past, and only feeble, self-conscious re-enactments remain. The decadent may see through the leveling mass culture surrounding him, but cannot face the isolation of alternatives, or the *Schwere* of constantly accepting that life can only be perceived aesthetically, not through inherited morality or religion.[13] Nietzsche also faced the paradoxes he had diagnosed: sickness is inevitable, but also the way to psychological and cultural health; amoral aestheticism runs against the ethical edge of his psycho-social critiques; true knowledge of the world is unattainable, and only artistic making (including metaphor and myth) is life-giving.[14] Nietzsche strove to be what Jacqueline Scott calls a "strong decadent," a thinker who acknowledges the depths of his own decadence and strives to overcome it without imagining that it can be erased and without retreating to rationalistic, systematic pseudo-solutions. Only art can console, thought Nietzsche, and many modernist artists, certainly including Mann, sought to follow that same path: move past sickness and skepticism, psychological and cultural, to reshape the world.

And then there was the analytic influence, Nietzsche's penetrating and wide-ranging "psychology," that Mann persisted in celebrating throughout his life. Nietzsche uses the term repeatedly to describe himself—a psychologist is one who unmasks the many dispiriting facets of decadence, and the painful alternatives left open to the artist who depicts their consequences. *Schwere* again: Nietzsche charted the inner life of those called to a task that seemed beyond them. Passages such as this from *Human, All Too Human* brought Mann's own struggle to create sharply into focus: "Isolated though I was, I took sides against myself and for everything that would hurt me, me especially, and be difficult for me … . Only under this pressure do I have a clear enough conscience to possess something few men have ever had—wings, so to speak" (*HH, P*, 4). The same book also posed challenges to the young writer, as in the critique of irony (*HH*, 372), Mann's favorite rhetorical, indeed philosophical stance. Further, it claimed that psychological acuity, depth, was something that the Germans specifically lacked, making its allure all the greater for the beginning writer.[15] Formally, the book's fragmentation and discontinuous juxtapositions prefigured modernism in both philosophy and literature.

Here's just one example. Take this oft-quoted passage from *Human, All Too Human*:

> But above all would I commend them to you whose burden is heaviest, you choice spirits, most encompassed with perils, most intellectual, most courageous, who must be the conscience of the modern soul and as such be versed in its science: in whom is concentrated all of disease, poison or danger that can exist to-day: whose lot decrees that you must be more sick than any individual because you are not "mere individuals": whose consolation it is to know and, ah! to walk the path to a new health, a health of to-morrow and the day after: you men of destiny, triumphant, conquerors of time, the healthiest and the strongest, you good Europeans! (*HH*, 376)

Then compare it with Mann's early short fiction "Der Bajazzo" ("The Clown" or "The Joker," translated with Mann's approval as "The Dilettante"). It was written in Italy in 1896, a first-person rewrite in fourteen small sections of an 1895 rejected third-person story, "Walter Weiler." A desolate young man, nameless except for his title, buys a notebook and sits down to transcribe the story of his emptiness. It begins this way:

> It can all be summed up, beginning, middle, and end—yes, and the fitting valediction too, perhaps—in the one word: "disgust" (*Ekel*). The disgust which I now feel for everything and for life as a whole, the disgust that chokes me, that shatters me, that hounds me out and pulls me down, and that one day may give me strength to break the whole fantastic and ridiculous situation across my knee and finish with it once and for all … . Outwardly my life may proceed as peacefully,

regularly and mechanically as it had been doing all this winter, in frightful contrast to the process of dry rot and dissolution going in within[16]

It's almost as though we're reading Nietzsche's own account of a knowing victim of cultural decline. The young man goes on to record his early pleasure in clowning for his family's guests, but a predictable failure in business and the death of his father leave him adrift. The story uses many elements from Mann's own life, among them his dreamy pleasure in his mother's melancholic playing of Chopin, his meticulous accounts of his expenses, and his passion for his childhood puppet theater. The Dilettante is satisfied for a time by inverting the work-ethic values of his family and society, achieving complete inactivity, every day a holiday. Then a solipsistic love affair—the young woman hardly knew of his existence—reveals his emptiness (the archetypal Canio of *Pagliacci* is nearby). Exposed as a pretender to aristocratic indolence, he achieves enough self-knowledge to unravel his wish-world and any prospects for achieving anything he might authentically admire. "What is destroying me is that hope has been destroyed with the destruction of all pleasure in myself."[17] He even imagines briefly that, like his creator, he might turn his woeful experience into literature.[18] Even the mock-triumph of suicide eludes him. "I cease to write, fling the pen from me—full of disgust, full of disgust! I will make an end of it—alas, that is an attitude too heroic for a dilettante. In the end I shall go on living … I shall gradually get used to the idea that I am dull, that I cut a wretched and ridiculous figure."[19] It's the tale's hidden author who exemplifies the Nietzschean "choice spirit," the "conscience of the modern soul," and who lays bare the subtleties of decadence for his peers.[20] Mann could, in dark moments, turn that same stripping psychology on himself, as in this confessional letter to Heinrich:

> My inability to find a proper intellectual and political orientation, as you have been able to do … . [My fate is] a growing sympathy with death, which is deeply inborn; my entire interest has always been captured by decay. … My time is up, I think, and I should probably never been allowed to become a writer. *Buddenbrooks* was a novel of the bourgeoisie and means nothing to the twentieth century. "Tonio Kröger" was merely lachrymose, *Royal Highness* vain, "Death in Venice" only half-cultivated and false.[21]

It was all well and good to create characters who anatomized decadence, but related attacks, like Nietzsche's on inorganic, decadent *literature* in *The Case of Wagner* (*CW*, 7), also threatened Mann's projected career and produced self-excoriating sentences like these.

The autobiographical form of "The Dilettante" leads to another central way in which Nietzsche undergirds Thomas Mann's oeuvre, one which connects both of them strongly to modernism: the exploration of the subtle turnings of consciousness. Neither Nietzsche nor Mann sought to present the stream of the mind directly—the quoted interior monologue most readily associated with modernism—but rather to dramatize its workings, as in Mann's story, or to evoke it, as in the Nietzsche passage.[22] Nietzsche explored the inner life of his era, unmoored from traditional values and unable to form fresh ones. And he particularly explored the psychology of isolation, weaving his autobiography into his philosophy. "The Dilettante" undertakes a similar task, dramatizing a character who, unlike Nietzsche, cannot turn his understanding of his isolation into meaningful action. To quote another of Nietzsche's many twentieth-century followers, Fernando Pessoa, "If you cannot live alone, then you were born a slave."

Mann always insisted that Nietzsche's stylistic influence was a central part of his heritage, and by "style" he meant at least two things. First was musicality: "His language itself was music; with a refinement of ear, a masterly sense of cadence and tempo, a rhythm that was unexampled in German prose and probably in European literature."[23] It was a musicality that Mann hoped carried over into his own writing. Second, Nietzsche's style entailed not just the fluidity of individual sentences and prose rhythms but a way of seeing the world. Mann could, in his essays, produce phrases and write with an edge that echoes Nietzsche's, but for the most part it was the unearthing quality of that style, its exposure of the papered-over hollowness of modern society, that impacted Mann's imagination most fruitfully. Over his career he gave us more than two dozen abject characters, souls mired in loss, in skepticism, in failed Romanticism, in impossible love, in "letting go," all of them rooted in Nietzsche's account of modernity's loss of inherited meanings. Their weak-willed aestheticism leads only to bankruptcy, as the Dilettante finally sees, not to the courageous affirmation Nietzsche claimed for his heroes.

Over the next decade Mann continued to explore how Nietzschean critique intersected with his artistic creativity. This led, among other projects, to a fragmented essay draft, "Mind and Art."[24] T. J. Reed has masterfully traced the entire process and its shifting historical context,[25] so I can concentrate on just a single aspect. In "Mind and Art" Mann takes up the tensions between intellectual critique and sensuous, "*Plastik*," visionary art. He argues that the border between them is in fact shifting and open and has always been so, even for Romantic artists, except for the few (like Wagner) who deliberately obscure that truth. The ensuing dilemma: Nietzsche obviously endorses critique, but also its contrary, vitalism, the spontaneous affirmation of "life" against the probing intellect. Dissection both enables and destroys, and Mann's well-practised critiques of the bourgeois world, he saw, could easily turn against their creator; after all, he too loves his bourgeois comforts and stability, and his narratives also contain unself-conscious moments of beauty, surface, and delight. Mann concludes:

> We who were born around 1870 are too close to Nietzsche, we participate too directly in his tragedy, his personal fate (perhaps the most terrible, most awe-inspiring fate in intellectual history). Our Nietzsche is Nietzsche Militant. Nietzsche Triumphant belongs to those born fifteen years after us. We have from him our psychological sensitivity, our lyrical criticism, the experience of Wagner, the experience of Christianity, the experience of "modernity"—from which we shall never completely break free, any more than Nietzsche himself ever did … . For *them* he is a prophet one doesn't know very exactly, whom one needs hardly

> to have read, and yet whose purified results one has instinctively in one. They have from him the affirmation of the earth, the affirmation of the body, the anti-Christian and anti-intellectual conception of nobility, which comprises health and serenity and beauty.[26]

Militant versus Triumphant: the comparison encapsulates Mann's complex view of Nietzsche. The "Triumphant" Nietzsche represents qualities that Mann increasingly rejected; indeed, the choice of "purified" directs Nietzschean irony against Nietzsche himself as well as the new generation. Several times in later work he wrote that he never took anything Nietzsche wrote "literally," meaning primarily what he wrote about masculinity as strength, power, and the "blond beast."[27] Most readers agree that Mann transposed Nietzsche's "extreme" vitalism into more harmonious keys: the "blond beast" became the blond lads and lasses who live uncritically and simply by their existence bedevil the divided, "diseased" imaginations of his outsider characters.

The place of Nietzsche in Mann's *Reflections of a Non-Political Man*, written during the war years, likewise deserves its own lengthy essay on our theme. I'll concentrate, of necessity, on just one aspect. *Reflections'* frame is provided by a book, *Nietzsche, Versuch einer Mythologie*, by Mann's good friend Ernst Bertram. Mann read portions of the book in manuscript, corresponded with and entertained the author. Briefly, Bertram gave Mann a Nietzsche—"the last great German"—consonant with his own predilections and artistic needs: a master of lived ambiguity and "psychological antimonies"; a believing skeptic; a celebrator of the mythic.

In his introduction, entitled "Legend," Bertram lays out his argument. Objectivity is unattainable, and subjectivity is the basis for understanding or "vision." Historians promote their own conscious (or unconscious) values and create images and myths that resonate for their contemporary readers. Life as it was actually lived in the past cannot be captured directly; "All of the past wants to become image, all that is living to become legend, all reality myth."[28] He emphasizes Nietzsche's ideas about Germanness and the Germans, and extols him as a figure of German cultural crisis: precisely the subjects of Mann's book. He gives evocative titles to the nineteen chapters of his book, all conjuring "Nietzsche" or linking him with other equally "mythic" figures and themes; representatives are "Ancestry," "Knight, Death, and Devil," "The German Becoming," "Justice," "Illness," "Judas," "Mask," "Claude Lorrain," "Venice," "Socrates," and "Eleusis." He outlines Nietzsche's own mythologizing of his philosophical ancestors. He regularly compiles quotations, constructing a kind of montage that elevates experience to myth, seen as recurring identification with historical figures or periods (e.g., "the Greek-obsessed German soul"[29]).

No surprise, then, that Mann depended heavily on Bertram in *Reflections'* polemical defense of German *Kultur*—always, for him, one of Nietzsche's fundamental subjects[30]—and therefore of the German cause against the French "man of civilization" and the economic pragmatists of England. He not only borrowed ideas, he borrowed entire sentences from Bertram's study. Bertram's book itself has aspects of a novel about it, and as he progressed Mann began to think of his own book as "more a work of fiction than a series of essays." One quotation from *Reflections* will have to suffice: Mann's high-flying, almost ecstatic tribute to Nietzsche.

> The *life concept*, this most German, most Goethean, and, in the highest religious sense, conservative concept, is the one that Nietzsche imbued with new feeling, reinvested with new beauty, strength and holy innocence, elevated to the highest rank, to intellectual dominance. ... If I were to reduce what I owe him spiritually to a formula, a key word—I would find no other than precisely this: the idea of life ... an antiradical, anti-nihilistic, anti-literary, most highly conservative German idea."[31]

In 1919 Bertram and Mann shared the "prize of honor" awarded by the Nietzsche Archive organization in Weimar.

The mention of Weimar gives me an ironic coda to this section, one worthy of Mann's fictional trickery, from two years after that award. His frequent alignment of his own life story with Nietzsche's took a surprisingly literal turn: After a public reading of his story "A Weary Hour" in Weimar on February 16, 1921, Mann breakfasted the next morning with the mayor of the city and another person from the audience: Elisabeth Föster-Nietzsche. They spoke for a half hour before sitting down to their meal. She created "a remarkable impression ... family resemblance in the eyes ... the oddity of his strikingly good manners even in advanced stages of his paralysis."[32] Had Mann known of the sister's Fascist politics and virulent anti-Semitism then, his impressions might not have been quite so "remarkable."

* * *

> *What Nietzsche offers is not only art—a special art is required to read him, and in reading him literalness and straightforwardness are of no avail. Rather cunning, irony, reserve are requisite.*
>
> —Thomas Mann. *Nietzsche in Light of Recent Events*

> [At Berkeley] *I spoke about Nietzsche, saying that were he alive he would be in America today and American tolerance would likewise have inducted him into the Phi Beta Kappa fraternity, in spite of his romantic sins. That brought laughter.**
>
> —Thomas Mann. Letter to Erich von Kahler, March 30, 1941

Mynheer Peeperkorn enters *The Magic Mountain* late in the saga of Hans Castorp, the unassuming young Hamburg engineer and subject of Mann's encyclopedic

Bildungsroman. A thumbnail overview: Hans travels from Hamburg to Davos to visit his cousin Joachim Ziemssen, a tuberculosis patient in the city's famous Sanatorium Berghof. But he soon discovers that he too is "susceptible" to the disease and the half-conscious affinities for death, the erotic, and "letting go" that it enables. His three weeks at the Sanatorium will turn into seven years (1907–14). By the time Peeperkorn appears Hans is deep into his adventure and has already encountered six remarkable pedagogues: Settembrini, the Enlightenment rationalist (who also, ironically, likes to quote Nietzsche on music); Hofrat Behrens, the melancholic medical man ("What is life? Oxidation … What is death? Oxidation"); Dr. Krokowski, the crank psychoanalyst and manipulative spiritualist; the brilliant and paradoxical Jewish Marxist Jesuit Leo Naphtha; Clavdia Chauchat, the Russian femme fatale who (well offstage) inaugurates Hans into sexual love before departing for "the East"; and finally, his cousin, the dedicated army lieutenant Joachim. All but the two doctors are themselves infected, and all can be seen in part through Nietzschean lenses, but none as fully or delightfully as Hans's seventh and final instructor, Pieter Peeperkorn.

Peeperkorn exemplifies Mann's conception of "Nietzschean modernism" in both technique and character conception: montage and parody coupled with vitalism, gnomic aphorisms, Pan-erotic desire. Peeperkorn "is" a Dionysus, a Rubensesque Silenus, complete with a "sybaritic dimple." He is a comi-tragic *Übermensch* who transcends all explanations of him, a powerful teacher who bypasses conventional arguments and explanations. He induces both mockery and reverence, paralleling Mann's mid-life understanding of Nietzsche. He is the most inventive character in the book, a riposte, perhaps, to a critic who termed Mann "uncreative" and "too cerebral and tradition-bound."[33] Never sympathetic with modernism's more radical avant-gardes (surrealism, expressionism, and futurism), Mann consistently sought interplay between traditional realism and his many artistic innovations (a mix that a good number of other modernist writers also undertook). For one, as he himself noted, even to set a *Bildungsroman* in a TB sanitarium parodies that tradition,[34] and he puts that parody to positive, and ultimately ethical use. With Peeperkorn Mann does not relegate the Dionysian to the destructive and the demonic, as he did with Aschenbach, Potiphar's wife in the *Joseph* novels, and his Faust, Adrian Leverkühn, but redirects it in surprisingly affirmative and Nietzsche-illuminating ways.

A retired colonial Dutchman from Java, Peeperkorn is a rich coffee magnate about sixty, tall and large—framed, with a nimbus of white-hair and a sparse beard framing his reddened face and that sybaritic dimple, and ill with quartan fever and perhaps other diseases. He arrives at the sanitarium with Clavdia as his consort, badly disconcerting a still-smitten Hans. Peeperkorn is "robust and spare."[35] His robustness is commanding. He is a presence, a universal force, a dynamo; not just Europeans but a newly arrived Egyptian princess and a young Chinese patient sense it immediately. And he is, to put it mildly, robust in talking—sometimes he speaks incessantly—but spare indeed in coherence. Other times he is silent, but his "exquisite gestures," like those of an orchestra conductor, convey meaning mysteriously; we're not far from *The Birth of Tragedy Out of the Spirit of Music*.[36] Hans's other pedagogues, Joachim excepted, have been impressive talkers, but Peeperkorn rarely utters a complete sentence in public arenas. Instead he ejaculates phrases, nostrums, gambits that seem to lead nowhere, speech and gestures that give nearly all his fellow patients great satisfaction in spite of, or perhaps because of, their incomprehensibility.[37]

> Ladies and gentlemen, Fine. How very fine. That *set*-tles it. And yet you must keep in mind and never—not for a moment—lose sight of the fact that—but enough on that topic. What is incumbent upon me to say is not so much *that*, but primarily and above all this: that we are duty-bound, that we are charged with an inviolable—I repeat with all due emphasis—*inviolable* obligation—*No*! No, ladies and gentlemen, not that I—oh, how very mistaken it would be to think that I—but that *set*-tles it, ladies and gentlemen. Settles it completely. I know that we are all of one kind, and so then, to the point.

Peeperkorn's character exemplifies modernist literary montage at its best, montage tinged with parody. He is a brilliant composite, an imaginative assemblage of overlays drawn from biography, myth, and philosophy. Biography: Peeperkorn's large features, small pale eyes, arabesque brows, gnomic stuttering, and prodigious consumption of alcohol are all playfully borrowed from Mann's erstwhile friend, playwright, and Nobel laureate Gerhardt Hauptmann; Peeperkorn's portrait is anchored in eccentric real life.[38] In addition, Hauptmann advocated Nietzsche's Dionysian vitalism in his 1908 travel journal *Greek Spring* and several other works. Beyond Hauptmann, Tolstoy and Whitman's different accounts of the "life-force" also contribute layers to the montage.

Mythically speaking, Peeperkorn is Dionysus in many guises, a montage within a montage. (As Hannalore Mundt observes, montage is an excellent technique for multiplying meanings.)[39] He's a wanderer from East to West; a celebrant of intoxication and rhapsodic speech. Reversing the ancient Greek pattern, he is a "dancing priest" of wintertime Delphi,[40] giving out gnomic utterances that his erstwhile priestess Clavdia sometimes translates.[41] He is the ruler of the Athenian festival of Anthesteria, at which he arrives unexpectedly, as Dionysus always does, a stranger from a distant port. In that festival the spirits of the dead are summoned to walk among the living before descending to the underworld again on the third day: a compelling mythic analog for how he enlivens the slowly dying inhabitants of the Berghof. Peeperkorn refers to both Hans and Clavdia as "children," and his attraction to them conjures yet another layer of the god's rich mythology: Erigone and the boy Ampelos, whom Dionysus loved (the homoerotic is rarely far away in a Thomas Mann fiction).[42] Peeperkorn also offers a vitalist, metaphoric theology: "Man himself is divine in that he feels. He is the very feeling of God. God created him in order to feel through him."[43]

Then there's the philosophical: He is not just a mythic representation but explicitly *Nietzsche*'s Dionysus, a comi-tragic affirmer of dark wisdom, and of vitality and potency, as the deepest expressions of life even as it closes. His face is often mask-like, conjuring classical drama and *The Birth of Tragedy*.[44] His many repetitions are godlike, a mark of majesty, "royal vigor."[45] He affirms life completely by living it to the hilt, willing it through his power. For him alcohol, far from being an addictive drug, comes purely from grain or grape and intensifies natural life; as Mann remarked of Nietzsche's chronic illnesses, it matter *who* is sick (or drinking).[46] He lectures on poisons that enhance life and love potions that could end it; sex—"the sacrament of lust"—expands to include every kind of fertility, the "Dionysian flood and excess" (*BT*, 21). He loves the mountains and the mountain air, as Nietzsche did, and exults in his bond with a soaring Zarathustrian eagle ("the king, of his race, the lion of the air!"[47]). In an enchanting variant on modernist characterization, Peeperkorn exists only the present, and any distinctions between his surface and his depths simply disappear. He is what he is: A genius of personality? A derelict old man? A god and a parody? "An artist-child? An intrinsically nonrealistic giant puppet who dwarfs all babblers"?[48] All these, and more.

The most well-known scene dramatizing Peeperkorn's inarticulate divinity takes place at a picnic he hosts beside the crashing "pandemonium" of a waterfall in the Flüela Valley.[49] Seven are assembled in his name, including the hyper-articulate debaters Naphta and Settembrini, but only he holds forth. No one can hear a word the majestic "grand stammerer" utters, but his sheer presence, "the ragged bitterness on his lips, the image of the Man of Sorrows" renders all the others silent.[50] But there's another, earlier scene that serves our theme even more directly. One evening Peeperkorn presides at a parodic Last Supper, where twelve patients, like disease-ridden disciple-bacchantes, congregate for games, endless wines and sweets, beef and omelets and gin, all consumed under the powerful aura of Peeperkorn's *Persönlichkeit.* Their outbursts—"hysterical fits of laughter ... exaltation or despair—were in genuine earnest," unself-conscious expressions of their most violent feelings; "they gladly allowed their emotions to wait upon him, and abandoned themselves with a passion"[51] And drunken Peeperkorn does the same, banging the dining table with his thundering fist. His "primitive, menacing pose" pronounces the "terror" that lies within or beneath his unbridled Bacchic celebration: impotence, the inability to honor Life's great gifts of sexual passion, bread and wine, and resilient, unmediated feeling. Without them there is only "shame and scornful laughter ... ruin and bankruptcy."[52] Nietzsche's Dionysian tragedy has rarely received such a powerful and sympathetic—and sympathetically parodic—dramatization. A final layer in the montage: Nietzsche's own deeply moving yet parodic signatures of 1888, "Dionysus" and "The Crucified," are given to Peeperkorn, who speaks of Gethsemane to his scattering, embarrassed (*beschämt*) guests, and cries, "Could you not watch with me one hour? ... Behold, the hour is at hand ... excruciating, heart-wrenching."[53] In his 1947 Nietzsche essay Mann affirms that "in mythological terms [Nietzsche's life] was a union of Dionysus with the Crucified One."[54] Nietzsche may have separated the Dionysian into the "Asiatic" and the "Greek," one leading to destruction and the other to oneness with life (*BT*, 2), but Mann weaves them together in Peeperkorn.

In Peeperkorn's final exchanges with Hans Castorp a different, and "unusually compact and precise" Dionysus emerges.[55] The old man is in bed, struck down by yet another fever attack, and Hans sits by his bedside, a loyal acolyte. Their ostensible topic is their shared love for and increasingly shared understanding of women, particularly Clavdia Chauchat, but their more intense exchange is about the ethics of brotherhood and friendship. Peeperkorn's magnetism induces a series of subtly balanced interpretations, then confessions from Hans. These culminate in his admission of his one night with Clavdia and so, despite the comical differences in their authority and grandeur, the men's common bond as her lovers. He ends by recounting the story of love-murder in *Carmen* (pertinently, Nietzsche's favorite opera after his break with Wagner). Taking Don Jose's knife as his prompt, the old man first offers to duel Hans for Clavdia—and it's a measure of Mann's achievement that the reader doesn't laugh—but sublimates that primitive will to power into a wine-christened offer of "the brotherhood of informal pronouns ... and feeling"[56] as her "traveling companions." And perhaps even more than brotherhood: "Leave me, my son" is Peeperkorn's farewell.[57]

Mann's coup in this dialogue is to bring together aesthetics and ethics in this outsized, monumental character, countering his conviction that Nietzsche divided them unnecessarily. He gives us a Dionysus as moral pedagogue, just as in the novel's earlier chapter, "Snow," he had given Hans Castorp a Nietzschean epiphany. By deriving the ethical from passion and unmediated feeling, Mann dramatizes his view that Nietzsche's worldview is finally not "beyond good and evil." It is reinforced by the perfect tone that Hans takes with Peeperkorn: deferential, yet playful; sincerely submissive, yet self-consciously preforming a role in a very serious, and comic, drama. He even parodies Peeperkorn's stammerings in a way that pays tribute to his magnificent *Persönlichkeit*. His love of and loyalty to his final teacher are sacrosanct. Mann called his novel "a very serious jest," and this rich dialogue bears out that conclusion.[58]

A few nights later, right after the decisive waterfall picnic, Peeperkorn, his vitality and virility entirely sapped, takes his own life. He employs an ingenious bit of technology worthy of a Futurist engineer: a tincture of strychnine embedded in a gold and ivory, steel and rubber reconstruction of the fangs of a cobra: as "natural" a passing, an infection, as can be imagined.

* * *

Philosophy is not a cold abstraction, but consists of experiencing, suffering, and sacrificing for humanity. This Nietzsche knew and demonstrated.

—Thomas Mann. *Nietzsche in Light of Recent Events*

In early February 1947, Thomas Mann, aged seventy-one, still residing in the elegant house he and Katia built in Pacific Palisades, California, began preparations for a long-postponed lecture tour. He had invitations to speak from the Library of Congress and Hunter College in America, and a number of cities in Europe, a list which he whittled down to London, Amsterdam, Zurich, and Berne (significantly and symbolically, he did not book any appearances in Germany). The lecture would be the centerpiece of his return to Europe as the standard-bearer of the best in German culture. For a topic he chose arguably the most challenging of subjects for his postwar audiences: "Nietzsche in the Light of Recent Events." A week earlier, on January 29, he had written the final words of what he rightly predicted would be his final major novel and the most important work of his life, *Doctor Faustus*.[59] After making final revisions to that manuscript, he turned directly to the Nietzsche project. The vast materials he had gathered for the writing of *Faustus* were still at hand. They included a great deal of material about Nietzsche's life because the philosopher was the unnamed, ghostly presence undergirding the character of the novel's composer-protagonist, Adrian Leverkühn. Everything from Leverkühn's basic biography and his tragic aestheticism right down to specific meals he ate in Italy come from Nietzsche's writings and history. Nearly all of Mann's essays across the decades either anticipate or intertwine with his fiction projects; this essay, almost alone, is an afterward—to *Doctor Faustus*, and the war.

Included in Mann's preparation was a rereading of a 1905 book by Karl Joël, *Nietzsche und die Romantik*, which he had first encountered as a young man and "learned a great deal."[60] Joël sharply contrasted Nietzsche's "manly spirit" with the "feminine soul" of the first-generation Romantics, emphasizing Nietzsche's call to "become hard" even to the point of brutality. This was the side of Nietzsche that Mann always rejected. At the same time Joël criticized what he termed Nietzsche's belated adherence to some Romantic ideals and advanced another view that Mann embraced: that Nietzsche's criticisms of the Germans was itself a prophetic incarnation of the German spirit. Joël also put forward ideas that the fascists would later twist into their service: Nietzsche's rejection of systems in favor of free, dynamic action; the joining of will and feeling; and the emphasis on "living dangerously" and "overcoming."

He worked hard on the lecture for more than a month, finishing on March 17, and producing twice the number of pages that could be performed in an hour on the stage. As always, his eldest daughter Erika helped edit the manuscript down to lecture-length—he half-jokingly called it "murdering"—in both English and German. The longer version, however, found a home at *Commentary* magazine, where it appeared in January and February of 1948 under the slightly altered title "Nietzsche in the Light of Modern Experience."[61] Nietzsche, then, had fully occupied Mann's mind since he began *Doctor Faustus* in 1943. But, as we shall see, the lecture's roots run deeper than even the depths of his Faust novel, and the essay seeks to pull together all Mann's half-century of reading and reflection on his subject: an all-but-impossible task.[62]

Mann's title makes clear his intention; this is not a philosophical analysis of Nietzsche's thought but a defense of his humanistic legacy to those all too familiar with the Nietzschean register, debased perhaps, but still all too recognizable in the mouths of Nazis.[63] For Mann, it's the Nietzsche that Americans and especially Europeans need to hear, and to remember. He was "a great critic and philosopher of culture, a European prose writer and essayist of the very first rank."[64] That is strong Nietzsche interpretation under political and historical pressure. Imagine facing a 1947 audience in, say, Amsterdam, with this subject matter. Mann wants to serve Nietzsche, and to rescue him for the future.

The 1947 essay begins not with Nietzsche's own beginnings but with his final collapse, and with Hamlet, "the observed of all observers." Once again Mann asserts the central force of suffering and isolation in Nietzsche's philosophy. Oscar Wilde[65] and Novalis soon make appearances, and the three give us the initial layers of Mann's montage of Nietzsche: the agonized, ascetic hero of thought, the beleaguered soul called to knowledge, the outsider aesthete set against conventional morality. He is the alpinist who overreached himself, his destiny shaped by his chronic illnesses. He may be "a phenomenon of vast cultural scope, a veritable resume of the European spirit," but like Mann's enervated Hamlet he is more martyr than *Übermensch*, more the Wildean aesthete than decisive actor, "a man who will be driven to saddle himself with insights crueler than his temperament can bear, and who will offer the world the heart-breaking spectacle of self-crucifixion."[66] Moving quickly to Nietzsche's earlier life, Mann accepts without reservation Dr. Paul Möbius's account of the philosopher's syphilitic infection in Köln, an infection thinly fictionalized in *Doctor Faustus*.[67] He cites as further evidence the seductive Dudu and Zuleika from "Among the Daughters of the Desert" in the fourth part of *Also Sprach Zarathustra* and Nietzsche's alleged statement to doctors in Jena, then Basel, that he had been infected ("some say deliberately, as self-punishment"[68]). He also quotes from Nietzsche's moving 1880 letter to a Dr. Eiser—"my existence is a frightful burden ... the constant pain and pressure in my head and on my eyes"—to intensify his portrait of chronic illness and genius developing together. There's reason to be skeptical of the entire syphilis narrative,[69] but Mann is wedded to it, and in no small part because of its pivotal role in *Doctor Faustus*.

Throughout the essay Mann counterpoints praise and celebration with critique, sometimes in the same paragraph. This is another aspect of his overall strategy to convince his audiences that he, like them, sees Nietzsche's naïveté and blindness "in the light of recent events" and so should trust his praise. First to be so judged is *Ecce Homo*, which he reread while writing his lecture. It receives high praise—"a stylistic masterpiece"—for the passage in which Nietzsche describes the exalted state in which he wrote his "Zarathustra poem"; once again, autobiography and psychology take center stage. But immediately Mann tells us that the work as a whole suffers from "delirious excesses of egotism."[70] Next to be celebrated are *Beyond Good and Evil* and *The Genealogy of Morals*; in them "his genius reached its height." But just two sentences later *Also Sprach Zarathustra* comes in for sharp criticism; Nietzsche was not, in his view, a strong or even a credible fiction writer. Mann mainly disparages Zarathustra as a character; he is "rhetoric, wild verbiage and puns ... often touching and usually embarrassing—a rollicking distortion [*Unfigur*] bordering on the ludicrous." Then he offers a moving account of Nietzsche's tragi-pathetic dilemma, the "desperate cruelty" with which he condemned "what he himself venerated: Wagner, music in general, morality, Christianity ... he seemed to regard the most rabid of the insults he hurled at them as a form of homage."[71]

Pivoting again, Mann puts forward Nietzsche's "two prime errors" (*es zwei Irrtümer*): his "willful misinterpretation of the relative power of instinct and intellect" and the related "treating life and morality ... as antagonists."[72] The first once again condemns Nietzsche's praise of strength and ruthlessness, his "crass hubris," that Mann from the beginning of his writing career has sought either to sublimate into a more uncritical love of life rather than power, or to simply eradicate from Nietzsche's thought.[73] Mann spends several pages granting Nietzsche's decriers their due: "All his ranting against morality, humanity, pity and Christianity, all his diseased enthusiasm for sublime amorality, war and evil, unfortunately found its place in the trashy ideology of fascism."[74] He examines other charges Nietzsche's opponents in 1947 might bring against him and declares them, finally, "aberrations." Still, in 1947, there is even greater reason to excise the "blond beast" of *On the Genealogy of Morality* from the "authentic" Nietzsche: the one-sided celebration of those highly selected passages by the Nazi ideologues. The second error encapsulates Mann's belief, stretching back to his earliest fictions, that, when taken whole, a coherent and future-oriented morality can be derived from Nietzsche's philosophy.

As the essay unfolds the reader comes to see that, by design or happenstance, the path follows the history of Mann's own relationship with Nietzsche: first the aestheticism and the critical psychology, rejecting historicism and positivistic science; then the shift to Nietzsche the defender of *Kultur* and German exceptionalism, and finally to autobiographical and historical justifications even for the aspects of his mentor that Mann had once derided. So, for example, his defense of instinct against reason and his aesthetic overvaluation of solitude were "proper for his time ... convenient to the German situation" then, but not now. "How time-bound, how theoretic and inexperienced, Nietzsche's romanticizing of evil seems to us today. We ... are no longer such aesthetes that we need to be ashamed of subscribing to the good." We now see that his aestheticism, "under whose banner freethinkers turned against bourgeois morality, itself belonged to the bourgeois age. ... He could not even have imagined such a phenomenon as fascism."[75]

But what does serve Europe, indeed the world, is Nietzsche's focus on the future. Mann not only places Nietzsche in the ethical humanist camp, but torques him into a socialist one, even though "he denounced it a hundred times over" (167; *GW* ix, 701). It is a necessary part of "the recasting of society to meet the global demands of the hour ... the transformation of the spiritual climate, a new feeling for the difficulty and the nobility of being human."[76] It's aesthetics and ethics one more time: Socialism is a "strictly moral world-view" and Nietzsche "the most uncompromisingly perfect aesthete in the history of thought,"[77] *but* "the socialistic element in his vision of life after the bourgeois era was just as strong as the element which has been called fascist."[78] The evidence may be slender—even the maligned Zarathustra's call to "remain faithful to the earth" is cited, together with the claim that Nietzsche was "prone to confuse morality in general with bourgeois morality"—but the political need is great. It may be "all up with Germany," as *Doctor Faustus's* narrator Serenus Zeitblom says repeatedly, but in 1947 Mann bravely enlists Nietzsche's aid in imagining a humanist Germany beyond the Fascist Holocaust.[79] Zarathustra sought to "permeate material things with human spirit. His is spiritual materialism—which I call socialism."[80] Mann always found himself, and his country, in Nietzsche's struggles.[81] In sum, Mann's 1947 Nietzsche, like his Peeperkorn, is a montage of Hamlet and Wilde, Novalis, Schopenhauer, and Mann's own autobiography, and stands as another example of his complex modernism: the uses of myth, montage and parody, subjectivity and philosophy, psychology and aesthetics, irony and the expansive middle grounds between realism and the aggressively avant-garde, to rescue Nietzsche's greatness for the future.

Mann's intellectual contributions to an understanding of Nietzsche's thought have been denigrated by nearly all his interpreters, including on several occasions himself.

Here's Michael Hamburger: "If Thomas Mann had not been a writer of fiction—however 'philosophical,' however ambitiously intent on dealing with the principal issues of the age—no one would have the slightest interest in his ideas."[82] It's true that Mann cherry-picked from Nietzsche's writings (and many other sources) to serve a current artistic project. This extends to his score of essays on the major figures in his "tradition," essays that when read in isolation sound solely like cultural and literary criticism but which were also always entangled with the purposes of an ongoing artistic project or the political situation. This was true especially between 1926 and 1947.[83] It's also true that Mann did not aspire to "do" philosophy or to contribute directly to the history of thought; his appropriation of Nietzsche was primarily aesthetic and aestheticizing, then ethical and political, enabling him to incarnate Nietzsche's critiques in figures of his own making. So, with caveats, nonetheless I offer that Mann did illuminate Nietzsche's thought primarily through his fictions, both those overtly connected with his mentor—"Death in Venice" and *Doctor Faustus*—but equally, as I have tried to show, in "Der Bajazzo" and the *Persönlichkeit* of the inimitable Peeperkorn. Mann loved Nietzsche as, in Mann's eyes, Nietzsche loved Wagner: both loves were laced with critique and rejection, but never faltered or were unfaithful.

I'll close with Mann's 1925 letter on Nietzsche, Wagner and himself, written in reply to composer and proto-fascist Hans Pfitzner, then a friend.[84] In a letter ostensibly celebrating Mann's fiftieth birthday Pfitzner had accused him of becoming a "Judas," a betrayer of the conservatism of *Reflections* and of Germany. Mann's rejoinder captures in content and especially in its subtle ironic tone his lifelong identification with and allegiance to Nietzsche. Pfitzner, ironically oblivious, published Mann's letter in 1933 in an attempt to "defame" its author before the fascists.

> Our play, dearest Maestro, speaking in the grand and representational sense of intellectual history, has long ago finished its run; we are only a latter-day journalistic acting-out of the case of Nietzsche vs. Wagner. Nietzsche's conscience made him free of Wagner, but he loved him unto death. And Nietzsche, like Wagner, was a late-born son of romanticism. But Wagner was a great and greatly fortunate self-glorifier and self-consummator, whereas Nietzsche was a revolutionary self-conqueror and "became a Judas." With the result that Wagner remained only the last glorifier and supremely effective consummator of an epoch, whereas Nietzsche became a seer and the leader for mankind toward a distant future.

Notes

1 The appended bibliography lists those who have especially helped shape my understanding: Reed first of all, then Lehnert, Picart, Corngold, Nicholls, Pütz, Scott, Stern, Mundt, and equally the biographers Heilbut, Hayman, Harpprecht, Prater, and Kurzke. But mainly I've turned to Mann himself.

2 Peter Pütz, "Thomas Mann und Nietzsche," in Bruno Hillebrand, *Nietzsche und die deutsche Literatur*, ed. Niemeyer Tübingen (1978), 132, T. J. Reed, "Thomas Mann

and Tradition: Some Clarifications," in *Critical Essays on Thomas Mann*, ed. Inta M. Ezergailis (Boston: G. K. Hall and Co., 1988), 222.

3 T. H. Reed's *Thomas Mann: The Uses of Tradition* is *the* book on this subject.

4 For example, *Last Essays*, 142: *Gesammelte Werke* ix, 676. (In subsequent citations I use the abbreviation "*GW*" for reference to Mann's collected works.) Mann does not elaborate on how Nietzsche's suffering specifically enriched his philosophy, but his letters and diaries are full of how his own lesser maladies both inhibited and advanced his own art.

5 Mann elaborates on this in his 1930 *A Sketch of My Life* (21–26; *GW* xi, 108–11).

6 For the early, and most transparent, account of montage in Mann's artistic practice, see the chapter "The Lofty Calling" in his 1909 novel *Royal Highness.*

7 This aspect of his fictions has received much attention, notably in the essays collected in *Thomas Mann's Doctor Faustus: A Novel at the Margins of Modernism*, edited by Herbert Lehnert and Peter C. Pfeiffer. Mann himself noted a parodic strain in Nietzsche's own writing.

8 Kurzke, 26. In *A Sketch of My Life* (22: *GW* xi, 108) Mann wrote that "the youth of twenty" was already clear "about the great moralist's immoralism," suggesting some time for reflection. See also Ronald Hayman, *Thomas Mann: A Biography* (New York: Scribner, 1995), 109.

9 Wysling's introduction to the brothers' correspondence (5). He also quotes from Heinrich's essay on Nietzsche (6): "At the time it [Nietzsche's writing] seemed to be a justification of ourselves; we understood it, including its extravagances, in terms of our own intellectual inclinations. We were happy to place our trust in the individualist—of which it offered an ultimate example—and in the opponent of the state, who would more likely be an anarchist than a devoted citizen of the 'Reich.' In 1890 and the following years this was an attitude of independence. We prepared ourselves in this way for our own accomplishments, and Nietzsche was extremely welcome to us as a philosopher. At the pinnacle of his ideal society he put the proud intellect—and why should that not be us?"

10 *Reflections of a Non-Political Man*, 54; *GW* xii, 79.

11 Stanley Corngold, "Mann as a Reader of Nietzsche," *Boundary* 2, vol. 9, no. 1 (Autumn, 1980): 47–74.

12 Stern, 207. Stern develops the metaphor-driven "anti-mimetic . . . aesthetic validation of the world" in Mann's writing, especially in *The Confessions of Felix Krull* (212ff).

13 On three different occasions in *The Birth of Tragedy* Nietzsche avers that "only as an aesthetic phenomenon is the world and the being of man eternally justified."

14 Nietzsche, "On Truth and Falsehood in an Extra-Moral Sense" (1873).

15 For example, see the foreword to *Nietzsche Contra Wagner* or *Beyond Good and Evil*, #254. Mann offers a tribute to *Human, All Too Human* in *Reflections of a Non-Political Man* (368; *GW*, xii, 499) that begins by praising the "magnificent, enchanting series of chapters ... in the first volume, followed with the spirit of true enlightenment, humanity and freedom, in which Nietzsche celebrates justice."

16 Thomas Mann, *Stories of Three Decades* (New York: Alfred A. Knopf, 1936), 28.

17 *Gesammelte Werke. I–XIII* (Frankfurt a. M.: S. Fischer, 1974), 1990, viii, 138.

18 Compare this paragraph that a young Mann, younger even than his Dilettante, sent to a magazine that had requested an autobiographical sketch: "Those who have leafed through my creative writings will remember that I have always regarded the artist's,

the creative writer's way of life with extreme mistrust. Indeed, my astonishment at the honors society grants this species will never end. I know what a creative writer is, for verifiably I am one myself. Briefly, a creative writer is a fellow who is completely useless in all fields of serious endeavor, only bent on making merry, not only not useful to the state, but even rebellious against it, who does not even have to possess special gifts of intelligence, but may be of as slow and dull an intellect as I have always been—for the rest, a childish charlatan inside, with a tendency to debauchery and in every way disreputable, who should have nothing else to expect from society—and basically expects nothing else—than quiet contempt." Quoted in *Reflections*, 423; *GW*, xii, 573–74.

19 *Gesammelte Werke. I–XIII* (Frankfurt a. M.: S. Fischer, 1974, 1990), viii, 140.

20 The French psychologist and writer Paul Bourget, whom Mann read in translation and quoted, also contributed to his understanding of decadence.

21 Thomas Mann, *Briefe I: 1889–1936*, ed. Erika Mann (Frankfurt a. M.: S. Fischer, 1961), 11/8/1913.

22 Only once did Mann use an extended interior monologue: in his Goethe-novel, *Lotte in Weimar*.

23 "Introduction to a Musical Celebration of Nietzsche," a short talk given at the Odeon in Munich on the occasion of Nietzsche's eightieth birthday anniversary: *Past Masters*, 142; *GW* x, 181.

24 "*Geist und Kunst*." Mann never completed the project, and it does not appear in the *Collected Works*.

25 Reed, "Thomas Mann and Tradition: Some Clarifications," 119–43.

26 Cited in T. J. Reed, "Thomas Mann and Tradition: Some Clarifications," in *Critical Essays on Thomas Mann*, ed. Inta M. Ezergailis (Boston: G. K. Hall and Co., 1988), 137–38.

27 The best example: "Nietzsche in the Light of Recent History," in *Last Essays*, 173; *GW* xi, 706.

28 Ernst Bertram, *Friedrich Nietzsche: Versuch einer Mythologie* (Berlin: G. Bondi, 1918), 5.

29 Bertram, *Friedrich Nietzsche: Versuch einer Mythologie*, 78.

30 Mann, *Last Essays*, 151: *GW* ix, 685–86.

31 Thomas Mann, *Reflections of a Nonpolitical Man*, trans. Walter D. Morris (New York: Frederick Ungar, 1983), 58; *Gesammelte Werke. I–XIII* (Frankfurt a. M.: S. Fischer, 1974), 1990 xii, 84–85: italics in original.

32 Thomas Mann, *Thomas Mann diaries 1918-1939: 1918-1921, 1933-1939*, trans. Hermann Kesten (London: Robin Clark, 1984), 2/21/1921.

33 Hugh Ridley, *The Problematic Bourgeois: Twentieth-Century Criticism on Thomas Mann's* Buddenbrooks *and* The Magic Mountain (Columbia, South Carolina: Camden House, 1994), 76ff.

34 Letter to Ernst Fischer, 5/25/1926; *Briefe I*, 256.

35 *Gesammelte Werke. I–XIII*. Frankfurt a. M.: S. Fischer, 1974, 1990, iii, 760.

36 Ibid., 761.

37 Ibid., 762–63.

38 There is an almost uncanny number of parallels between Hauptmann's and Mann's biographies, from family relations to time in Italy to their marriages, and beyond.

39 Hannelore Mundt, *Understanding Thomas Mann* (Columbia, South Carolina: University of South Carolina Press, 2004), 17.

40 *Gesammelte Werke. I–XIII* (Frankfurt a. M.: S. Fischer, 1974, 1990), iii, 795.
41 Ibid., 776.
42 Ibid., 778.
43 Ibid., 837.
44 Ibid., 846.
45 His most characteristic gesture is to form a circle with his thumb and forefinger, then extend his other three long-nailed fingers: in German signing it signifies "F" and in several contexts *ficken* seems a right inference (542, 562: *GW* iii, 763, 792): "and the emotions this [sign] evoked were much like those one might feel watching an elderly priest of some alien cult hitch up his robes and dance with strange grace before the sacrificial altar." He also likens his lance-nailed hand directly to Zarathustra's eagle-claw (582; *GW* iii, 821).
46 *Gesammelte Werke. I–XIII* (Frankfurt a. M.: S. Fischer, 1974, 1990), iii, 821.
47 Mann to Gerhart Hauptmann, April 11, 1925; *Briefe II*, 234–35.
48 *Gesammelte Werke. I–XIII* (Frankfurt a. M.: S. Fischer, 1974, 1990), iii, 851–63.
49 Compare Roberto Calasso's account of Dionysus: "Dionysus is the river we hear flowing by in the distance, an incessant booming from far away; then one day it rises and floods everything, as if the normal above-water state of things, the sober delimitation of our existence, were but a brief parenthesis overwhelmed in an instant" (45).
50 *Gesammelte Werke. I–XIII* (Frankfurt a. M.: S. Fischer, 1974, 1990), iii, 779.
51 Ibid., 784, 787.
52 Ibid., 789.
53 Ibid., ix, 692.
54 Ibid., 840.
55 Ibid., 849.
56 Ibid., 850.
57 Hans shows the same subtle spirit when he makes a pact with his former lover Clavdia to serve the failing god as best they can together: Hans's death-inspired passion for her, and her fetishized X-ray image, converted into a life-affirming alliance.
58 Donald Prater, *Thomas Mann* (London and New York: Oxford University Press, 1995), 395.
59 *The Story of a Novel*, 223; *GW* xi, 295.
60 "*Nietzsche's Philosophie im Lichte Unserer Erfahrung*." The Winstons's translation of the title in *Last Essays* certainly captures its meaning, and Mann would presumably have approved this similar translation used by *Commentary*. But a literal rendering of *unserer Erfahrung*, "*our* experience," suggests that Mann wants to make common cause, especially with his European audiences who had suffered through the war directly.
61 He even apologized, in English, to *Commentary* editor Elliot Cohen that the essay was "too simple on Nietzsche's spiritual development" (*Letters*, 552). Mann had already expressed the same criticism to Heinrich, on 5/22/47: "The Nietzsche lecture, simplistic as it is" (526: *Briefe* II, 536).
62 Reed (1988) points out that Mann had before him selections from Nietzsche made by Nazi supporter Alfred Bäumler: clearly direct refutation was the task (233, 237).
63 *Gesammelte Werke. I–XIII* (Frankfurt a. M.: S. Fischer, 1974, 1990), xi, 682.

64 Readers may well remember the great popularity of Wilde in early-twentieth-century Germany, where, for example, *Salome*, in Alfred Linder's weak poetic translation, was performed more than 100 times in 1903–04 alone.
65 *Gesammelte Werke. I–XIII* (Frankfurt a. M.: S. Fischer, 1974, 1990), ix, 680.
66 Mann owed a 1909 copy of Möbius's book. He first took up the idea of an artist infected with syphilis in his projected early work, "Maja," a novella whose actual completion he would credit to the protagonist of "Death in Venice," Gustave von Aschenbach.
67 *Gesammelte Werke. I–XIII* (Frankfurt a. M.: S. Fischer, 1974, 1990), ix, 680.
68 Hayman, *Thomas Mann: A Biography*, 518.
69 *Gesammelte Werke. I–XIII* (Frankfurt a. M.: S. Fischer, 1974, 1990), ix, 682.
70 Ibid., 683.
71 Ibid., 695–96.
72 For example, from "On Myself" (1938): "What was his theorem of might and the 'blond beast' to me? Almost an embarrassment. His glorification of life at the expense of the spirit, which had such precarious consequences in German thought—there was only one possibility of my assimilating it—as irony. It is true—the "blond beast" also haunts my early writing, but it is fairly well stripped of its brutish character, and what is left is nothing but the blondness together with a lack of spirit. … The personal metamorphosis which Nietzsche experienced in me may indeed have meant making him bourgeois. This bourgeois interpretation seemed to me and still seems today deeper and of more consequence than all the heroic-aesthetic delirium that Nietzsche fanned up elsewhere" (43; *GW*, xiii, 143). Several of these sentences also appear in the earlier *A Sketch of My Life* (232; *GW* xi, 110).
73 *Gesammelte Werke. I–XIII* (Frankfurt a. M.: S. Fischer, 1974, 1990), ix, 702.
74 Ibid., 702, 710. Picard puts this even more strongly: "Ultimately, Mann's denial of Nietzsche's influence is inescapably Nietzschean, as it is the closest approximation of the type of 'discipleship' Nietzsche cultivated in both *Also Sprach Zarathustra* and *Ecce Homo*. Nietzsche warned against the worship of a dying idol and exhorted his followers to deny him, that they might find themselves. Mann, in this slaying of his teacher, claims his heritage" (108).
75 *Gesammelte Werke. I–XIII* (Frankfurt a. M.: S. Fischer, 1974, 1990), ix, 711–12.
76 Ibid., 706.
77 Ibid., 703.
78 Debates over Nietzsche's role in the Nazi era were lively in Germany throughout the war era and into the 1950s. For example, in the late 1930s Walter Benjamin, fearing ideological criticism, disguised his quotations from the philosopher. See Ridley, 135.
79 *Gesammelte Werke. I–XIII* (Frankfurt a. M.: S. Fischer, 1974, 1990, ix, 704).
80 Mann's diary entry for August 3,1935, ends with a passage he copied from one of Nietzsche's letters to Peter Gast: "If Germany does not fulfill her moral duty and fails to renounce her national egotism, if she does not disavow the doctrine of Might makes Right, and refuses to believe that Right makes Might—if she does not strive with all her strength and honesty for freedom and truth, then her fate is already sealed."
81 Michael Hamburger, *From Prophesy to Exorcism* (London, Longmans, 1965), 84.
82 I try to show this in my study of *Joseph and His Brothers*. Mann took from Freud, Kleist, Lessing, Schopenhauer, Goethe, and Wagner—his great subjects of those

years—what the *Joseph* novels, *Lotte in Weimar*, and *Doctor Faustus* required. He also sometimes ignored or even suppressed ideas that might menace his current project, or for that matter himself. Nietzsche's psychology had given Mann a perspective for developing characters; Freud's threatened to unmask the artist who created them.

83 Thomas Mann, *Briefe II: 1937–1947*, ed. Erika Mann (Frankfurt a. M.: S. Fischer, 1963), 241–42.

Part Three

Glossary

17

Dionysiac

Douglas Burnham

Dionysus is a Greek mythological figure with a complicated and not entirely consistent set of narratives and symbols attached. Of particular importance for Nietzsche are Dionysus's association with intoxication (especially wine), fertility (of which the grape vine is a symbol), dissolute and destructive religious practices, the cycle of death and rebirth (in one myth, Dionysus is torn apart by the Titans, to be reborn after a sojourn in the underworld), and finally his marriage with Ariadne (daughter of Minos, who helped Theseus through the labyrinth, only to be abandoned by him on Naxos). Important for Nietzsche also is the fact that, as god of wine, Dionysus is associated with a number of festivals in the ancient Greek calendar correlated to the phases of wine production, and above all with the great *Dionysia*, the festival at which new tragedies were performed.

In *The Birth of Tragedy*, Nietzsche is attempting to understand the inner connection between the figure of Dionysus and the nature of tragedy. Dionysus represents a basic cultural drive, Nietzsche argues, in contrast to the Apollonian and the Socratic. Specifically, Dionysus is the drive to sweep aside beautiful illusions and identify oneself with the underlying Will, yielding joy and profound wisdom perhaps, but at the cost of all individuality. This ecstatic loss of individuality is evoked by the mythic symbols of intoxication, violent ritual, and being torn apart. The union of Dionysus and Apollo is the secret to the phenomenon of tragedy.

In his later writings, the figure of Dionysus has evolved, and becomes another name for Nietzsche's philosophy overall. Nietzsche's own account of this evolution can be found neatly expressed at *The Gay of Science*, 370. His earlier view of Dionysus in relation to tragedy was a mistake founded upon his misunderstanding of "romanticism." There, romanticism is defined as that condition in which tragedy is reduced to a mere means of escape for those whose life is essentially impoverished. Schopenhauer and Wagner are both named in this connection. This romantic need for tragedy (and thus for Dionysus) is contrasted to that of the one "who is richest in fullness of life," who welcomes both the beautiful and destructive as aspects of creativity. Other key passages where Dionysus is explicitly evoked in Nietzsche's late works, either as mythic symbol or a philosophical concept, include the following: Z part three, *On the Great*

Yearning; part four *The Sorcerer*; *BGE*, 294–95; and the last chapter of *Twilight of the Idols*. Frequently in these passages, Nietzsche also evokes the figure of Ariadne, who stands for the human who has recognized the poverty of knowledge that only serves the preservation of the human (i.e., guiding Theseus through the labyrinth), and now yearns for that Dionysian mode of life described above.

18

Decadence

Jack Brookes

Nietzsche writes in his preface to the *Case of Wagner*: "My greatest preoccupation hitherto has been the problem of *decadence*" (*CW*, *P*). Taking him at his word, a full account of this problem would therefore require volumes. Despite this formidable task, I will attempt a concise sketch of what Nietzsche defines this problem to be with remarks drawn from his unpublished notebooks and the *Twilight of the Idols*.

Décadence implies two things upon etymological analysis: a *decay* and a *fall down* (*de-cadere*). Nietzsche's use of this middle French term is attuned to the connotations of its origin. We can thus initially characterize Nietzsche's conception as related to both a kind of general physical decay—such as weak immunity—and a psycho-spiritual one, such as the existential disorder that comes by way of the fall from idealized, conceptual height. Nietzsche's use of decadence is most often in the language of the body, specifically its degeneration into illness:

> One loses one's power of resistance against stimuli—and comes to be at the mercy of accidents ..."depersonalization," disintegration of the will ... One longs for a condition in which one no longer suffers ... one esteems unconscious states, without feeling, (sleep, fainting) as incomparably more valuable than conscious ones. (*KSA*, 13:17[6])

Decadence is therefore not the lavish consumption of goods, but *that which* weakens essential powers that promote an active state of feeling and willing. "Life" is experienced as the "ground of ills" (*KSA*, 13:17[6]), to the point where narcosis is sought over wakefulness. Sickness or exhaustion become primary, and initiate the disengagement of the essential human instincts for life—which, for Nietzsche, is primarily the instinct for seeking one's advantage. This instinct toward advantage is what we either allow ourselves to follow—thereby potentially rescuing ourselves from disintegration—or choose to battle: "To *have* to fight the instincts—that is the formula for decadence" (*TI*, *The Problem of Socrates*, 11).

As a "physiological condition" (*KSA*, 13:17[6]), decadence makes one subject to the immoderate reactions it promotes. One might liken this situation to an addict staving off withdrawal by maintaining a small amount of the same, poisonous substance whose absence induced withdrawal in the first place. Such a substance to which we might be addicted, however, could be the moralities found in philosophy or religion.[1] Decadence is therefore both a cause and an effect, in that it is equally a predisposition to sickness as it is a sickness in its own right:[2]

> Philosophers and moralists are lying to themselves when they think that they are going to extricate themselves from decadence by waging war on it. Extrication is not in their power: what they choose as a remedy, as an escape, is itself only *another expression* of decadence. (*TI, The Problem of Socrates*, 11; emphasis added)

But what might such a reaction to this condition—a *depersonalization*—look like, exactly? To sketch this concept more concretely, we should turn to two figures that Nietzsche gives significant attention to in *Twilight of the Idols* and elsewhere: Socrates and the Christian, both of whom he calls "decadents" (*TI, The Problem of Socrates, 35*). What these two figures share is their experience of life as primarily constituted of suffering. This experience induces a decadent condition, since to suffer to such an extent is, for Nietzsche, a sign that "you are a piece of reality that has *gone wrong*. … The preponderance of feelings of displeasure over feelings of pleasure … provides the formula for decadence" (*A*, 15).

Socrates, Nietzsche claims, was depersonalized by the tyrannical employment of his reason against a preexisting condition of "anarchic" desire (*TI, The Problem of Socrates, 4, 10*). As further evidence that Socrates suffered from the illness of the decadent, Nietzsche claims that Socrates suffered life as if it were a source of illness: "[Life]," for such wise men, "*is no good*" (*TI, The Problem of Socrates, 1*).[3] What makes Socrates's decadence unique, however, was his immoderate use of rationality to control the instincts he thought would obscure a mental vision of otherworldly, higher Forms.[4] Such a reaction served to keep Socrates in painful relation with the chaos of his instincts, and compelled him to attempt a perverse and inhumane self-mastery.

The Christian succumbs to decadence by her implicit condemnation of the instincts she holds responsible for her experience of a pitiable, persecuted life. Due to humanity's fall from grace, our natural instincts are to be regarded as the cause for our sinful nature and its works, all of which contrast with those of God. Unlike Socrates's attempt to generate an inner tyrannical rationality to master himself—which is properly a sublimation of instinct rather than strict negation—the Christian's decadence lies in her irrational *eradication* of instinct which serves to preserve her misery. Where Socrates sought an extreme and austere reformation to inner anarchy, the Christian seeks to exterminate altogether those instincts she holds responsible for her present suffering:

> [The Christian Church] never asks: "how can a desire be spiritualized, beautified, deified?"—it has always laid the weight of its discipline on eradication (of sensuality, of pride, of greed, of the thirst to dominate and exact revenge). But attacking the root of the passions means attacking the root of life; the practices of the church are *hostile to life*. (*TI, Morality as Anti-Nature*, 1)

Combining these two accounts of Socrates and the Christian, we can therefore say that decadence for Nietzsche is a general state of tension toward our instincts borne through an inability to bear the instability such instincts promote.

The fates of these two "decadents" have important consequences that reflect onto Nietzsche's unique understanding of rationality. For Nietzsche, "*reason* demands" that one "do justice" to decadence by not condemning it (*KSA*, 13:14[75]). By giving the instincts and their urges their due, one experiences a harmony that falls into neither Stoic resignation nor Epicurean ecstasy, but that of *amor fati.*[5] Nietzsche's concern with decadence is thus equally a concern for an integrated person, within whom the instincts are oriented to the task of fully living, and eventually loving, the natural consequences of human life.

Nietzsche's concern with decadence is foundational to his concern for value and, ultimately, nihilism. The loss of privileged ideals resulting in the moralistic folly of ever-stricter value judgment stems from a decadent condition, and lays the foundation for those values to eventually devalue themselves. Moreover, "Nihilism," Nietzsche writes in his notebooks, is "no cause, but merely the logical result of decadence" (*KSA*, 13:14[86]). One can therefore use decadence as a guide to explore vast regions of Nietzsche's work to witness his profound preoccupation with the subject.

Notes

1 Cf. *GM*, *What Is the Meaning of Ascetic Ideals?*, 21–22 for an exposition of how Nietzsche views the connection between moralities and their detriment to general health.

2 Cf. *Antichrist, Ecce Homo, Twilight of the Idols& Other Writings* (Cambridge, 2005); Introduction, xxvi. In these terms, decadence can be understood as a kind of general weakness Cf. *KSA*, 13:17[6].

3 Some of Nietzsche's evidence for this is drawn from Plato's *Phaedo* where Socrates is said to have requested, while dying, that Crito offer a rooster to the god of health, Asclepius, for curing him of the illness of life. Cf. *GS*, 340, and Plato's *Phaedo*, 118a.

4 Cf. *Phaedo*, 64c.

5 Cf. *GS*, 276. An interesting facet of Nietzsche's medicine for decadence is his willingness to extend his *Yea-saying* spirit to an illness he sees as having such disastrous consequences. Indeed, it's difficult to see how such medicine could be rational, if by rationality we mean a calculating activity aimed at a security of whatever type. Such a medicine, however, is prescribed only if one holds that the fruits of life are coextensive with the natural and precarious elements of life. Building one's cities on the slopes of Mount Vesuvius could be where one meets an untimely death, or where one is more aware of the uncertainty of life and thereby more *able* to appreciate the view.

19

From Zoroaster to Zarathustra

Matthew John Grabowski

Zoroastrianism is perhaps the world's oldest revealed religion. Ancient sources date its founder and prophet—Zoroaster (Zarathustra)—to the seventh millennium BCE, though modern scholars date him between 1400 and 1000 BCE.[1] Zoroastrianism became the state religion of Persia during the Achaemenid Empire (553–330 BCE), remained influential through Parthian times (247 BCE–224 CE), and reached its cultural zenith in the Sassanid Empire (224–661 CE). The religion was then suppressed and its adherents persecuted following the Muslim conquest of Persia in the seventh century.

Translations of Zoroastrian texts became accessible to Europeans in the late eighteenth century, and while early interpretations understood Zoroaster's teaching to be a "rigid monotheism," this approach required a careful extenuation of its dualistic and henotheistic doctrines.[2] In the *Gathas*—a collection of seventeen hymns attributed to Zoroaster himself—the cosmos is depicted as an unfolding conflict between good and evil in which mankind has a unique role to play. From this cosmogony emerges a moral system that values truth above all else. By speaking the truth and opposing falsehood, each of us can orient ourselves toward the good and thereby contribute to an ultimate victory over evil.[3]

There are many soteriological doctrines inherent in Zoroaster's metaphysics, such as the belief in an immortal soul, the resurrection of the body, and the bestowal of rewards and punishments in an afterlife. These otherworldly ideas—which have inspired both saints and zealots for millenia—were deeply rooted into the Judeo-Christian culture of modern Europe; nevertheless, they derive from Zoroaster and were incorporated into the Abrahamic faiths through religious syncretism.[4]

In light of this revelation, several German scholars came to view Zoroastrianism as the source of what seemed to them to be a moral confusion within the Judeo-Christian ethos. A relevant example is the cultural historian Friedrich von Hellwald, who writes in *The Story of Culture from Its Natural Development to the Present* (1874), "We thus for the first time encounter among the ancient Iranians the delusion of a *moral world order*, an idea to which only higher developed peoples reach, and which influence on the development of culture has been of incalculable value."[5] Nietzsche, who evidently read Hellwald's book three times,[6] echoes this claim in *Ecce Homo* (1888) when he writes, "Zarathustra was the first to see in the struggle between good and evil the essential wheel in the working of things. The translation of morality into metaphysics, as force, first cause, end-in-itself, is his work. ... Zarathustra created this most fateful of all errors—morality" (*EH*, *Why I Am a Destiny*, 3).

Further evidence of Hellwald's influence on Nietzsche is found in the following introduction of the Persian prophet: "Zarathustra ... was born into the city of Urmia by the same named lake. In his thirtieth year of life he left the homeland and moved East to the province Aria and occupied himself for ten years in the loneliness of the mountain range, busying himself with the drafting of the Avesta. After this time had passed he wandered away."[7] Nietzsche transforms this passage on three occasions, the first in an unpublished note from August 1881—a date that coincides with his reading of Hellwald and his experience near the pyramidal rock on the shore of Lake Silvaplana, when the idea of Zarathustra first came to him (*EH*, *Thus Spoke Zarathustra*, 1)—and the second in aphorism 342 from *The Gay Science* (1882). In its third and most popular version—the opening lines of *Thus Spoke Zarathustra* (1883)—Nietzsche's introduction reads: "When Zarathustra was thirty years old he left his home and the lake of his home and went into the mountains. Here he enjoyed his spirit and his solitude, and for ten years did not tire of it. But at last a change came over his heart" (*Z*, *P*, 1).

In these and other examples, Hellwald's influence on Nietzsche's Zarathustra is apparent, but he was by no means the only source of inspiration. Sources from antiquity include Herodotus, Xenophon, and Diogenes Laërtius; other modern contributors include Nietzsche's favorite philosopher Ralph Waldo Emerson, and his contemporary and fellow philologist Max Müller.[8] In spite of these many influences, Nietzsche's Zarathustra is nevertheless the child of his own eccentricity.[9] In *Ecce Homo* we learn that Zarathustra's mission is his alone to undertake: since the historical Zoroaster "created this most fateful of all errors—morality," Nietzsche's Zarathustra must "be the first to recognize it as an error" (*EH*, *Why I Am a Destiny*, 3).[10]

So when Zarathustra announces the death of God (*Z*, *P*, 2), and then proceeds to offer us an antiquated morality in a uniquely modern guise, we ought to take note of the irony.[11] Indeed, truth is still the highest virtue, but it is a truth now free of the exigencies of otherworldly doctrines. Zarathustra thus implores us to "remain faithful to the earth" and "not believe those who speak ... of otherworldly hopes!" (*Z*, *P*, 3). When God died, so did the morality of soteriological theology.[12] A new morality was needed, one based on values that affirm this life and this world. And so Zarathustra heralds the Übermensch as "the meaning of the earth," for the values he creates are life- and world-affirming (*Z*, *P*, 3).[13] "For the game of creation ... a sacred 'Yes' is needed: the spirit now wills his own will, and he who has been lost to the world now conquers his own world" (*Z*, *The Three Metamorphoses*).[14]

What Nietzsche's Zarathustra shows us, then, is that piety can survive even the death of God. It can survive in those who—following Zoroaster and Nietzsche's Zarathustra—uphold the "Persian virtues": "to tell the truth and to shoot straight" (*EH*, *Why I Am a Destiny*, 3).[15] Armed with the clarity of truth, the authentically pious will aim beyond man and his otherworldly morality. "Is it not your very piousness that no longer allows you to believe in a god? And your overly great honesty will yet lead you away beyond good and evil!" (*Z*, *Retired*). Honesty is of course limited by the domain of truth, so to those inauthentic "higher men" of modernity whose sanctimony inclines them to parade their virtues, Zarathustra offers this admonition: "Will nothing beyond your capacity: there is a wicked falseness among those who will beyond their capacity. Especially if they will great things! For they arouse mistrust against great things, these subtle counterfeiters and actors—until finally they are false before themselves ... cloaked with strong words, with display-virtues, with splendid false deeds. Take good care there, you higher men! For nothing today is more precious to me and rarer than honesty" (*Z*, *The Higher Man*, 8).

Notes

1 Pliny the Elder writes: "Eudoxus ... informs us that this Zoroaster existed six thousand years before the death of Plato, an assertion in which he is supported by Aristotle. Hermippus...an author who has written with the greatest exactness on all particulars connected with [the art of magic] ... has left a statement, that Agonaces was the name of the master from whom Zoroaster derived his doctrines, and that he lived five thousand years before the time of the Trojan War." *NaturalHistory, Vol. XXX, Ch. 2* (AD 77). For a modern dating of Zoroaster, see Mary Boyce, *A History of Zoroastrianism, Vol. 1* (Leiden: E.J. Brill, 1975), 190 (hereinafter abbreviated *HZ:1*).

2 On the "rigid monotheism" interpretation, Boyce writes: "This approach, by which a European scholar, however gifted, could set his judgment, slenderly based on the study of one group of texts alone (and deeply enigmatic texts at that), against all the later scripture, tradition and observances of the once mighty Zoroastrian church, now seems astonishingly presumptuous; but Europe in the nineteenth century was very sure of itself and ready to instruct the world, and for a variety of reasons Haug's [monotheistic] interpretation was widely accepted. It established Zoroaster, so long fabled for wisdom, as a teacher of whom the contemporary West could approve—a rational theist, making minimal demands for observance." "The Continuity of the Zoroastrian Quest," *Man's Religious Quest*, ed. Whitfield Foy (London: Croom Helm, 1978), 604.One wonders if this was not rather an inadvertent Trollope ploy that many nineteenth-century Parsee reformers eagerly accepted, perhaps due to a history of persecution, perhaps in an attempt to legitimize themselves in the eyes of Europeans, perhaps for some other reason. In any case, the monotheistic interpretation is no longer popular among scholars.

3 At the cosmic level, this struggle is between two opposing spirits: the beneficent Wise Lord (Ahura Mazda) and the malevolent Hostile Spirit (Angra Mainyu). Aiding the Wise Lord in this struggle against the Hostile Spirit is a pantheon of six lesser divinities, each hypostatizing a particular desirable quality or attribute. Together they form a divine heptad that corresponds to the seven stages of creation. Mankind, the sixth creation and specially endowed with the power to speak the truth and oppose falsehood, can thus contribute to the fulfillment of the Wise Lord's plan. See Zoroaster's *Gathas,* Yasna 30. See also Boyce, *HZ:1*, 204. Cf. Gen. 1:26-31.The phrase "orient ourselves toward the good" is borrowed from Jordan B. Peterson, who connects the ideas of truth and self-worth to Nietzsche in his book *12 Rules for Life: An Antidote to Chaos* (Random House Canada, 2018), 223. Rule 8 is "Tell

the truth—or at least don't lie." After quoting the Sermon on the Mount in his coda Peterson asks: "What does all that mean? Orient yourself properly. Then—and only then—concentrate on the day. Set your sights at the Good, the Beautiful, and the True, and then focus pointedly and carefully on the concerns of each moment. Aim continually at Heaven while you work diligently on Earth. Attend fully to the future, in that manner, while attending fully to the present. Then you have the best chance of perfecting both." Ibid., 359.

4 Max Müller, who oversaw the first English translations of the sacred texts of Zoroastrianism, writes: "It is well known that these [soteriological] doctrines were entirely, or almost entirely, absent from the oldest phase of religion among the Jews. ... Here there are no chronological difficulties. These doctrines exist, as we shall see, in their germinal stage, in the Gathas, while of the more minute details added to these old doctrines in the later portions of the Avesta, or in the still later Pehlevi writings, there is no trace even in post-exilic books of the Old Testament." *Theosophy or Psychological Religion* (London: Longman, Green & Co., 1895), 47–48.Müller speculates this syncretic assimilation took place following the Assyrian conquest of Samaria (~721 BC), when the Jews were exiled to the cities of the Medes (2 Kings 18:11). This is at least plausible chronologically, as the arrival of Zoroastrianism to the Medes dates to the seventh century BC (see Boyce, *HZ:1*, 191). For a detailed list of Zoroastrian doctrines assimilated into Judaism, Christianity, and Islam, see Boyce's *HZ:3* (Leiden: E.J. Brill, 1991), 361–68. For an interesting comparison, see Freud's hypothesis in *Moses and Monotheism* (1939).

5 Friedrich von Hellwald, *The Story of Culture from Its Natural Development to the Present* (Augsburg, 1874), 128 (quoted in Thomas Brobjer, "*Thus Spoke Zarathustra* as Nietzsche's Autobiography," *Nietzsche's Thus Spoke Zarathustra: Before Sunrise*, ed. James Luchte (London: Bloomsbury Academic, 2008), 35).

6 Brobjer, "*Thus Spoke Zarathustra* as Nietzsche's Autobiography," 35.

7 Hellwald, *The Story of Culture from Its Natural Development to the Present*, 169 (quoted in Constantine Sandis, "*Why did Nietzsche choose Zarathustra as a Mask?,*" *Hamazor*, no. 1 (2013): 13).

8 For a detailed list of known and possible influences on Nietzsche's writing of *Thus Spoke Zarathustra*, see Brobjer, "*Thus Spoke Zarathustra* as Nietzsche's Autobiography," 38–39. For an interesting survey of some influences on his choice of Zarathustra in particular, see Sandis, "*Why did Nietzsche choose Zarathustra as a Mask?,*" 11–16. A possible source not mentioned by either author is the *Clavis Artis*, a Zoroastrian alchemical manuscript published in Germany in the late seventeenth or early eighteenth century which features numerous watercolor illustrations, including several of a lion and a dragon (see *Z:I, Metamorphoses*).

9 In his article "Nietzsche's Dance with Zarathustra" (Philosophy Now, no. 93 (2012): 13–15), Constantine Sandis writes: "In May 1882, Nietzsche's friend Paul Rée introduced him to Lou Salomé (with whom he was immediately smitten). Nietzsche soon confessed to her that he had conceived of a figure called Zarathustra partly as a substitute for the son he would never have. Some days later, he told his friends the Overbecks of his aspiration to create 'a filial figure artistically.' In a letter to Peter Gast written the following year, Nietzsche again calls himself 'the father of Zarathustra.' … 'It would be a mistake to identify Nietzsche the father with Zarathustra the son. In a letter written to his sister Elisabeth upon the completion of the final part of *Thus Spoke Zarathustra*, Nietzsche warns against being identified

with his character: "By no means believe that my son Zarathustra voices my opinions. He is one of my presentations and an interlude." . . .Thus, Zarathustra is not so much a mouthpiece for Nietzsche's views, but a mask he wears with mischievous intent, with the dual aim both of using Zarathustra to express himself and to hide behind' Whether mask or mouthpiece, Nietzsche's voice is heard through the *persona* of his Zarathustra.

10 Cf. *TI, World*, which ends with the proclamation: "INCIPT ZARATHUSTRA." Jung attributes this reversal to a kind of enantiodromia. See Carl Jung, *Jung's Seminar on Zarathustra*, ed. James Jarrett (Princeton: Princeton University Press, 1997 [1934]), 14–15.

11 Walter Kaufmann hints at this irony in his biography *Nietzsche: Philosopher, Psychologist, Antichrist* (Princeton: Princeton University Press, 1950), 383, fn. 9: "Nietzsche's sister relates . . . that he himself remarked that his Zarathustra proclaimed a view which was the very opposite of the real Zarathustra's." Nietzsche added that he chose Zarathustra as his protagonist because he was the first one to commit "the error": therefore, he had to be the first one to repudiate it. It seems to have gone unnoticed, however, *how close Nietzsche himself had come to the real Zarathustra's view.*" (italics in the original)

12 Nietzsche stresses that God did not simply die, rather: "*We have killed him*—you and I . . . How shall we, the murderers of all murderers, comfort ourselves? . . . Must not we ourselves become gods simply to seem worthy of it?" (*GS*, 125). In his short essay "The Murder of God" (1968), Eric Voegelin remarks, "The murder of God is committed speculatively by explaining divine being as the work of man. Let us consider what Nietzsche's Zarathustra has to say on this point: "Alas, my brothers, that God whom I created was human work and human madness, like all gods' Man should stop creating gods because this sets absurd limits to his will and action. . . . It does not suffice, therefore, to replace the old world of God with a new world of man: the world of God itself must have been a world of man, and God a work of man which can therefore be destroyed if it prevents man from reigning over the order of being." *Science, Politics, & Gnosticism* (Wilmington: ISI Books, 2007), 40–41.A similar point is made by Martin Heidegger in his essay "Who is Nietzsche's Zarathustra?" (1954): "The question is: is man, as man in his nature till now, prepared to assume dominion over the whole earth? If not, what must happen to man as he is, so that he may be able to 'subject' the earth and thereby fulfill the word of the Old Testament? Must man as he is then not be brought *beyond* himself if he is to fulfill his task? If so, then the 'super-man' rightly understood cannot be the product of an unbridled and degenerate imagination rushing headlong into the void. Nor, however, can the superman species be discovered historically through an analysis of the modern age." *Review of Metaphysics*, 20:3 (New York: Harper and Row, 1967), 415–16.

13 Regarding the history of his book *Thus Spoke Zarathustra*, Nietzsche writes: "Its fundamental conception, the idea of the *Eternal Recurrence*, [is] the highest formula of affirmation that can ever be attained" (*EH, Thus Spoke Zarathuatra*, 1). See *The Gay Science* 341 for an interesting comparison. Since neither of the two key concepts that Zarathustra teaches—the eternal recurrence and the Übermensch—are novel ideas, it is worth exploring their origins. For a detailed study of the history of the eternal recurrence, see Mircea Eliade's *Cosmos and History: The Myth of the Eternal Return* (New York: Bollingen, 1954). The idea of an Übermensch-type character goes back to at least Plato's *Republic*, but could arguably be traced even further to the

Saoshyant figure of Zoroastrian eschatology. These historical nuances provide a much needed context that helps us understand the character of Zarathustra. Without such context, one can sympathize with the reactions of early critics such as Santayana, who found Nietzsche's ethics to be nothing more than the "foolish, incoherent, disastrous" musings of "an immature, half-playful mind" (George Santayana, *Egotism in German Philosophy* (New York: Charles Scribner's Sons, 1916), 135), as well as postmodern critics like MacIntyre, who sees the Übermensch as "an absurd and dangerous fantasy" (Alasdair MacIntyre, *After Virtue* (Notre Dame: University of Notre Dame, 2007), 113).

14 On the creation of values, Jordan B. Peterson offers an interesting perspective—one he attributes to Jung—when he writes, "Nietzsche ... posited that individual human beings would have to invent their own values in the aftermath of God's death. But this is the element of his thinking that appears weakest, psychologically: *we cannot invent our own values, because we cannot merely impose what we believe on our souls. ...* We rebel against our own totalitarianism, as much as that of others. ... I cannot merely make myself over in the image constructed by my intellect (particularly if that intellect is possessed by an ideology)." *12 Rules for Life: An Antidote to Chaos* (Random House Canada, 2018), 193.

15 Cf. Herodotus' *Histories* 1.136.2 (440 BC): "They [the Persians] educate their boys from five to twenty years old, and teach them only three things: riding and archery and honesty." Hellwald echoes this: "It was important for the Iranians to speak the truth about everything." *Story of Culture*, 171. (quoted in Sandis, 14)

20

Figuration and Imagery

Gill Zimmerman

One of Nietzsche's greatest discoveries is the basic predominance of the visual in philosophy. In his work he points out how the visual seems not only metaphorically to have absorbed thought, knowledge, desire, and even the other sensual faculties. At the center of his critique of the visual stands Platonic idealism. Since Nietzsche is sometimes reduced to a mere iconoclast, who must be held responsible for the death of God and possibly even for the still coming death of humanism, it seems to be worthwhile to generally put a finger on the problem of the image in his philosophy and more specifically onto its relation to Plato's conception of it.

Plato developed a comprehensive definition of pictorialities whose declared goal was to introduce a division-method between permissible and impermissible pictorial forms. The admissibility of images was, for the most part, defined due to their intrinsic similarity to certain primordial images, the so-called ideas, which were at the same time concealed and revealed by iconic images, and maintained a pure and transcendent identity with themselves. In the famous *Analogy of the Divided Line* Plato makes Socrates and Glaucon discuss the iconological division-method, in which even true images are nothing but attempts to acquire knowledge about the ideas.

> And do you not know also that although they [students of geometry and arithmetic] make use of the visible forms and reason about them, they are thinking not of these, but of the ideals which they resemble; not of the figures which they draw, but of the absolute square and the absolute diameter, and so on—the forms which they draw or make, and which have shadows and reflections in water of their own, are converted by them into images, but they are really seeking to behold the things themselves, which can only be seen with the eye of the mind? *(Republic*, 510d–511a)

While even by using an analogy to explain the relation between appearances and ideas should suggest that Plato's philosophy fundamentally relies on an analogical conception of truth, the analogical relation between those elements makes this conclusion inevitable.

In early 1870, Nietzsche writes: "My philosophy is reversed Platonism: the farther away from the true being, the purer, the more beautiful, the better is it. Life in appearance as a goal" (*KSA*, 7:7[156]). It is clear from the cited passage that Nietzsche's philosophy (while obviously being determined by the Platonic logic of images) evolves a quite distinct schema for thinking about the image and its relation to truth. As a reversal of the schema underlying Platonic ideal forms, for Nietzsche, the deviation or dissimilarity to any assumed true being supersedes the significance of similarity. Appearance itself supersedes the necessary abolition of every appearance.

To not merely dismiss these inverting operations as the celebration of a libelous jest or a mere disruptive act, we must first try to contextualize them.

From Platonic icons to Nietzschean idols

In a famous chapter of *Twilight of Idols* titled "How the 'True World' Finally Became a Fable" Nietzsche depicts the history of the Platonic iconology as a process of devaluation. When the "true world" as a figuration of the iconically represented and concealed ideal reality is excluded from the vicinity of human knowledge, it does not only become useless, but can be recognized as an idol or simulacrum that forces people to hold to a certain framework, in which the distinction of truth and untruth is produced. Since the "true world" is partially suspended, Nietzsche argues, we can also no longer assume the existence of its counterpart, and must therefore abolish the iconic-division method, which the platonic imaginary-space was founded on. But what remains of philosophy and of the realm of images, if it is withdrawn from its iconological horizon?

A possible answer could, for instance, be indicated by the title *Twilight of Idols* itself. The German term *Dämmerung* translated into "twilight," makes a temporal reference to both dusk and dawn, so that the "night" of the Platonic icons, revealed as idols, simultaneously indicates the daybreak of new idols, of a new imaginary-space. This imaginary-space can be found in Nietzsche's *Zarathustra*. Even if the Zarathustra prima facie at least stylistically recalls the great occidental epics, a closer look shows that precisely this formal similarity allows Nietzsche to transcend the icono-platonic paradigm, for only in the space of images the function of images can be transformed, because only in it the image can become dissimilar to its traditional configuration.

Still the question lingers, why should it be the notion of "dissimilarity," that builds the main parameter for the constitution of the mentioned imaginary-space? And if there is neither a "true world" nor an "apparent world" left, what can be taken as the reference point of the dissimilarity of the image? Nietzsche comes with a seemingly odd answer to the second question. He argues that even if the iconic division-method of Plato has exceeded its validity it has not yet lost influence and continues to be represented in a realm, which is no longer its own. Representations and images, in fact, are still assessed by their similarity to an assumed but never reached fiction of truth or reality. The Nietzschean idols thus in their dissimilarity refer to a powerful intersubjective fiction or simulation, which is not yet overcome. To overcome the power of Platonic iconology, philosophy, for Nietzsche, has to surpass its *academic* limits and become political and artistic at the same time, which means to create and implement a new imaginary space. This leads us to a possible answer to the question of dissimilarity. If the above-indicated intersubjective fiction forces people to search for an iconic representation of reality, it excludes transformation, excludes becoming dissimilar to one's self. For this reason, the future imaginary-space has to foster transformation by idols constituted by their dissimilarity to what is perceived as a fixed and common reality,

Under this reading, the figure of the overman for instance becomes understandable, as a transfiguration of the iconic figure of the "human." The overman cannot be reduced to a similarity-based definition of an enhanced human. If anything it can be construed as the projection of a figure which is thought to open up a new horizon for transformation. Thus the Nietzschean imaginary-space seems to implement a rather indexical function of imagery and figuration, pointing to a possibility of change, which is not directed toward an ideal image, but toward the contingency or necessity of transformation itself. What one might miss though in Nietzsche's conception of imagery must thus be a finalizing transparency that leaves no space for future modifications.

21

Danger

SJ Cowan and Brian Pines

"Danger" is a concept that arises frequently in Nietzsche's writings, and is often associated with terms such as "risk," "experiment," or "chance." He will use this term quite literally in some instances, as an immediate threat to one's physical body or person. Nietzsche saves some of his rare praise for the military daredevils of history: Cæsar (*TI, Skirmishes of an Untimely Man*, 38), Napoleon (*GM*, *'Good and Evil,' 'Good and Bad,'* 16), Alexander (*D*, 549). He will also associate danger with thinking, for example:

> The Will to Truth, that still seduces us into taking so many risks ... And could it be believed that it at last seems to us as if the problem had never been propounded before, as if we were the first to discern it, get a sight of it, and risk raising it. For there is risk in raising it, perhaps there is no greater risk. (*BGE*, 1)

Here Nietzsche is considering the ways that the desire for truth leads thinkers to potentially dangerous lines of questioning. In passages such as this Nietzsche was trying to recapture and romanticize a kind of dangerous thinking from a bygone era; namely, the kind of unsafe thinking practiced by Socrates or Camille Desmoulins, both of whom were killed for their thoughts.

Yet as one continues to read Nietzsche it becomes clear that danger—along with risk, chance, and experiment—encompasses more than just the risk of bodily harm. There are points at which Nietzsche drives this conjunction of danger and thought even further down, locating risk within the heart of thinking itself. He writes in *Twilight of the Idols*, "The unfamiliar involves danger, anxiety and care,—the fundamental instinct is to get rid of these painful circumstances. First principle: any explanation is better than none at all" (*TI*, *The Four Great Errors*, 5). Importantly, Nietzsche calls this desire for safety an "instinct." This demonstrates that Nietzsche does not advocate danger for purely romantic purposes, but rather that he finds the concept to be embedded both in the principle of human life and of the organism itself.

On the one hand, Nietzsche argues that the development of human life, of culture, has sprung from the natural world purely by chance. Early in his career, in his 1874 *Schopenhauer as Educator*, he characterized nature as a process of pure chance, one "bent on squandering" (*SE*, 2). Not only does he believe that the existence of human life is accidental, but so too is a culture's production of great thinkers: nature merely propels great thinkers, like an arrow, "it takes no aim but hopes the arrow will stick somewhere" (*SE*, 7). Countless times, the arrows do not stick; but nature continues its blind risk, occasionally hitting a target. Noteworthy here is the cavalier attitude he ascribes to nature. The "blind" arrow "bent on squandering" gives us an image of risk as involving a certain carefree attitude. From Nietzsche's perspective there is a principle at the heart of life that demands that life risk itself: that, in order to experiment and develop, a living being must squander itself in the face of death.

> In all commanding there is experiment and risk; and always when it commands the living risks itself doing so. And as the smaller gives way to the greater, in order for it to have its pleasure and power over the smallest, so too the greatest gives way, and for the sake of power risks—life itself. That is the giving-way of the greatest, that it is a risk and a danger and a tossing of dice unto death. (*Z*, *On Self-Overcoming*)

In the early 1880s Nietzsche begins using the image of the "dice-throw" as a way of referring to the concept of danger. This is an allusion to Julius Cæsar, who is so instructive an example of how Nietzsche meant the term "risk" to be understood, that it is worth explaining the event in his life that Nietzsche is referencing.

At the age of fifty, Cæsar had conquered the province of Gaul and expanded what had always been a Mediterranean empire into Central Europe. He was one of the wealthiest men in the world and was surrounded by ten loyal and experienced legions. However, his second Proconsulship was ending, and so was his immunity from legal prosecution. Negotiations to ensure his second Consulship had broken down between his faction and his conservative enemies back in Rome, led by Pompey the Great. He now faced the choice of a lengthy court battle—which could ultimately involve exile or execution—or abandoning the legal system entirely and using his armies to march on Rome. The river Rubicon marked the boundary seperating Cæsar's province of *Gallia Cisalpina* from *Italia*. As he crossed this river with the *Legio XIII* (thirteenth legion) at his back he supposedly uttered "ἀνερρίφθω κύβος [the die is cast]" (Plutarch, *Parallel lives*. Pompey.60.2). This phrase has since gained immense fame: in addition to being referenced by Nietzsche it has been repeated by such absurd figures as King George III, who reportedly quoted Cæsar once he heard the demands of the first Continental Congress.

George, however, seems to have misunderstood the significance of the fact that Cæsar spoke this phrase in Greek, and not Latin. When Cæsar spoke, he was himself quoting a line from "The Flutist," a comedic play by Menander. The context of the line is that one man is advising another not to marry; the other acts as if the matter is already decided, and says *ἀνερρίφθω κύβος*. Although we only have this small fragment from this play, we know that Menander was a Greek comedian associated with "New Comedy," which eschewed the deeper questions posed by the "old comedians" like Aristophanes. The New Comedians preferred light-hearted subjects, such as love affairs and other family matters that today usually take place in daytime television and sitcoms. So with the weight of tens of millions of lives on his heart, with the Republican governmental system on which Roman civilization rested at stake, Cæsar rode across Rubicon and plunged the Mediterranean into civil war with a reference to a cheerful comedian.

Nietzsche does not admire Cæsar because he was a conqueror, but because of the joviality, the cheerfulness, and nonchalance that he incorporated into the most immense and serious gamble of his life.[1] This folding of the ridiculous into the sublime is precisely the spirit in which Nietzsche writes about the nature of danger. He claims in his own autobiography, "I know of no other manner of dealing with great tasks than as play: this as a sign of greatness, is an essential prerequisite" (*EH*, *Why I Am So Clever*, 10). The prerequisite for an individual to throw the dice, the prerequisite to living or thinking experimentally, dangerously, is that one must cheerfully embrace nihilism's destruction of meaning. To throw the dice means to participate affirmatively in life in full consciousness of its absurdity. The image of the spirit who hazards to "dance even on the verge of abysses" (*GS*, 347) may therefore represent the courageous or dangerous thinker, the one who intentionally seeks the unknown and cultivates the abyss that is their own self. This is an "approach" to life, or an "attitude" toward life that Nietzsche is advocating—an attitude which courts danger.

This attitude—embodied in the metaphor of the dice throw—was picked up by some of Nietzsche's most enthusiastic interpreters in the twentieth century. Georges Bataille, for example, was particularly taken by Nietzsche's insistence on the "necessity of endless chance" involved in human thought and life. For Bataille, the risk of throwing the dice reveals the way.

> Existence as a whole situates itself beyond any one meaning, it is the conscious presence of man in the world insofar as a human being is *nonsense*, with nothing to do but be what it is, no long able to surpass itself, to offer itself some meaning by acting.[2]

This nihilistic half of this attitude allows one to see that the entirety of existence could never have a single meaning. The comedic half of this attitude values the otherwise valueless nonsense of human life. From this perspective, as Nietzsche put it, "even the *blunders* of life have their own meaning and value" (*EH*, *Why I Am So Clever*, 9). It is precisely the blunders of life which can be approached either as the most tragic, or the most comedic.

Similarly, Gilles Deleuze stresses the way that Nietzsche's appreciation of risk allows him to develop a life-affirming philosophy. As he states, Nietzsche's "dice-throw affirms the being of becoming," and celebrates the fact that chance-based processes sit at the heart of nature. For Deleuze, moreover, "to know how to affirm chance is to know how to play"; that is, to know how to not take the obligations of life so seriously.[3] Nietzsche's own affirmation of human life and thought has thus exceeded the confines of his books, and has allowed others to endure life's seemingly meaninglessness with an attitude of joy. "Let accidents come to me," said Zarathustra, "they are innocent as little children" (*Z*, *Upon the Mount of Olives*).

Notes

1 Nietzsche would have been pondering similar concepts when reading this same story, writing to Peter Gast: "I myself have not gotten beyond experiments and daring, over preludes and promises of all kinds. ... I found in Plutarch the means with which Caesar defended himself against sickness and headache: tremendous marches, a simple way of life, uninterrupted outdoor living, exertions" (*KGB*, February 1888, III.5:991).
2 Georges Bataille, *On Nietzsche*, trans. Stuart Kendall (Albany: SUNY Press, 2015), 12.
3 Gilles Deleuze, *Nietzsche & Philosophy*, trans. Hugh Tomlinson (New York: Columbia University Press, 1983), 25–26.

22

The Eternal Recurrence

Karl Laderoute

The eternal recurrence is a key idea in Nietzsche's thought, even though it receives few explicit articulations in his published works. While the idea may be formulated succinctly, what Nietzsche meant by it has been the subject of long scholarly debate. The debate runs along two primary axes. The first axis concerns the status of the recurrence itself, that is, whether or not all things—including events, people, thoughts, desires, and so on—are supposed to repeat deterministically in the same way, forever. Most commentators concur that this is the basic idea of the recurrence, although Gilles Deleuze offers an idiosyncratic interpretation that regards the recurrence as fundamentally rejecting the Platonic metaphysics of identity, and thus is incompatible with the infinite repetition of the same events.[1] The second axis concerns the practical implications of the thought of recurrence. Some commentators, such as Martin Heidegger, believe that Nietzsche intends the eternal recurrence as a metaphysical doctrine.[2] Many others see the recurrence mainly as a psychological test that only requires an individual take the idea of recurrence seriously, even if it is literally false that all things repeat identically an infinite number of times. Although Nietzsche offered some attempted "proofs" of the eternal recurrence in his notebooks, the published references to the idea do not contain such proofs. What follows is a brief articulation of the eternal recurrence along both axes.[3]

The idea first appears in *The Gay Science*, 341, entitled "The heaviest weight," where it is given an explicit articulation, although not dubbed "eternal recurrence" by name. There Nietzsche forms the idea conditionally:

> What if some day or night a demon were to steal into your loneliest loneliness and say to you: "This life as you now live it and have lived it you will have to live once again and innumerable times again; and there will be nothing new in it, but every pain and every joy and every thought and sigh and everything unspeakably small or great in your life must return to you, all in the same succession and sequence—even this spider and this moonlight between the trees, and event his moment and I myself. The eternal hourglass of existence is turned over again and again, and you with it, speck of dust!"

In this passage it is clear that the basic idea is that all things recur eternally, that is, eternally repeat in the exact same way. However, this passage does not affirm that all things do eternally recur. Instead, this passage's emphasis concerns how the reader would react to such an idea. Two options are presented. First, the individual may reject the idea and "curse the demon who spoke thus." Second, the individual may react positively and will that all things repeat eternally. The conditional formulation of the eternal recurrence here suggests that in this initial formulation Nietzsche placed more emphasis on how one would react to the idea of recurrence than on whether or not all things do recur eternally.

In *Ecce Homo*, Nietzsche claims that "the basic idea of [*Thus Spoke Zarathustra*], *the thought of eternal return*, [is] the highest possible formula of affirmation" (*EH*, *Thus Spoke Zarathustra*, 1). Given that Nietzsche holds *Zarathustra* in such high regard, one would expect that its "basic idea" would be prevalent throughout the work. However, eternal recurrence only (explicitly) appears twice in the four books of *Zarathustra*.[4] In its first appearance Zarathustra offers a formulation of the eternal recurrence reminiscent to the articulation provided in "the heaviest weight," though in this case it is addressed to the spirit of gravity.[5] Here Zarathustra calls it his "abysmal thought" and the reader is presented with the image of a shepherd choking on a long, black snake. Zarathustra instructs the shepherd to bite off the snake's head, after which he was "no longer shepherd, no longer human—a transformed, illuminated, *laughing* being! (*Z*, *On the Vision and the Riddle*). Later, Zarathustra claims that this "abysmal thought" nauseates him. His animals laud his idea of the eternal recurrence, which Zarathustra now clarifies is the "monster [that] crawled into my throat and choked me! But I bit off its head and spat it away from me." We learn that Zarathustra was choked by his "great surfeit of human beings," his nausea at the thought that "the small human beings recur eternally!" (*Z*, *The Convalescent*). Zarathustra chastises both his animals and the spirit of gravity for not taking the idea seriously enough; the spirit of gravity is chastised for making the idea too easy (*Z*, *On the Vision and the Riddle*, 2) while Zarathustra's animals are chastised for making a "hurdy-gurdy song of it" (*Z*, *The Convalescent*, 2). These admonishments, and the two reactions examined in GS 341, suggest that the idea of the eternal recurrence ought to be countenanced quite seriously.

In *Twilight of the Idols*, Nietzsche claims to be "the teacher of the eternal recurrence" (*TI*, *What I Owe the Ancients*, 5). There the eternal recurrence is given a less metaphysical articulation and is instead equated with affirming earthly human existence, including its attendant pain and suffering as well as its joyousness. A positive reaction to the eternal recurrence is what Nietzsche dubs *amor fati* (the love of fate). As Nietzsche explains, "My formula for human greatness is *amor fati*: that you do not want anything to be different, not forwards, not backwards, not for all eternity. Not just to tolerate necessity, still less to conceal it ... but to *love* it" (*EH*, *Why I Am So Clever*, 10).[6]

The eternal recurrence is best contrasted with the idea of the Christian afterlife. Pessimists (such as Schopenhauer and Christians), in Nietzsche's view, degrade earthly existence by regarding it as something terrible.[7] For a pessimist who views earthly life as something negative, nothing could be worse than its eternal repeated occurrence. Christians posit a blissful afterlife as antithetical to the suffering of earthly existence.[8]

The eternal recurrence, by contrast, posits that all things will repeat exactly as they have already occurred. When the idea of eternal recurrence is countenanced seriously, a person's reaction to the idea elucidates their basic evaluative stance toward earthly life.[9]

Notes

1 See Gilles Deleuze's *Nietzsche and Philosophy*, trans. Hugh Tomlinson (New York: Columbia University Press, 2006) and *Difference and Repetition*, trans. Paul Patton (New York: Columbia University Press, 1994).

2 "Nietzsche's fundamental metaphysical position is captured in his doctrine of *the eternal return of the same*." Martin Heidegger, *Nietzsche*: Volume II: *The Eternal Recurrence of the Same*, trans. David Farrell Krell (San Francisco: Harper & Row, 1984), 5.

3 One's stance on the status of the eternal recurrence must be related to one's stance concerning the status of Nietzsche's notebook material. Those who regard the notebook material as on par with Nietzsche's published texts will have far more resources to buttress an interpretation such as Heidegger's of Deleuze's than will someone who regards the works Nietzsche decided to publish as authoritative.

4 Eternity is a theme that runs throughout the work, and there is more explicit discussion of eternity than of eternal recurrence in the text. There are also allusions to eternal recurrence in places throughout the text. For example, compare "Was *that* life? Well then! One More Time!" (*Z*, *On the Vision and the Riddle*, 1) with "'Was *that*—life?' I want to say to death. 'Well then! One More Time!'" (*Z*, *The Sleepwalker Song*, 1).

5 The formulation of the eternal recurrence in *The Gay Science* 341 also describes it as "the heaviest weight."

6 Cf. *The Gay Science*, 276; *NCW*, *Epilogue*, 1.

7 See *TI*, *What I Owe the Ancients*, 4–5 and *A* 15 for articulations of this point.

8 *On the Genealogy of Morality*, "*'Good and Evil,' 'Good and Bad',*" 15.

9 In an affirmative voice, Nietzsche declares that "you will the eternal recurrence of war and peace" (*GS*, 285). Compare that claim with Nietzsche's positive assessment of the spiritualization of hostility that "involves a deep appreciation of the value of having enemies" (*TI*, *Morality as Anti-Nature*, 3). See also *On the Genealogy of Morality*, "*'Good and Evil,' 'Good and Bad',*" 10.

23

The Will to Power

Karl Laderoute

The will to power is one of Nietzsche's most infamous ideas. The origin of the idea lays in Schopenhauer's great work, *The World as Will and Presentation* (1819). In 1865, Nietzsche stumbled across a copy of Schopenhauer's great work in a used bookstore in Leipzig, and quickly became a devotee of Schopenhauer's thought. Although he later came to break from Schopenhauer and criticize him, Nietzsche's thinking was influenced by his early devotion, which was reinforced by Wagner, who was also a committed disciple of Schopenhauer. *The Birth of Tragedy* (1872) bears traces of the heavy influence of both Schopenhauer and Wagner on Nietzsche's early thought.[1]

Schopenhauer's aim was to complete Kant's philosophy. Like Kant, Schopenhauer holds that the external world is a phenomenon, that is, a presentation (*Vorstellung*) to a subject. While Kant maintained that the thing in itself (the world as it really is) was unknowable, Schopenhauer claims that it is knowable. Schopenhauer's central idea is that the thing in itself is the Will, accessible to all humans through simple introspection. Ultimately, Schopenhauer maintains that it is a single, intrinsically undifferentiated, eternal, endlessly striving Will that produces the entire disparate world of phenomena, including all people, objects, actions, and effects.[2] Although Nietzsche later attacks Schopenhauer's claim that the Will is immediately knowable to humans through mere introspection (*BGE*, 19), the core idea that willing plays a central explanatory role in human—and perhaps worldly—activity remained a key theme throughout Nietzsche's mature thought.[3] The key alteration Nietzsche makes to Schopenhauer's idea of will is relating it to power. In the (so-called) Middle Period works—*Human, All Too Human* and its sequels, *Daybreak*, and *The Gay Science*—Nietzsche engages in multiple psychological investigations, arguing that seemingly disparate psychological phenomena are actually all manifestations of a desire for power (e.g., *HH*, 50, 348, 415, 478, 595, 603; *WS*, 22, 26, 251; *D*, 18, 112-113, 187, 189, 204, 262, 271, 356; *GS*, 13, 349).

The phrase "will to power" appears sparsely in Nietzsche's notebooks from 1880 to 1883. It is in notebook entries from 1884 to 1887 that the phrase is mentioned most frequently in Nietzsche's notes. The idea first appears in Nietzsche's published work in *Thus Spoke Zarathustra*, albeit it is hard to determine what role, exactly, it plays in that cryptic and allegorical text (*Z*, *On a Thousand and One Goals*, *On Self-Overcoming*,

On Redemption). The will to power also appears in the three works published after *Zarathustra*, namely *Beyond Good and Evil* (*BGE*, 10, 13, 22–23, 36, 51, 186, 198, 211, 259), the fifth book of *The Gay Science* (*GS*, 349), and *On the Genealogy of Morals* (*GM*, *'Guilt,' 'Bad Conscience,' and the Like*, 12, 18; *What Is the Meaning of Ascetic Ideals?*, 15, 17–18, 27). During this period the term is also ubiquitous in Nietzsche's notebooks, along with plans to produce a masterwork titled *The Will to Power*. By Nietzsche's late period (1888), his commitment to the idea, and its promise to act as a unifying explanation of disparate phenomena, appears to have waned. The idea is mentioned less in his notebooks of this period and finds fewer expressions in his works (*CW*, *Epilogue*; *TI*, *Maxims and Barbs*, 11, 20, 38, *What I Owe the Ancients*, 2; *A* 2, 6, 9, 16–17; *EH*, *P*, 4, *The Birth of Tragedy*, 4, *The Case of Wagner* 1, *Why I Am a Destiny*, 1). By the middle of 1888 Nietzsche appears to have abandoned his plan to produce a work titled *The Will to Power*, opting instead to produce a masterwork *Revaluation of All Values*, material for which was eventually published in *Twilight of the Idols* and *The Antichrist*.[4]

In both the published works and the notebooks it is suggested that the idea can play a unifying explanatory role. A key question that scholars have debated is what *explananda*, exactly, Nietzsche thought the will to power was supposed to unify. Minimally, it seems that the idea was originally thought to offer a unifying account of human willing, that is, all human activity ultimately aims at attaining or expressing power, even if that is not what an agent consciously believes themselves to be doing. The next level of generality interprets the concept as offering a unifying account of all intentional agency, both human and nonhuman. The next level posits that power is the ultimate aim of all life, even that which is non-sentient. The maximal intended explanatory scope of the will to power is that all things desire (to express) power, even natural forces such as gravity. By Nietzsche's late period, the idea appears to pick out a particular, human psychological phenomenon, namely the desire for (or expression of) power, control, or strength.

Notes

1 On these points, see Julian Young, *Friedrich Nietzsche: A Philosophical Biography* (Cambridge: Cambridge University Press, 2010), chapters 5 and 7.

2 On the various points about Schopenhauer's view, see Arthur Schopenhauer, *The World as Will and Presentation*, vol. 1, trans. Richard E. Aquila in collaboration with David Carus (New York: Pearson Longman, 2008), 17–24. As Young points out, Schopenhauer does undermine his own, earlier view in the second volume of *The World as Will and Presentation*, there maintaining that while will underlies all appearances, reality is ultimately unknowable in itself, as Kant originally maintained. See Arthur Schopenhauer, *The World as Will and Presentation*, vol. 2, trans. David Carus and Richard E. Aquila (New York: Pearson Longman, 2011), chapter 18 and Young, *Friedrich Nietzsche*, 91–95.

3 For example, in his diagnosis of the ascetic ideal and nihilism in *On the Genealogy of Morals*, Nietzsche opens by claiming "*that* the ascetic ideal has meant so many things

to man expresses above all the fundamental truth about human will, its *horror vacui*: *it must have a goal*–and it would even will *nothingness* rather than *not* will at all" (*GM*, *What Is the Meaning of Ascetic Ideals?*, 1).

4 The book *The Will to Power* is a compilation of Nietzsche's notebook entries, organized according to a discarded draft plan of his masterwork, *Revaluation of Values*. On the details of these changes in Nietzsche's plans, see the next glossary definition.

24

The Revaluation of All Values

Brian Pines

The following will be an atypical definition. Instead of explaining a key concept in Nietzsche's work I intend to recount and reexamine the history behind the alleged "magnum opus" that Nietzsche had conceived of writing. The story behind what he had called his *Hauptwerk* (literally "main work") was originally distorted by Elisabeth Förster-Nietzsche, who edited and published a handpicked collection of Nietzsche's notes in 1901 under the title *The Will to Power*, and presented the work as an intended magnum opus. Authors such as Kaufmann,[1] Bittner,[2] Magnus,[3] Colli, and Montinari all worked to correct Elisabeth's distortions and establish what is now generally considered to be the facts: that Nietzsche revised and reworked his plans for this masterwork several times until, in frustration, he abandoned the idea of it in 1888.

According to Colli and Montinari, Nietzsche first conceived of writing a *Hauptwerk* titled *The Will to Power* in August 1885 (*KSA*, 12:39[1]). Beginning in the summer of 1886 he began to think of it as four books, and gave it the subtitle *The Revaluation of All Values* (*KSA*, 12:5[75]). He would work on it in spurts, and the plan for the books fluctuated, sometimes dramatically. Colli and Montinari observe that at the very beginning of September 1888, Nietzsche decided to scrap the title *The Will to Power* and make the subtitle, *The Revaluation of All Values*, the full title (*KSA*, 14, p. 398). They believe that he subsequently gave up the entire plan for a *Hauptwerk*, stating that "N's Nachlaß in total represents an attempt, aborted because of his sickness" (*KSA*, 14, p.389). There are two occasions where Nietzsche puts in writing something like an intention to discard the idea of a *Revaluation of All Values*. The most important instance is a portion of a letter to Heinrich Köselitz (Peter Gast) that Colli and Montinari quote: "I have the first transcript of my 'Attempt [*Versuchs*] at a Revaluation' finished: it was, all in all, a torture. Also, I do not quite yet have the courage for it. Ten years from now I will make it better" (*KGB*, February 1888, III.5:991).[4]

The notion of a ten-year hiatus is significant in this letter. At the time Nietzsche wrote this he was roughly half a year away from his forty-fourth birthday. In the forty-fourth year of *his* life Richard Wagner became disheartened by the progress of *his Hauptwerk*: *The Ring Cycle*. In 1847 he placed the manuscript for Act II of *Siegfried* in a drawer and didn't begin writing again until a little over eleven years later.[5] It would be hard to overstate the claim that the deceased Wagner still made to Nietzsche's thoughts. In 1888 Nietzsche published two books specifically on Wagner

(Nietzsche contra Wagner, The Case of Wagner), and the title of a third publication is an allusion to Wagner's *Ring* (*GötzenDämmerung*). Writing again to Köselitz, Nietzsche says of a fourth book published that year, "Wagner is absolutely the first name that appears in *Ecce homo*" (*KGB*, December 1888, III.5:1228). Given these circumstances, this hiatus Nietzsche writes of quite likely was an imitation of the recess that Wagner had taken when composing his own magnum opus.[6]

As a second piece of evidence that Nietzsche abandoned the idea of a *Hauptwerk*, Colli and Montinari discuss another letter Nietzsche wrote to Köselitz thirteen days after the first, "What occurs now, dear friend? I promised myself that I would take nothing seriously for a long time. Also, you may not believe that I have remade 'literature,' this manuscript was for me; I want to make a manuscript for myself every winter from now on—the thought of 'publication' being actually eliminated" (*KGB*, February 1888, III.5:1000).[7] Colli and Montinari take this to mean that Nietzsche is ruling out the prospect of any future manuscript of *The Revaluation of All Values* being published. However, these four lines of the second letter are preceded by twenty-eight lines of extended discussion of Wagner, who is the main subject of the contents of the letter. An alternative reading of this letter could place more emphasis on the use of the word "seriously." "Seriousness" is a significant concept in Nietzsche's work, especially in relation to Wagner (see *NCW*, *Wagner as the Apostle of Chastity*, 3). Nietzsche's intention to commit to creating experimental manuscripts every winter, which, by eliminating the thought of publishing them, would not be "serious" work, can only be understood in the context of his philosophy.[8] Without spending too much space speculating on this subject (see SJ Cowan's chapter in Part one of this collection for a more detailed discussion of "seriousness") we can assert that perhaps Nietzsche's *Hauptwerk* itself would not necessarily aim to be "serious," and therefore that this letter is also far from presenting an unambiguous abandonment of the *Hauptwerk*, but might just be presenting us with a *quality* of the *Hauptwerk*.

Intertwined with the history of Nietzsche's *Hauptwerk* is the history of his penultimate book *Der Antichrist*. This book may represent our most polished window into the direction and scope of Nietzsche's *Revaluation of All Values*, or it even might represent the entire *Revlauation of All Values*. There are at least four plans Nietzsche made in his 1888 notes where he places *Antichrist* as first book of his *Revaluation of all Values* (*KSA*, 13:11[416], 13:19[8], 13:22[14], 13:22[24]), there are also a couple of outlines in which something resembling the *Antichrist* is made the first book of this *Hauptwerk* ("1: *Critique of previous values*" *KSA*, 13:14[136]; "First book: *The declining values* [Die Niedergangswerth]" *KSA*, 13:15[100]). Despite his earlier commitment to a cessation of 'serious' work on *The Revaluation*, Nietzsche began to write *Antichrist* on September 3, 1888, the same day he composed one of these plans for the *Revaluation* just mentioned. In this plan *Antichrist* features as the first book, this plan is also the first to use *The Revaluation of all Values* instead of *The Will to Power* as a main title for the *Hauptwerk* (*KSA*, 13:19[8]). Nietzsche claims he wrote the entirety of *Antichrist* in twenty-seven days (*EH*, *Twilight of the Idols*, 3 and *TI*, *P*) although he made extensive notes for it the previous spring and summer. From September 3-30, he will continually refer to *Antichrist* in his letters as the first book of the *Revaluation*,[9] and continue to do so even after it is completed.[10]

He will then draw up two fairly extensive plans in his notes for a book titled *The Immoralist* in mid October (*KSA*, 13:23[4], 13:23[5]). This is the same title that appears as "Book Two" of the *Revaluation* in several of its recently planned incarnations (*KSA*, 13:22[14], 13:22[24], 13:22[25]). This seems to suggest that he conceived of the first book of *The Revaluation* as finished, and was beginning work on the second. What follows is a set of lengthy notes in which he ponders the specific problems that he will discuss in *The Immoralist*. Immediately following these notes we find the last plan for his *Hauptwerk* he will write, it lists the three remaining books in the *Revaluation* (*KSA*, 13:23[13]). This last plan moves *The Immoralist* to the third book, behind *The Free Spirit*, reflective of plans he had made the past September and even earlier (*KSA*, 13:19[18], 13:11[416]). This can perhaps be taken as an indication that he was once again distancing himself from this project as a whole, because it is the last mention of any of the three missing *Revaluation* books in his letters or notes. This is very auspicious time to cease working on his *Hauptwerk*: right as he turns forty-four, and right as he has finished the first of the four parts and begun work on the second. Wagner's masterwork was likewise structured into four parts, put it away in his forty-fourth year after he had completed a similar amount of work.

The very next note, and the last of this notebook, can be dated to October 15, 1888 because he claims it is his forty-fourth birthday. This note is a draft of the dedication in Ecce Homo in which he calls *Antichrist* the first book of *Revaluation of all Values* (*KSA*, 13:23[14]). This differs from the published dedication of *Ecce Homo*, where *Antichrist* is referred to simply as *The Revaluation of all Values*. This is perhaps the strangest aspect of *Antichrist*. Sometime in the month between his forty-fourth birthday and the 20th of November, while Nietzsche was composing *Ecce Homo*, he reconsidered what *Antichrist* represented. He appears to have made the decision that this book he had just written the previous month *was* the entire *Revaluation* that he had been planning for years. He communicates this reassessment through his letters, writing to George Brandes on the 20th of November that he has finished *Ecce Homo*, which was, "a prelude to *The Revaluation of All Values*, the work that lies completed before me."[11] He later claims to Brandes to have a manuscript ready: "Antichrist, The Revaluation of All Values."[12] He also begins a letter he sent to Deussen claiming, "My *Revaluation of All Values* with the main title *Antichrist* is finished."[13]

The claim that *Antichrist* is even a partial representation of Nietzsche's *Hauptwerk* is controversial. Not only because on the final draft of the title page for *Antichrist*, the subtitle "*Umwerthung aller Werthe* [Revaluation of all Values]" was crossed out and replaced with "*Fluch auf das Christenthum* [A Curse on Christianity]." The first few generations of Nietzsche scholars had a distaste for *Antichrist*'s style, and didn't consider it to be as philosophically valuable as his other works. It was therefore puzzling to scholars that Nietzsche would claim either that *Antichrist* represented his *Hauptwerk* on its own, or it was the preparatory work that groomed its readers for the rest of *The Revaluation of All Values*. Even when these claims come from Nietzsche's own pen, they were taken as evidence that madness had already shaken his mind.

Recently, Thomas Brobjer[14] and Reto Winteler[15] have worked on revising the story of Nietzsche's magnum opus. Brobjer convincingly argues that Nietzsche never abandoned the idea of a *Hauptwerk*, or that if he did, it was only during his last weeks of semi-sanity. Brobjer argues that Nietzsche had not made up his mind whether to subtitle *Antichrist* as *The Revaluation of All Values* or not, but he also asserts that even if Nietzsche did decide that *Antichrist* was *The Revaluation*, he never gave up the idea of writing three more books which would make up his *Hauptwerk*. That is, if *Antichrist* was *The Revaluation* then *The Revaluation* was not the *Hauptwerk*.

Winteler does an excellent job investigating what Nietzsche was writing during this time period, and connecting it to his decision to make *Antichrist* the whole of his *Revaluation*. Winteler demonstrates that Nietzsche was rereading his own works while drafting chapters about them for *Ecce Homo*, putting particular emphasis on Nietzsche's rereading of *Zarathustra*. Winteler claims that while rereading his own work—something that Nietzsche almost never did—he came to the conclusion that *Zarathustra* represented the positive, constructive aspect of his philosophy, while *Antichrist* represented the negative, destructive aspect. Winteler asserts that Nietzsche decision was that, taken together, these two works constituted his magnum opus.

Notes

1 Kaufman writes that Nietzsche abandoned the project of the will to power in 1888 in his introduction to *The Will to Power* as well as an appendix to *Nietzsche: Philosopher, Psychologist, Antichrist*. His evidence is similar to Colli and Montinari's: he finds portions of Nietzsche's notes for *The Will to Power* which were subsequently edited and used instead for *Twilight of the Idols*.

2 Bittner relies on Colli and Montinari analysis (Friedrich Nietzsche, *Writings from the Late Notebooks*, eds. Rüdiger Bittner, trans. Kate Sturge (New York: Cambridge University Press, 2007), xi).

3 Magnus also relies almost entirely on Colli and Montinari analyses, and concentrates his article on discrediting the general practice of analyzing Nietzsche's *Nachlass*. He felt that instead concentration should be placed on his published works.

4 Quoted by Colli and Montinari in (*KSA*, 14 p. 393). He sent this letter many months before *Antichrist* was composed, and so when he says "I have the first transcript" he is most likely referencing the extensive notes that he made during this time period.

5 Wagner himself claims in *Mein Leben* that he put the work on hold in mid-1857, and judging by his notes in *The Brown Book* it appears to resume in full force at the beginning of 1869 (Richard Wagner, *The Diary of Richard Wagner 1865-1882: The Brown Book*, trans. Joachim Bergfeld (Cambridge: Cambridge university press, 1980), 171). Ten years is also the length of time Odysseus wandered, and Zarathustra spent in his cave.

6 The identity of the recipient of this letter, Köselitz, further identifies Nietzsche with Wagner. Nietzsche referred to Köselitz as his "shadow," and had referred to himself as Wagner's "shadow." Thus the old adage that the student becomes the master.

7 Quoted by Colli and Montinari in *KSA*, 14 p. 393.

8 Colli and Montinari's theory is that Nietzsche made the decision that this unpublished material should be a "summary" or an "abstract" of his work as a whole, and that *Twilight of the Idols* and *Antichrist* absorbed the important material from

the plans for a *Revaluation of All Values*. They cite for example that at one point Nietzsche begins to write a preface for the *Revaluation* which he titles, "Musings of a Psychologist," close to the original title for *Twilight*. Also, one of his later plans for the contents of *Revaluation* is very similar to the combined contents of *Twilight*, and *Antichrist*.

9 *KGB*, September 1888, *KGB* III.5:1102; September 1888, III.5:1104; September 1888, III.5:1112; September 1888, III.5:1115; *KSA, 13:22[14]*.

10 *KGB*, November 1888, III.5:1126.

11 *KGB*, November 1888, III.5:1151.

12 *KGB*, December 1888, III.5:1170.

13 *KGB*, November 1888, III.5:1159. Further mentions: December 1888, III.5:1180; December 1888, III.5:1196.

14 T. Brobjer, Nietzsche's magnum opus. *History of European Ideas*, 32, no. 3 (2006): 278–94.

15 R. Winteler, Nietzsches Antichrist als (ganze) Umwerthung aller Werthe. Bemerkungen zum "Scheitern" eines "Hauptwerks." *Nietzsche-Studien*, 38 (2009).

Index

Lightning Source UK Ltd.
Milton Keynes UK
UKHW020928190921
390607UK00014B/418

9 781501 367595